Crises in Authoritarian Regimes

Jörg Baberowski is Professor of East European History at Humboldt-Universität zu Berlin.

Martin Wagner is a research fellow and Ph.D. candidate at Humboldt-Universität zu Berlin.

Jörg Baberowski, Martin Wagner (eds.)

Crises in Authoritarian Regimes

Fragile Orders and Contested Power

Campus Verlag
Frankfurt/New York

This volume was generously supported by a joint Princeton-Humboldt Strategic Partnership Grant.

PRINCETON UNIVERSITY

HUMBOLDT-UNIVERSITÄT ZU BERLIN

ISBN 978-3-593-51494-9 Print
ISBN 978-3-593-44968-5 E-Book (PDF)

Cover design: Campus Verlag GmbH, Frankfurt-on-Main
Cover illustration: Chilean dictator Augusto Pinochet surrounded by members of the military junta after the putsch against Salvador Allende (1973) © Ullstein Bild (00232315)
Typesetting: Campus Verlag GmbH, Frankfurt-on-Main
Printing office and bookbinder: CPI books Leck, GmbH
Printed in Germany

www.campus.de
www.press.uchicago.edu

Contents

II. (Dis-)Continuity of Crisis—The Interwar Period

III. Identities and Ideologies of Crisis

IV. Violent Crises, Crises of Violence

Acknowledgments

Crises reveal the fragility of political orders and academic writing alike. Long before the current Covid-19 crisis, political scientists, sociologists, and historians from Princeton University and Humboldt-Universität zu Berlin united to collaboratively study authoritarian regimes. From the outset in early 2018, Stephen Kotkin and Deborah Kaple were keen on such an endeavor and we are grateful that they supported a joint grant application and made a workshop at Princeton possible in March 2019. Without Jonathan Raspe, who put great effort into the initial stages, this project would not have begun. When we invited scholars to contribute to "Crises in Authoritarian Regimes" in January 2020, however, we could not have foreseen that our topic of interest—crises—would affect our own project in such a profound way. A conference at Humboldt-Universität zu Berlin scheduled for June 2020 had to be postponed, cancelled, and finally held digitally. We owe much gratitude to all the scholars who agreed to contribute before the outbreak of the pandemic and ultimately did so despite inconceivable hardships. We are grateful to Murmann Verlag for allowing a revised translation of Armin Nassehi's essay to be included in this volume. And we are honored that Princeton University and Humboldt-Universität zu Berlin bestowed a Strategic Partnership Grant. Without Anastasia Vrachnos and Christin Bohnke who benevolently prolonged funding, we would not be reading these chapters. Jürgen Hotz accompanied the project from the beginning to publication, Linda O'Grady put great effort into making it a readable piece, and Tabea Nasaroff typeset the manuscript—we want to thank them all for turning these words into a volume.

June 2021 *Jörg Baberowski and Martin Wagner*

Crises in Authoritarian Regimes: An Introduction

Jörg Baberowski and Martin Wagner

Crises are a fundamental human experience. At any time, humans perceive and master them, even in non-democratic regimes that do not necessarily perish in crises as is usually assumed, but, on the contrary, can emerge empowered. Dictators can face crises in two ways—either overcoming or perpetuating them. Depending on what they are striving for, their *raison d'être*, legal basis, and political mission differ. For ancient Rome, German historian Theodor Mommsen distinguished a republican from a post-Sullan dictatorship, both of which were characterized by unlimited power to cope with crisis: Limited in time, the republican dictatorship aimed at restoring a chaos-ridden political order, whereas dictators following Sulla reigned indefinitely amidst a seemingly never-ending crisis.[1] Drawing on Mommsen, German legal scholar Carl Schmitt explored the sources of sovereignty in order to define two modes of dictatorial rule. In the Roman Republic (509 BC–27 BC), the consul appointed a dictator to resolve an extraordinary situation, like war or internal rebellion, and thus restore the *status quo ante*. Upon accomplishing its mandate, or after six months at the latest, this "commissarial dictatorship" was terminated. A regime, on the contrary, that aimed at eliminating the current political order and establishing an entirely new body politic can be called a "sovereign dictatorship": It acquired its sovereignty from a yet to be adopted constitution.[2] But since this sovereignty remains challenged by external threats or internal opponents, sovereign dictators, one may add, need to perpetuate a sense of crisis—as the situation to

1 Theodor Mommsen, *Römisches Staatsrecht*, Vol. 2:1 (Leipzig: S. Hirzel, 1874), 142–144, 152. On dictators in the Roman Republic, cf. Gregory K. Golden, *Crisis Management During the Roman Republic: The Role of Political Institutions in Emergencies* (Cambridge: Cambridge University Press, 2013), 11–41.

2 Carl Schmitt, *Die Diktatur: Von den Anfängen des modernen Souveränitätsgedankens bis zum proletarischen Klassenkampf*, 8th ed. (Berlin: Duncker & Humblot, 2015), 1, 134, 142.

be overcome that legitimates any measure of power.[3] When encountering the fragility of political order displayed by crises, dictatorships can thus appear as either an emergency regime to cope with crisis or a regime of self-empowerment to cultivate crisis.

How do modern authoritarian regimes deal with the duality of crisis as they often aim at both—preserving stability *amidst crisis* and reviving their political order *via crisis*? Claiming their regime to be an alternative to the crisis-ridden period of the past, a certain sense of crisis remains an ever-present companion to authoritarian legitimacy. In many cases, authoritarian regimes not only come into power or lose power after severe political crises, but also arise from crises in a more consolidated form. So, what are their strengths and weaknesses in coping with crises? Are they at a (dis-)advantage compared to democratic or even totalitarian regimes?[4] And how does adaptability towards internal and external challenges enable authoritarian regimes to perform and remain in power?[5]

Crises

Crises seem to be threatening and urgent moments of critical decision and, as such, the notion of crisis discloses both a contemporary perception of a particular situation and a present-day fascination with allegedly extraordinary circumstances. According to current diagnoses, liberal democracy, the capitalist economy, and global finance, as well as public health, the natural environment, and our personal selves are in the throes of a crisis.[6] Each crisis,

3 Jörg Baberowski, "Diktatur und Gewalt," in *Diktaturen: Perspektiven der zeithistorischen Forschung*, ed. Johannes Hürter and Hermann Wentker (Berlin: De Gruyter/Oldenbourg, 2019), 156–66, here: 157.

4 For recent studies on democratic crisis management, cf. Arjen Boin, Paul 't Hart, Erik Stern and Bengt Sundelius, *The Politics of Crisis Management: Public Leadership Under Pressure* (Cambridge: Cambridge University Press, 2017); Matthias Lemke, *Demokratie im Ausnahmezustand: Wie Regierungen ihre Macht ausweiten* (Frankfurt: Campus Verlag, 2017).

5 Johannes Gerschewski highlights the importance of "endogenous sources of change", cf. Johannes Gerschewski, "Analyzing Crises in Autocratic Regimes," in *Crisis in Autocratic Regimes*, ed. Johannes Gerschewski and Christoph H. Stefes (Boulder: Lynne Rienner Publishers, 2018), 1–19, here: 9.

6 For recent studies of various crisis phenomena inter alia, cf. Manuel Castells, *Rupture: The Crisis of Liberal Democracy* (Cambridge: Polity Press, 2019); Vandad Sohrabi, *Risikoethik der Banken: Große Banken, systemische Risiken und globale Finanzkrisen als Herausforderungen einer*

however, obeys its own rules. Thus, instead of applying a well-balanced overall definition, one might approach the matter of interest by touching upon its manifold traits in order to excavate its contextual complexity.

Crises appear as "*phenomena of perception*"—only by an *ex post* comparison of a current situation with an alleged state of normalcy do individuals gain the conviction that they are amidst a crisis. On a personal level, people detect crises by feeling a sense of loss in terms of control, confidence, and stability.[7] Rather than qualifying as a clear-cut objective category, the notion of crisis stems from individual comprehension within a specific social and cultural context. Thus, a situation that appears threatening and urgent to one person does not necessarily bother another.[8] Crises, however, are not a product of mere opinion. To be plausible, crisis perceptions need to be communicated and reconciled with other people's expectations in a shared environment.[9]

A looming situation, on the other hand, becomes a crisis only when an authoritative voice deems it to be a pressing threat needing to be resolved. As *phenomena of construction*, crises depend on a claim offered by government or societal elites.[10] It is the powerful who identify crises in order to legitimate their actions. Conversely, a government can claim a certain situation not to be a crisis in order to absolve itself of responsibility. In any case, this construction is not independent from individual crisis perception, since it buttresses allegiance only among people who believe in the rulers' narrative.

---

modernen Ethik des Risikos (Tübingen: Mohr Siebeck, 2020); Forum "The Financial Crisis and its Legacies," *Journal of Modern European History* 19, no. 1 (2021): 3–39; Susanne Schmidt, *Midlife Crisis: The Feminist Origins of a Chauvinist Cliché* (Chicago, London: The University of Chicago Press, 2020); Martin Florack, Karl-Rudolf Korte, and Julia Schwanholz, *Coronakratie: Demokratisches Regieren in Ausnahmezeiten* (Frankfurt, New York: Campus Verlag, 2021).

7 Looking at national crises via the prism of "personal crises", as Jared M. Diamond called for, however, is not convincing: By regarding nations as monolithic subjects, Diamond presumes elites and ordinary people alike all wish for the same; further, it blurs the relationship between individual and context, cf. Jared M. Diamond, *Upheaval: How Nations Cope with Crisis and Change* (London: Penguin Books, 2020).

8 Thomas Mergel, "Einleitung," in *Krisen verstehen: Historische und kulturwissenschaftliche Annäherungen*, ed. Thomas Mergel (Frankfurt: Campus, 2012), 9–22, here: 13.

9 Frank Bösch, Nicole Deitelhoff, Stefan Kroll, and Thorsten Thiel, "Für eine reflexive Krisenforschung: Zur Einführung," in *Handbuch Krisenforschung*, ed. Frank Bösch, Nicole Deitelhoff and Stefan Kroll (Wiesbaden: Springer Fachmedien, 2020) 3–16, here: 3–5.

10 Bert Spector, *Constructing Crisis: Leaders, Crises, and Claims of Urgency* (Cambridge: Cambridge University Press, 2019), 16. Cf. Bert Spector, "There Is No Such Thing as a Crisis: A Critique of and Alterative to the Dominant Crisis Management Model," *Journal of Contingencies and Crisis Management* 61, no. 1 (2019): 274–79, here: 276.

Coining new vocabulary and inventing forms of communication is seen to foster these claims.[11] Framing facts, however, does not belong to the past only: Obviously, crises also appear as a "historiographical construction of the past" by scholars projecting their perceptions of a chaotic present into the past.[12] This is why scholarship on previous crises peaks with scholars facing crisis themselves.

In its ancient Greek origin, *krisis* referred to a "'decision' in the sense of a final determination".[13] Despite gaining additional layers of meaning throughout the centuries, the concept has retained its core. As *phenomena of decision*, crises appear as situations in urgent need of an ultimate verdict. Marking a period of time that awaits a decision not yet taken, crises aspire toward a definitive choice granting success or failure, even life or death.[14] Thus, the range of an imagined decision mirrors the magnitude of the crisis perceived—either a singular judgment to resolve a concrete juncture or the grand decision of history to bring essential relief. In any case, they "nurture an appetite for radical change."[15]

The pressure to decide confers power. In an urgent state of emergency, when any quick decision is preferable to a well-balanced though lengthy decision-making process, the government cannot pay regard to particular interests, hesitant voices, or opposing forces. As *phenomena of power*, crises call for definitive answers and thus allow authorities to acquire power beyond the realm of ordinary duty. By staging crises, on the contrary, elites demonstrate power to their subordinates and legitimate their reign. By doing so,

11 Heidrun Kämper, "Krise und Sprache: Theoretische Anmerkungen," in *Krisen verstehen: Historische und kulturwissenschaftliche Annäherungen*, ed. Thomas Mergel (Frankfurt: Campus, 2012), 241–55, here: 244.

12 Lutz Raphael, "'Gescheiterte Krisen': Geschichtswissenschaftliche Krisensemantiken in Zeiten postmoderner Risikoerwartung und Fortschrittsskepsis," in *Geschichte intellektuell: Theoriegeschichtliche Perspektiven*, ed. Friedrich W. Graf, Edith Hanke and Barbara Picht (Tübingen: Mohr Siebeck, 2015), 78–92, here: 79.

13 Reinhart Koselleck, "Krise," in *Geschichtliche Grundbegriffe: Historisches Lexikon zur politisch-sozialen Sprache in Deutschland*, ed. Otto Brunner, Werner Conze and Reinhart Koselleck, Vol. 3. (Stuttgart: Klett-Cotta, 1982), 617–50, here: 617.

14 Reinhart Koselleck, "Einige Fragen an die Begriffsgeschichte von 'Krise,'" in *Begriffsgeschichten: Studien zur Semantik und Pragmatik der politischen und sozialen Sprache*, 4th ed. (Frankfurt am Main: Suhrkamp, 2019), 203–17, here: 204.

15 Boin et al., *The Politics of Crisis Management*, 4.

they also reify their abilities to themselves.[16] "A crisis strengthens the power of the manager just as an external enemy strengthens the dictator."[17]

Crises follow their own times. They appear as assumptions of "non-simultaneity", i.e., a perceived difference between past normalcy and present chaos, that express themselves both in a sense of acceleration towards change and in a sense of halt in the light of uncertainty.[18] As *phenomena of temporality*, crises are perceived (and conceptualized) as having different time horizons. Marking either a sharp break or a short period of transition, crises appear as watershed developments—usually seen from an *ex post* perspective. In this sense, "what leads to a crisis does not necessarily matter in a crisis."[19] With the Age of Enlightenment, as German historian Reinhart Koselleck pointed out, the concept of crisis was also applied to history itself. Becoming a concept of the philosophy of history, crisis represents a permanent state of history, an epochal transition or the "last crisis in history".[20] For Hegel and Marx, history appeared as an infinite series of sequential crises that each brings about the conditions for the following crisis.

As *phenomena of contingency*, crises force us to face the future. Revealing the openness and uncertainty of future times, crises compel us to imagine a world beyond today. Thus, preparing and preventing are expressions of the necessity to actively encounter an unknown tomorrow—coping with crisis is no less than coping with contingency.[21] These projections into the future mirror experiences of previous crises. Regardless of their accuracy, assumptions about upcoming events help us to endure the uncertainty and thus make the present feasible.[22] As a result of the Enlightenment, narratives of

16 Jörg Baberowski, *Scorched Earth: Stalin's Reign of Terror* (New Haven: Yale University Press, 2016), 11.

17 Gunter Dueck, "Ich hasse Krisen: Denn Krisen geben Macht, die keiner braucht," *Kursbuch* 48, no. 170 (2012): 84–100, here: 85.

18 Mergel, "Einleitung," 15.

19 Frédéric Volpi and Johannes Gerschewski, "Crises and Critical Junctures in Authoritarian Regimes: Addressing Uprisings, Temporalities and Discontinuities," *Third World Quarterly* 41, no. 6 (2020): 1030–45, here: 1032.

20 Koselleck, "Einige Fragen an die Begriffsgeschichte von 'Krise,'" 207–208.

21 Stefan Brakensiek, "Ermöglichen und Verhindern – Vom Umgang mit Kontingenz: Zur Einführung," in *Ermöglichen und Verhindern: Vom Umgang mit Kontingenz*, ed. Markus Bernhardt, Stefan Brakensiek and Benjamin Scheller (Frankfurt, New York: Campus Verlag, 2016), 9–22, here: 11–12.

22 Laetitia Lenel, Roman Köster, and Ulrich Fritsche, "Introduction," in *Futures Past: Economic Forecasting in the 20th and 21st Century*, ed. Ulrich Fritsche, Roman Köster and Laetitia Lenel (Berlin: Peter Lang, 2020), 11–29, here: 18. Cf. Laetitia Lenel, "The Hopeful

contingency management had to be drawn from the human capability to act and not a transcendent entity anymore.[23]

Crises reveal the relationship between critique and decision. While the ancient Greek term *krisis* comprised both of these dimensions, the modern concept of the former had taken over the strand of assessment and evaluation leaving the latter to merely represent a situation in need of decision.[24] As *phenomena of critique*, crises disclose the fragility of political orders that derives from eternal "truths" being called into question or regarded beyond doubt. The Roman Republic faced this dilemma: While a structural crisis was looming large, its elites refrained from addressing it and, on the contrary, worsened it by criticizing those who strove for reform.[25] The early modern French absolutist state and the Soviet Union went down a different path: Here, crisis did not stem from structural conditions but emerged as the consequence of elites criticizing the political order that had stabilized their regime.[26] But what do we mean when we speak of authoritarian regimes?

Authoritarian Regimes

After the exterminatory excesses of Stalinism and National Socialism that turned the permanent state of emergency into the norm, no one could affirm dictatorships and authoritarian orders any longer. National Socialists and Bolsheviks did not want to preserve order but, on the contrary, to change, move, and mobilize societies. They tried to enforce their ideas of the new (world) order with repression and exterminatory power. Their representatives invoked history, race, and nature, but without abandoning the idea that their rule was the "true" expression of the people's will. Lenin summed up

Science: A Transatlantic History of Business Forecasting, 1920–1960," (Ph.D. Dissertation, Humboldt-Universität zu Berlin, 2021).

23 Armin Nassehi, "Der Ausnahmezustand als Normalfall," *Kursbuch* 48, no. 170 (2012): 34–49, here: 35. Cf. Armin Nassehi, *Unbehagen: Theorie Der Überforderten Gesellschaft* (München: C.H.Beck, 2021).

24 Koselleck, "Krise," 618.

25 Christian Meier, *Res publica amissa: Eine Studie zu Verfassung und Geschichte der späten römischen Republik*, 4th ed. (Stuttgart: Franz Steiner Verlag, 2017), 13, 302–303.

26 Reinhart Koselleck, *Kritik und Krise: Eine Studie zur Pathogenese der bürgerlichen Welt*, 14th ed. (Frankfurt am Main: Suhrkamp, 2018), 66, 82, 86; Stephen Kotkin, *Armageddon Averted: The Soviet Collapse*, 1970–2000 (Oxford: Oxford University Press, 2001), 2.

the essence of modern totalitarian dictatorship when he confessed that dictatorship was "nothing more or less than authority untrammeled by any laws, [...] and based directly on force."[27]

Comparative research on dictatorships emerged from astonishment at the unprecedented exterminatory excesses of Nazi and Bolshevik rule. The modern "total state," Sigmund Neumann concluded in 1942, derived its stability from the promise to represent the will of the people and was based on the acclamation of those who profited from its advantages.[28] In the 1950s, the "totalitarian model" focused on the dictatorships in Germany and the Soviet Union.[29] It was not until decolonization in the 1960s and 1970s that the political regimes in Africa, Asia, and Latin America became a matter of scholarship. To grasp them, comparative political science introduced the term "developmental dictatorship".[30] Indeed, this was a modern form of dictatorship invoking the will of the people and claiming to embody "true" democracy. At the same time, however, it was also a promise to rescue society from the chaos that would have ensued from people being allowed to decide their own destinies.

Authoritarian regimes differ from totalitarian regimes in the limitation of their claims. They do not aim at destroying and annihilating, but preserving what the order promises to preserve. Even democratic procedures are tolerated where they do not threaten the ruler. In this sense, both models of dictatorship are embodied in authoritarian developmental orders: The emergency regime and tyranny. Political science has since emphasized the diversity of authoritarian orders.[31] Reflections on regime change, however,

---

27 Cited in Mark Mazower, *Dark Continent: Europe's Twentieth Century* (New York: A.A. Knopf, 1999), 12. Cf. Enzo Traverso, *Im Bann der Gewalt: Der europäische Bürgerkrieg, 1914–1945* (München: Siedler Verlag, 2008), 111–118; Michael Geyer and Sheila Fitzpatrick, *Beyond Totalitarianism: Stalinism and Nazism Compared* (Cambridge: Cambridge University Press, 2009).

28 Sigmund Neumann, *Permanent Revolution: The Total State in a World at War* (New York and London: Harper & Brothers, 1942).

29 Hannah Arendt, *The Origins of Totalitarianism* (New York: Harcourt Brace & Co., 1951); Carl J. Friedrich and Zbigniew K. Brzezinski, *Totalitarian Dictatorship and Autocracy* (Cambridge, MA.: Harvard University Press, 1956).

30 Hans F. Illy, Rüdiger Sielaff and Nikolaus Werz, *Diktatur: Staatsmodell für die Dritte Welt?* (Freiburg: Ploetz Verlag, 1980).

31 Juan J. Linz, "Totalitarian and Authoritarian Regimes," in *Handbook of Political Science*, ed. Fred I. Greenstein and Nelson J. Polsby, Vol. 3 (Reading, MA.: Addison-Wesley, 1975); Richard Snyder, "Beyond Electoral Authoritarianism: The Spectrum of Non-Democratic Regimes," in *Electoral Authoritarianism: The Dynamics of Unfree Competition*, ed. Andreas Schedler (Boulder: Lynne Rienner Publishers, 2006), 219–231.

were long based on the premise that dictatorships would linearly transform into democracies.[32] Certainly, structuralist theories have emphasized the importance of economic and social conditions and the diversity of political cultures in explaining different paths to democracy.[33] However, they too have held to the view that authoritarian regimes are deviations, democracies normality.

Why did authoritarian orders remain in power in some regions of the world longer than others? And why has the number of authoritarian regimes increased rather than decreased in the last twenty years?[34] In 2002, when Thomas Carothers finally announced the end of the transformation paradigm, a theoretical shift occurred.[35] Now, the matter of interest became why they are stable and how they can adapt.[36] The concept of "electoral authoritarianism", for example, refers to regimes that are neither exclusively authoritarian nor exclusively democratic.[37] Seen in this light, authoritarian regimes are historically complex political, social, and cultural configurations that are not based solely on violence, oppression, and a lack of freedom.

---

32 Dankwart Rustow, "Transitions to Democracy: Toward a Dynamic Model," *Comparative Politics* 2, no. 3 (April 1970): 337–363; Guillermo O'Donnell, Philippe Schmitter and Laurence Whitehead, *Transitions from Authoritarian Rule*, Vol. 1–4 (Baltimore: John Hopkins University Press, 1986); Samuel Huntington, *The Third Wave: Democratization in the Late Twentieth Century* (Norman: University of Oklahoma Press, 1991); Larry Diamond. et al., *Consolidating the Third Wave Democracies*, Vol. 1–2 (Baltimore: John Hopkins University Press, 1997).

33 Seymour M. Lipset, "Some Social Requisites of Democracy: Economic Development and Political Legitimacy," in *American Political Science Review* 53, no. 1 (March 1959): 69–105; Barrington Moore, *Social Origins of Dictatorship and Democracy* (Boston: Beacon Press, 1966); James M. Malloy and Mitchell A. Seligson, *Authoritarians and Democrats: Regime Transition in Latin America* (Pittsburgh: University of Pittsburgh Press, 1987).

34 Barbara Geddes, "What Do We Know about Democratization after Twenty Years?," in *Annual Review of Political Science* 2 (January 1999): 115–144; Larry Diamond, "Thinking about Hybrid Regimes," in *Journal of Democracy* 13, no. 2 (April 2002): 21–35.

35 Thomas Carothers, "The End of the Transition Paradigm," in *Journal of Democracy* 13, no. 1 (January 2002): 5–21.

36 Holger Albrecht and Rolf Frankenberger, "Autoritarismus Reloaded: Konzeptionelle Anmerkungen zur Vergleichenden Analyse politischer Systeme," in *Autoritarismus Reloaded: Neuere Ansätze und Erkenntnisse der Autokratieforschung*, ed. Holger Albrecht und Rolf Frankenberger (Baden-Baden: Nomos Verlag, 2010) 37–61; David Art, "What Do We Know about Authoritarianism After Ten Years?," in *Comparative Politics* 44, no. 3 (April 2012): 351–373; Uwe Backes and Steffan Kailitz, *Ideokratien im Vergleich: Legitimation, Kooptation, Repression* (Göttingen: Vandenhoeck & Ruprecht, 2014).

37 Andreas Schedler, *Electoral Authoritarianism: The Dynamics of Unfree Competition* (Boulder, CO.: Lynne Rienner Publishers, 2006).

Why do people adjust to authoritarian orders? Sociological action theory, political science research on authoritarianism, and historical research on dictatorship have identified three reasons: The fear of repression, the belief in regime legitimacy, and the benefits to be gained from cooperating.[38] These are the three pillars any authoritarian regime rests upon.[39] Repression, however, cannot be separated from belief and benefit, since people often face all three aspects simultaneously. Dictatorships that do not fulfill their promises resort to violence because they can no longer prevail in any other way; supporters can turn into opponents, perpetrators into victims. This reality, however, is only revealed if we turn to everyday life and ask how people perceived their environment. Regardless of how authoritarian orders imagine themselves, they depend on asserting themselves against resistance and on mobilizing followers. They need approval and acclamation, but they also know that without violence they would be powerless. Thus, fear and participation are two sides of power.[40] But people subordinate to other people not only out of fear, but also because they have an interest in obeying. A regulated power relationship simplifies social relations since it relieves people of decision-making constraints and conflicts. Therefore, there are reasons to adjust to power relations that offer security, even in dictatorships.[41]

In all authoritarian orders, rule is enforced by repression. Fear is a source of subordination and obedience; it is generated through threats, arrests, and the public performance of violent and stigmatizing practices. But this would only tell half the truth about the effectiveness of fear. Authoritarian regimes that have emerged in situations of crisis mobilize support by naming and eliminating those who allegedly caused the crisis. For the representatives of the regime, securing order also means eliminating those who do not fit into

38 Hartmut Esser, *Soziologie: Spezielle Grundlagen, Vol. 5: Institutionen* (Frankfurt am Main: Campus Verlag, 2000), 9; Johannes Gerschewski et al., "Warum überleben Diktaturen?," in *Politische Vierteljahresschrift* 47, no. 1 (2012): 1–26, here: 7–8; Jochen Hellbeck, *Revolution on My Mind: Writing a Diary under Stalin* (Cambridge, MA.: Harvard University Press, 2006); Peter Fritzsche, *Life and Death in the Third Reich* (Cambridge, MA.: Belknap Press of Harvard University Press, 2008).

39 Johannes Gerschewski, "The Three Pillars of Stability: Legitimation, Repression, and Co-Optation in Autocratic Regimes," *Democratization* 20, no. 1 (2013): 13–38.

40 Max Weber, *Wirtschaft und Gesellschaft: Grundriß der verstehenden Soziologie*, 5th ed. (Tübingen: Mohr Siebeck, 1972), 28.

41 Heinrich Popitz, *Phänomene der Macht*, 2nd ed. (Tübingen: Mohr Siebeck, 1992), 236–240; Niklas Luhmann, *Macht im System* (Frankfurt am Main: Suhrkamp Verlag, 2013). Cf. Jörg Baberowski, *Räume der Gewalt* (Frankfurt am Main: S. Fischer Verlag, 2015).

the order. Images of the "enemy" mobilize support and approval. In all authoritarian regimes, opportunities arise to participate in violence, to denounce adversaries as "enemies", or to fill the posts of victims. Thus, the people become a link in the hierarchy of domination.[42]

The rulers do not know what their subjects think and want. They can never be sure of the loyalty of their subordinates. Without co-optation, without followers and profiteers, they cannot survive. No authoritarian order that invokes the will of the people can do so without instruments of (limited) participation and pluralism.[43] As long as such systems succeed in compensating for the unequal distribution of power opportunities through privileges and in creating a sense of certainty of expectation, they will be able to assert themselves as legitimate orders, especially if the authoritarian order can claim to have put an end to civil wars, chaos, and anarchy. However, the regime does not always succeed in manipulating and directing the public. Some people adjust, others do not; today they obey, tomorrow they oppose. Authoritarian regimes are thus dependent on moods and opinions that they cannot ignore.

Authoritarian orders need to buttress legitimation in order to perpetuate their claim to rule. Non-democratic regimes foster their legitimacy by legal procedures, such as elections, or by efficiently solving problems or managing crises to gain "output legality".[44] Legitimacy is not decreed, but established through communication between the rulers and the ruled. "If a political order claims to apply to *many*, it must be recognizable to *many* in order to be heeded by *all who are affected*."[45] This is all the more true when the authoritarian regime declares that it is the only one capable of managing crises and

---

42 Moshe Lewin, "The Social Background of Stalinism," in *The Making of the Soviet System*, ed. Moshe Lewin (New York: Pantheon Books, 1985), 258–285, here: 266–268; Sheila Fitzpatrick, *Everyday Stalinism: Ordinary Life in Extraordinary Times. Soviet Russia in the 1930s* (New York: Oxford University Press, 1999); Michael Wildt, *Volksgemeinschaft als Selbstermächtigung: Gewalt gegen Juden in der deutschen Provinz, 1919 bis 1939* (Hamburg: Hamburger Edition, 2007), 370–374.

43 Paul Brooker, *Non-Democratic Regimes* (New York: Palgrave Macmillan, 2000); Robert I. Rotberg, "Repressive, Aggressive, and Rogue Nation-States: How Odious? How Dangerous?," in *Worst of the Worst: Dealing with Repressive and Rogue Nations*, ed. Robert I. Rotberg (Cambridge: Brookings Institution Press, 2007), 1–39.

44 On "output legality", cf. Utz Schliesky, *Souveränität und Legitimität von Herrschaftsgewalt: Die Weiterentwicklung von Begriffen der Staatslehre und des Staatsrechts im europäischen Mehrebenensystem* (Tübingen: Mohr Siebeck, 2004), 125–153.

45 Volker Gerhardt, *Öffentlichkeit: Die politische Form des Bewusstseins* (München: C.H. Beck, 2012), 347.

creating order. Then, the reasons for an authoritarian "solution" to the crisis must be presented in a publicly convincing way. No authoritarian regime refrains from getting the media, such as the press, radio, and later also television, under its control to shape and dominate public opinion. The addressees, however, acquire these messages on their own terms, reshape them, change them, and thus create their own belief in legitimacy. So the idea of a homogeneous public sphere must be abandoned. Rather, it is a matter of "segmentation" (Wehler) or "fragmentation" (Mergel) of the public sphere, of the plurality of public spaces of communication, i.e., of those "small public spheres" (Gerhards/Niedhardt) which, especially under repressive conditions, are difficult to control for the government.[46]

Almost all authoritarian regimes respond not only repressively but also "responsively" to their subjects' demands for prosperity, security, and participation. As soon as they combine their claim to rule with the promise of prosperity, they are obliged to engage in state welfare or lose credibility. Thus, the fulfillment of promises creates trust and consent. Those who want to benefit from the authoritarian blessings in everyday life have to adjust to the regime and cooperate with its representatives. The rulers, on the other hand, must accommodate the interests of groups and individuals relevant to the regime to be successful. All authoritarian rulers, thus, must respond to expectations and find appropriate answers to people's needs in order to avoid systemic crises and not put stability at risk.[47] And as long as they accomplish what other regimes fail to do, people have reason to consider these orders legitimate.[48] Until the crisis comes that calls everything into question.

46 Hans-Ulrich Wehler, *Deutsche Gesellschaftsgeschichte: Vol. 4: Vom Beginn des Ersten Weltkrieges bis zur Gründung der beiden deutschen Staaten, 1914–1949* (C.H. Beck: München, 2003), 474; Thomas Mergel, *Parlamentarische Kultur in der Weimarer Republik: Politische Kommunikation, symbolische Politik und Öffentlichkeit im Reichstag* (Düsseldorf: Droste Verlag, 2002), 336; Jürgen Gerhards and Friedhelm Neidhardt, "Strukturen und Funktionen moderner Öffentlichkeit: Fragestellungen und Ansätze," in *Öffentlichkeit – Kultur – Massenkommunikation*, ed. Stefan Müller-Doohm and Klaus Neumann-Braun (Oldenburg: BIS-Verlag, 1991), 31–89.

47 Daniel Lambach and Christian Göbel, "Die Responsivität autoritärer Regie," in *Autoritarismus Reloaded: Neuere Ansätze und Erkenntnisse der Autokratieforschung*, ed. Holger Albrecht and Rolf Frankenberger (Baden-Baden: Nomos Verlag, 2010) 79–92, here: 79.

48 Holger Albrecht and Rolf Frankenberger, "Autoritarismus," 57.

Crises in Authoritarian Regimes

Authoritarian regimes are remarkably durable—even when facing severe crises. While the political science literature of the 1990s believed that authoritarian regimes would democratize as a result of their immanent shortcomings, the absence of a wave of regime transitions posed the question of authoritarian stability anew.[49] Current scholarship has mapped out three ways to conceptualize *stability*: "Persistence" as time in power, "continuity" as adjusting to authoritarianism's deficits, and "adaptability" as the capability to master internal and external challenges. Authoritarian regimes, for instance, often tend to palliate their weaknesses with (pseudo-)democratic institutions, like parties, courts, and elections which, however, can also increase their political vulnerabilities. In any case, maintaining stability is not passive but should rather be considered an "active process".[50] In encountering extraordinary situations, authoritarian elites have to engage with various crises phenomena; naturally, some do so more actively than others.

At least for current crises, it is rather difficult to empirically verify whether, and if so when, political leaders perceive a certain situation to be a crisis. As long as archives have not brought minutes or memoranda to light, scholars approach crises as *phenomena of perception* by investigating first reactions, such as repression or denial.[51] By providing inadequate incentives, on the other hand, authoritarian leaders often suffer from insufficient information to perceive a situation's severity. Given the lack of independent media outlets, a bureaucracy that has little interest in reporting full or entirely true information is the only channel of communication.[52] In the past, however, asymmetric communication also turned out to be an advantage, since information suppression could only operate effectively where there were no alternative sources of information; social media, however, has filled this gap.

49 Andrew J. Nathan, "China's Changing of the Guard: Authoritarian Resilience," *Journal of Democracy* 14, no. 1 (2003): 6–17, here: 6.

50 Johannes Gerschewski, "Persistenz – Kontinuität – Adaptivität: Konzeptionen Politischer Stabilität in der vergleichenden Autokratieforschung," in *Politische Stabilität: Ordnungsversprechen, Demokratiegefährdung, Kampfbegriff*, ed. Eva M. Hausteiner, Grit Straßenberger and Felix Wassermann (Baden-Baden: Nomos, 2020), 39–55, here: 42–46, 40 (quote).

51 Christoph H. Stefes, "Crisis? What Crisis? Concluding Thoughts," in *Crisis in Autocratic Regimes*, ed. Johannes Gerschewski and Christoph H. Stefes (Boulder: Lynne Rienner Publishers, 2018) 217–28, here: 218.

52 Cf. Alexander Libman's chapter in this volume.

To be sure, elites and ordinary people alike also observe developments in neighboring countries that help them to grasp what is at stake domestically.[53]

Authoritarian leaders, however, often tend to confirm crisis rather late—despite being sufficiently informed—, since the cost of confessing a "crisis" that does not become evident in the long term is higher than being late in confirming what is just beginning to be visible. By actively claiming or denying a crisis, authoritarian elites, on the other hand, demonstrate their sovereignty of interpretation as they force a genuine way of perceiving the present on their subordinates.[54] As *phenomena of construction*, authoritarian regimes impose their own language and narrative of crisis in order to silence opposing voices and alternative interpretations.[55] Any tale, of course, can also be undermined by the silence of the ruled.[56] On the other hand, authoritarian regimes can construct "normalcy" amidst crisis to conceal a chaotic situation that its elites had caused in order to prevent it from looming large and harming regime legitimacy.

A decision can have value regardless of its content. As *phenomena of decision*, crises disclose the cost of hesitating, since refraining from taking decisions in the long term calls into question the functionality of the political order itself. Thus, urgency demands firmness—firm decisions and firm conditions. The fact that one can learn to value the stability of a body politic as such, even if one rejects the political program associated with it, is what German sociologist Heinrich Popitz called: "'the regulative virtue of the existing order.'"[57] Authoritarian parties and governments make their mark by pointing to the supposed weakness of democracies in crisis-induced decision making.[58] Whether non-democratic regimes, however, are at an advantage in coming to decisive answers more quickly is doubtful. Even though they have less need to involve many stakeholders, which can lead to delay, highly personalized decision making in many cases is not less prone to hesitant decisions, since wrong decisions carry a higher cost.[59] And authoritarian rulers know that inefficient crisis management can not only deepen and accelerate crisis but, even more harmful to their rule, can trigger the ruled to question the rulers' ability to secure order.

53 Cf. Stephen G. F. Hall's chapter.

54 Cf. Bertram Lang's chapter.

55 Cf. Jakob Zollmann's and Janis Nalbadidacis' chapters.

56 Cf. Chan Yong Bu's chapter.

57 Popitz, Phänomene der Macht, 226: "'Der Ordnungswert der bestehenden Ordnung'".

58 Bösch et al., "Für eine reflexive Krisenforschung: Zur Einführung," 6.

59 Cf. Alexander Libman's chapter.

Crises allow authoritarian leaders to demonstrate power, illustrate their coping capabilities, and legitimize themselves by referring to alleged achievements. As *phenomena of power*, crises enable the powerful to identify new kinds of "enemies" to be fought against in order to prove their claim to power is still plausible. The idea that authoritarian rule might come to an end at some stage is, thus, a strong motive for non-democratic leaders to apply force.[60] While authoritarian orders have certain disadvantages compared to democratic orders in perceiving crisis, they can have advantages in implementing concrete measures.[61] In many cases, they also have internal "veto players", but those forces that can (under certain circumstances) prevent measures being implemented are far less institutionalized. At the same time, insufficient institutionalization is also a disadvantage: If government bodies beyond the center are weak, this can lead to measures being implemented slowly or inadequately. Weak or disposed statehood, however, can partly be compensated for by emergency measures or promises of salvation.[62]

In many cases, authoritarian regimes draw legitimacy from having overcome severe political crises in the past. As *phenomena of temporality*, every new crisis can become a reminder of how the regime came into power and why it is still in power. Thus, authoritarian leaders have to constantly maintain their promise of stability and the population's anxiety of potentially recurring turmoil. On the other hand, authoritarian regimes often lack "mechanisms of de-escalation" to end the crisis mode and find a way back to normalcy.[63] On a narrative level, interpreting crises as mere interruptions on the path towards something better is much more difficult for authoritarian elites than for totalitarian. Since they are far less utopian, authoritarian regimes can hardly narrate crises as a necessary intermediate stage in linear progress.[64] Thus, crises can de-legitimize their promise of stability in a much severer way.

As *phenomena of contingency*, crises reveal how fragile and vulnerable political regimes are—not least authoritarian ones. Although governments engage in crisis prevention, being well-prepared for the unknown is hardly

60 Jörg Baberowski and Robert Kindler, "Disziplinieren und Strafen: Vom Leben mit der Diktatur," in *Disziplinieren und Strafen: Dimensionen politischer Repression in der DDR*, ed. Jörg Baberowski, Robert Kindler and Stefan Donth (Frankfurt: Campus, 2021), 11–21, here: 14.

61 Cf. Carolin Kautz's chapter.

62 Cf. Amerigo Caruso's and Stefan Schubert's chapters.

63 Volpi and Gerschewski, "Crises and Critical Junctures in Authoritarian Regimes," 1034.

64 Cf. Grzegorz Krzywiec's chapter.

achievable. Little is known, however, about how authoritarian regimes anticipate crises and brace themselves to cope.[65] As the British political scientist Stephen Hall has proven for countries in Eastern Europe, authoritarian elites prepare and adapt by learning from similar constellations in neighboring regimes.[66] In times of crisis, they can also join forces to solve common problems and minimize the risk of possible failure in the future.[67]

Authoritarian regimes are not only challenged by their critics. They often fail to deal with criticism and thus "manufacture" the crises that endanger their rule themselves.[68] Inadequately dealing with the opposition, insufficiently coping with international pressures, or simply losing the authority to impose undisputed narratives are factors that engulf authoritarian regimes in crises. As *phenomena of critique*, crises reveal how fragile authoritarian legitimacy is, as opposing voices are often answered with mere repression. Increasing violence, however, exacerbates criticism. In this vein, some regimes manage to remain in power even after they have lost credibility and public belief in their rule. Conversely, crises also reveal that the object of oppositional criticism often does not disappear even after the unpopular regime has vanished.[69]

***

This volume aims to assemble a broad variety of perspectives in analyzing crises in authoritarian regimes. Instead of focusing on "regime crises", its chapters deal with political crises and their implications for power in a broader sense.[70] Stemming from the internal deficits of authoritarianism or external developments (or both), the crises we analyze cover unique challenges, long-term decline, or crisis amidst crisis. Rather than putting forth a particular approach, we apply questions of political science, history,

65 Stefes, "Crisis? What Crisis? Concluding Thoughts," 224.

66 Stephen G. F. Hall, "*Tracing Authoritarian Learning in Belarus, Moldova, Russia and Ukraine*," (Ph.D. Dissertation, University College London, 2020).

67 Cf. Rob Konkel's chapter.

68 Cf. Alexander Libman's chapter.

69 Cf. Duygu Coşkuntuna's and Meher Ali's chapters.

70 For an insightful first study of crises in authoritarian regimes that centers around "regime crises", cf. Johannes Gerschewski and Christoph H. Stefes, eds. *Crisis in Autocratic Regimes* (Boulder: Lynne Rienner Publishers, 2018). For a study of "governance crisis" in authoritarian regimes, cf. Chan Hin-yeung, "Crisis Politics in Authoritarian Regimes: How Crises Catalyse Changes Under the State-Society Interactive Framework," *Journal of Contingencies and Crisis Management* 21, no. 4 (2013): 200–210.

literature studies, sociology, and area studies. Examining case studies from the entire 20th and 21st centuries, we try to understand crises in authoritarian regimes in Africa, East and Central Asia, Eastern and Western Europe, and Latin America. Most of these regimes had never been democracies before, having neither a strong tradition of rule of law nor a liberal public sphere to serve as corrective. Each crisis thus is important in itself—as an example of the concentration of the extraordinary and the authoritarian responses to it.

I. Contemporary Crises and Authoritarian Response

A Manufactured Crisis? How Authoritarian Regimes Undermine their Own Legitimacy—The Case of Putin's Russia in 2018–2020

Alexander Libman

Introduction

Authoritarian regimes in many parts of the world have proven to be astonishingly resilient to external challenges and shocks, and able to survive even in an inhospitable environment. The studies of authoritarian resilience in the Middle East,[1] East Asia[2] and the post-Soviet Eurasia[3] emphasize the ability of authoritarian regimes to flexibly adapt to the challenges they face, or suggest that the apparent weaknesses observed from time to time may be a temporary phenomenon and a natural part of the regime's lifecycle. Information manipulation[4] and cooptation of elites[5] reduce the need to use outright repression as a tool of control and increase the longevity of regimes. Unsurprisingly, the expectations of the inevitable demise of authoritarian

---

1 Holger Albrecht and Oliver Schlumberger, "Waiting for Godot: Regime Change without Democratization in the Middle East," *International Political Science Review* 25, no. 4 (2004): 371–392; Michelle Pace and Francesco Cavatorta, "The Arab Uprisings in Theoretical Perspective: An Introduction," *Mediterranean Politics* 17, no. 2 (2012): 125–138; Steven Heydemann and Reinoud Leenders, "Authoritarian Learning and Authoritarian Resilience: Regime Responses to the 'Arab Awakening,'" *Globalizations* 8, no. 5 (2011): 647–653.

2 Cheng Li, "The End of the CCP's Resilient Authoritarianism? A Tripartite Assessment of Shifting Power in China," *China Quarterly* 211 (2012): 595–623; Bruce Gilley, "Taxation and Authoritarian Resilience," *Journal of Contemporary China* 26, no.105 (2017): 452–464; Haifeng Huang, Serra Boranbay-Akan and Ling Huang, "Media, Protest Diffusion, and Authoritarian Resilience," *Political Science Research and Methods* 7, no. 1 (2019): 23–42.

3 Henry Hale, "Regime Cycles: Democracy, Autocracy, and Revolution in Post-Soviet Eurasia," *World Politics* 58, no. 1 (2005): 133–165.

4 Sergei Guriev and Daniel Treisman, "A Theory of Informational Autocracy," *Journal of Public Economics* 186 (2020), Article 104158.

5 Carles Boix and Milan Svolik, "The Foundations of Limited Authoritarian Government: Institutions, Commitment, and Power-Sharing in Dictatorships," *Journal of Politics* 75, no. 2 (2013): 300–316.

regimes, as they were formulated after the fall of Communism or after the Arab Spring, are frequently overly optimistic.

However, while successfully managing external shocks, both short-term (like economic crises or wars) and long-term (like technological progress), authoritarian regimes are frequently vulnerable to other types of crises—those produced by the regimes themselves. Daniel Treisman, in studying the experience of democratic transitions over the last two hundred years, suggests that about two thirds of those occurred not as a consequence of a deliberate choice by the rulers but because the rulers made mistakes—miscalculated the optimal strategy, incorrectly reacted to the challenges their countries faced, or ignored the available information.[6] Examples of these mistakes include both excessive concessions to the opposition and excessive repression, ultimately leading to the radicalization of protest, avoidable alienation of elites, and obvious policy mistakes. A prominent example of the latter is the decision by Mikhail Gorbachev to take a vacation in Crimea in August 1991, which allowed his opponents in the Communist Party, KGB, and the armed forces to stage a coup (which ultimately led to the dissolution of the USSR). In some cases, authoritarian leaders react suboptimally to the challenges their regime faces. In some cases, however, the situation is even worse for the authoritarian rulers—they produce challenges which, without the erroneous policy choices, would not even exist.

In this chapter, we will refer to the latter situation as *manufactured crises*. We will investigate using the case of the Russian authoritarian regime of Vladimir Putin and, specifically, its policy *vis-à-vis* governing sub-national regions in 2018–2020. Students of the Russian regime regularly allude to "Putin's plan",[7] implying the ability of the regime to carefully navigate the challenges it faces in order to remain in control of Russia. At the same time, there have always been doubts as to whether the "plan" actually exists; whether there is indeed a pattern one would ascertain by trying to "connect the dots" available to observers of Russian politics. And even if there is a "plan", should we infer that the complex Russian bureaucracy with numerous interest groups is diligently executing it? This chapter aims to demonstrate that Putin's regime systematically makes suboptimal decisions, and

6 Daniel Treisman, "Democracy by Mistake: How the Errors of Autocrats Trigger Transitions to Freer Government," *American Political Science Review* 114, no. 3 (2020): 792–810.

7 Clifford Gaddy and Andrew Kuchins, "Putin's Plan," *Washington Quarterly* 31, no. 2 (2008): 117–129.

that similar miscalculations repeat themselves time and again, leading to similar crises. These mistakes will be linked to several important features of the Russian regime—high centralization of power, inflexible bureaucracy, and the growing personalization of Putin's rule.

Historical Context and the Notion of Crises

While the attribution of the Russian Federation to a particular type of regime in the 1990s under Boris Yeltsin is a topic for debate,[8] most observers agree that Russia under Putin (who came to power in 2000) is a consolidated (electoral) authoritarian regime.[9] The regime regularly conducts elections at local, regional and federal levels and uses election victory to legitimize its rule. However, the elections are frequently falsified; undesirable candidates are not allowed to run for office.[10] In fact, the victory of Putin and pro-Kremlin candidates is almost always assured. The Russian state does not shy away from using repression against its political opponents.[11] Most news-papers and major TV channels are under governmental control.[12] Putin has successfully managed to eliminate most alternative power centers, which existed

8 Dmitriy Furman, *Dvizhenie po Spirali: Politicheskaya Sistema Rossii v Ryadu Drugikh Sistem* (Moscow: Ves Mir, 2010).

9 Timothy Frye, *Weak Strongman: The Limits of Power in Putin's Russia* (Princeton: Princeton University Press, 2021); Vladimir Gel'man, *Authoritarian Russia: Analyzing Post-Soviet Regime Changes* (Pittsburgh: University of Pittsburgh Press, 2015); Steven Levitsky and Lucan Way, *Competitive Authoritarianism: Hybrid Regimes after the Cold War* (Cambridge: Cambridge University Press, 2010); M. Steven Fisch, "What Has Russia Become?" *Comparative Politics* 50, no. 3 (2018): 327–346.

10 Mikhail Myagkov, Peter C. Ordeshook, and Dimitry Shakin, "Fraud or Fairytales: Russia and Ukraine's Electoral Experience," *Post-Soviet Affairs* 21, no. 2 (2005): 91–131; Cole Harvey, "Changes in the Menu of Manipulation: Electoral Fraud, Ballot Stuffing, and Voter Pressure in the 2011 Russian Election," *Electoral Studies* 41 (2016): 105–117; Rodion Skovoroda and Tomila Lankina, "Fabricating Votes for Putin: New Tests of Fraud and Electoral Manipulations from Russia," *Post-Soviet Affairs* 33, no. 2 (2017): 100–123; Robert Moser and Allison C. White, "Does Electoral Fraud Spread? The Expansion of Electoral Manipulation in Russia," *Post-Soviet Affairs* 33, no. 2 (2017): 85–99.

11 Kirill Rogov, "The Art of Coercion: Repressions and Repressiveness in Putin's Russia," *Russian Politics* 3, no. 2 (2018): 151–174.

12 Anna Litvinenko and Florian Toepfl, "The 'Gardening' of an Authoritarian Public at Large: How Russia's Ruling Elites Transformed the Country's Media Landscape After the 2011/12 Protests 'For Fair Elections,'" *Publizistik* 64, no. 2 (2019): 225–240.

in the 1990s, or to integrate them into his regime—regional governors, wealthy businessmen, and opposition parties.

The Russian regime belongs to the group of personalist authoritarian systems, with most major decisions made by Putin and his inner circle. There is constant speculation about the possible coalitions and groups influencing Russian politics (which are identified based on ideological grounds—conservatives versus liberals—or career background and institutional affiliation—*siloviki*, or representatives of the military and security services or high-ranked officials of state-owned corporations), yet ultimately the balance of power within the elite remains unknown. Over time, formal political institutions and even informal power coalitions seem to decline in importance.[13] At the same time, Putin's attention to individual policy areas also varies; since the Ukrainian crisis of 2014, many have argued that Putin concentrates more on foreign policy issues, leaving many domestic issues in the hands of the elites or the technocratic bureaucracy.[14]

The notion of crises examined in this chapter focuses on individual events, which at least potentially threaten the control of the authoritarian regime over society. Typically, these crises are associated with public protests, especially if they have a political agenda. These protests are occasionally driven by election fraud (which in other cases, however, is silently accepted by the public). Even if the protests are localized, they can create spillover effects (leading to more protests in other regions, industries, or spheres of life) and trigger learning by the opposition (informing it about optimal strategies to counteract the regime)—and therefore become dangerous to the regime as a whole. As a result, the regime is interested in undermining these protests before they get out of control. The main argument in this chapter is that, in many cases, the protests are triggered by the decisions of the regime itself rather than by objective circumstances, and that the actions of the elites and bureaucrats aiming to control the protests only aggravate matters.

13 Regina Smyth, "The Putin Factor: Personalism, Protest, and Regime Stability in Russia," *Politics & Policy* 42.4 (2014): 567–592; Alexander Baturo and Johan A. Elkink, "Dynamics of Regime Personalization and Patron: Client Networks in Russia, 1999–2014," *Post-Soviet Affairs* 32, no. 1 (2016): 75–98.

14 Arnold Khachaturov, "Putin Uzhe Znaet Kto Preemnik," *Novaya Gazeta*, accessed April 22, 2021, https://novayagazeta.ru/articles/2020/01/23/83585-politolog-tatyana-stanovaya-o-profile-novogo-kabineta-ministrov-konflikte-medvedeva-s-putinym-i-konturah-novoy-politicheskoy-sistemy.

Causes of Manufactured Crises

Why do authoritarian leaders make mistakes? As such, the question appears to be trivial; mistakes are natural in any decision-making process, including in authoritarian regimes. However, there are at least three reasons which make mistakes (and thus manufactured crises) particularly likely in certain types of authoritarian regimes: (a) Lack of information, (b) bureaucratic inflexibility and complexity and (c) personalization of decision making.

The lack of reliable information on developments in the country is inherent in many authoritarian regimes. On the one hand, the regime is unaware of whether its subjects really support it, or express their approval of the regime out of fear of repression and would immediately defect if the opportunity arose.[15] On the other hand, the lack of free media leads to the inability of authoritarian rulers to quickly collect information on grievances or, more generally, on economic and political problems. Certainly, authoritarian regimes create organizations and institutions to deal with information collection, but they are also likely to provide incorrect information to the leader—either because of principal-agent problems[16] or because reporting good news to the leader is more likely to be rewarded.[17] However, not all authoritarian regimes suffer from the problem of information collection to the same extent. Some manage to keep some open and free discussion[18] or encourage citizens to report any problems they encounter to the authorities.[19]

Therefore, it is possible to hypothesize that the stronger communication and information collection constraints in authoritarian regimes are, the more likely they are to lead to erroneous decisions and manufactured crises. In the case of Russia, one characteristic which exacerbates information collection

15 Timur Kuran, *Private Truths, Public Lies: The Social Consequences of Preference Falsification* (Cambridge: Harvard University Press, 1995); Ronald Wintrobe, *The Political Economy of Dictatorship* (Cambridge: Cambridge University Press, 2000).

16 Jeremy Wallace, "Juking the Stats? Authoritarian Information Problems in China," *British Journal of Political Science* 46, no. 1 (2016): 1129.

17 Canice Prendergast, "A Theory of 'Yes Men,'" *American Economic Review* 83, no. 4 (1993): 757–770.

18 Jidong Chen and Yiqing Xu, "Why Do Authoritarian Regimes Allow Citizens to Voice Opinions Publicly?" *Journal of Politics* 79, no. 3 (2017): 792–803.

19 Jidong Chen, Jennifer Pan, and Yiqing Xu, "Sources of Authoritarian Responsiveness: A Field Experiment in China," *American Journal of Political Science* 60, no. 2 (2016): 383–400; Alexander Libman and Vladimir Kozlov, "The Legacy of Compliant Activism in Autocracies: Post-Communist Experience," *Contemporary Politics* 23, no. 2 (2017): 195–213.

constraints must be emphasized—excessive centralization of power. In more centralized systems, the likelihood that correct information reaches the level at which decisions are made is less likely—while in a decentralized system many issues can be resolved at the local level, where collecting information is easier. In centralized systems, local bureaucrats can be powerless or disinterested in taking the initiative. Fundamentally, decentralization is an important factor in reducing information asymmetries in politics.[20] In authoritarian regimes where information collection is generally problematic, decentralization can be even more important—the case of post-Mao China is traditionally used as an example of how decentralization improves the quality of public policy in an authoritarian system. Russia, under Vladimir Putin, experienced a strong trend towards centralization, which most likely made the problems with information more severe.[21]

Paradoxically, excessive centralization does not guarantee that local officials act *exactly* as the federal government expects them to: The principal-agent problems allow them to deviate from central guidelines to engage in rent-seeking[22] or to minimize their efforts. However, the incentives local officials receive preclude them from taking the interests of their constituency into account; it is more important to give the illusion of performance in the eyes of the typically poorly informed central government, which lacks understanding of local problems.[23]

Bureaucratic inflexibility is yet another reason why authoritarian regimes make the wrong choices. Even if the political leadership makes a fundamentally correct assessment of a situation, it may fail to implement the necessary measures because of slow and inefficient bureaucracy. Sometimes, bureaucracy turns the envisioned measures into their exact opposite. For example, economic assistance for the population can be associated with cumbersome official requirements, making it almost impossible for ordinary people to gain access to it; propaganda can misrepresent facts, use questionable analogies and concepts, and thus even increase public mistrust towards the

20 Friedrich von Hayek, "The Use of Knowledge in Society," *American Economic Review* 35, no. 4 (1945): 519–530.

21 Alexander Libman and Michael Rochlitz, *Federalism in China and Russia* (Basingstoke: Edward Elgar, 2019).

22 In political science and economics, the concept of "rent-seeking" is used to describe the use of political office for personal enrichment leading to overall losses for society. See Gordon Tullock, "The Welfare Costs of Tariffs, Monopolies, and Theft," *Western Economic Journal* 5 (1967): 224–232.

23 Alexander Libman, *Consequences of Informal Autonomy* (Frankfurt/Main: Peter Lang, 2016).

government.[24] The problem is that the incompetence and inflexibility of public officials is an inherent feature of authoritarian states due to the loyalty-versus-competence trade-off.[25] Competent bureaucrats pose a threat to authoritarian leaders since they can grab power for themselves; therefore, appointing incompetent bureaucrats is an attractive option. In the worst case, there is a downward spiral of decreasing competence in decision making in an authoritarian regime.[26] Incompetence specifically manifests itself in the inability to adjust to a changing environment and to deal with new challenges which emerge as the crisis develops.

Nevertheless, the extent of bureaucratic inflexibility also differs across authoritarian regimes. Some authoritarian regimes rely heavily on bureaucratic hierarchy in implementing their policies, while in other regimes bureaucracy plays a relatively limited role. Modern Russia is an example of bureaucratic authoritarianism.[27] Furthermore, the quality of bureaucracy differs across authoritarian regimes—while some authoritarian regimes manage to reduce corruption and improve bureaucratic flexibility, public administration is inflexible and poorly governed in others. In Russia, the quality of bureaucracy has traditionally been rather low, and it has not improved under Putin. Taking this into account, Russian authoritarianism is particularly likely to face problems associated with bureaucratic mistakes.

Finally, political leaders in authoritarian regimes also make mistakes—even if they have accurate information and their decisions are executed

24 There have been multiple instances in modern Russia where posters produced as official propaganda for the World War II Victory Celebration—a key element in Putin's historical narrative—depicted Wehrmacht soldiers and military equipment rather than Soviet ones ("Fashisty na Plakatakh ko Dnyu Pobedy," *Yandex Zen,* accessed April 22, 2021, https://zen.yandex.ru/media/mugska9i_territori9i/fashisty-na-plakatah-ko-dniu-pobedy-5c98c5ed59be0f00b291486a; "Na Plakatakh k 75-Letiyu Podey pod Stalingradom Vnov' Poyavilas' Nemetskaya Tekhnika," *Novye Izvestiya,* accessed April 22, 2021, https://newizv.ru/news/society/01-02-2018/na-plakatah-k-75-letiyu-pobedy-pod-stalingradom-vnov-poyavilas-nemetskaya-tehnika).

25 Georgy Egorov and Konstantin Sonin, "Dictators and Their Viziers: Endogenizing the Loyalty: Competence Trade-Off," *Journal of the European Economic Association* 9, no. 5 (2011): 903–930; Debin Ma and Jared Rubin, "The Paradox of Power: Principal-Agent Problems and Administrative Capacity in Imperial China (and Other Absolutist Regimes)," *Journal of Comparative Economics* 47, no. 2 (2019): 277–294.

26 Yinan Li, *Institutions, Political Cycles and Corruption: Essays on Dynamic Political Economy of Government* (Stockholm: Stockholm University, 2012).

27 Eugene Huskey, "Elite Recruitment and State-Society Relations in Technocratic Authoritarian Regimes: The Russian Case," *Communist and Post-Communist Studies* 43, no. 4 (2010): 363–372.

promptly and correctly. As previously mentioned, politicians make mistakes in all political systems; they are (just like everyone else) subject to various cognitive and behavioral biases.[28] In authoritarian regimes, however, politicians' mistakes could be more significant than in democracies for two reasons. The first is the *imitational nature* of modern authoritarianism. To gain legitimacy, many authoritarian regimes today present themselves as democracies, conduct regular elections and imitate other democratic political practices.[29] Lucan Way shows that, in many cases, authoritarian leaders engage in these imitational practices without any real understanding of the practices they want to imitate, and this leads to mistakes.[30] Secondly, authoritarian regimes are typically characterized by a higher level of *personalization* in the decision-making process than democracies. In democracies, politicians are constrained by institutions and rules. In authoritarian regimes, these institutions are much weaker; essentially, this means that one person (or a small group of individuals) makes all the decisions—therefore, their possible mistakes carry larger weight. However, authoritarian regimes differ in their levels of personalization—in some regimes, the leaders are constrained by informal rules and other power centers.[31] The weaker the degree of regime institutionalization, therefore, the higher the likelihood of mistakes being made.

In summary, there seem to be three important factors leading to the increased likelihood of mistakes in authoritarian states—the degree of personalization of the political decisions; the level of (excessive) centralization; and the reliance on (inflexible and low quality) bureaucracy. It would appear that these factors have contributed to the emergence of "manufactured crises" in Russia.

---

28 Niklas Berggren, "Time for Behavioral Political Economy? An Analysis of Articles in Behavioral Economics," *Review of Austrian Economics* 25, no. 3 (2012): 199–221.

29 Andreas Schedler, "Elections without Democracy: The Menu of Manipulation," *Journal of Democracy* 13, no. 2 (2002): 36–50.

30 Lucan Way, "Deer in Headlights: Incompetence and Weak Authoritarianism after the Cold War," *Slavic Review* 71, no. 3 (2012): 619–646.

31 Dawn Brancati, "Democratic Authoritarianism: Origins and Effects," *Annual Review of Political Science* 17 (2014): 313–326. Precisely these "institutional authoritarian regimes" have been at the core of research on authoritarian regimes in recent decades. See David Art, "What Do We Know about Authoritarianism after Ten Years?" *Comparative Politics* 44.3 (2012): 351–373; Thomas Pepinsky, "The Institutional Turn in Comparative Authoritarianism," *British Journal of Political Science* 44, no. 3 (2014): 631–653.

Manufactured Crises in the Russian Far East

Elections in Primorskiy Kray (2018)

One of the key steps Putin's regime implemented to reestablish control over regional elites was replacing the public election of provincial governors with appointments from Moscow. In 2012, following mass protests caused by falsified federal Duma elections,[32] Russia reinstated the direct election of governors. However, the outcomes of the supposedly open elections were almost entirely predetermined by the federal government. Institutional safeguards were introduced, prohibiting unacceptable opposition candidates from running.[33] An attractive strategy many incumbent governors pursued was to resign ahead of their official end of term; in this case, the elections took place earlier than originally scheduled, which prevented the opposition from devising successful campaign plans.[34] After Russia introduced a *single elections day*—a requirement that all regional and federal elections take place simultaneously once a year—another strategy became popular; after the resignation of the old governor, Putin appointed a new provisional governor to run the region until election day. Thus, Putin candidates had enough time prior to elections to consolidate their power and to make sure that they won. Elections in Russia became a formal instrument of legitimizing candidates selected by the Kremlin—with only minor exceptions, governors remained fully dependent on the center and entirely loyal to it.[35] In short, the

32 Graeme Robertson, "Protesting Putinism: The Election Protests of 2011–2012 in Broader Perspective," *Problems of Post-Communism* 60, no. 2 (2013): 11–23; Paul Chaisty and Stephen Whitefield, "Forward to Democracy or Back to Authoritarianism? The Attitudinal Bases of Mass Support for the Russian Election Protests of 2011–2012," *Post-Soviet Affairs* 29, no. 5 (2013): 387–403; Stephen White and Ian McAllister, "Did Russia (Nearly) Have a Facebook Revolution in 2011? Social Media's Challenge to Authoritarianism," *Politics* 34, no. 1 (2014): 72–84.

33 Such as the *municipal filter*. The requirement to collect a certain number of signatures by the members of municipal councils in the region—in Russia, municipalities are very weak and typically rely heavily on the executive.

34 Grigorii Golosov and Tatiana Tkacheva, "Let My People Run: Pre-election Resignations of Russia's Governors, 2013–2015," *Problems of Post-Communism* 65, no. 4 (2018): 243–252.

35 Joan DeBardeleben and Mikhail Zherebtsov, "The Reinstated Gubernatorial Elections in Russia: A Return to Open Politics?" *REGION* 3, no. 1 (2014): 3–36; Helge Blakkisrud, "Governing the Governors: Legitimacy vs. Control in the Reform of the Russian Regional Executive," *East European Politics* 31, no. 1 (2015): 104–121; Alexander Libman, *Russische Regionen: Sichere Basis oder Quelle der Instabilität für den Kreml?* (Berlin: SWP, 2016); Grigorii Golosov, "Russia's Centralized Authoritarianism in the Disguise of Democratic

reintroduction of gubernatorial elections in Russia turned into a perfect case of authoritarian resilience—superficial liberalization meeting the demands of the opposition at the same time as keeping the political leadership in control.

In 2018, however, the mechanism of authoritarian resilience failed; in several Russian regions, opposition candidates managed to gain the majority of votes. There were multiple reasons for this development. Firstly, by 2018, the Russian economy had experienced a lengthy period of stagnation, along with declining income and consumption.[36] Throughout the 2000s, Putin's public support was closely linked to economic growth;[37] in 2014, he managed to obtain a major popularity boost after the annexation of Crimea.[38] By 2018, these two factors were unable to sustain the popularity of the regime. Secondly, in 2018, the Russian government implemented a hugely unpopular pension reform increasing the retirement age.[39] The reform was almost unanimously rejected by the Russian population.[40] While Putin himself avoided making any direct statements about the pension reform for a long time, the ruling party, United Russia, (and regional governors who are, in many cases, members of the party) was forced to voice support.[41]

The fact that opposition candidates won regional elections *per se* is unpleasant but not particularly problematic for the federal center. The municipal filter and other rules exclude the real opposition (with a strong

---

Federalism: Evidence from the September 2017 Sub-National Elections," *International Area Studies Review* 21, no. 3 (2018): 231–248; Aleksandr Kynev, *Gubernatory v Rossii: Mezhdu Vyborarmi i Naznacheniyami* (Moscow: Liberal'naya Missiya, 2020).

36 Janis Kluge, *Mounting Pressure on Russia's Government Budget: Financial and Political Risks of Stagnation* (Berlin: SWP, 2019); Laura Solanko, *From Reforms to Stagnation—20 Years of Economic Policies in Putin's Russia* (Helsinki: BOFIT, 2020).

37 Daniel Treisman, "Presidential Popularity in a Hybrid Regime: Russia under Yeltsin and Putin," *American Journal of Political Science* 55, no. 3 (2011): 590–609.

38 Derek Hutcheson and Bo Petersson, "Shortcut to Legitimacy: Popularity in Putin's Russia," *Europe-Asia Studies* 68, no. 7 (2016): 1107–1126.

39 Igor Logvinenko, "Authoritarian Welfare State, Regime Stability, and the 2018 Pension Reform in Russia," *Communist and Post-Communist Studies* 53, no. 1 (2020): 100–116.

40 According to a survey by the Levada Center, 89 percent of the respondents had a negative attitude towards the increase in the retirement age for the male population ("Pensionnaya Reforma," *Levada*, accessed April 22, 2021, https://www.levada.ru/2018/07/05/pensionnaya-reforma-3/).

41 Vladimir Dergachev, Elisaveta Antonova, Mariya Kokoreva, Igor Gubernatorov and Yulia Lymar, "Kakie Regiony Uklonilis' ot Podderzhki Pensionnoy Reformy," *RBC*, accessed April 22, 2021, https://www.rbc.ru/politics/18/07/2018/5b4dfd109a79470e38d581a2.

negative attitude towards Putin) from participating in gubernatorial elections, so that the only opposition parties to have even a hypothetical chance of winning are the so-called "systemic opposition" (*sistemnaya oppozitsiya*) —specifically, the Communist Party of the Russian Federation (CPRF) and the Liberal-Democratic Party of Russia (LDPR). Both are implicitly loyal to Putin's regime, support its initiatives (although they occasionally allow some minor critique of individual aspects of the government's policy), and even frequently refrain from nominating candidates with a real chance of succeeding at regional elections to make sure United Russia wins.[42] Given that Russia is a highly centralized state, regional budgets are heavily dependent on federal subsidies, which provides an additional means of control. However, in spite of this, in the case of one of the regions—Primorskiy Kray—the situation escalated towards a full-fledged crisis with negative consequences for the regime in general.

Primorskiy Kray is located in the Far East of Russia, and borders China, North Korea and Japan. In the 1990s, without any real support from Moscow, the region developed a viable, almost self-sustainable economy based on economic ties with its neighboring Asian states and the exploitation of natural resources. This regional economic model was also accompanied by rampant corruption and the importance of organized crime.[43] In the 2000s, the federal government successfully closed most of the legal loopholes and increased control over the region—this limited the development of this regional economic model without providing any viable substitutes (the federal measures aimed at developing the Far Eastern provinces turned out to be less successful).[44] This contributed to growing dissatisfaction with the central government, which had already led to protests in the past.[45]

Throughout the 1990s, Primorskiy Kray was run by independent politicians who frequently criticized federal policies, as well as by those with likely

---

42 Cameron Ross (ed.), *Systemic and Non-Systemic Opposition in the Russian Federation: Civil Society Awakens?* (Abingdon: Routledge, 2015).

43 Tobias Holzlehner, *Shadow Networks: Border Economies, Informal Markets and Organized Crime in the Russian Far East* (Münster: Lit, 2014).

44 Alexander Libman and Andrei Yakovlev, "A Centralist Approach to Regional Development: The Case of the Russian Ministry for the Development of the Far East," *Europe-Asia Studies*, forthcoming.

45 Alexander Libman, "Russian Federalism and Post-Soviet Integration: Divergence of Development Paths," *Europe-Asia Studies* 63, no. 8 (2011): 1323–1355.

ties to organized crime.[46] In 2012–2017, the governor was Vladimir Miklushevskiy, former rector of the Far East Federal University and a loyal member of United Russia. In October 2017, he resigned, and Putin appointed Andrei Tarasenko temporary governor of the Kray. While born in Primorskiy Kray, Tarasenko had spent most of his career outside the region in the European part of Russia (St. Petersburg, Moscow and the Murmansk regions). Tarasenko was a loyal member of United Russia, and enthusiastically supported the pension reform, claiming that refusing to support the reform would "kill future development" and that "we [people of the region] can be patient, can wait."[47] As such, Tarasenko embodied a number of characteristics which were very likely to make him an unpopular candidate—an outsider (in a remote region with a relatively strong identity and a tradition of criticizing the incompetence and lack of attention from the center), and a politician in favor of highly unpopular policy measures. At the same time, in 2018, Tarasenko also had hardly any rivals in the regional elections. All four challengers admitted to the elections (scheduled for September 2018) represented the systemic opposition. The most important opposition candidate, the CPRF representative, Andrei Ishchenko, was, according to the available polls, much less popular than Tarasenko.[48] In the Far East, communists are traditionally quite weak; the nationalist LDPR is the most relevant opposition party.

The election turned out to be not quite as straightforward as the federal leadership had expected. On September 9, none of the candidates received the 50 percent of the votes necessary to win the elections: Ishchenko received 24.6 percent and Tarasenko 46.6 percent. According to the Russian news agency RBC, this result was already entirely unexpected for the federal administration, which linked it to poor weather conditions (typhoon Jeby

46 Peter Kirkow, "Regional Warlordism in Russia: The Case of Primorskii Krai," *Europe-Asia Studies* 47, no. 6 (1995): 923–947.

47 "VRIO Glavy Primor'ya Tarasenko Podderzhal Izmeneniya Pensionnogo Vozrasta," *RIA*, accessed April 22, 2021, https://ria.ru/20180714/1524575014.html. The comment by Tarasenko caused massive disapproval in the region, also because Tarasenko himself, with his wealthy businessman background, did not appear as a credible politician able to ask people to "wait," ("Millioner Tarasenko Velel Bedneyushchim Primortsam Terpet' i Izobrazhat' Bogachei," *Vostok.Today*, accessed April 22, 2021, https://vostok.today/23012-millioner-tarasenko-velel-bedneyuschim-primorcam-terpet-i-izobrazhat-bogachey.html).

48 "Primorskiy Kray Pered Vyborami Gubernatora," *Tsentr Issledovaniy Politicheskoy Kultury Rossii*, accessed April 22, 2021, http://cipkr.ru/2018/09/03/primorskij-kraj-pered-vyborami-gubernatora-po-materialam-monitoringovogo-oprosa/.

prevented people from voting in some of the affected polling stations). Federal officials claimed that the results of the second round of elections, scheduled for September 16, were unlikely to be problematic for the center (as opposed to several other regions in Russia, where a second round of elections also became necessary). On September 11, Tarasenko had a personal meeting with Putin, who endorsed his campaign claiming that he "thinks that everything will be all right."[49] Tarasenko received major support from Moscow in terms of the organization of his election campaign; local observers doubted that these outsiders had a good grasp of the situation in the region.[50] All parties in the systemic opposition, except the CPRF, directly or indirectly supported Tarasenko.[51]

On September 16, the second round of elections took place. After the polling stations were closed, the vote count started; the results of the count were published in real time on the website of the regional elections committee. After 95 percent of the votes had been counted, Ishchenko appeared to be the unexpected winner (52 percent versus 46 percent of votes). After 97.87 percent of the votes had been counted, the elections committee stopped updating the website for about two hours (Ishchenko was still in the lead at that time); when the publication of information continued, Tarasenko took the lead. The outcome was a highly unlikely one—a small fraction of votes counted towards the end appeared to have been cast for Tarasenko only. There are no systemic reasons for this abnormality (for example, specific features of polling stations counted towards the end or differences in voting procedures). The representatives of the Communist Party accused Tarasenko of falsification, which is rather unusual—typically, the systemic opposition does not openly question the rules of the game in the Russian political system.[52] The open accusations could have been linked

49 Elisaveta Antonova, "Temnoe Delo: Kak Nochyu na Vyborakh v Primor'e Smenilsya Lider," *RBC,* accessed April 22, 2021, https://www.rbc.ru/politics/16/09/2018/5b9e6acb9a79475b1a2578f4.

50 "Shtab Tarasenko – Eto Sborishche Neprofessionalov – Politolog," *REGNUM,* accessed April 22, 2021, https://regnum.ru/news/polit/2483794.html.

51 Aleksey Chernyshov and Ekaterina Grobman, "Khvatili Cherez Kray," *Kommersant,* accessed April 22, 2021, https://www.kommersant.ru/doc/3743969.

52 Olga Korelina, "Samye Strannye Vybory 2018 Goda," *Meduza,* accessed April 22, 2021, https://meduza.io/feature/2018/09/17/samye-strannye-vybory-2018-goda-kommunist-ischenko-protiv-edinorossa-tarasenko-v-primorie-glavnoe. A detailed report summarizing the evidence of falsifications can be found here: Ivan Shukshin, "Pokhishchenie Vyborov," *Novaya Gazeta,* accessed April 22, 2021, https://novayagazeta.ru/articles/2019/07/23/81340-pohischenie-vyborov.

to both the unprecedented audacity of the manipulations (obvious to everybody following the elections), and uncertainty about how Russian political leadership would react to the actions of its local bureaucrats.

On September 17, protests against Tarasenko started in Vladivostok (the capital of Primorskiy Kray). The federal government reacted almost immediately. On September 20, the regional elections committee, upon the recommendation of the federal elections committee, declared the second round of elections invalid, given multiple violations. The region then declared that new elections would take place on December 16. Ishchenko protested this decision, arguing that evidence of electoral fraud had only been observed in selected polling stations, so that new elections were not necessary; he also filed a lawsuit against the elections committee, which was dismissed by the courts. Although Ishchenko had initially planned to participate in the new elections as well, the CPRF revoked its support for him,[53] and he ultimately failed to pass the municipal filter.[54] In September, Putin appointed a new temporary governor, Oleg Kozhemyako, who had experience of running multiple regions in the Far East.[55] Kozhemyako successfully won the elections (however, not as an official candidate of United Russia but as an independent candidate—this is most likely linked to the extremely low level of support for United Russia in the region[56]). There is some evidence of election fraud in favor of Kozhemyako, but this time the falsifications were more subtle and did not seem to have such an enormous impact on the outcome of the election.[57]

The developments in Primorskiy Kray are driven by the structural preconditions likely to produce negative electoral outcomes for the regime.[58]

---

53 Aleksey Chernyshov, "Andrey Ishchenko ne Poslushalsya KPRF," *Kommersant*, accessed April 22, 2021, https://www.kommersant.ru/doc/3792902.

54 "Politolog Andreyu Ishchenko Nikto ne Chinil Prepyatstviy," *REGNUM*, accessed April 22, 2021, https://regnum.ru/news/polit/2522925.html.

55 Taisiya Bekbulatova, "Mister Okey," *Meduza*, accessed April 22, 2021, https://meduza.io/feature/2018/10/12/mister-okey.

56 Vladimir Degrachev, Margarita Devyatkina and Elisaveta Antonova, "Edinoross Kozhemyako Poidet na Vybory Gubernatory Primor'ya Samovydvizhentsem," *RBC*, April 22, 2021, https://www.rbc.ru/politics/27/09/2018/5bacc2f19a794700e1dc9386.

57 "Eksperty Uvideli v Nekotorykh Itogakh Golosovaniya za Kozhemyako Priznaki Falsifikatsii," *Obzor.Press*, accessed April 22, 2021, https://obzor.press/regions/83691-ekspertyi-uvideli-v-nekotoryix-itogax-golosovaniya-za-kozhemyako-priznaki-falsifikaczii.

58 Although it is possible to treat the pension reform itself as yet another manufactured crisis, the necessity of increasing the retirement age has been acknowledged by many Russian economists due to the ageing population of the country.

However, the fact that the elections turned into a full-scale crisis, ultimately affecting other Russian regions as well, is a product of multiple miscalculations by the federal center. Firstly, the federal government underestimated the willingness of the regional population to vote against representatives of United Russia—essentially, the voters were willing to support any candidate but the one representing the party in power. Secondly, the center overestimated the positive effects of Putin's endorsement, which did not increase support for the incumbent governor. Thirdly, the center firmly believed that large international events in the region would increase support for the incumbent. In September 2018, Primoskiy Kray hosted the Far Eastern Economic Forum, a major event with multiple guests from Moscow and from other countries. The Forum did not boost support for Tarasenko, implying that people in the region were more concerned about the domestic rather than the international agenda.[59] And finally, the falsification of the elections was done in such a blatant and outrageous manner that the cancellation of elections became inevitable. According to Aleksandr Kynev, a well-known Russian expert specializing in sub-national governance: "One could only have acted like this if one did not understand anything about public opinion, political institutions, and the Far East. It is simply meaningless barbarism."[60]

The excessive falsification of the elections was probably also driven by an unwillingness to acknowledge that Putin is capable of wrongly assessing a situation and of making mistakes.[61] After the public endorsement of Tarasenko, Russian bureaucrats had no choice but to ensure his electoral victory, no matter the cost. According to the editorial of the leading liberal newspaper in Russia, *Vedomosti*: "The doctrine of power the Kremlin is following suggests that turning back and recognizing one's mistakes is nothing else but the recognition of weakness, which is inappropriate for a strong president."[62]

---

59 Elisaveta Antonova, "Temnoe Delo: Kak Nochyu na Vyborakh v Primor'e Smenilsya Lider," *RBC*, accessed April 22, 2021, https://www.rbc.ru/politics/16/09/2018/5b9e6acb9a79475b1a2578f4.

60 Elena Mukhametshina and Anastasiya Agamalova, "Vybory v Primor'e Okazalis' Samymi Skandal'nymi s Dumskoi Kampanii 2011 Goda," *Vedomosti*, accessed April 22, 2021, https://www.vedomosti.ru/politics/articles/2018/09/17/781115-vibori-glavi-primorya-okazalis-samimi-skandalnimi.

61 Oleg Savin, "Vybory v Primor'e—Prosto Bessmyslennaya Dikost," *BBC*, accessed April 22, 2021, https://www.bbc.com/russian/features-45556846.

62 Maria Zheleznova, "Chto Delat', Esli Prezident Vse-Taki Oshibsya," *Vedomosti*, accessed April 22, 2021, https://www.vedomosti.ru/opinion/articles/2018/09/17/781127-chto-delat-esli-prezident-oshibsya.

Thus, one can interpret the crisis in Primoskiy Kray through the lens of (at least) two of the three factors described in the previous section. Bureaucratic inflexibility prevented it from finding a better solution or even seeking one—instead, the bureaucracy ignored the warning signs and focused on making the original scenario of Tarasenko's victory a reality, no matter the cost. Principal-agent problems and information asymmetry prevented the center from correctly assessing the situation in Primorskiy Kray, and the geographic distance between Moscow and Vladivostok of over 6,000 kilometers probably exacerbated the information deficit problem. A series of mistakes emerged, leading to a much more severe crisis than one could have expected. At the same time, the center managed to avoid public protests and ultimately kept the situation under control—unlike the crisis in another Far Eastern region, Khabarovskiy Kray, which unfolded about two years later.

Arrest of the Governor of Khabarovsk (2020)

Since the mid-2010s, Russian governors and mayors have routinely been fired and sent to prison, mainly for corruption.[63] Typically these arrests rarely result in any form of public disapproval—on the contrary, measures against allegedly corrupt officials are highly popular in Russia. To some extent, regular arrests allow Putin to stay ahead of the accusations of corruption coming from the opposition. They also discipline elites (although loyalty does not actually protect a governor from prosecution). The level of corruption in the high ranks of the Russian elites is very high, so finding reasons for arrests is typically not a difficult task.

The arrest of the governor of Khabarovsk in July 2020, however, differs substantially from previous incidents. In 2018, Sergey Furgal was elected governor of Khabarovsk, another Far Eastern region of Russia; similarly to Primorskiy Kray, he was a candidate from the systemic opposition (this time, the LDPR), who unexpectedly won against the incumbent United Russia candidate, although Furgal did not really try to win the elections and even openly declared his willingness to work as deputy governor on the team of

---

63 Joel Moses, "Russian Center-Periphery Relations from Khrushchev to Putin, 1957–2018," *Demokratizatsiya* 27, no. 2 (2019): 215–236; Noah Buckley, Ora John Reuter, Michael Rochlitz and Anton Aisin, "Staying Out of Trouble: Criminal Cases Against Russian Mayors," *Bremen Papers on Economics & Innovation* 2013 (2020).

his opponent. According to some accounts of the elections, at some point Furgal was willing to revoke his candidacy for the governor's office. However, after winning the elections, Furgal quickly gained popularity in Khabarovsk, regularly criticizing the federal government and engaging in dialogue with the opposition (including the "non-systemic" opposition).[64] The LDPR in Khabarovsk developed into a "party of Furgal", bound by personal loyalty to the governor. They managed to win regional elections, significantly weakening the position of United Russia in the region.[65]

Since mid-2019, the federal government has instigated a series of criminal investigations in Khabarovsk. On July 9, 2020, Furgal himself was arrested and transported to Moscow. The federal prosecution charged him with multiple counts of murder in 2004–2005 (during that period, Furgal was an entrepreneur in Khabarovsk and in the Amur Oblast). As of March 2021, the criminal investigations are ongoing, with Furgal being held in prison in Moscow; on July 20, 2020, Putin fired Furgal from the office of the governor.

Furgal's arrest was met with massive disapproval by the people of the region. On July 11, between 30,000 and 35,000 people in Khabarovsk protested the actions of the center (this was the largest protest in the history of the region; the city of Khabarovsk has about 600,000 inhabitants).[66] The spontaneous protests were not endorsed by the regional administration or by the LDPR. Since July, protests have taken place every day in Khabarovsk. Furthermore, demonstrations took place in other cities in Russia, including Moscow and St. Petersburg.[67] A public opinion survey implemented by the Levada Center in July 2020 demonstrated that 81 percent of Russians were, to some extent, informed about the protests in Khabarovsk, and 45 percent approved of the protests (only 17 percent of the respondents claimed to

---

64 Andrey Perzev, "Slishkom Narodnyy Gubernator," *Meduza,* accessed April 22, 2021, https://meduza.io/feature/2020/07/09/slishkom-narodnyy-gubernator.

65 Andrey Perzev, "Drugoe Bolshinstvo: Kak v Khabarovske Proveryayut Populyarnost' Putina," *Moscow Carnegie Center,* accessed April 22, 2021, https://carnegie.ru/commentary/82387.

66 Konstantin Groshin, "Aktsiya Protesta posle Aresta Furgala Stala Samoi Massovoy v Istorii Khabarovska," *Kommersant,* accessed April 22, 2021, https://www.kommersant.ru/doc/4415230.

67 "Zhiteli Rossiyskikh Gorodov Vyshli na Aktsii Solidarnosti s Khabarovchanami: Est' Zaderzhannye," *Novaya Gazeta,* accessed April 22, 2021, https://novayagazeta.ru/news/2020/08/01/163449-zhiteli-rossiyskih-gorodov-vyshli-na-aktsii-solidarnosti-s-habarovchanami.

have a negative attitude towards the protests).[68] The protesters not only called for stopping investigations into Furgal but also criticized Putin and the federal administration.

Another factor that made the situation even worse was Putin's decision to replace Furgal with Mikhail Degtyarev as a temporary governor. Degtyarev also officially represents the LDPR but, unlike Furgal, had no biographical connections to the Far East. The appointment prompted even more criticism from protesters,[69] which became even stronger after Degtyarev publicly refused to engage in any form of dialogue with the protesters (and presented himself as a person able to lobby for resources for the region through his personal connections in Moscow—a stance which did not increase his popularity in Khabarovsk).[70]

Protests in Khabarovsk turned out to be a serious problem for Putin's administration. Firstly, they again demonstrated that Putin's endorsement does not automatically guarantee public support. Secondly, the protests showed the importance and the strength of regional identities, potentially weakening the centralized approach of Putin's administration to governing Russia. Thirdly, again, as in the case of the Primorskiy Kray elections, the fact that Furgal was personally loyal to Putin to a large extent (and the fact that he, as with most businessmen starting their careers in the 1990s, was most likely involved in questionable activities in the past) did not prevent the protests from developing. In fact, the protests showed that even relatively insignificant regional politicians have the potential to become the focal point of protests—in an entirely unexpected way for Putin.[71]

In the case of Furgal's arrest and the protests, the mistakes made by the central government are even more obvious. First of all, the arrest itself was not inevitable; on the contrary, Furgal, as mentioned, remained loyal to Moscow and the center was still able to implement its policies in the region (for example, Khabarovsk supported the constitutional reform in a referendum in early July 2020, which allows Putin to run for a new presidential term

68 "Protesty v Khabarovske," *Levada,* accessed April 22, 2021, https://www.levada.ru/2020/07/28/protesty-v-habarovske/.

69 Anastasiya Yakoreva, "Eto Plevok so Storony Putina," *Meduza,* accessed April 22, 2021, https://meduza.io/feature/2020/07/25/eto-plevok-so-storony-putina.

70 Ekaterina Kuznetsova, "Khabarovsk Protiv Degtyareva," *TJ,* accessed April 22, 2021, https://tjournal.ru/analysis/190973-habarovsk-protiv-degtyareva-on-ignoriruet-protestuyushchih-no-obeshchaet-hodit-v-banyu-s-nachalnikami-radi-zhiteley.

71 Dmitriy Travin, "Opasen Li Dlya Putina Khabarovsk," *ROSBALT,* accessed April 22, 2021, https://www.rosbalt.ru/blogs/2020/07/29/1856178.html.

after the end of the current one).[72] The dominance of the LDPR probably required some adjustments in the way the center interacted with the Khabarovsk elites; however, these adjustments would have been less costly than mass protests spilling over to other parts of Russia. Second of all, the appointment of Degtyarev and his subsequent actions only intensified the protests—although officially he represented the same party as Furgal (but for the people in the Far East, Furgal's local origins were more important than his official party affiliation).

Most importantly, the central government underestimated the robustness of the protests, and faced significant difficulties in understanding it—the protests were not organized by the regional administration and were entirely spontaneous. They had a strong political agenda but, at the same time, did not fall under the group of "liberal protests" by the democratic opposition, which Putin's regime has been dealing with for the last fifteen years or more.[73] The protesters did not call for democratic reforms in Russia, improving relationships with the west, or market reforms—all these items on the agenda of liberal opposition are well known to Putin's administration, which has developed effective ways of counteracting them.[74] The typical rhetorical tools used against the opposition (for example, claims that protests are organized by foreign actors) obviously missed the target in the case of Khabarovsk.[75] And, finally, the protests in Khabarovsk demonstrated a lack of understanding of spontaneous protests by Putin's administration,

72 "V Khabarovskom Krae Popravki k Konstitutsii Poddezhali 62.28% Progolosovavshikh," *TASS,* accessed April 22, 2021, https://tass.ru/politika/8863317.

73 Tatyana Stanovaya, "Kognitivnyy Dissonans Kremlya," *Forbes Russia,* accessed April 22, 2021, https://www.forbes.ru/obshchestvo/406003-kognitivnyy-dissonans-kremlya-chem-habarovskiy-protest-opasen-dlya-vlasti.

74 For example, referring to the painful experience of the 1990s, which in the eyes of most Russians was a period of national humiliation and extreme poverty. See Alessandro Belmonte and Michael Rochlitz, "The Political Economy of Collective Memories: Evidence from Russian Politics," *Journal of Economic Behavior & Organization* 168 (2019): 229–250; Olga Malinova, "Framing the Collective Memory of the 1990s as a Legitimation Tool for Putin's Regime," *Problems of Post-Communism*, forthcoming.

75 The claim that protests, to some extent, are organized by foreign citizens was made by Degtyarev ("Degtyarev: K Organizatsii Poslednikh Mitingov v Khabarovskom Krae Prichastny Inostrannye Grazhdane," *BFM,* accessed April 22, 2021, https://www.bfm.ru/news/449121); Putin's spokesperson, Dmitriy Peskov, on the contrary, claimed that protests are not organized by foreigners but that over time "professional rowdies" joined the protests ("V Kremle Isklyuchili, Chto Mitingi v Khabarovske Organizovany Iz-za Rubezha," *RIA,* accessed April 22, 2021, https://ria.ru/20200724/1574865238.html).

who were unable to grasp and to deal with protests without a clear center and group of organizers.

Thus, a pattern similar to the one already documented for the elections in Primorskiy Kray in 2018 can be observed. Putin's regime fails to correctly assess the situation in the region and to devise effective tools to counteract it. The inflexible bureaucracy is unable to effectively deal with the protests and often reacts in a way that only fuels the flames—for example, the demands of Putin's representative, Yuriy Trutnev, directed at regional officials to immediately stop the protests (which the regional administration did not organize in the first place)[76] or the rhetoric of Degtyarev. Over time, the protests died down and, on October 10, the police used force to disband the demonstrations. Still, the protests continued, although with a much smaller number of participants—the most recent protest took place on January 23, 2021, in spite of the ongoing Covid-19 pandemic.

Discussion

The two cases presented in this chapter share one common characteristic—while there are structural reasons behind poor electoral outcomes or protests, the reaction of the central government aggravated the situation. In the case of Khabarovsk, Furgal's arrest even provided the population with a "focal point" to mobilize protesters, which otherwise would have been absent. In the past, there have been cases of corruption accusations and arrests against governors from United Russia, like Aleksandr Khoroshavin (Sakhalin, 2015) or Vyacheslav Gayzer (Komi, 2015), and from the systemic opposition, like Nikita Belykh (Perm, 2016), but they did not lead to protests. However, in the case of Primorksiy Kray, the elections constituted a natural focal point present in many electoral authoritarian regimes.[77] In both cases, the central government had a poor understanding of the situation in the region, underestimated disapproval of the center, and the strength of regionalist sentiments (the latter point is astonishing given how important it was

76 "Polpred Prezidenta Provel Zakrytye Soveshchaniya v Khabarovske i Potreboval Podavit' Protesty," *BUSINESS Online,* accessed April 22, 2021, https://www.business-gazeta.ru/news/474571.

77 Carl Knutsen, Håvard Nygård and Tore Wig, "Autocratic Elections: Stabilizing Tool or Force for Change?" *World Politics* 69, no. 1 (2017): 98–143.

for Putin's administration to deal with possible autonomist movements in the regions from the start). In both cases, the tools used to deal with the problem were inadequate. And, in both cases, the center overestimated the power of Putin's popularity, which is evidently unable to resolve any conflicts in the Russian regions anymore.

The situation in the Russian Far East fits at least two theoretical predictions formulated in this chapter. Firstly, it appears to be a probable case of information asymmetries, in the case of Russia, exacerbated by the enormous dimensions of the country. While the digital era simplifies information transmission from, and communication with, remote regions, it does not solve the problem of information collection constraints. The local knowledge required to fully understand the expectations of the regional population and elites is a *tacit* one and can only be obtained through regular and informal interactions with local actors and casual observations of regional politics and social life. Secondly, Russian bureaucracy did not respond to the crises in an optimal way. The governance system established in Russia under Putin discourages public officials from taking the initiative and makes them focus on manipulating reporting rather than actually solving the problems they face.[78] The centralization of Russian bureaucracy, which took place over two decades of Putin's rule, robbed it of "local knowledge" and understanding of the situations in individual regions.[79] A bureaucratic, centralized, authoritarian state thus shows lower resilience (and higher likelihood of "manufacturing" crises).

An interesting question is whether the third factor—the personalization of the regime—also contributed to the emergence of manufactured crises. Under Putin, the Russian regime became more personalized over time, and it would be tempting to link the crises with the misperceptions of, and mistakes made by Putin personally. However, given the highly untransparent decision-making process in modern Russia, there is hardly any evidence available to corroborate this issue. Putin commented on Furgal's case only in December 2020, claiming that he personally "never had problems" with him and perceived him as "loyal", yet considers the criminal charges to be

78 Ella Paneyakh, "The Overregulated State," *Social Sciences* 45, no. 1 (2014): 20–33; Alexander Kalgin, "Implementation of Performance Management in Regional Government in Russia: Evidence of Data Manipulation," *Public Management Review* 18, no. 1 (2016): 110–138.

79 Andre Schultz and Alexander Libman, "Is There a Local Knowledge Advantage in Federations? Evidence from a Natural Experiment," *Public Choice* 162, no. 1–2 (2015): 25–42.

very serious ones.[80] As for the Primorskiy Kray elections, Putin described the situation as a "normal" one.[81] In both cases, Putin's personal decisions (for example, the appointment of temporary governors) instead escalated the crisis. Russian observers frequently suggest that Putin overestimates the stability of his regime.[82] Nevertheless, it is difficult to go beyond mere speculation in this respect. (Putin's calm behavior during the crises, and confident and nonchalant comments in the aftermath, could be a strategic move to signal his full control over the situation in the country.)

As a caveat, authoritarian regimes occasionally create artificial crises (or situations which look like crises to an external observer) to test the loyalty of their subjects or to remove bureaucrats they are dissatisfied with. The cases examined here, however, do not seem to be examples of these artificial crises. Firstly, the Kremlin seems to have been genuinely concerned about the situation and unable to understand the reasons for the protests (as Trutnev's reaction to the Khabarovsk protests shows). Furthermore, the crises had a chance to spill over to other parts of Russia (some reaction—for example, public actions in defense of Furgal—was observed in other regions of Russia as well), and one can hardly expect Putin's regime to accept such a risk. Finally, for Putin, from the very beginning of his rule, loss of control over regional situations seems to have been the major challenge he wanted to avoid at all costs.[83] It is therefore unlikely that he would consciously provoke a crisis in a region, especially one he considers strategically important (like the Far East).

In conclusion, "manufactured crises" are an important issue for at least certain varieties of authoritarian regimes. Russia is—by far—not the only case of an authoritarian regime facing this challenge. Other examples include the reaction of Belarusian President Alyaksandr Lukashenka to the Covid-19 pandemic in 2020 (the denial of the severity of the problem led to growing dissatisfaction with Lukashenka's policy and unprecedented public protests followed the falsified 2020 elections); Saddam Hussein's decision to

---

80 "Loyal'nyy Byl Chelovek. Problem u Menya s Nim Ne Voznikalo. Putin o Dele Furgala," *Meduza,* accessed April 22, 2021, https://meduza.io/news/2020/12/17/loyalnyy-byl-chelovek-problem-u-menya-s-nim-ne-voznikalo-putin-o-dele-furgala.

81 "Putin Prokommentiroval Situatsiyu s Vyborami v Primor'e," *AMIC,* accessed April 22, 2021, https://www.amic.ru/news/424156/.

82 Tatyana Stanovaya, "Presidentskie Itogi Goda," *Moscow Carnegie Center,* accessed April 22, 2021, https://carnegie.ru/commentary/83492.

83 Natal'ya Gevorkyan, Natal'ya Timakov and Andrey Kolsesnikov, *Ot Pervogo Litsa* (Moscow: Vagrius, 2001).

occupy Kuwait in 1990 (which triggered an international response the dictator did not expect and made him a pariah in international relations until the end of his rule); and the decision of Augusto Pinochet to organize a national plebiscite to reaffirm his position as President of Chile in 1988 (which he, contrary to his expectations, lost). Stephen Hall, in his chapter in this edited volume, discusses the reaction of Lukashenka's regime to the 2020 crisis and shows that the regime ignored any lessons previously learned from similar events in post-Soviet Eurasia, citing the growing inflexibility of the regime—similarly to what has been observed in this chapter.

"Manufactured crises" are not inevitable—one could imagine an authoritarian regime that meets all the conditions discussed in this chapter but, by chance, manages to avoid making mistakes for a prolonged period of time. However, the stronger the features of authoritarian regimes favoring "manufactured crises" are—personalism, centralism and inflexibility of bureaucracy—the more *probable* "manufactured crises" become. The cases of manufactured crises presented in this chapter are not unique. In Russia, there were similar cases of reform initiatives triggering protests (like those of truck drivers in 2015 following the introduction of the poorly designed road tax collection system[84]) and of inadequate reaction to protests by failing to understand the causes and organizers of the protests.[85] However, the considerations presented in this chapter allow one to infer that instances of strategic miscalculation will reoccur in the future, and may even become more frequent—ultimately, with unpredictable consequences for Putin's regime.

---

84 Ekaterina Fomina, "We Have Plenty of Reasons to Protest Apart from Platon," *Open Democracy,* accessed April 22, 2021, https://www.opendemocracy.net/en/odr/russia-truck-driver-protest/.

85 Alexander Libman, "Putin and the Costs of Being Wrong," *Verfassungsblog,* accessed April 22, 2021, https://verfassungsblog.de/putin-and-the-costs-of-being-wrong/.

Learning from a Neighboring Crisis: Did the Belarusian and Kazakh Regimes Learn from the Ukrainian Revolution of Dignity, 2013–2014?

Stephen G. F. Hall

Introduction

The Euromaidan[1] was typified by a regional disparity which saw most protesters come from Western and Central Ukraine, predominantly from Kyiv and Lviv. This discrepancy was found in surveys conducted during the protests between December 2013 and February 2014.[2] It is for other studies to analyze these geographical disparities, but they further confirm Ukraine's geographical cleavages—among others—a situation further emphasized by the ease of the Russian annexation of Crimea and the war in the Donbas. While the Donbas war was originally led by Russians, the majority of fighters were always Ukrainian, further highlighting these geographical cleavages.

The problems of a cohesive Ukrainian national identity were watched closely by the Belarusian and Kazakh governments. The geographical divides in Ukraine were easily exploited by Russia to annex Crimea and create a frozen conflict in the Donbas, and these worried the Belarusian and Kazakh authorities who feared possible Russian-sponsored separatism in Belarus and Kazakhstan. During his 2014 National Assembly address,

1 The Euromaidan was a protest that occurred from November 2013 to February 2014. For the most part, it occurred in central Kyiv in the main square—Maidan Nezalezhnosti (Independence Square). This square has been the setting for most major protests in Ukraine: The Revolution on Granite (1990), the Orange Revolution (2004–2005) and the Euromaidan (2013–2014). The Euromaidan was the protest in central Kyiv that eventually resulted in President Viktor Yanukovych fleeing the presidency for Russia. The Euromaidan was the catalyst for the wider Revolution of Dignity, which centered on the belief that the state should treat its citizenry as citizens and not subjects.

2 Daryna Shevchenko, "Poll discovers Euromaidan evolution from dreamy to radical," *Kyiv Post*, accessed November 19, 2020, https://www.kyivpost.com/article/content/ukraine-politics/poll-discovers-euromaidan-evolution-from-dreamy-to-radical-336389.html.

Belarusian President Alyaksandr Lukashenka[3] stated that "Ukraine is seething [...] Old boundaries are crumbling before our eyes and, for the first time in many years, smoke from explosions is again happening in Europe." The Belarusian authorities particularly feared that the eastern *Mahilioŭskaya voblast* (Mogilev region) could be annexed by Russia due to the region's close ties to Russia.[4] Similarly, Kazakh President, Nursultan Nazarbayev, claimed on Kazakhstan's Unity Day in 2014 that the Ukrainian events had occurred due to a lack of national unity.[5] As with the Belarusian authorities, there was real fear in the Kazakh government that a sizeable minority of Kazakhs remained in the Russian sphere of influence, which the Russian regime could use to justify annexing parts of Kazakhstan.[6]

Events in Ukraine, from the Euromaidan and the Donbas war, provided the Belarusian and Kazakh regimes with at least one lesson—the necessity of enhancing national unity. As authoritarian regimes, the Belarusian and Kazakh governments are wary of any large-scale protests or other crises, especially ones in a neighboring post-Soviet state where protest spillover to Minsk and Astana is possible.[7] Using the bank-run analogy, where during times of financial crisis banks use money to prop themselves up, authoritarian regimes have to stop any potential threat as any danger left alone could spiral out of control and result in the collapse of the regime. Consequently, it is likely that the Belarusian and Kazakh regimes were concerned by events in Ukraine in late 2013 and 2014 and developed best practices to restrict the chance of such events occurring in Belarus or Kazakhstan. In the 2000s, both regimes saw the Color Revolutions in the post-Soviet space as a crisis that needed to be tackled in order to prevent such events from happening

3 Alyaksandr Lukashenka, "Poslanie Prezidenta belorusskomu narodu i Natsional'nomu sobraniyu," *Presidential Portal of the Republic of Belarus*, accessed November 19, 2020, http://president.gov.by/ru/news_ru/view/aleksandr-lukashenko-obraschaetsja-s-ezhegodnym-poslaniem-k-belorusskomu-narodu-i-natsionalnomu-sobraniju-8549/.

4 Interview: S91GA11/12/2016; Interview: MMD04/05/2017; Interview: AprA90SR03/05/2017; Interview: PMA12/12/2017.

5 Olzhas Auyezov and Shamil Zhumatov, "Kazakh leader evokes Ukraine as land protests spread," Reuters, accessed November 19, 2020, https://www.reuters.com/article/us-kazakhstan-protests-president-idUSKCN0XS1E1.

6 Petr Trotsenko, "Uroki ukrainskogo: Evormaidan i kazakhstanskoe obshchestvo," *Radio Azattyk*, accessed November 19, 2020, https://rus.azattyq.org/a/ukraine-euromaidan-2014-kazakhstan/29612134.html.

7 Astana was re-named Nur-Sultan in honor of Nazarbayev after he left the presidency in 2019. To maintain historical consistency, I use Astana unless referring to events after March 2019 when the city was re-named to Nur-Sultan.

in Minsk and Astana, and the Euromaidan was perceived in a similar way.[8] The Color Revolutions, as popular protests supporting democracy, were a direct threat to the legitimacy of authoritarian regimes that may have mimicked democracy but controlled the system to such an extent that elections were a foregone conclusion.

Although Freedom House has certain potential methodological and ideological problems, it has consistently placed Belarus and Kazakhstan in the bracket of unfree states. In 2020, Belarus scored 19 out of 100[9] and Kazakhstan 23 out of 100[10], with scores closer to zero highlighting the unfree nature of a state. This outside assertion of the authoritarian nature of each state is further corroborated by outside researchers.[11] Even Belarusian and Kazakh officials say the same,[12] epitomized by statements from Lukashenka that democracy is too *bourgeois* and leads to instability, and Nazarbayev's continual advocating for stability before democracy can be implemented.[13] Both regimes are known as electoral authoritarian regimes where elections are held, but these "violate the liberal-democratic principles of freedom and fairness [...] profoundly and systematically [...] to render elections instruments of authoritarian rule rather than 'instruments of democracy'".[14] While both regimes do use all three pillars of authoritarian stability—

---

8 Interview: PVR/20/11/2020; Interview: S91GA/18/11/2020.

9 Freedom House, "Freedom in the World 2020: Belarus," *Freedom House*, accessed November 19, 2020, https://freedomhouse.org/country/belarus/freedom-world/2020.

10 Freedom House, "Freedom in the World 2020: Kazakhstan," *Freedom House*, accessed November 19, 2020, https://freedomhouse.org/country/kazakhstan/freedom-world/2020.

11 For Belarus, see: Andrew Wilson, *Belarus: The Last European Dictatorship* (New Haven and London: Yale University Press, 2011); Matthew Frear, *Belarus under Lukashenka: Adaptive Authoritarianism* (London and New York: Routledge, 2019). For Kazakhstan, see: Edward Schatz, "The Soft Authoritarian Toolkit: Agenda-Setting Power in Kazakhstan and Kyrgyzstan," *Comparative Politics* 41, no. 2 (January 2009): 203–222; Ernesto Gallo, "Globalisation, Authoritarianism and the Post-Soviet State in Kazakhstan and Uzbekistan," *Europe-Asia Studies* 73, no. 2 (March 2021): 340–363.

12 Interview: PVR/20/11/2020; Interview: S91GA/18/11/2020.

13 Alyaksandr Lukashenka, "Rabochaya vstrecha s prem'er-ministrom Belarusi Andreem Kobyakovym," *Presidential Portal of the Republic of Belarus*, accessed December 30, 2020, http://president.gov.by/ru/news_ru/view/rabochaja-vstrecha-s-premjer-ministrom-belarusi-andreem-kobjakovym-11890/; Vremya, "Nursultan Nazarbayev: Vrazhdauyut ne religii, a lyudi i gosudarstva," *Vremya*, accessed December 30, 2020, https://time.kz/news/archive/2012/06/02/nursultan-nazarbaev-vrazhduyut-ne-religii-a-lyudi-i-gosudarstva.

14 Andreas Schedler, "The Logic of Electoral Authoritarianism," in *Electoral Authoritarianism: The Dynamics of Unfree Competition*, ed Andreas Schedler (Boulder and London: Lynne Rienner Publishers, 2006). 1–26.

incorporating repression, co-optation and legitimacy[15]—the Kazakh authorities are subtler in their practices having established a regime-controlled, multi-party system using the law to reduce the capacity of opposition groups to operate.[16] While the Kazakh authorities still use repression, there is less reliance on it than in the Belarusian regime, which resorts to repression at the slightest threat.[17] While the Belarusian regime does have state-controlled parties, these play very little role in the political system because of the fear among the authorities that these organizations could become independent.[18]

To test the argument of Belarusian and Kazakh reactions to crises—specifically the Euromaidan—and how the Belarusian regime has recently failed to use practices developed in the 2000s, we firstly address existing literature on authoritarian learning to provide an understanding of what is meant by the concept. Secondly, we investigate Belarusian and Kazakh reactions to this protest, ascertaining what lessons were drawn by both regimes. Thirdly, we then address the practices that were developed to limit a possible Maidan-like revolution in Astana or Minsk. Finally, we analyze the current protests happening in Belarus, and the lessons that the regime learnt from past Color Revolutions for use in 2020.

A quick note to explain that the methodology used is in order here. Process-tracing attempts to "validate a causal relationship between independent and dependent variables"[19] and unpacks "causality, that aims at studying what happens between X and Y and beyond."[20] When analyzing authori-tarian regimes, there is difficulty in accessing information, as these regimes do not publish much evidence. Therefore, it is only possible to provide some evidence and infer from this data that learning in authoritarian regimes happens. We also rely on interviews to gather appropriate evidence. As au-thoritarian regimes are being dealt with here, interviewees are

---

15 Johannes Gerschewski, "The three pillars of stability: legitimation, repression, and co-optation in autocratic regimes," *Democratization* 20, no. 1 (January 2013): 13–38.

16 Interview: PVR/20/11/2020.

17 Interview: S91GA/18/11/2020.

18 Interview: AugP86VY/24/11/2020.

19 Thomas Ambrosio and Jakob Tolstrup, "How do we tell authoritarian diffusion from illusion? Exploring methodological issues of qualitative research on authoritarian diffusion," *Quality & Quantity* 53, no. 6 (June 2019): 2741–2763.

20 Christine Trampusch and Bruno Palier, "Between X and Y: how process tracing contributes to opening the black box of causality," *New Political Economy*, 21, no. 5 (February 2016): 437–454.

anonymized to offer some protection.[21] However, it can be disclosed that the inter-viewees come from the world of journalism and research, and that analysis of both regimes is their daily focus.

Towards Authoritarian Learning in Belarus and Kazakhstan, and Belarusian Pre-Emptive Authoritarianism

The existing authoritarian learning literature has investigated how authoritarian regimes learn to develop best practices for keeping power. This literature originated from analyzing the Arab Spring and how some authoritarian regimes there learnt from the failure of other authoritarian regimes, such as Egypt and Tunisia, to maintain power.[22] Authoritarian learning involves a mixture of policy-transfer and diffusion, with diffusion being particularly crucial.[23] Elkins and Simmons[24] see diffusion as the "policy decisions of one government alter[ing] the conditions under which other governments base their decisions." Ambrosio[25] argued that authoritarian regimes diffuse information, trying to locate appropriate policies, ideas and models to ensure a continuation of power. We follow the definition of authoritarian learning provided by Hall and Ambrosio[26], who see authoritarian learning as "a process in which authoritarian regimes adopt survival strategies based upon the prior successes and failures of other governments."

---

21 The coding system uses a mixture of birth date, birth month, and year, where the interviewee was born or currently resides, where the interview occurred, either online or the city, and the first letter of the interviewee's name and surname, and the date that the interview happened. As not all information is available, I use what is available to provide anonymity.

22 Steven Heydemann and Reinoud Leenders, "Authoritarian Learning and Authoritarian Resilience: Regime Responses to the 'Arab Awakening,'" *Globalizations* 8, no. 5 (November 2011): 647–653.

23 Stephen G. F. Hall and Thomas Ambrosio, "Authoritarian Learning: A Conceptual Overview," *East European Politics* 33, no. 2 (February 2017): 143–161.

24 Zachary Elkins and Beth Simmons, "On waves, clusters, and diffusion: a conceptual framework," *Annals of the American Academy of Political and Social Science*, 598, no. 1 (March 2005): 33–51, here: 40.

25 Thomas Ambrosio, "Constructing a Framework of Authoritarian Diffusion: Concepts, Dynamics, and Future Research," *International Studies Perspectives* 11, no. 4 (November 2010): 375–392.

26 Hall and Ambrosio, "Authoritarian Learning," 143.

Existing literature on authoritarian learning offers an extensive analysis of how authoritarian regimes learn from the failures of others. This is applicable in analyzing the Belarusian and Kazakh learning from the Euromaidan, and the learning from the failures of Ukrainian President, Viktor Yanukovych.

To better understand the Belarusian regime's use of certain practices during the 2020 protests, we investigate the literature on pre-emptive authoritarianism, as the Belarusian authorities were particularly adept at using pre-emptive tactics to maintain power in the 2000s. Pre-emptive authoritarianism allows the regime to pre-empt potential external democratization efforts. Another type of literature is that of adaptive authoritarianism, which is relevant to understanding how the Belarusian regime reacts to events. Adaptive authoritarianism is about how a regime constantly adapts to ever-changing external and internal developments.

During the 2000s, the Belarusian regime was adept at pre-empting democratization practices instigated by external actors, with the authorities perceiving any challenge as a zero-sum game needing elimination.[27] Rather than allow pressure to build, and opposition groups, civil society and independent media to be established and exert influence, the government used targeted repression against any challenge, however small and inconsequential, fearing that by not doing so these challenges could become a major issue later.[28] After the first Color Revolution[29] in 2000 in Serbia, the Belarusian regime quickly devised practices to prevent such events from happening in Belarus.[30] Due to the rapidity of the authorities' reaction, Belarus became a testing ground for developing best practices for post-Soviet authoritarian regimes to maintain power in the face of democratic protests.[31] The development of adaptive authoritarianism in Belarus allowed the regime to continually maneuver in an ever-changing world.[32] However, it is fascinating to

27 Vitali Silitski, "Contagion Deterred: Preemptive Authoritarianism in the Former Soviet Union (the Case of Belarus)," *Center on Democracy, Development and the Rule of Law*, accessed November 26, 2020, https://fsi-live.s3.us-west-1.amazonaws.com/s3fs-public/Silitski_No_66.pdf.

28 Interview: OctM17BD/12/09/2017.

29 The Color Revolutions were a series of democratic revolutions across the post-Soviet space and Eastern Europe starting in Serbia in 2000, and then in Georgia 2003, Ukraine, 2004, and Kyrgyzstan, 2005.

30 Stephen G. F. Hall, "Preventing a Colour Revolution: the Belarusian example as an illustration for the Kremlin," *East European Politics* 33, no. 2 (February 2017): 162–183.

31 Wilson, *Belarus*, 209.

32 Frear, *Belarus under Lukashenka.*

consider that a regime which relied heavily on its capacity to adapt in the 2000s allowed its methods of doing so to disintegrate so quickly after 2017.[33] Although there are nuances between pre-emptive and adaptive authoritarianism, the two concepts are similar and will be used interchangeably here.

Belarusian and Kazakh Learning from the Euromaidan

Of course, the Belarusian and Kazakh regimes are established authoritarian regimes and so had already established best practices in developing tools to better consolidate power. Certainly, the Belarusian regime had created methods to counteract protests before the Euromaidan. Due to domestic protests in 2006 and 2010, the regime had learnt from mistakes made during these events, such as allowing protesters to set up tents in 2006, leading to police clearing central Minsk quickly in 2010.[34] Similarly, the Kazakh authorities had developed effective tactics to hold power prior to the Euromaidan. As Kazakhstan is not a direct neighbor of Ukraine, the regime was less affected by events in Kyiv. The authorities were more concerned with devising best practices after domestic events, or analyzing events in neighboring Kyrgyzstan in 2005, 2010 and 2020.[35] However, as authoritarian regimes always have to be prepared, fearing that if they are not, then events may spiral out of control, the downfall of any other authoritarian regime provides an example for copycat attempts domestically, so neighboring authoritarian regimes have to stay ahead. Although the Belarusian and Kazakh authorities were established authoritarian regimes with developed, effective best practices to maintain power, the Ukrainian events resulted in learning by both regimes.

The Euromaidan was of particular concern to certain state institutions in both regimes, with both regimes' *siloviki*[36] (literally "strongmen") taking particular interest in these events. For example, the Belarusian security services, even today, get personnel to watch videos of the mistakes made by the

33 Interview: AugP86VY/22/09/2020.

34 Interview: S91GA/18/11/2020; Interview: UMP/18/11/2020.

35 Interview: BAA/24/11/2020.

36 This term refers to senior officials of state institutions, such as the Interior Ministry, Presidential Administration, Security Council and Security Service. I use the Russian spelling for ease, rather than interchanging between the Belarusian and Kazakh spellings.

Ukrainian security forces during the Euromaidan, highlighting that, if the Belarusian security forces do not use full repressive measures, then the protesters will win. Privately, the Belarusian security forces constantly discuss the Euromaidan and develop tactics to counter a potential Minsk Maidan. There is the realization that the authorities must use maximum repression against protesters, which came from learning about the failures of Yanukovych at the Euromaidan.[37] During the Euromaidan, Yanukovych procrastinated about using repression, trying to placate protesters while using off-screen repression away from the Maidan. This radicalized the protesters, making it increasingly difficult for the regime to maintain power. Currently, the Belarusian regime is experiencing state-wide protests and it is uncertain whether full repression is effective, as it has radicalized protesters after six years of limited coercion. While the Belarusian regime has long had high repressive capacity and relies on this, the need to use maximum repressive capabilities was a lesson from the Euromaidan.

Although far more hidden regarding available information, members of the Kazakh *siloviki* developed practices from the Euromaidan to enhance the consolidation practices that the regime already possessed. Soon after the Euromaidan, existing legislation on protests, political parties and non-Governmental organizations (NGOs) were all changed to further restrict the activities of political parties, NGOs and future protests.[38] While getting inside the black box of an authoritarian regime and gleaning information on the activities of regime institutions is a challenge, in particular *siloviki* structures, there is evidence that the Belarusian and Kazakh regimes hold regular meetings with one another.[39] It is likely that events, such as the Euromaidan, result in dialogue between both regimes on how to stop potential Maidans in Astana and Minsk. According to one interviewee,[40] representatives of the Kazakh Interior Ministry met with their Tajik, Turkmen and Uzbek counterparts to discuss the Euromaidan and to develop tactics to stop such an event happening in Central Asia.

37 Interview: S91GA/18/11/2020; Interview: AugJ16DSB/19/11/2020.

38 Interview: JulN18AN/24/11/2020.

39 Igor' Vinyavsky, "Pochemu Belorusam nuzhny uroki kazakhskoi istorii," *Belsat*, accessed November 25, 2020, https://vot-tak.tv/novosti/pochemu-belorusam-nuzhny-uroki-kazahskoj-istorii/; Andrey Tikhomirov, "Kazakhstan dlya Belarusi—partner, o kotorom mozhno tol'ko mechtat,"" *Naviny.by*, accessed November 25, 2020, https://naviny.media/rubrics/politic/2013/02/03/ic_articles_112_180718.

40 Interview: JulN18AN/24/11/2020.

Social media had been a key aspect of mobilizing protesters during the Euromaidan, with the protests allegedly started by a Facebook post, although this is somewhat of a romanticized view.[41] In December 2014, the Belarusian authorities updated the Law on Mass Media, allowing the government to close websites that did not delete information deemed inaccurate by the state media watchdog.[42] Likewise, the Kazakh regime updated media legislation in 2014, directly after the Euromaidan, that increased fines for Internet sites that published offensive information—as determined by the authorities—and allowed the government to block websites without appeal.[43] These actions were a direct consequence of how social media had helped organize, coordinate and maintain the Maidan protests. That the Kazakh law change on fines occurred in June 2014 also points to the Euromaidan being a direct cause of this development.

Both regimes used control of television media to portray the Euromaidan as violent and to convey that only the authorities could maintain stability.[44] In 2015, there was a presidential election in Belarus and the necessity for stability, which apparently only the regime could offer, became the regime's key election campaign message. The message was that, without Lukashenka, Belarus would have a Maidan and anarchy,[45] epitomized in the election campaign slogan "For the Future of Independent Belarus." This was in contrast to the 2010 presidential election campaign slogan "For a Prosperous and Strong Belarus." Kazakh state media emphasized the Donbas conflict with the narrative that, without Nazarbayev, a similar scenario would occur in northern Kazakhstan.[46] During protests in 2014 over

41 Olga Onuch, "'Facebook helped me do it': Understanding the Euromaidan Protester 'Tool-Kit,'" *Studies in Ethnicity and Nationalism* 15, no.1 (April 2015): 170–184.

42 Interview: HMA/19/08/2016.

43 Daily News.kz, "Kazakhstantsev budut shtrafovat' za oskorbitel'nye kommentarii v internete," *Dailynews.kz*, accessed November 27, 2020, http://www.dailynews.kz/society/kazahstantsev_budut_shtrafovat_za_oskorbitelnye_kommentarii_v_internete; Khabr, "V Kazakhstane massovo blokiruyut populyarnye veb-saity," [Popular websites are often blocked in Kazakhstan], *Khabr.com*, accessed November 27, 2020, https://habr.com/ru/news/t/355880/.

44 Interview: UMP/18/11/2020; Interview: DMM/18/11/2020; Interview: AugJ16DSB/19/11/2020; Interview: BAA/24/11/2020.

45 Interview: UMP/18/11/2020; Interview: DMM/18/11/2020.

46 Interview: BAA/24/11/2020.

land ownership, state media continually referenced and used footage of Ukraine's conflict to keep protest numbers small and disunited.[47]

Corruption was a major aspect of the Yanukovych regime in Ukraine, with the Yanukovych "family" of close allies taking close to eight billion dollars out of the economy annually between 2010 and 2013.[48] An end to corruption had been one of the demands of the Euromaidan. Although the Kazakh authorities had announced the Strategy Kazakhstan-2050[49] in 2012, the government had focused on governance issues until 2014. After the Euromaidan, the course changed to concentrate on anti-corruption initiatives and nominally strengthen government anti-corruption bodies, increasing their powers on paper.[50] Similarly, the Belarusian regime instigated an anti-corruption drive, with Lukashenka publicly dressing down politicians for corrupt practices live on television. That this occurred in 2014 soon after the Euromaidan, and that it was done so publicly, points to direct learning from the venality of the Yanukovych regime and the fear that Belarusians may become disenchanted by the authorities' own corruption. Through an anti-corruption drive, Lukashenka could show that he still had the interests of the populace at heart, thereby increasing regime legitimacy.[51]

Although Lukashenka had previously referred to protesters and the political opposition as fascists, the Euromaidan gave him another opening to continue this rhetoric domestically. The Euromaidan was portrayed by Yanukovych and the Russian authorities as a fascist coup. The message of the Euromaidan being organized by fascists was an effective propagandistic tool by the Russian regime to distort facts and engage fellow travelers in Europe to misrepresent the Euromaidan to the wider public[52]. This gave Lukashenka an avenue of discourse during the 2017 state-wide protests

47 Reuters, "Kazakh leader evokes Ukraine as land protests spread," *Reuters*, accessed November 25, 2020, https://www.reuters.com/article/us-kazakhstan-protests-president-idUSKCN0XS1E1.

48 Andrew Wilson, "Supporting the Ukrainian Revolution," *European Council on Foreign Relations*, accessed November 25, 2020, http://www.ecfr.eu/page/-/ECFR96_UKRAINE_MEMO.pdf.

49 An initiative to turn Kazakhstan into one of the 30 most developed global economies by 2050.

50 Interview: PVR/20/11/2020.

51 Interview: UMP/18/11/2020.

52 Olexiy Haran, "Don't believe the Russian propaganda about Ukraine's 'fascist protesters,'" *The Guardian*, accessed November 25, 2020, https://www.theguardian.com/commentisfree/2014/mar/13/russian-propaganda-ukraine-fascist-protesters-euromaidan.

against "social parasites",[53] with the re-creation of the *Belyy Legion* (White Legion) to serve as a Belarusian version of the Ukrainian fascist organization, *Pravy Sektor*,[54] to taint all protesters as fascists and link this to the Euromaidan. The re-creation of the *Belyy Legion*, which had been successfully terminated after being accused of the 2010 Minsk metro bombings, was a signal to the Russian authorities to support Lukashenka. The fascist discourse was a direct lesson for the Belarusian regime from the Euromaidan.

Geo-politically, the annexation of Crimea and the war in Donbas instigated by Russia forced the Belarusian regime to seek better relations with the European Union for fear that, without external support, Belarus would be prey to Russian annexation. However, it was only ever an association of convenience because the Belarusian authorities, perceiving that the European Union and western states instigated the Euromaidan, could not trust these governments knowing that they would support democratic protesters. For the Belarusian authorities, the Euromaidan was a coup that was not just supported by western states, but that was instigated by these governments.[55]

There was a very real fear in the Belarusian regime that the Russian authorities may at least try to annex the Mogilev Oblast.[56] Belarusian society was largely polarized into those who supported Russian actions and those that did not. This worried the regime, who feared that the Russian authorities could use this support to justify annexing Belarus or Belarusian territory. Therefore, to re-engage popular support for the regime, the Belarusian authorities looked to "patriotic initiatives that avoid accentuating ideological differences."[57] This policy to enhance Belarusian identity was known as soft-Belarusianization, and the program moved away from the glories of the partisans in World War II and close alignment to Russia, to an identity that emphasized Belarusian achievements and re-interpreted history. Belarusian was promoted in schools[58] but this new identity was malleable, with Lithuanian Grand Duke Algirdas re-cast as an early Belarusian freedom

---

53 In 2015, the regime passed legislation known as the "social parasite law," which was a tax on the unemployed. This became law in 2017 and led to state-wide protests.

54 BelGazeta, "'Belyy Legion' on 'Eurovision,'" *BelGazeta*, April 18, 2017.

55 Interview: AugJ16DSB/19/11/2020.

56 Interview: S91GA11/12/2016; Interview: MMD04/05/2017; Interview: AprA90SR03/05/2017; Interview: PMA12/12/2017.

57 Volha Chrnysh, "War of Ideology: The Ukrainian Conflict Polarizes Belarusians," *Belarus Digest*, accessed March 3, 2021, https://belarusdigest.com/story/war-of-ideology-the-ukrainian-conflict-polarizes-belarusians/.

58 Interview: MMD/04/05/2017.

fighter against Muscovy.[59] The regime allowed the opposition to openly celebrate the 1918 Declaration of Independence to emphasize 100 years of independent Belarusian statehood. The old Kyivan Rus' Principality of Polotsk was portrayed as a distinct entity to Kyiv and Muscovy, allowing the regime to contend that Belarus had a thousand years of statehood.[60]

Soft-Belarusianization[61] was an answer to the Russian concept of *Russkiy Mir*—an initiative to engage with Russian speakers and countries in the post-Soviet region—especially those deemed by the Russian authorities to be ethnically and linguistically close to Russia, such as Belarus. However, soft-Belarusianization was incoherent and poorly planned, due to Lukashenka still viewing Belarusian identity as an opposition issue that, if left uncontrolled, would galvanize the public against his rule which remained closely tied to Russia and the Soviet past. Soft-Belarusianization was a way to increase domestic support for the regime and to highlight to an international audience that Belarus was not an appendage of Russia. However, Lukashenka still fundamentally believed that western states could not be trusted as they supported the opposition and ultimately wanted regime change in Belarus. This perception of western intransigence and the belief that the Belarusian identity was dangerous kept Lukashenka close to Russia.[62] Although in 2014 Belarusian had a mini-resurgence in Belarusian-language education, it has since declined in favor of Russian. It is questionable whether the Belarusian army would even fight the Russian army, due to the former's close allegiance to the High Command in Moscow.[63] However,

59 Vadim Mojeiko, "Soft Belarusianization: A New Shift in Lukashenka's Domestic Policy?" *Belarus Digest*, accessed November 25, 2020, https://belarusdigest.com/story/soft-belarusization-a-new-shift-in-lukashenkas-domestic-policy/.

60 Andrew Wilson, "Softly, softly Belarus," *New Eastern Europe* 33, no. 5 (September 2018): 7–13.

61 Soft-Belarusianization represented Belarus as a state with a long, prominent history. It also promoted the language. This was in contrast to Belarusian identity in the Soviet Union, where the state had promoted some distinct Belarusian characteristics, but had couched these in Marxist-Leninist terms and superseded Russian culture in importance to Belarusian, viewing the latter as an appendage of Russian identity. The promotion of Belarusian identity, promoted by groups like the Belarusian Popular Front in the late 1980s and early 1990s, dissolved Soviet monikers replacing these with a flag, symbols and cultural references largely alien to the wider population. This helped Lukashenka come to power, as he advocated a closer alignment to Russia and the Soviet era. Soft-Belarusianization kept the idea of Belarus being close to Russia but being distinct. In this regard, it was closer to the Soviet variant of Belarusian identity than the early 1990s option.

62 Interview: UMP/18/11/2020; Interview: S91GA/18/11/2020.

63 Interview: UMP/18/11/2020.

the instigation of a soft-Belarusianization policy, which stemmed directly from events in Ukraine, was a process of learning by the Belarusian regime, to counteract a Belarusian Donbas scenario. The authorities feared that public attitudes were too pro-Russian and supportive of Crimea's annexation and the war in the Donbas. Therefore, the regime instigated the soft-Belarusianization policy to differentiate Belarus from Russia for both internal and external audiences.[64] The identity policy was a means to increase popular legitimacy domestically, and raise Belarus's profile internationally as distinct from Russia. However, because of the current protests, Lukashenka has reverted to a more pro-Russian identity policy to gain the support of the authorities in Moscow.

Officially, the Kazakh regime continues a pro-Russian discourse as, like Belarus, Kazakhstan is a member of many Russian-dominated, post-Soviet regional organizations. However, some parliamentary delegates vocally attacked Russia for the Crimean annexation. Due to regime control of parliament, these statements were an unofficial regime statement on the annexation.[65] Unlike Belarusian society, which largely supported the Russian annexation of Crimea, Kazakh society was more divided,[66] thereby forcing the Kazakh government to promote state unity. Yet, Russian practices in Crimea and the war in Donbas allowed the Kazakh authorities to run a drive to promote Kazakh statehood.

In the 1990s and 2000s, the need to improve the "Kazakh" identity to incorporate all people in Kazakhstan had not been a pressing issue for the government. However, following the events in Ukraine, this identity promotion went into overdrive after 2014. This situation was not helped by comments from Russian politicians, such as Putin, that Kazakhstan had never been a state until Nazarabayev, who had created "a state in a territory that had never had a state before," and that Kazakhstan should "remain in the greater Russian world."[67] The Kazakh government instigated policies to

64 Interview: S91GA/18/11/2020.

65 Interview: JulN18AN/24/11/2020.

66 Andrey Chebotarev, "Publikatsii: Analitika," *Alternativa*, accessed November 25, 2020, http://www.alternativakz.com/index.php?nid=274.

67 Frangis Najibullah, "Putin Downplays Kazakh Independence, Sparks Angry Reaction," RFE/RL, accessed November 25, 2020, https://www.rferl.org/a/kazakhstan-putin-history-reaction-nation/26565141.html. This was a gross misrepresentation of Kazakh identity and state-building, which had already begun under Soviet rule. In 1920, an Autonomous Soviet Socialist Republic was established within the Russian Soviet Federative Socialist Republic. In 1936, then, the Kazakh Soviet Socialist Republic (Kazakh SSR)

enhance Kazakh statehood.[68] After the events in Ukraine, coupled with the threats emanating from Moscow over Kazakh statehood, the authorities instigated a number of Kazakh identity policies.

Ethnic Kazakhs, traditionally located in the country's south were offered subsidies to re-locate to the more ethnically Russian north.[69] Unlike the Belarusian regime, which allowed the opposition to celebrate the 1918 Independence Day unimpeded, the Kazakh authorities instigated a state celebration in 2015 on the establishment of the Kazakh Khanate in 1465.[70] In a further dissimilar stance to the Belarusian regime, the Kazakh authorities took a far stronger stance on promoting national identity. While the regime has maintained the narrative of Kazakhstan being home to 130 ethnic groups,[71] after 2014, the authorities designed a new slogan "Kazakhstan for the Kazakhs." While this slogan could accommodate all 130 ethnic groups, the implication was that ethnic Kazakhs were now the dominant state group.[72] The authorities restricted access to key institutions for some ethnic groups, such as denying ethnic Russians the right to join the Kazakh army or be employed in the civil service.[73]

Belarusian Regime Reactions to the 2020 Protests—Learning from the Past?

Having investigated the Belarusian and Kazakh regimes' reaction to the Euromaidan, we address Belarusian reactions to the 2020 protests, investigating how the authorities used tactics developed from previous protests during the current events. While the political elites learnt little from the Euromaidan, with soft-Belarusianization being at best an incoherent policy, the Belarusian security services did assess the Euromaidan and the failures of the Ukrainian security services.[74] On two separate occasions in 2014,

---

became a constituent republic, gaining political institutions which provided it with viable statehood.

68 Interview: BAA/24/11/2020.

69 Interview: BAA/24/11/2020.

70 Interview: BAA/24/11/2020.

71 Interview: BAA/24/11/2020.

72 Interview: PVR/20/11/2020.

73 Interview: PVR/20/11/2020.

74 Interview: S91GA/18/11/2020.

Lukashenka stated that "events in Ukraine do not pose direct threats to...Belarus,"[75] and that events like the Maidan were not new as the regime had had to counteract a "similar Maidan in Belarus" in 2010, with the 2004 Orange Revolution having already provided valuable learning opportunities for the regime.[76] If we take Lukashenka's statement at face value, it is likely that previous external and internal protests were of more relevance to the Belarusian regime than the Euromaidan.

The first Color Revolution occurred in 2000 in Serbia and saw the collapse of its President, Slobodan Milošević, a person who had been a close ally of Lukashenka.[77] One slogan of the Serbian revolution was "today Milošević[...]tomorrow Lukashenka,"[78] which sent the Belarusian regime into overdrive to stop a Serbian scenario in Belarus. The authorities created a pro-regime youth movement—the Belarusian Republican Youth Union (BRSM—Belarusian acronym)—to galvanize younger Belarusians to support the regime.[79] Another point linking Belarusian learning from Serbia was the restrictions placed on Non-Governmental Organizations (NGOs) in 2001, which saw limitations placed on NGOs operating without regime approval.[80] Although the regime had largely taken control of media outlets by 2001, the authorities passed legislation on defamation and publishing of "false" information, as defined by the regime, and foreign financing of media was further restricted.[81] In 2001, the presidential administration set up the Information Analytic Centre (IAC), to conduct public opinion polls and become an early warning system for the regime as to what could lead to future

75 Alyaksandr Lukashenka, "Aleksandr Lukashenko provel zasedanie Soveta Bezopasnosti Respubliki Belarus,'" *Presidential Portal of the Republic of Belarus*, accessed November 26, 2020, http://president.gov.by/ru/news_ru/view/aleksandr-lukashenko-provedet-zasedanie-soveta-bezopasnosti-respubliki-belarus-8449/.

76 Alyaksandr Lukashenko, "Aleksandr Lukashenko prinyal uchastie v torzhestvennykh meropriyatiyakh po sluchayu Dnya zashchitnikov Otechestva," *Presidential Portal of the Republic of Belarus*, accessed November 26, 2020, http://president.gov.by/ru/news_ru/view/aleksandr-lukashenko-prinjal-uchastie-v-torzhestvennyx-meroprijatijax-po-sluchaju-dnja-zaschitnikov-otechestva-8098/.

77 Feduta, Aleksandr, *Lukashenko: Politicheskaya Biografiya* (Moscow: Referendum, 2005), 442.

78 Jonathan Steele, "Serbia is Just the First of the Post-communist States to Fall," *The Guardian*, accessed November 26, 2020, http://www.theguardian.com/world/2000/nov/20/serbia.comment.

79 Hall, "Preventing a Colour Revolution," 169.

80 Ibid, 173.

81 Ibid, 168.

protests.[82] To maintain support, Lukashenka promoted close allies who would support the regime at all costs. The authorities continued to refine tactics in a process of constant adaptation after 2001.[83]

While legislative changes occurred and further restrictions were placed on independent entities between 2001 and 2006, there was limited significant change. It is likely that the 2004 Orange Revolution in Kyiv, a neighboring state, was a key catalyst. This, combined with the build-up to the 2006 presidential election, meant that the regime had been building up security forces and increasing training exercises against protesters.[84] As part of the reaction to the Orange Revolution and 2006 presidential elections, the regime passed legislation which ended foreign funding for NGOs.[85] The authorities developed a system of early voting after the 2004 Orange Revolution, which forced state employees and students to vote early and allowed the regime to change the result if necessary, without worrying about the concerns of election observers. Another lesson from the Orange Revolution was the necessity to get "independent" electoral polls claiming the regime's electoral victory. This tactic was used to good effect during the 2006 presidential election where so-called independent electoral polls confused the situation and made it harder to organize protests over electoral fraud.[86] Although the Belarusian regime had located an external enemy in the past, it was in 2006 that the regime really developed this tactic. As opposition leader Alyaksandr Milinkevich spoke Polish, the Belarusian security services "discovered" that the Polish security forces were working with Milinkevich to violently remove Lukashenka.[87]

The protests after the 2006 presidential election gave the regime a clear lesson in the run up to the 2010 presidential elections. In 2006, the authorities had allowed protesters to set up a tent city reminiscent of the Orange Revolution in Kyiv. Even worse, the security services had allowed protesters to congregate again in central Minsk after initially clearing demonstrators.[88] Therefore, the regime resorted to excessive force in 2010 to clear protesters,

82 Interview: DECJ22DB/21/11/2016; Interview: JanK31MA/26/08/2016; Interview: AugT84BY/29/01/2018.

83 Feduta, *Lukashenko*, 535, 567.

84 Vitali Silitski "Belarus: Learning from Defeat," *Journal of Democracy* 17, no 4 (October 2006): 138–152.

85 Interview: JanK23J/21/11/2016; Interview: AprY79MA/23/08/2016.

86 Hall, "Colour Revolution," 170.

87 Yelena Ankudo, "Shpiony "spalilis"" na flesh-karte," *BelGazeta*, September 17, 2007.

88 Interview: JanK23J/21/11/2016.

especially after receiving the green light from Russia.[89] Devised by the security services, the regime instigated new tactics, learnt from the mistakes the authorities made in 2006.[90] Having addressed the lessons that the regime learnt from earlier Color Revolutions and domestic protests, we turn to address the tactics that the authorities used during the current protests.

Color Tactics in the 2020 Protests?

The Belarusian regime had been a highly adaptive authoritarianism, preempting external efforts at democratization throughout the 2000s and developing a range of practices to counter a potential Color Revolution. However, did the regime use tactics developed against previous external and internal protests during the current protests in Minsk? We show that the authorities failed to use many of the tactics. This is partly because the current protests have been state-wide, and because of the changed geo-political situation, but primarily, it is due to a growing regime disconnect, brought on by regime longevity and increasing miscommunication within the regime and to the populace. This fits with Alexander Libman's chapter on "manufactured crises" in this volume. As the tenure of an authoritarian regime becomes increasingly long, the state structures begin to break down, thereby resulting in more and more crises. The longevity of the Lukashenka regime in Belarus points to this breakdown scenario as a likely factor in the current crisis. Increasingly, the regime lacks information channels on events in the country, there is a growing inflexibility, and the regime has long been personalized in the figure of Lukashenka—represented as *bat'ka* or the father of the nation. While the authorities have survived past crises and remain capable of adaptation, the longevity of the regime has resulted in an example of manufactured crisis *par excellence*.

During the Color Revolutions of the 2000s, the regime restricted capacity and limited foreign funding for NGOs. Similarly, media outlets were constrained through a two-strike system, where two warnings resulted in

89 Uladzimir M Padhol and David R Marples, "The 2010 Presidential Election in Belarus," *Problems of Post-Communism* 58, no. 1 (January 2011): 3–16, here: 7.

90 Jarábik Balázs, Jana Kobzova, and Andrew Wilson, "The EU and Belarus After the Election," *European Council on Foreign Relations*, accessed November 26, 2020, http://www.ecfr.eu/page/-/Belarus%20memo%20Jan%202011.pdf.

closure, leading to self-censorship. The authorities had the power to close an outlet for "inaccurate" information, with the inaccuracy being determined by the government. Public opinion polling capacity was another effective tool in the regime's preventive arsenal, providing an early warning system as to what may lead to protests. The regime established an extensive repressive capacity and, with fourteen different security institutions, coercion was used regularly against any threat.[91] It was this extensive repressive capacity that the regime developed to ensure retention of power. Certainly, the regime was a testing ground for developing best practices to counter Color Revolutions, with the authorities adept at adaptation and constant improvements in expanding anti-Color Revolution methods.

However, I contend that there was little that the regime used during the current protests that came from its anti-Color Revolution playbook. After the state-wide protests about the legislation labeled the "Social Parasite Law" in 2017, the authorities placed further restrictions on the Internet, passing legislation to make it difficult to post comments online anonymously as all commentators had to provide personal data before posting.[92] Even TUT.by—a nominally independent Internet news portal—had its wings clipped. Before 2017, TUT.by was relatively independent without criticizing the regime—allowing its readers to let off steam without becoming opposition[93]—but after the social parasite protests, the authorities moved against TUT.by. Editor-in-chief, Mariya Zolotova, was accused of using services from the state news agency, BelTA, without paying for them. This was a message that even the pro-regime TUT.by was considered too independent.[94] While the regime has long had an effective preventive revolution arsenal that it used against protesters concentrated in one square in Minsk, it had less capacity to repress state-wide protests.[95]

Throughout the 2020 protests, the authorities did not use their palette of anti-protest tactics developed in the 2000s. There has been no new anti-NGO or media legislation at the time of writing in March 2021. Of course,

91 Interview: DMM/04/05/2017.

92 Tat'yana Korovenkova, "Internet v Belarusi perestaet byt' zonoi svobody," Naviny.by, accessed November 27, 2020, https://naviny.media/article/20181209/1544345453-internet-v-belarusi-perestaet-byt-zonoy-svobody.

93 Interview: HMA/19/08/2016.

94 Evgeny Zhukov and Ekaterina Venkina, "V Belarusi osvobozhden ryad zhurnalistov po "delu BELTA," *Deutsche Welle*, accessed November 27, 2020, https://www.dw.com/ru/в-беларуси-освобожден-ряд-жуналистов-по-делу-белта/a-45027797.

95 Interview: AugT84BY/29/09/2020.

it takes time to pass legislation but, in a personalized regime like Belarus, and with a parliament with no independent deputies, laws can be passed quickly. However, this has not happened to date. Rather, the authorities have concentrated on the Internet and developing repressive tactics. The regime had long realized that it does not have control over the Internet and so it began increasing control over the Internet and creating a regime presence online.[96] During the current protests, the Presidential Administration's Operational Analytical Centre (OAC) disabled 80 percent of available Internet access, thereby limiting access to most websites. Even encrypted websites and social media channels like NEXTA—which is a crucial protest organizing channel—were affected.[97] However, the authorities fell back on their number one practice of using repression during the protests. As mentioned, the Belarusian regime perceived that the Yanukovych regime during the Euromaidan had not used sufficient force and that only full repression would maintain regime survival.[98] Coercion had been the regime's go-to tactic in the past, using this as a message to the rest of the electorate that the government possesses coercive capacity and will use it if necessary.[99] The authorities have perfected an extensive palette of repression developed from counteracting the Color Revolutions, and this has included extensive—and effective—tactics of riot control. Therefore, there has been little so far that is ostensibly new in how the regime has dealt with protesters during the current crisis, as the authorities already possess appropriate practices for crowd control.[100]

As mentioned earlier, the Belarusian security services analyzed the Euromaidan and the failure of the Ukrainian security services to end the protest, using videos of these events to train Belarusian security personnel in the mistakes of the Ukrainian government. One key Belarusian lesson from the Euromaidan was that protest had to be met with full repression.[101] The necessity of using all the regime's repressive capacity learnt from the Euromaidan led to the authorities resorting to torture and beatings of protesters

96 Interview: AugT84BY/29/09/2020.

97 Tadviser, "Kontol' povedeniya pol'zovatelei v internete v Belorussi," *Tadviser*, accessed November 27, 2020, https://www.tadviser.ru/index.php/Статья:Контроль_поведения_пользователей_в_интернете_в_Белоруссии#.

98 Interview: S91GA/18/11/2020.

99 Interview: P85WA/09/08/2016.

100 Interview: AugT84BY/29/09/2020.

101 Interview: S91GA/18/11/2020; Interview: UMP/18/11/2020.

during the current protests.[102] However, the use of the regime's full palette of repression has failed to clear the protests, bringing more people onto the streets to protest the use of repression.[103]

It appears that the Belarusian regime's learning from the Euromaidan was poorly absorbed. Yanukovych used as much coercive capacity as the Ukrainian regime possessed, and yet all these practices did was bring more people onto Kyiv's streets. As Lukashenka stated, Belarus had already had a Maidan in 2010,[104] which had been put down by significant repression by the authorities. The Euromaidan likely confirmed the need for a coercive approach by the regime. Nevertheless, then Interior Minister, Igar Shunevich, stated that the security services had not needed to train against possible protests during the 2015 presidential elections, having learnt all they needed after the protests in 2006 and 2010.[105] While meant as a threat to the opposition, it highlighted that there had only been limited learning by the regime from the Euromaidan. Therefore, the authorities were fighting the last war, concentrating on Color Revolutions and missing the nuances of the Euromaidan, which had largely been leaderless in organization.[106]

Whereas the Color Revolutions, and the 2006 and 2010 protests had had leaders, the 2020 protests followed a similar trajectory to the Euromaidan in that they were largely leaderless. The authorities have jailed or exiled the three women widely seen as the leaders of the 2020 protests, Svyatala Tsikanhouskaya, Marya Kalesnikava and Veranika Tsapkala. However, whereas the arrest of opposition leader Alyaksandr Milinkevich in 2006 and Andrei Sannikau in 2010 largely precipitated the collapse of protests, the arrest and exile of Tsikanhouskaya, Kalesnikava and Tsapkala in 2020 has not had the same effect. While parts of the Belarusian regime drew some lessons from the Euromaidan, the nuances of the Euromaidan appear to have been missed.

---

102 Tanya Lokshina, "Justice is Needed for Belarus. International Scrutiny is the Way to Get it," *The Moscow Times*, accessed November 27, 2020, https://www.themoscowtimes.com/2020/09/16/justice-is-needed-for-belarus-international-scrutiny-is-the-way-to-get-it-a71454.

103 Interview: AugT84BY/29/09/2020; Interview: DecJ22DSJ/19/11/2020.

104 Lukashenka, "uchastie v torzhestvennyky".

105 BelTA, "Shunevich: MVD k vyboram gotovo," *BELTA*, accessed November 27, 2020, https://news.tut.by/society/456168.html.

106 Dmitry Dagaev, Natalia Lamberova, Anton Sobolev and Konstantin Sonin, "The Arab Spring Logic of the Ukrainian Revolution," *Free Policy Briefs*, accessed November 27, 2020, https://freepolicybriefs.org/2014/03/31/the-arab-spring-logic-of-the-ukrainian-revolution/.

Similarly, it appears that the Belarusian regime has not initiated its counter-revolutionary playbook learnt from reaction to the Color Revolutions of the 2000s. Legislation takes time to pass and so it is likely that further anti-NGO, protest and media legislation is coming, but the authorities have been reactive rather than proactive. Currently, the regime has relied heavily on the use of repression to maintain control, but this has had the opposite effect. Repression has led to greater protest numbers, which has led to more coercion, again increasing protest numbers. As seen in 2017, the authorities are less adept at coping with state-wide protests than clearing a square in central Minsk.[107] However, the state-wide protests of 2017 were several years ago and surely an adaptive authoritarianism, such as Belarus, should have instigated methods to counter such events.

Why was this not the case? After all, the regime was considered in the 2000s to be adept at adaptation and pre-empting external democratization pressures, having developed an effective palette of preventive revolution tactics. I argue that this is due to a range of factors that can be labeled as static authoritarianism, where a growing disconnect has affected the ability of the regime to adapt. Firstly, Lukashenka is increasingly reliant on a small group of personnel tied to the security services, such as the presidential guard.[108] For example, one interviewee stated that Lukashenka gets economic policy from the security services rather than from personnel from the Ministry of Economics.[109] This is a problem for the regime, as security personnel and Lukashenka hold similar world views and largely ignore information that does not fit that understanding.[110] The lack of information reaching Lukashenka is highlighted by the example of former Head of the Presidential Administration, Natallya Kacahanava, and Lukashenka's Press Secretary, Natallya Eismant. According to an interviewee, both Natallyas re-interpret information, putting a positive spin on material before passing it to Lukashenka,[111] which has adversely affected the regime. This information disconnect is an issue in such a personalized regime. Most regime decisions are made by the presidential administration and Lukashenka and, if negative

107 Interview: AugT84BY/29/09/2020.

108 Yuri Tsaryk "Lukashenka's recent appointments: in search of efficacy," *Belarus Digest*, accessed November 27, 2020, https://belarusdigest.com/story/lukashenkas-recent-appointments-in-search-of-efficacy/.

109 Interview: AugT84BY/29/01/2018.

110 Interview: DecZ10MJ/29/09/2020; Interview: S91GA/21/09/2020; Interview: AugT84BY/29/09/2020.

111 Interview: AugT84BY/29/09/2020, Skype.

information is kept from Lukashenka and he is closer to personnel who share his world view, then this is a significant problem for the regime and how it functions.

Secondly, the regime has been faced with a stagnating economy since the global recession of 2008. This, coupled with a society increasingly less reliant on the state due to a growing private sector, has become a problem for the regime. Belarusian society has become increasingly middle class, with a younger generation less susceptible to quasi-Soviet propaganda reaching political maturity. The image of the patrician father, epitomized by Lukashenka, increasingly no longer resonates. This situation was made worse by Lukashenka's backtracking over the Social Parasite Law,[112] highlighting that the emperor had no clothes. Within Belarus, increasingly, younger people are concerned with single issue politics, rather than joining the opposition.[113] However, the regime believed that society had become uninterested in politics because opposition numbers were decreasing. Therefore, when faced with single issue problems, such as the social parasite protests and the current protests, the authorities have been unable to react other than to use repression, which increases protest numbers.[114] This is a problem for all authoritarian regimes that want to remain in power long-term—how to remain relevant to the public and keep the same leader in power without the whole *façade* appearing stale. Changing a leader can be traumatic for an authoritarian regime, as few authoritarian leaders are willing to countenance an alternative and so will make sure that only they are kept in power. Similarly, gentlemen's agreements, where leaders step down after a certain period in power and are replaced by the next generation are one option, but this is dependent on the leader following the agreement. This system was in operation in China and Vietnam, but the current leaders—Xi Jinping and Nguyen Xuan Phuc—have recently reneged on the deal. Citizen apathy is one crisis a regime cannot plan for as it is not certain when the indifference will happen, and a

112 Dmitry Kysnets, "Lukashenko pravit 26 let—i, navernoe, budet pravit' eshche kakoe-to vremy. No za poslednyuyu "pyatletku" ego rezhim lishilsya glavnykh opor," *Meduza*, accessed November 27, 2020, https://meduza.io/feature/2020/08/12/lukashenko-pravit-26-let-i-navernoe-budet-pravit-esche-kakoe-to-vremya-no-za-poslednyuyu-pyatiletku-ego-rezhim-lishilsya-glavnyh-opor.

113 Interview: KT/26/08/2016.

114 Stephanie Höppner, "Belarus protests have roots in Lukashenko's repression," *Deutsche Welle*, accessed November 27, 2020, https://www.dw.com/en/belarus-protests-have-roots-in-lukashenkos-repression/a-54627793.

palace coup against the incumbent leader may not actually resolve the problem.

A part of the misunderstanding problem in Belarus was the demise of the IAC. Natallya Eysmant believed that the regime needed to get online and win hearts and minds there[115] and so she restricted IAC funding. This change in policy drastically affected the regime's early warning system. While the IAC had methodological issues and did not account for societal changes by polling people in the private sector,[116] it was the regime's alarm system to predict future protests. In 2019, the IAC was split into the Belarusian Institute for Strategic Studies (BISD—Belarusian acronym) and the Sociology Department of the Academy of Sciences. The BISD was tasked with writing policy reports on changes the regime could make, although these were apparently ignored,[117] and the Sociology Department ran public opinion polls. However, the Sociology Department lacked finances, access to sensitive information, and continued to ask questions of little relevance to the present.[118] When, in 2019, the Sociology Department conducted a test poll of Minsk residents on how they would vote at the 2020 presidential elections, the findings, which saw Lukashenka receiving a low vote percentage were ignored by the regime,[119] highlighting again the informational disconnect.

With the Russian annexation of Crimea, the Belarusian authorities began a limited rapprochement with western states. This resulted in the regime limiting its use of repression, resorting to fines, administrative arrests and, if necessary, the use of tax authorities and child services.[120] Historically, the regime always relied on repression when faced by any issue, and so any curbing of the regime's coercive apparatus was seen as a signal that the authorities were less willing to repress. This notion was epitomized by the authorities' reaction to protests over a battery factory in Brest. Rather than clear the protesters, the authorities involved negotiated a peaceful solution. This happened in early 2020 and highlighted that the regime was changing and was less reliant on repression. This sheathing of the regime's repressive capacity likely made Belarusians more willing to protest.[121] However, when

115 Interview: AugT84BY/29/09/2020.

116 Interview: FMA/29/09/2020.

117 Interview: DecZ10MJ/29/09/2020.

118 Interview: DecZ10MJ/29/09/2020; Interview: FMA/29/09/2020.

119 Interview: JunA26MY/10/11/2020.

120 Interview: DecL23MV/27/11/2016; Interview: AugP86VY/18/08/2016; Interview: Ł72MA/04/05/2017.

121 Interview: AugT84BY/29/09/2020.

the regime uses repression now, this angers many Belarusians and increases willingness to protest. The use of coercion and torture, which the authorities had learnt was a necessity from the Euromaidan, created a zero-sum game between the authorities and protesters.

Finally, the lack of a government reaction to the coronavirus pandemic further galvanized society. The pandemic caused an economic recession which the authorities failed to react to, and this further alienated society.[122] Lukashenka's statement that the coronavirus was a mass psychosis appeared insensitive at the very least, but the regime's decision to press ahead with the May 9 Victory Day celebrations, when even Russia delayed its own celebrations, was incredibly obtuse.[123] This callous approach by the authorities was made worse by the fact that deaths from the virus rose throughout June, a month before the election.[124] The pandemic acted as a single issue giving the opposition an unprecedented opportunity to unite society against the regime. The pandemic helped galvanize the protests which were further animated by Lukashenka's fraudulent electoral victory of 80.1 percent.

Conclusion

As has been shown here, there were lessons that both the Belarusian and Kazakh regimes took from the Euromaidan to cope with this neighboring crisis, such as building up security forces, controlling the Internet, and devising a stronger Belarusian and Kazakh national identity. The Belarusian regime concentrated on the security issues of the Euromaidan, examining the failures of the Ukrainian security services, and training their own security personnel to avoid the mistakes made during the Euromaidan. By contrast, the Kazakh regime engaged in re-defining Kazakhstan and strengthening

---

122 BEROC, "BEROC: Velika veroyatnost' otsrochennoi i rastyanutoi retsessii," *BEROC*, accessed November 27, 2020, http://beroc.by/media/press/beroc-velika-veroyatnost-otsrochennoy-i-rastyanutoy-retsessii/?sphrase_id=682.

123 RBK, "Lukashenko nazval pandemiyu COVID-19 politicheskoi i ekonomicheskoi voinoi," *RBK*, accessed November 27, 2020, https://www.rbc.ru/politics/07/08/2020/5f2d3ca09a794754ca49849b; Marina Elistratova, "Edinstvennyi v Evrope parad—v otrazhenii Belorusskikh media," *UDF.by*, accessed November 27, 2020, https://udf.by/news/main_news/212339-edinstvennyj-v-evrope-parad-v-otrazhenii-belorusskih-media.html.

124 Interview: FMA/29/09/2020.

national identity. While the Belarusian regime devised a soft-Belarusianization policy, it was largely ineffectual. Both regimes implemented stricter policies towards the Internet, taking greater control over websites and social media.

After a comparison of Belarus and Kazakhstan, we investigated what lessons from the past Color Revolutions the Belarusian regime used to better cope with the current protests. The existing literature has heaped praise on the Belarusian authorities for devising practices to pre-empt democracy, offering learning opportunities to other post-Soviet authoritarian regimes and adapting to whatever issues of the day exist. However, we have shown that while the regime used some anti-Color Revolutionary tactics in 2020, these methods have been ineffective due to what is called static authoritarianism, a growing disconnect in the regime. We analyzed a range of factors explaining why this is the case. While it is too early to predict the end of the Lukashenka regime, it appears that, in the near future, there will be political and economic stagnation. Lukashenka may survive in the short-term, but it is difficult to gauge how the regime will get out of this impasse. It appears that a regime that had consistently adapted to previous crises, been a testing ground for other post-Soviet authoritarian regimes and developed a range of best practices to reduce the possibility of a proverbial run on the bank has, in 2020, not adapted to the current crisis.

The current Belarusian regime has been in power since 1994, and this longevity has resulted in a growing stagnation. Lukashenka has long had the capacity to change his colors, chameleon-like, to react to the changing international situation. However, the regime appears to have lost its adaptability becoming increasingly sluggish. Due to increasing inertia, the authorities are generating a manufactured crisis brought on by the increasing lack of information channels to understand a changing country, an inflexibility to keep evolving, and a personalized regime through a representation of Lukashenka that no longer resonates. Lukashenka has been one of the best political survivors in the post-Soviet space, with a strong capacity to adapt and change whenever needed. However, in the current crisis this flexibility appears elusive and, having burnt bridges with western states, there are very few options other than further integration with Russia. This is a situation that the regime has long been averse to, but there are few other options.

However, Lukashenka has managed to retain the support of the majority of the political elites. There were splits within the regime but these have been covered-up, at least on the surface. Similarly, some defections did occur but, for the most part, the elite have remained supportive of Lukashenka. One of the earliest ploys that Lukashenka used was to award medals to security officials live on television without their faces being pixelated. The message was clearly highlighting that if Lukashenka goes down, then the rest of the political elite will follow. This has resulted in the regime remaining relatively cohesive. We have detailed why this is the case, and it appears that adaptation to crises in Belarus is a thing of the past, and that the new normal will be a trajectory of increasing manufactured crises. However, the end of the Lukashenka regime has been predicted before and this remains unlikely. Rather, stagnation, non-adaptation and manufactured crises are the likely short-term future for Belarus.

China's "Anti-Corruption" Campaign Under Xi Jinping: Framing Catastrophe and Catharsis in a Never-Ending Crisis

Bertram Lang

Introduction[1]

> Over the past years, due to their long-term accumulation of contradictions, several countries have attracted their people's wrath, social turbulences, and political regime collapse […] and corruption has been a very important cause of this. All facts tell us that, as the corruption problem is growing ever more serious, eventually it will inevitably lead to the death of Party and nation. We must be on our guard.[2]

Approaching the end of General Secretary Hu Jintao's second term in office, the Chinese Communist Party (CCP) was in a state of internal disarray. It was beset by factional infighting, widespread disorientation, and fundamental disagreements over the long-term economic and political trajectory.[3] Building on popular grievances about economic inequality and flagrant social injustices, an egalitarian, neo-Maoist populism that denounced moral

1 Supplementary material for this chapter is made available in online annexes which can be accessed via the Center for Open Science's OSF repository (https://osf.io/7ymfp/).

2 Xi Jinping, quoted in the Oriental Morning Post, "Xi Jinping Summarizes Lessons from Soviet Communist Party Collapse to Embody Anti-Corruption Determination," February 28, 2013. Henceforth, all articles from the CorCris Corpus described below are quoted by their unique text id ("2013_146"). Annex 3 on OSF contains full references to original Chinese corpus articles quoted in the paper. Unless otherwise indicated, all translations from Chinese are my own.

3 In 2012, Cheng Li observed the most profound CCP legitimacy crisis since 1989 (Cheng Li, "The End of the CCP's Resilient Authoritarianism? A Tripartite Assessment of Shifting Power in China," *The China Quarterly* 211 (September 2012): 595–623). See further, Nimrod Baranovitch, "A Strong Leader for a Time of Crisis: Xi Jinping's Strongman Politics as a Collective Response to Regime Weakness," *Journal of Contemporary China* 30, no. 128 (2020): 249–65.; Brantly Womack, "Xi Jinping and Continuing Political Reform in China," *Journal of Chinese Political Science* 22, no. 3 (2017): 393–406, here: 397; Ruoyun Bai, *Staging Corruption: Chinese Television and Politics,* (Vancouver: UBC Press, 2015).

degeneration due to capitalist economic reforms was thriving.[4] It centered around the popular Party Secretary of Chongqing, Bo Xilai, who notoriously went down on bribery and abuse of power charges in early 2012. In turn, Bo's trial in summer 2013 marked an early milestone in incoming General Secretary Xi Jinping's subsequent drive to present himself as a heroic "tiger-fighter", determined to eliminate both petty and grand corruption in his fearless struggle against corruption and for "the soul of the Party".[5]

That Xi Jinping, in large part, owed his rise to supreme power within the Chinese Party-state to his ability to claim and authoritatively define an existential corruption crisis while simultaneously presenting himself as the one credible leader able to overcome and "solve" this regime crisis has been well established.[6] By contrast, much less attention has been paid to the longer-term implications and resulting challenges created by the crisis moment staged at the 18th Party Congress in 2012 for regime legitimation in the "new era" subsequently proclaimed by Xi.

This chapter seeks to establish whether and how the corruption crisis, which fundamentally shaped the early years of Xi's reign, was overcome and replaced with a new, post-crisis framing of the corruption problem. Since a regime crisis is temporary by definition (lest it transform into irreversible regime decay), a discursive shift away from "crisis mode" to some sort of "success mode" is hypothesized here, in which official Party propaganda turns away from highlighting problems and towards stressing successful crisis management and the decisive progress achieved by the new leadership. In addition to testing this basic hypothesis, this analysis seeks to answer the following sub-questions: How did the Chinese media frame this postulated shift, and how do they deal with the challenging fact that abuses of power by Party-state officials have—obviously—not suddenly disappeared?[7]

---

4 Li He, "Debating China's Economic Reform: New Leftists vs. Liberals," *Journal of Chinese Political Science* 15, no. 1 (2010): 1–23.

5 Kerry Brown, "The Anti-Corruption Struggle in Xi Jinping's China: An Alternative Political Narrative," *Asian Affairs* 49, no.1 (2018): 1–10.

6 Kerry Brown, "The Powers of Xi Jinping," *Asian Affairs* 48, no. 1 (2017): 17–26; Womack, *Xi Jinping*, 402; Lutgard Lams, "Examining Strategic Narratives in Chinese Official Discourse under Xi Jinping," *Journal of Chinese Political Science* 23, no. 3 (2018): 387–411, here: 404.

7 Much research effort has been dedicated to gauging the effectiveness of Xi's campaign, which is obviously impressive in terms of the sheer number of convictions and sanctions but whose longer-term, systemic impact on corruption remains controversial. Cf. e.g., Li Li and Peng Wang, "From Institutional Interaction to Institutional Integration: The National Supervisory Commission and China's New Anti-corruption Model," *The China*

Following a claim-based understanding of crises, this chapter will examine the discursive strategies not only for proclaiming but also for "solving" a corruption crisis, and discuss the implications for authoritarian regime legitimation.[8] I combine quantitative and qualitative content analysis techniques on a corpus of 6,957 articles published in major Chinese newspapers on (anti-)corruption and bribery between January 2007 and December 2020, complemented by 33 Xi speeches on anti-corruption gathered in the *People's Daily* online, "Series of Xi Jinping's important speeches".[9] The core hypothesis is that the public discourse on (anti-)corruption has indeed shifted significantly from a "pre-crisis era" under Hu Jintao to a "crisis era" during Xi's early years in power, and then again towards a "post-crisis era", characterized by the impression of success in the fight against an existential crisis to "Party and nation". I have, therefore, divided my observation period into three eras, and have applied structural topic modeling and sentiment analysis to the segmented corpus to test this assumption. Then, alternating between quantitative pattern detection and in-depth qualitative follow-up, I develop more nuanced patterns showing how the discourse on corruption has evolved throughout these different crisis stages, which corruption-related topics have gained and lost in prevalence, and which parts of the vast anti-corruption toolbox have been foregrounded or de-emphasized.

Corruption and Crisis in Authoritarian Regimes

In light of the overarching topic—"Crises in Authoritarian Regimes"—corruption in contemporary China presents an intriguing yet conceptually

---

Quarterly 240 (2019): 967–989.; Andrew Wedeman, "The Evolution of China's Anticorruption Strategy," in *The Political Logics of Anticorruption Efforts in Asia*, ed. Cheng Chen and Meredith Weiss (Albany: State University of New York Press, 2019), 201–228. In fact, China's score in Transparency International's widely used Corruption Perceptions Index (CPI) has barely budged between 2012 and 2020. Notwithstanding the methodological caveats regarding the CPI's subjective nature, this indicates that bribing public officials is still a very common way of doing business, even if the methods for doing so have become more sophisticated.

8 Following Beetham, legitimation should be studied as an ongoing process involving legitimacy "not in the private recesses of people's minds" but based on "the evidence […] available in the public sphere," see David Beetham, *The Legitimation of Power*, 2nd ed. (Basingstoke: Palgrave Macmillan, 2013), 18.

9 The database is available online at http://jhsjk.people.cn/ (accessed May 10, 2021).

challenging case: There is widespread agreement in the literature that egregious corruption has always been part and parcel of the Communist one-party system,[10] and that it has both amplified and intensified in line with China's frantic economic development during the reform era.[11] At various points in history, Mao Zedong and Deng Xiaoping themselves asserted that corruption threatened to undermine the Party's ruling legitimacy and very existence.[12]

A Process- and Claim-Driven Understanding of Crises

Urgency is often seen as "the most compelling crisis characteristic".[13] However crises, especially human-made ones, never suddenly appear but are part of an ongoing process and thus "need to be viewed in the context of broader streams of time".[14] Urgency need not be induced by a sudden situational change: From a crisis-as-claim perspective, it is the leaders' aptitude to instill a *sense of urgency* in decision makers and the population at large for a crisis to be perceived and accepted as such.[15]

Such a claim-based understanding is particularly pertinent in the study of corruption as a regime crisis: Unlike a financial crisis, a pandemic, or a leadership succession crisis, a "corruption crisis" does not *break out* in the sense of a sudden, disruptive change to the *status quo* that forces political decision makers to respond. Corruption is a looming and enduring problem, and

10 Alan Liu, "The Politics of Corruption in the People's Republic of China," *American Political Science Review* 77, no. 3 (1983): 602–623.

11 Shaomin Li, "Assessment of and Outlook on China's Corruption and Anticorruption Campaigns: Stagnation in the Authoritarian Trap," *Modern China Studies* 24, no. 2 (2017): 139–157; Andrew Wedeman, *Double Paradox: Rapid Growth and Rising Corruption in China* (Ithaca: Cornell University Press, 2012).

12 Jon S. T. Quah, *Hunting the Corrupt "Tigers" and "Flies" in China: An Evaluation of Xi Jinping's Anti-Corruption Campaign (November 2012 to March 2015)* (Baltimore: University of Maryland, 2015), 33–49.

13 Uriel Rosenthal and Alexander Kouzmin, "Globalizing an Agenda for Contingencies and Crisis Management: An Editorial Statement," *Journal of Contingencies and Crisis Management* 1, no.1 (1993): 1–12, here: 5.

14 Ibid.

15 Bert Spector, "There is No Such Thing as a Crisis: A Critique of and Alternative to the Dominant Crisis Management Model," *Journal of Contingencies and Crisis Management* 61, no. 1 (2019): 274–279, here: 276.

success stories in fighting it worldwide are few and far between.[16] Its aggravation or improvement is a longer-term trend that is hard to observe, let alone reliably measure, and is therefore prone to subjective judgment.[17] Various analysts have therefore focused on "critical junctures" to explain countries' historical anti-corruption success cases.[18] However, while the retrospective analysis of critical junctures is "inherently biased towards 'positive' cases" with lasting institutional impact, a crisis episode "is a moment of fluidity and openness".[19] A crisis moment is defined precisely by the (perceived) contingency of events, where things may move in either direction—or not move at all.

Who Defines a Corruption Crisis?

In "normal" times, high-level political corruption is often suspected by ordinary citizens or critical media but can hardly be proven in the absence of an independent, effective, and legitimate judiciary.[20] In democratic and hybrid regimes, major corruption crises are typically sparked by the emergence of a high-level scandal that galvanizes public anger and thus leads to protests. In authoritarian systems, and particularly in the context of a strong authoritarian state with sophisticated central-level censorship and an "opinion guidance" system, the uncontrolled outbreak of such a "corruption crisis" against the leadership's will is unlikely. Indeed, the last such incident arguably occurred in 1989 and the CCP leadership, terrified by the scale of public

16 Anna Persson, Bo Rothstein, and Jan Teorell, "Why Anticorruption Reforms Fail—Systemic Corruption as a Collective Action Problem," *Governance* 26, no. 3 (2013): 449–471; Jon S. T. Quah, *Curbing Corruption in Asian Countries: An Impossible Dream?* (Bradford: Emerald Group Publishing Limited, 2011); Christian Göbel, "Warriors Unchained: Critical Junctures and Anticorruption in Taiwan and South Korea," *Zeitschrift für Vergleichende Politikwissenschaft* 7 (2013): 219–242, here: 223.

17 Kin-man Chan, *Popular Perception of Corruption in Post-Mao China* (Dissertation, Yale University, 1995); Christian Göbel, "(Anti-)Corruption and Partisan Bias in Taiwan's Newspapers," in *The Political Logics of Anticorruption Efforts in Asia*, ed. Cheng Chen and Meredith Weiss (Albany: State University of New York Press, 2019).

18 See notably Göbel's study on Taiwan and South Korea: Göbel, *Warriors Unchained.*

19 Frédéric Volpi and Johannes Gerschewski, "Crises and Critical Junctures in Authoritarian Regimes: Addressing Uprisings' Temporalities and Discontinuities," *Third World Quarterly* 41, no. 6 (2020): 1030–1045, here: 1031.

20 Michael Johnston, "Building a Social Movement Against Corruption," *Brown Journal of World Affairs* 18, no. 2 (2012): 57–74, here: 57.

anger vented at their regime, has made it a paramount priority to avoid any repetition of such a popular challenge at national level.[21] At the local level, popular protests involving anti-corruption issues remain common; but whether such local crises escalate again depends on the central-level reaction to them.[22] Instead, in China's one-party regime, the definition of what constitutes "corruption", particularly in the political sense of *fubai* 腐败 (moral decay) and when specific forms reach a crisis level that warrants decisive, radical counter-measures, is mostly an outcome of political struggles within the ruling party.[23]

Although the personal or collective perception of crisis by authoritarian leaders is unobservable at least for contemporary analysts, what we can observe and analyze is the discursive construction and management of a crisis in the public sphere. I aim to achieve this by examining Chinese newspaper reports and identifying systematic differences in the public discussion of (anti-)corruption prior to, during, and after the crisis moment staged around Xi's coming to supreme power in 2012/2013. From the above discussion, we can retain the following defining elements of a crisis discourse: An existential danger or threat perception, a sense of urgency for decisive all-out action, as well as a high degree of contingency and sense of uncertainty among contemporary actors regarding the future trajectory.

Data Collection and Pre-Processing

The main reasons for adopting a mixed-methods approach to media discourse analysis here are complementarity and triangulation:[24] While qualitative in-depth analyses of political speeches and media articles can

21 Elizabeth A. Quade, "The Logic of Anticorruption Enforcement Campaigns in Contemporary China," *Journal of Contemporary China* 16, no. 50 (2007): 65–77.

22 Christian Göbel, "The Political Logic of Protest Repression in China," *Journal of Contemporary China* 30, no. 128 (2021): 169–185.

23 Cf. also Yan Sun, "The Politics of Conceptualizing Corruption in Reform China," *Crime, Law and Social Change* 35 (2001): 245–270; Kilkon Ko and Cuifen Weng, "Critical Review of Conceptual Definitions of Chinese Corruption: A Formal-legal Perspective," *Journal of Contemporary China* 20, no. 70 (2011): 359–378.

24 Alan Bryman, "Integrating Quantitative and Qualitative Research: How is it Done?" *Qualitative Research* 6, no. 1 (2006): 97–113.

heuristically decode complex meaning structures, quantitative text analyses (QTA) excel at identifying patterns across large text corpora.[25]

Corpus Construction and Pre-Processing

The main corpus of corruption-related Chinese news reports was retrieved from the newspapers (报刊) section of WiseSearch, a large database covering over 12,000 Chinese language outlets. After experimenting with various search parameters, the search was limited to articles with at least one of the following terms in their headline: 腐败 (fubai, corruption/decay), 反腐 (fanfu, anti-corruption), 贪污 (tanwu, graft/embezzlement), 贪腐 (tanfu, corruption), 防腐 (fangfu, corruption prevention) or 贿赂 (huilu, bribery). I chose 2007, the year of the 17th Party Congress, as the starting year to obtain a baseline for comparing anti-corruption discourses during Xi's reign. I limited the search to six outlets with differing regional backgrounds and ownership structures, all with wide coverage and relatively consistent data availability.[26] The resulting corruption-crisis corpus ("CorCris") comprises 6,957 articles covering a period of three National CCP Congresses.

25 Göbel, *(Anti-)Corruption and Partisan Bias*, 99; Daniela Stockmann, "Information Overload? Collecting, Managing, and Analyzing Chinese Media Content", in *Contemporary Chinese Politics. New sources, methods, and field strategies*, ed. Allen Carlson et al. (New York: Cambridge University Press, 2010): 107–125.

26 By drawing a conscious sample among the newspapers in terms of reach and consistency, the full set of articles from the chosen sources can be used, thereby avoiding additional random sampling challenges discussed in Chinese media content analyses by Stockmann (Stockmann, *Information Overload*).

Table 1: Corpus overview by newspaper

Newspaper (Chinese)	Newspaper (English)	Affiliation	Articles in corpus
东方早报	Oriental Morning Post	Shanghai United Media Group	876
北京青年报	Beijing Youth Daily	CCP Youth League	902
南方都市报	Southern Metropolis Daily	Nanfang Media Group, Guangzhou	1840
新京报	The Beijing Times	Beijing CCP newspaper	1617
环球时报	Global Times	People's Daily tabloid spin-off	611
羊城晚报	Yangcheng Evening News	Guangzhou	1111

Source (here and for all following): Bertram Lang

I used the programming language R[27] and its extension packages *tidyverse*[28] and *quanteda*[29] for all corpus processing and text modeling tasks.[30] After cleaning the raw text files downloaded from WiseSearch and extracting publication dates, outlet, and headlines using regular expressions, I pre-processed the articles for topic modeling and sentiment analysis using a customized version of the *jieba* algorithm, implemented in R's *jiebaR* package,[31] to segment and tokenize the texts which represent particular challenges in Chinese.

27 R Core Team, "R: A Language and Environment for Statistical Computing. R Foundation for Statistical Computing," Vienna, Austria (2020), accessed May 10, 2021, https://www.R-project.org/.

28 Hadley Wickham et al., "Welcome to the tidyverse," *Journal of Open Source Software* 4, no. 43, (2019): 1686–1692.

29 Ken Benoit et al., "Quanteda: An R Package for the Quantitative Analysis of Textual Data," *Journal of Open Source Software* 3, no. 30 (2018):774–778.

30 All relevant pre-processing and content analysis steps are explained in full detail in Annex 2 (online on OSF).

31 Qin Wenfeng and Wu Yanyi, "jiebaR: Chinese Text Segmentation" (2019), accessed May 10, 2021, https://CRAN.R-project.org/package=jiebaR.

Classification: To distinguish between articles discussing corruption in a "Domestic" versus a "Foreign" context, I classified the corpus into two categories using a combination of keyword search and a Naïve Bayes classifier. 1,081 articles were classified as relating to "Foreign" topics, with 5,876 articles remaining in the "Domestic" corpus.

Grouping into eras: To test the core hypothesis, the corpus was divided into three eras. The first (2007–2011) captures the later Hu/Wen period as a baseline "pre-crisis" era. The second (2012–2014) covers the launch of Xi's campaign, accompanied by a sense of urgency, contingency, and existential threat ("crisis" era). 2014 marked the arrests of General Xu Caihou and former Security Chief Zhou Yongkang, two of the most powerful "tigers" to be trialed for corruption in PRC history, after which external observers started to opine that the campaign had now passed its climax.[32] I therefore hypothesize a shift from crisis to "post-crisis" mode around the end of 2014.[33]

Table 2: Corpus grouping into three eras

Date	Era	N articles	Explanation of cut-off points
2007–2011	Pre-crisis: ("Hu")	2699	2nd Hu Jintao era, 17th to 18th Party Congress
2012–2014	Crisis ("Xi1")	2535	Launch and apex of Xi's anti-corruption crisis discourse
2015–2020	Post-crisis ("Xi2")	1723	Presumed shift to post-crisis discourse after high-level arrests

Finally, I added a dummy variable ("Xi") to indicate whether an article quotes Xi Jinping. The underlying assumption is that articles making direct reference to Xi show systematic differences regarding choice of topics and ways of reporting (anti-)corruption.

32 Carolin Kautz, "Power Struggle or Strengthening the Party: Perspectives on Xi Jinping's Anticorruption Campaign," *Journal of Chinese Political Science* 25, no. 3 (2020): 501–511, here: 502.

33 The difference in length between these periods is not a problem for the present approach, which is interested in the *relative* prevalence of terms and topics per article or per year, rather than in comparing absolute frequencies over an entire administration.

Data Analysis

Keyword Dictionary: I constructed a 68-word Chinese-English dictionary for targeted keyword analysis[34] based on terms derived from conceptual articles on Chinese (anti-)corruption[35] and my qualitative analysis of Xi's speeches. A word frequency analysis by year was carried out on the whole corpus. Interesting quantitative patterns were followed up with qualitative keyword-in-context (KWIC) analysis to understand not only how much certain terms are used over time, but also in which context and to what purpose.

Sentiment analysis: To implement a Chinese-language sentiment analysis to quantitatively extract evaluations and emotions, I relied on the augmented NTU sentiment dictionary (ANTUSD) developed at Academia Sinica.[36] After testing different calculation methods to ensure the relative robustness of results (cf. Annex 2), I calculated the sentiment score for each document as the sum of all CopeOpi score points assigned to tokens matched between the text and the ANTUSD dictionary, divided by the total number of tokens in a text.

Structural Topic Modeling: Topic models use unsupervised machine learning algorithms to discover latent themes from text documents. Unlike clustering algorithms, they are mixed-membership models, where topics are probabilistic sets of words, and documents are represented as mixtures of topics. The "structural topic model" implemented in R's *stm* package enhances probabilistic topic models by integrating covariates from the corpus metadata to structure the corpus beyond a group of exchangeable documents. Its goal is to "discover topics and estimate their relationship

34 The full dictionary is available in Annex 1 online on OSF.

35 Kilkon Ko and Cuifen Weng, "Structural Changes in Chinese Corruption," *The China Quarterly* 211 (2012): 718–740; T'ing Gong, *The Politics of Corruption in Contemporary China: An Analysis of Policy Outcomes* (Westport, Conn.: Praeger, 1994); Xuezhi Guo, "Controlling Corruption in the Party: China's Central Discipline Inspection Commission," *The China Quarterly* 219 (2014): 597–624.

36 Shih-Ming Wang and Lun-wei Ku, "ANTUSD: A large Chinese sentiment dictionary," *Proceedings of the Tenth International Conference on Language Resources and Evaluation* (2016): 2697–2702.

to document metadata. Outputs of the model can be used to conduct hypothesis testing about these relationships."[37]

The appropriate number of topics, *k*, needs to be determined by the analyst. While this is largely a heuristic task,[38] stm provides a *searchK* function which calculates key metrics such as semantic coherence, exclusivity, held-out likelihood and a residual test for different values of *k*.[39] Based on these metrics, I opted for k=80 topics (cf. Annex 2) and estimated the stm model with *era* (Hu/Xi1/Xi2) and *class* (Foreign/Domestic) as topic prevalence covariates, since I want to test the effect of publication time while assuming that this relationship is moderated by whether the articles relate to corruption topics within China or abroad. To ascertain that "the semantic concept covered by the topic is reflected in the text",[40] I first examined the ten words most associated with each topic to assess their coherence, assigned meaningful English summary labels and filtered out irrelevant or senseless topics.[41] Selecting only topics with a significant ($p<0.05$) effect of *era* (mediated by *class*) on topic prevalence, I then compiled a table of the top ten documents for each topic (by theta/gamma value) for closer examination.

---

37 Margaret Roberts et al., "stm: An R Package for Structural Topic Models," *Journal of Statistical Software* 91, no. 2 (2019): 1–40, here: 2.

38 Justin Grimmer and BM Stewart, "Text as Data: The Promise and Pitfalls of Automatic Content Analysis Methods for Political Texts," *Political Analysis* 21, no. 3 (2013): 267–297.

39 Roberts, *stm*: 12.

40 Margaret Roberts, BM Stewart and E. Airoldi, "A Model of Text for Experimentation in the Social Sciences," *Journal of the American Statistical Association* 11, no. 515 (2016): 988–1003.

41 The stm package offers different methods for calculating the top words on a given topic—I rely on the 'FREX' statistic, which calculates the harmonic mean of a term's frequency with its exclusivity to a given topic to ensure that chosen terms are both prominent and topic-specific, rather than simply an extreme on a single dimension. While 18 topics related exclusively to overseas events, only one incoherent topic had to be removed; all others were related to (anti-)corruption in the PRC and semantically sufficiently coherent.

Historical Context: Anti-Corruption in the PRC

"Corruption", from a CCP perspective, includes all sorts of behavior by Party cadres and members seen as undermining the ruling Party's legitimacy and governing capacity.[42] Consequently, "anti-corruption" (反腐败) efforts in the Chinese context traditionally cover a wide range of measures to enforce Party discipline and pursue ideological rectification, including in government, social organizations, and the private sector.[43] In official CCP propaganda and external analyses alike, the "newness" of Xi Jinping's anti-corruption campaign and rhetoric has often been overstated. Thus, before turning to the empirical analysis, this chapter provides some historical context to contemporary CCP anti-corruption politics and rhetoric.

Anti-Corruption Campaigns in Maoist Tradition

Even by communist country standards, the PRC has implemented an extraordinary number of anti-corruption campaigns since Maoist times.[44] These campaigns have always been used simultaneously as a means of purging political enemies (within the ruling Party as well as in other social strata) and of restoring or reinforcing the popular image of a leadership concerned about social justice.[45] Corruption was routinely portrayed as a problem of bureaucracy and individuals' moral degeneration (变质), rather than being due to systemic weaknesses in the current political system.[46] This pre-valent moralistic framing reduced corruption to individual "corrupt acts" that "violate the ideal that a Communist cadre ought to be a revolutionary ascetic."[47]

Consequently, anti-corruption focused heavily on mass campaigns involving the mobilization of the public by Party cadres to expose and attack perceived corruption[48] and disciplinary inspection tours by Party

42 Yongshun Cai, *State and Agents in China: Disciplining Government Officials* (Stanford: Stanford Univ. Press, 2015); Ko and Weng, *Critical Review*.

43 Wedeman, *Double Paradox*.

44 Quah, *Hunting the corrupt*, 33.

45 Quah, *Hunting the corrupt*, 34.

46 Alan Liu, "Mass Campaigns and Political Development in China," *Current Scene Developments in Mainland China* 11, no. 8 (1973): 1–9.

47 Liu, *Politics of Corruption*, 603.

48 Wedeman, *Evolution of China's Anticorruption Strategy*, 203–205.

investigators into administrative departments.[49] Even the metaphoric allusion to the supreme leader's heroic fight against the corrupt, high-level "tigers"[50] in the Party bureaucracy, presented in recent analyses as a core feature of Xi Jinping's self-legitimization,[51] had already been used by Mao Zedong in his earliest political purge, namely the "Three-Anti" (三反) campaign against the "three evils" of "corruption", "bureaucratism" and "waste" in 1951–1952.[52]

The anti-corruption rhetoric promoted by the leadership and propagated in mass media changed significantly in the Deng Xiaoping era. Suddenly, corruption was indeed portrayed as a systemic problem, however one exclusively associated with the excrescences of Maoist times. This can be explained by Deng's (eventually successful) efforts to delegitimize the "radical left" in a seminal fight for the country's future direction.[53]

However, along with frantic economic development and the rapid expansion of material opportunities for self-enrichment, corruption also soared despite the almost ritualistic occurrence of anti-corruption campaigns.[54] Most importantly, the expansion of market structures and new possibilities to transfer embezzled wealth into safe havens abroad facilitated a new form of systematic collusion between political office holders on the one hand, and private entrepreneurs and land developers on the other.[55] Not only did corruption become more widespread, it also qualitatively "intensified", in-creasingly involving well-institutionalized, self-serving, elite networks with the ability to systematically extract huge sums from the system.[56]

---

49 Anthony B.L. Cheung, "Combating corruption as a political strategy to rebuild trust and legitimacy: Can China learn from Hong Kong?" in *Research in PublicPpolicy Analysis and Management: Democracy, Corruption, and Government Trust*, ed. Phitthayā Bọwọ̄nwatthanā and Clay Wescott (Bingley: Emerald/JAI, 2008), 63.

50 The term "tiger" (老虎) usually refers to corrupt senior officials at or above vice-ministerial level.

51 Zhuo Jing-Schmidt and Xinjia Peng, "Winds and Tigers: Metaphor Choice in China's Anti-corruption Discourse," *Lingua Sinica* 3, no. 1 (2017): 295–322, here: 312–314.

52 Liu, *Politics of Corruption*, 610.

53 Liu, *Politics of Corruption*, 603.

54 Cheung, *Combating Corruption*, 56.

55 Melanie Manion, *Corruption by Design: Building Clean Government in Mainland China and Hong Kong* (Cambridge: Harvard University Press, 2004), 93; Yuen Yuen Ang, *China's Gilded Age: The Paradox of Economic Boom and Vast Corruption* (Cambridge: Cambridge University Press, 2020).

56 Andrew Wedeman, "The Intensification of Corruption in China," *The China Quarterly* 180 (2004): 895–921, here: 896.

Corruption and Political Legitimacy since 1989

While corruption has apparently been less harmful to economic growth in China (and other Asian developmental states) than in other world regions,[57] its severe political threat potential to the CCP's ruling legitimacy was acknowledged well before Xi took center-stage.[58] As early as 1982, the CCP's disciplinary inspection organs officially recognized that "corruption had reached crisis levels".[59] In the 1980s, however, corruption was mainly construed as an economic challenge to development, with the recovery of stolen assets at the center of the leadership's attention.[60] After the violent regime consolidation in the wake of the Tian'anmen protests, which were at least as much an anti-corruption as a democracy movement,[61] corruption was explicitly defined as posing an acute risk of "organizational breakdown" to the CCP[62] and the pledge to get rid of "corrupt elements" within the Party became a core element of authoritarian regime legitimation.[63]

After China signed up to the United Nations Convention against Corruption (UNCAC) in 2003, criminal laws were further tightened, new legislation against transnational bribery and money laundering was introduced, and a national anti-corruption coordination agency was established with explicit reference to international norms.[64] However, all these measures and campaigns undertaken throughout the Reform-and-Opening-Up era clearly did not prevent a further spike in corruption,[65] which many analysts have

57 Michael Johnston, "Japan, Korea, the Philippines, China: Four Syndromes of Corruption," *Crime, Law and Social Change* 49, no. 3 (2008): 205–223.

58 Yufan Hao and Michael Johnston, "Corruption and the Future of Economic Reform in China," in *Political Corruption: Concepts & Contexts*, ed. Arnold J. Heidenheimer and Michael Johnston, 3rd ed. (New Brunswick, N.J.: Transaction Publishers, 2007), 583.

59 Manion, *Corruption by Design*, 84.

60 Manion, *Corruption by Design*, 110–116.

61 Hsu, for instance, has shown how, throughout the late 1980s, "political dissidents used corruption narratives to advocate a version of political liberalism, and they forced the ruling regime into a defensive position," Carolyn L. Hsu, "Political Narratives and the Production of Legitimacy: The Case of Corruption in Post-Mao China," *Qualitative Sociology* 24, no. 1 (2001): 25–54, here: 26.

62 Cheung, *Combating Corruption*, 66.

63 Manion, *Corruption by Design*, 117; Hsu, *Political Narratives.*

64 Margaret K. Lewis, "Corruption: Spurring China to Engage in International Law," *China Rights Forum* 1 (2009): 90–96, here: 91–92; Bertram Lang, "China's anti-graft campaign and international anti-corruption norms: Towards a 'new international anti-corruption order'?" *Crime, Law and Social Change* 70, no. 3 (2018): 331–347.

65 Wedeman, *Double Paradox.*

shown to be intrinsically linked to the *sui generis* path of economic reform and development on which China embarked in the 1980s and 1990s.[66]

More fundamentally, the potential of authoritarian, campaign-style anti-corruption efforts to actually reign in systemic corruption is subject to controversial debate. Dominant international anti-corruption norms hold that this can only be achieved based on liberal rule of law principles, independent anti-corruption agencies, government transparency, and collective action. In 2005, Wedeman described the CCP's recurring campaigns as utterly ineffective and portrayed them as "a form of Beijing Opera."[67]

Xi's Campaign: Continuity or Break with the Past?

Xi Jinping's dire warnings about corruption's destructive potential thus stand in a long tradition of incoming leaders' use of existential threat rhetoric to rally the Party behind their respective reform agenda. However, Xi went much further than his predecessors by making the anti-corruption and disciplinary drive his landmark domestic policy campaign.[68] He thereby tied his personal authority closely to his credibility as a crisis manager and his ability to not only temporarily cut back excesses—as had been the traditional function of recurring anti-corruption campaigns[69]—but to fundamentally restore "the Party's purity".[70]

Analysts continue to disagree over the ulterior motives of Xi's campaign, variously focusing on his recentralization of decision making as a personal "power grab", on more widespread factional struggles among competing Party elites, or on reform efforts to rebuild an internally disaggregated Party with a new identity and morality.[71] These understandings are, however, not necessarily incompatible[72] but rather stress different levels and aspects of a far-reaching and inevitably multi-faceted organizational remolding effort in the world's largest political organization. Whatever the relative weight of these underlying drivers, the discursive use of existential crisis rhetoric and

66 Gong, *Politics of Corruption*; Ang, *China's Gilded Age*.

67 Andrew Wedeman, "Anticorruption Campaigns and the Intensification of Corruption in China," *Journal of Contemporary China* 14, no. 42 (2005): 93–116, here: 94.

68 Baranovitch, *A Strong Leader*; Lams, *Examining Strategic Narratives*.

69 Wedeman, *Anticorruption Campaigns*, 97.

70 Xi Jinping, quoted in 2012_123.

71 See Kautz, *Power Struggle*, for an up-to-date review of these academic controversies.

72 Ibid., 509.

the ensuing anti-corruption campaign—cast as the inevitable "solution"—can be viewed as an effort to restore regime legitimacy[73] at a time when the CCP was internally considered to have become ungovernable due to "too many players who had veto powers in their areas of interest",[74] and GDP growth alone was increasingly seen as a nonviable basis for appeasing an ever more exigent population, disgruntled by the exuberant privileges brazenly displayed by many cadres.[75]

Framing a Crisis: From Hu's "Fourth Danger" to Xi's Threat of "Death to Party and Nation"

It was the outgoing General Secretary Hu Jintao who, at a high-level disciplinary inspection meeting in 2011, defined the "danger of rampant corruption" as one of the "four big dangers" (四大危险) to Party survival, together with "laxness of spirit", "lack of force" and "abandonment of the masses", and called for a shift "from awareness of misery to awareness of crisis."[76] Back in 2008, Hu had already warned that "in peaceful times, if there is anything that may inflict a mortal wound upon the party, corruption clearly stands out."[77] Most people agreed, so much so that (local) Party-state officials' venality and cases of bribery and convictions were prominently discussed in Chinese media and the slogan of "fighting corruption, promoting integrity" (反腐倡廉) was *en vogue* throughout Hu's second term in office.

Xi Jinping's own efforts to style himself as an anti-corruption hero also started long before he was made CCP General Secretary. In spring 2012, Xi penned a seminal article in the Party's authoritative theory magazine, *Qiushi*, in which he called on the Party to "decisively eliminate the degenerate

73 Suisheng Zhao, "The Ideological Campaign in Xi's China: Rebuilding Regime Legitimacy," *Asian Survey* 56, no. 6 (2016): 1168–1193; Cheung, *Combating Corruption*; Bai, *Staging Corruption*.

74 Womack, *Xi Jinping*, 397.

75 Heike Holbig and Bruce Gilley, "In Search of Legitimacy in Post-Revolutionary China: Bringing Ideology and Governance Back in," *GIGA Working Paper* 127 (Hamburg, 2010), accessed May 10, 2021, https://www.giga-hamburg.de/en/publications/11572189-search-legitimacy-post-revolutionary-china-bringing-ideology-governance-back/, 24–27; Baranovitch, *A Strong Leader*, 2.

76 2012_268.

77 2011_011.

corrupt members".[78] Thus, the CCP leaders choosing him as Hu's successor were well aware of his priorities. This supports the idea that the perception of an existential crisis was widespread internally and Xi was chosen precisely for his credentials as a crisis manager, as opposed to the "personal power grab theory" which has him conjuring up a "corruption crisis" in order to selectively purge his own enemies and usurp personal power once in office.

But it was the 18th Party Congress in November 2012, including both Xi's inaugural speech and the official work report (prepared under Hu's aegis), which unambiguously elevated corruption to the "dominant political problem in the people's eyes [which], if not resolved, will mortally wound (致命伤害) the Party, and even lead to the death of Party and nation (亡党亡国)."[79] Xi's close ally and top corruption fighter, Wang Qishan, followed up, stating that "the Party's work style determines the people's support or opposition, it determines whether the Party lives or dies, exists or perishes (生死存亡)."[80]

This threat discourse was bolstered with ominous historical "lessons that incarnate our anti-corruption determination": In a widely reported speech given at the dawn of his crowning as President in March 2013, Xi reminded his Party of the "rise, decline and replacement of feudal dynasties" and "the historical lesson of the Soviet Communist Party's decay" to demonstrate the "harmfulness of rampant corruption and improper workstyle image."[81]

From the beginning, the scope of Xi's campaign went far beyond fighting corruption, as shown by both the "Eight Regulations of the Center" (中央八项规定) and the new slogan of fighting the evil "four winds" (四风),[82] referring to the four undesirable "work styles" (作风) of "formalism" (形式主义), "bureaucratism" (官僚主义), "hedonism" (享乐主义), and "extravagance" (奢靡) among Party cadres.

Well aware of the long history of previous, largely ineffectual campaigns launched with similar fanfare, Xi also sought to distance himself from his predecessors by vowing to "hit tigers and flies together", thus directing the spotlight explicitly on grand corruption in the upper Party-state echelons. During Xi's first two years as General Secretary, more "tigers" were

78 2012_124.

79 2012_525, 2012_531, 2012_532.

80 2012_571.

81 2013_146.

82 For an in-depth analysis of the use of metaphors in Xi's anti-corruption fight, cf. Jing-Schmidt and Peng, *Winds and Tigers*, 305–306.

investigated, questioned, demoted, expelled, and convicted than at any time since the Cultural Revolution (1966–1976).[83] In October 2014, Xi further upped the ante at a CCDI meeting, by defining corruption as "a struggle that cannot be lost" (输不起的斗争)[84]—a phrase frequently repeated in the media in late 2014 and early 2015 but which disappears entirely from the corpus after that.

Media Framing of Corruption in Pre-Crisis, Crisis and Post-Crisis Eras

From this top-down construction of a crisis discourse between 2012 and 2014, we will now turn to the analysis of corruption framing in the wider media landscape. Given the CCP's extraordinary capacity for discourse guidance and control, the core framing of politically sensitive topics, such as corruption, is defined by top-level authorities and then subject to further interpretation by other discourse participants. The leeway for interpretation will, in turn, depend on the (varying) political sensitivity and ideological status of a topic.

Figure 1 presents an overview of the 20 most prevalent CorCris topics according to the above-defined stm model with 80 topics, along with their five most closely associated terms according to stm's frequency-exclusiveness (FREX) measure.[85]

83 Wedeman, *The Evolution*, 216.
84 2014_825.
85 Roberts et al, *A Model of Text for Experimentation.*

Figure 1: Prevalent topics in CorCris corpus with five most associated words

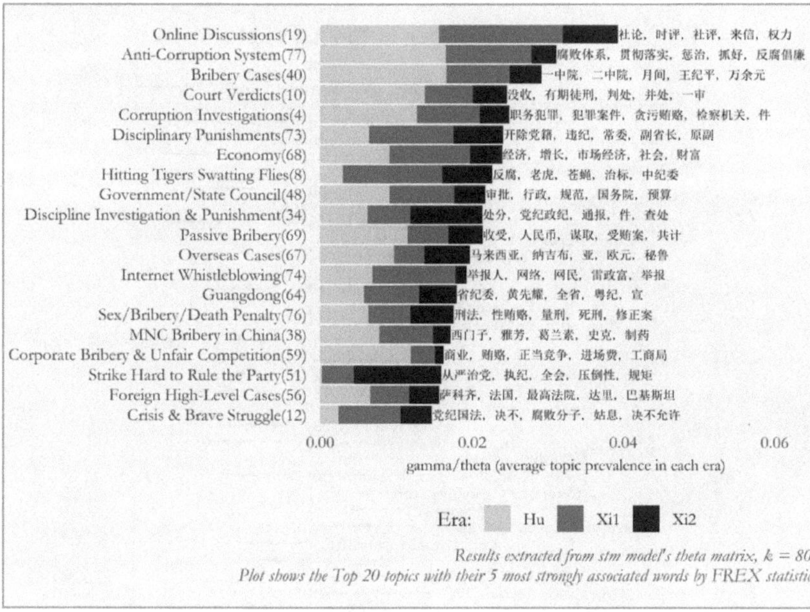

Figure 2 displays all topics whose prevalence has been significantly affected by the shift from the pre-crisis era (Hu) to the crisis era (Xi1). This is true for 35 out of 80 topics, which suggests an impressive change in Chinese media discourse on corruption. Topics 8, 31, 58, 5, 47, 73 and 36 all relate to Xi's campaign and his emphasis on the Party's disciplinary system to address the internal crisis. As opposed to Hu Jintao, Xi also directly and publicly tackled corruption in the People's Liberation Army (46). Conversely, topics involving real-life occurrences of corruption (69, 40, 10, 5, 4), as well as its negative repercussions for ordinary citizens—namely, forced resettlements (25) and workplace/railroad accidents (70)—were significantly toned down, with the notorious exception of Bo Xilai's trial, which was assigned its own topic by the stm algorithm.

Figure 2: Topic prevalence in crisis vs pre-crisis era

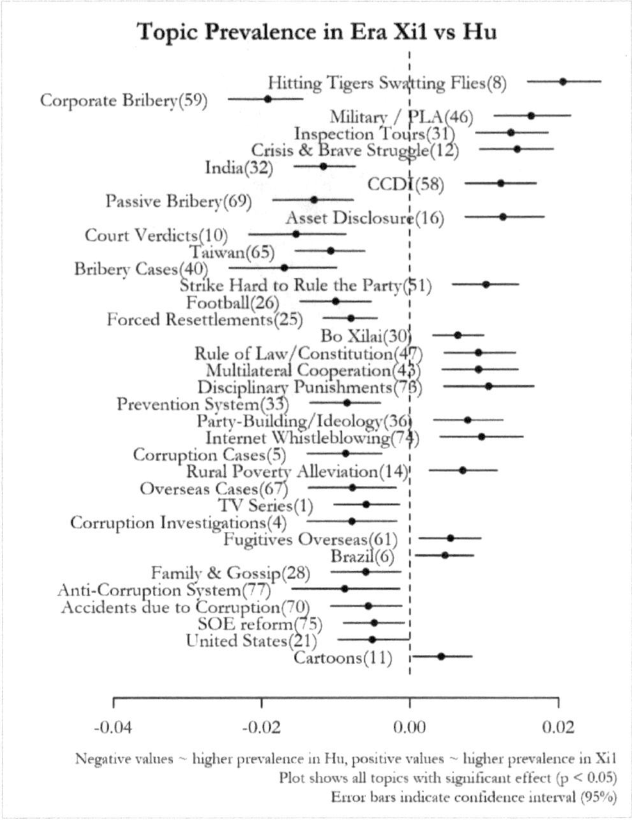

Next, we can calculate which topics are most closely associated with the crisis vocabulary collected in the manual dictionary: From the stm model's beta matrix, which gives the likelihood of belonging to each topic for all terms, the twenty most likely topics are selected for each keyword of interest. Figure 4 confirms that Topic 12, intuitively labeled "Crisis & Brave Struggle", is by far the one most associated with crisis terms, notably "danger", "death to Party and nation", "matter of life or death" and "mortal (wound)". FREX terms and top documents further show that this theme conflates notions of urgency and danger with the description of Xi's courageous efforts to address this situation. That these terms have been automatically lumped into one topic shows how closely these notions—threat and heroic solution—are associated in Chinese articles. A topic correlation analysis (using stm's *topicCorr* function) reveals that Topic 12 is closely associated with other themes relating to Xi's resolve and capability to govern the Party, namely "Strike Hard to Rule the Party" (51), "Hitting Tigers, Swatting Flies" (8) and "Party-Building/Ideology" (36).

Figure 3: Topics most associated with crisis terms

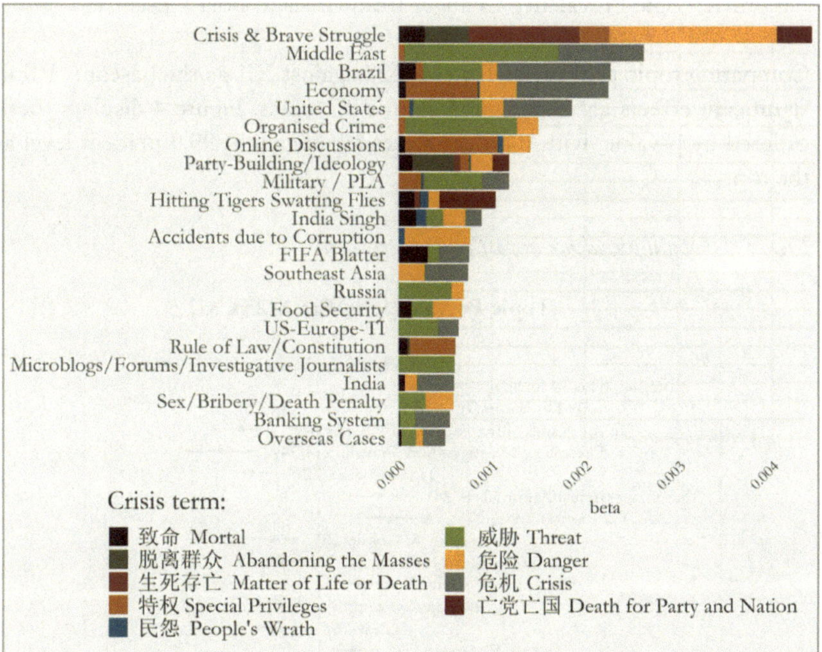

Author's calculation based on dictionary terms and stm output, k = 80
Full CorCris Corpus (6957 articles)

Interestingly, the term "crisis" (危机) itself most commonly appears in foreign topics (Middle East, Brazil, United States) as well as economy-related themes, whereas domestic problems are described predominantly in "CCP speak", in addition to the common words—"danger" and "threat". A closer qualitative examination shows that international corruption stories are mostly factual reports of scandals and investigations that use wording similar to other international news outlets. Reporting on corruption in China, by contrast, is heavily codified and subjected to ideological terms defined and controlled by the Party-state.

The Challenge of Claiming Victory Against a Structural Crisis

Turning to the hypothesized second shift from the crisis era ("Xi1") to a post-crisis era ("Xi2"), several patterns deserve to be highlighted.

Pattern 1: Topic Prevalence Changes from Crisis to Post-Crisis Era

Comparing topic prevalence for era=Xi2 against Xi1 as the baseline, I find significant effects at 95 percent level for 27 topics. Figure 4 displays these ordered by p-value, with the nine topics significant at 99.9 percent level at the top.

Figure 4: Topical prevalence in post-crisis vs crisis era

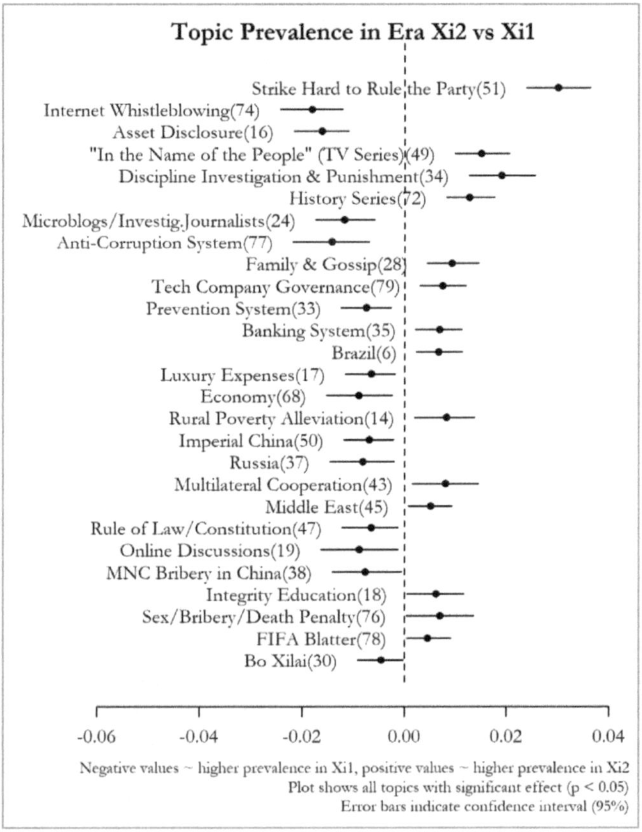

The two topics most obviously dominating the post-crisis era (51&34) both relate to the need for strict(er) enforcement of Party discipline. The former is labeled by its top FREX word— "Strike Hard to Rule the Party" (从严治党)—a new slogan that dominated official anti-corruption discourse in 2016 and 2017, ahead of the 19th Party Congress where Xi consolidated his own power and smashed what remained of collective leadership norms. Most top articles here report on speeches by Xi and Wang Qishan stressing the need to "maintain a high-pressure attitude without relaxing"[86] or declaring the extension of the campaign to other sectors and government bodies,[87] as well as editorial appeals to Party members' "confidence" in "the center's unswerving anti-corruption determination."[88] Thus, the emphasis is on upholding the morale of party members in an ongoing "struggle". Other rising topics comprise efforts to boost popular support and instill anti-corruption norms in the wider population through "Integrity Education" (18) and TV series—namely the very successful anti-corruption propaganda series "In the Name of the People" (人民的名义)(49), which stars heroic public prosecutors hunting down morally deficit cadres, and several history series (72), equally reinforcing the narrative of corruption as the action of a few degenerate individuals rather than a systemic failure. Other topics relating to systemic corruption prevention (33, 77, 47) have further declined, as have all topics related to popular checks on power (74, 16, 24, 19) and the extravagant lifestyle of CCP officials (17). Instead, there is a significant rise in non-political tabloid stories about corruption (28, 76), as well as a new focus on corruption in China's banking system (35) and, most recently, in private tech companies (namely Jingdong and Alibaba) (79).

86 2015_035.
87 2016_018, 2017_013.
88 2016_015.

Pattern 2: De-Emphasizing (Anti-)Corruption Across the Board

Figure 5: Salience of corruption in sharp decline

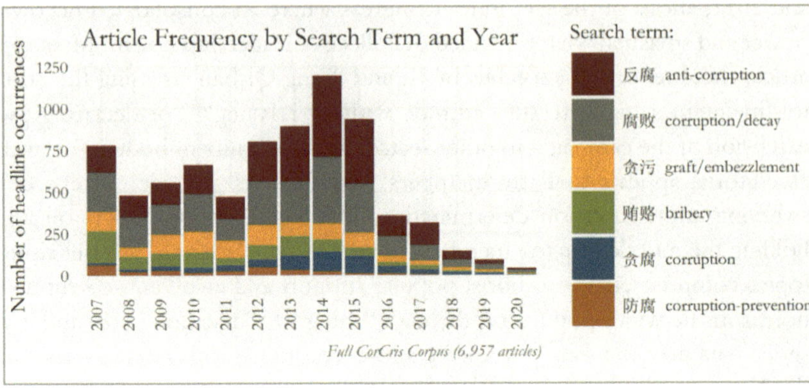

The simplest corpus metric, namely the number of articles per year, shows a more fundamental pattern: The salience of all (anti-)corruption-related topics sharply declined after 2015, not only compared to the crisis, but also to the pre-crisis period. By 2019, corruption appears to have almost disappeared from media headlines. This sharp decline in media salience is different from the shift to an all-out "crushing victory" framing I had expected based on analyzing Xi's speeches.[89] Instead, these results suggest that the dearth of demonstrable results (apart from constantly high investigation and conviction numbers, which could also be read as proof that corruption is still rampant) makes the topic increasingly ill-suited to the kind of "positive energy" (正能量) propaganda framing that is expected from Chinese media outlets nowadays.[90]

89 See, for example, People's Daily, 取得全面从严治党更大战略性成果，巩固发展反腐败斗争压倒性胜利 (Obtaining More Strategic Results from Comprehensive Strict Enforcement of Party Discipline, Consolidating the Crushing Victory in the Struggle Against Corruption), January 12, 2019, accessed March 14, 2021, http://politics.people.com.cn/n1/2019/0112/c1024-30523582.html.

90 Qiushi Theory, 习近平：推动媒体融合向纵深发展，巩固全党全国人民共同思想基础 (Xi Jinping: Advancing Towards Deeper Media Integration, Consolidating a Common Thought Basis for the Whole Party, Whole Nation and the People), January 26, 2019, accessed January 10, 2021, http://www.qstheory.cn/yaowen/2019-01/26/c_1124046672.htm.

Pattern 3: From Crisis to Success Framing?

My initial assumption was that corruption reporting should be more negative during the crisis era, compared to both the pre-crisis and, notably, a presumed post-crisis era where I expected to find more positive sentiment terms related to a proclaimed success in fighting corruption. Based on the explanations in Section 3, I estimate a multivariate linear regression model for the sentiment scores of all 6,957 articles, with the era (baseline=Xi1) as the explanatory variable, and both the classification result *class* and the dummy variable *Xi* as interaction variables.

Table 3: Regression Results for Sentiment Scores

Call: lm(formula = ANTscore_toks ~ era * Xi * class, data = df_scored)

Residuals:	Min	1Q	Median	3Q	Max
	-11.7937	-1.1399	0.0166	1.1365	8.7442

Coefficients: (1 not defined because of singularities)

	Estimate	Std. Error	t value	Pr(>|t|)
(Intercept)	1.20898	0.04192	28837	< 2e-16 ***
eraHu	-0.20245	0.05773	-3507	0.000456 ***
eraXi2	-0.21188	0.06863	-3087	0.002027 **
XiTRUE	0.94714	0.14071	6731	1.82e-11 ***
classForeign	-0.81150	0.11318	-7170	8.26e-13 ***
eraHu:XiTRUE	2.15088	0.72566	2964	0.003047 **
eraXi2:XiTRUE	0.41353	0.19761	2093	0.036413 *
eraHu:classForeign	0.11253	0.14937	753	0.451251
eraXi2:classForeign	0.31426	0.16646	1888	0.059080 .
XiTRUE:classForeign	0.02976	0.73216	41	0.967578
eraHu:XiTRUE:classForeign	NA	NA	NA	NA
eraXi2:XiTRUE:classForeign	1.58820	0.92841	1711	0.087188 .

Signif. codes: 0 '***' 0.001 '**' 0.01 '*' 0.05 '.' 0.1 ' ' 1

Residual standard error: 1.881 on 6946 degrees of freedom

Multiple R-squared: 0.04945, Adjusted R-squared: 0.04808

F-statistic: 36.13 on 10 and 6946 DF, p-value: < 2.2e-16

Reports on corruption overseas have significantly more negative sentiment, which was to be expected, and supports the validity of the dictionary-based sentiment-scoring method. Similarly, articles mentioning Xi Jinping have significantly higher sentiment scores throughout. However, the model's coefficient of determination is rather poor—there is clearly a lot of variation between individual articles it cannot explain. What it does show, however, is that the hypothesized improvement in article sentiment from Xi1 to Xi2 only holds for domestic articles mentioning Xi Jinping (*eraXi2:XiTRUE*). The estimate *eraXi2* is negative (and significant at 99 percent level), meaning that the tonality of articles not mentioning Xi has become decisively more negative in the "post-crisis" era. The time series in Figure 6 illustrates the more complex pattern at play: Whereas articles mentioning Xi show a clear upwards trend in sentiment from 2012/13, the opposite is true for other domestic articles.

Figure 6: Timeline of Article Sentiment Scores

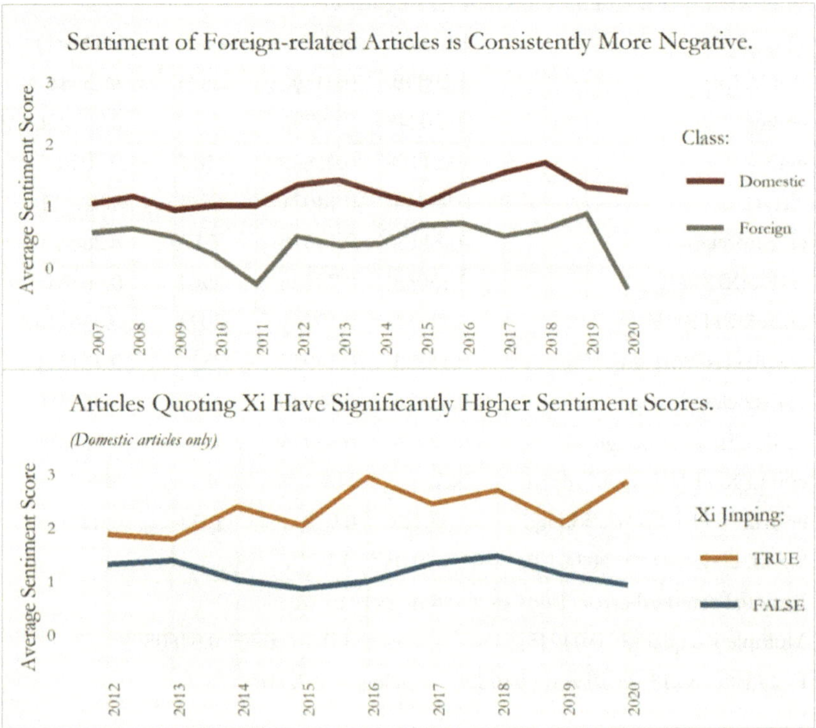

Going beyond a singular sentiment metric, which is necessarily coarse, we can further examine the use of specific crisis- and success-related terms over time. A frequency analysis of domestic articles, based on the manually constructed dictionary, confirms that the use of crisis-related terms indeed peaked in 2012, before declining sharply except for an intriguing outlier in 2018. Crisis terms that were extensively used by Xi (and reiterated across Chinese media) at the onset of his first term in 2012/2013 include the warning that the Party is "abandoning the masses" (脱离群众) and attracting the "people's wrath" (民怨) due to the corrupt and reckless behavior of certain cadres.[91] Both these sensitive terms acknowledging a severe legitimacy crisis disappeared entirely from public discourse afterwards. (A follow-up qualitative examination revealed that the exceptions are articles from 2018 reminding the public about Xi's mission by reprinting his "important speeches" (重要讲话) from 2012–2014.)

Figure 7: Salience of Crisis Vocabulary in Anti-Corruption Articles over Time

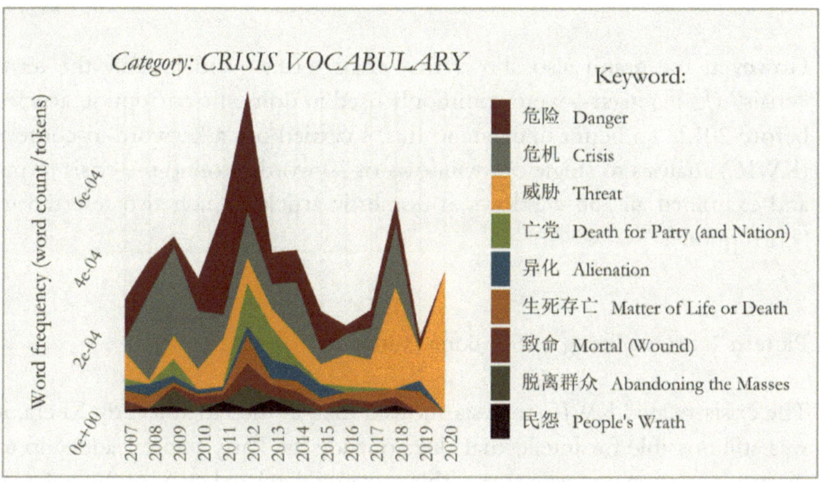

91 2013_146.

Figure 8: Salience of Success Vocabulary in Anti-Corruption Articles over Time

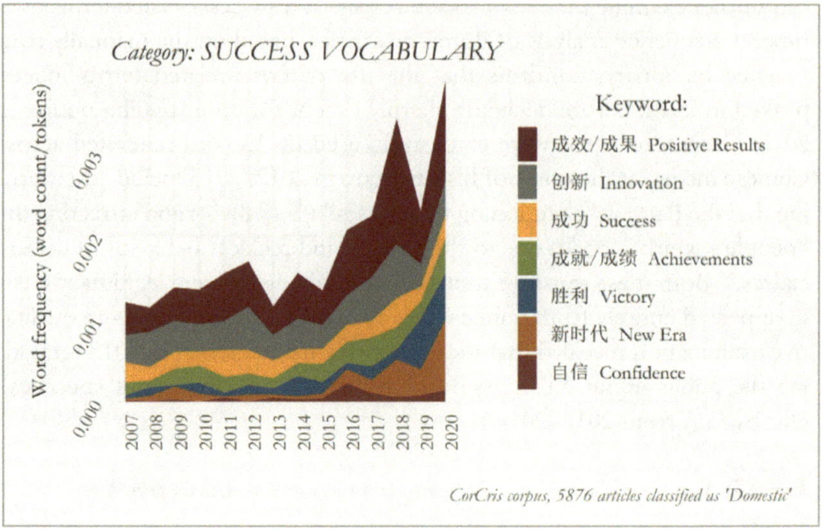

However, the graph also shows that crisis terms—and notably the term "crisis" (危机) itself—were commonly used in domestic corruption articles before 2012. To better understand this, I carried out a keyword-in-context (KWIC) analysis to single out windows of 30 words around the crisis terms and examined all 258 windows in domestic articles which also referred to "corruption".

Pattern 4: Streamlining of Speaking Authority

The crisis-related KWIC analysis showed that, in the Hu and early Xi era, it was still possible for intellectual elites outside the Party's core leadership to discuss, and even critically assess, the corruption-related crisis of the political system (without quoting Xi). In 2008 and 2009, most "crisis" occurrences naturally relate to the financial and economic crises. But they also include provocative articles such as an opinion piece in the Southern Metropolis Daily arguing that what people really cared about was systemic corruption in the Chinese system, rather than the global financial crisis.[92]

92 2009_108.

From 2010 to 2012, warnings about a "trust crisis" (信任危机) due to staggering levels of political corruption and calls for a "sense of crisis" (危机感) in anti-corruption work multiplied. In December 2012, The Global Times published an op-ed comparing China's current situation to corruption in the French 18th century *ancien régime* to stress systemic corruption's potential to "undermine and even break a political regime's legitimacy", inferring that anti-corruption must not be limited to its "political function" (政治作用) and urging the leadership to take swift action instead of engaging in a protracted campaign.[93]

Large media outlets even picked up on investigative journalism and micro-blogs (Topic 24). In response, "netizen whistle-blowing" (网友举报), i.e., online corruption reporting (Topic 74), was hijacked and actively promoted by the central leadership from late 2012. This served both to display the center's willingness to go hard on local cadre corruption, and to reign in the thriving community of online bloggers and investigative citizen journalists by offering them an official, approved, and controlled channel for complaining about corruption. However, more systemic, underlying problems were also brought up in debates around mandatory asset disclosure for Party-state officials (Topic 16). In this context, The Beijing News opined that "if there is no disclosure of officials' fortunes, the trust crisis (信任危机) will only increase, and without institutionalized anti-corruption, [internet anti-corruption] will not go far."[94] Again, these topics largely disappeared in the post-crisis era, together with discussions about the need for rule-of-law reform (47) and systemic anti-corruption (77).

Finally, the sharp rise in sentiment of articles mentioning Xi Jinping (cf. Figure 6 above) can be qualitatively explained by the fact that articles in the crisis era tended to commend Xi's declared resolve before turning to descriptions of urgency and criticism of the dire situation, abuses of power, etc. By contrast, recent articles mentioning Xi by name almost always fall into two categories—direct quotes or paraphrases of Xi speeches (thus frequently containing Xi's recent claim of a "crushing victory" (压倒性胜利) over corruption), or sycophantic praises of Xi Jinping Thought and the "unique linguistic charm" (独特的语言魅力)[95] of his speeches, rather than any direct discussions of the actual subject matter, corruption.

93 2012_641.
94 2012_607.
95 2019_064.

Pattern 5: From Institution-Building (back) to Punishment

A recurring question in assessments of Xi's anti-corruption drive has been whether it was moving from an initial focus on prosecuting "tigers and flies" towards "institutionalization". This question has interested both Chinese and foreign scholars looking for signs of a longer-term transformation of China's anti-corruption system, beyond the ritualistic campaign-style enforcement efforts known from previous administrations.[96] Judging purely by the media discourse, the opposite is true: Concepts derived from internationally established anti-corruption norms, such as "clean governance", "government integrity", "transparency" and other institutional mechanisms viewed as essential parts of an effective corruption prevention system were present in Chinese debates in the later Hu era and still enjoyed popularity in the early Xi years. Initial (mis)readings of Xi's announcements of a law-based approach to ruling the country (依法治国) contributed to a peak in debates over necessary reforms to China's legal system and the importance of rule-of-law for sustainable anti-corruption efforts in 2014/15.[97]

These findings correspond to the great enthusiasm among Chinese intellectual elites, reported by Guo, who perceived a window of opportunity for—finally—moving from a campaign-based, short-term enforcement strategy to durable, "institutionalized anti-corruption measures".[98] This "window of opportunity" (反腐突破口)[99] is also reflected in the corpus, however it quickly closed, with references to institution-building and other key components of liberal anti-corruption recipes overall declining sharply after 2015 (cf. Annex 4).

96 Quah, *Hunting the Corrupt*; Wedeman, *Evolution of China's Anticorruption Strategy*, 217–218; Li and Wang, *From Institutional Interaction*, Melanie Manion, "Taking China's anticorruption campaign seriously," *Economic and Political Studies* 4, no. 1 (2016): 3–18.

97 2014_063, 2014_145, 2014_283, 2014_420.

98 Guo, *Controlling Corruption*, 621.

99 2012_590.

Figure 9: The Rise and Fall of Institutionalized Anti-Corruption

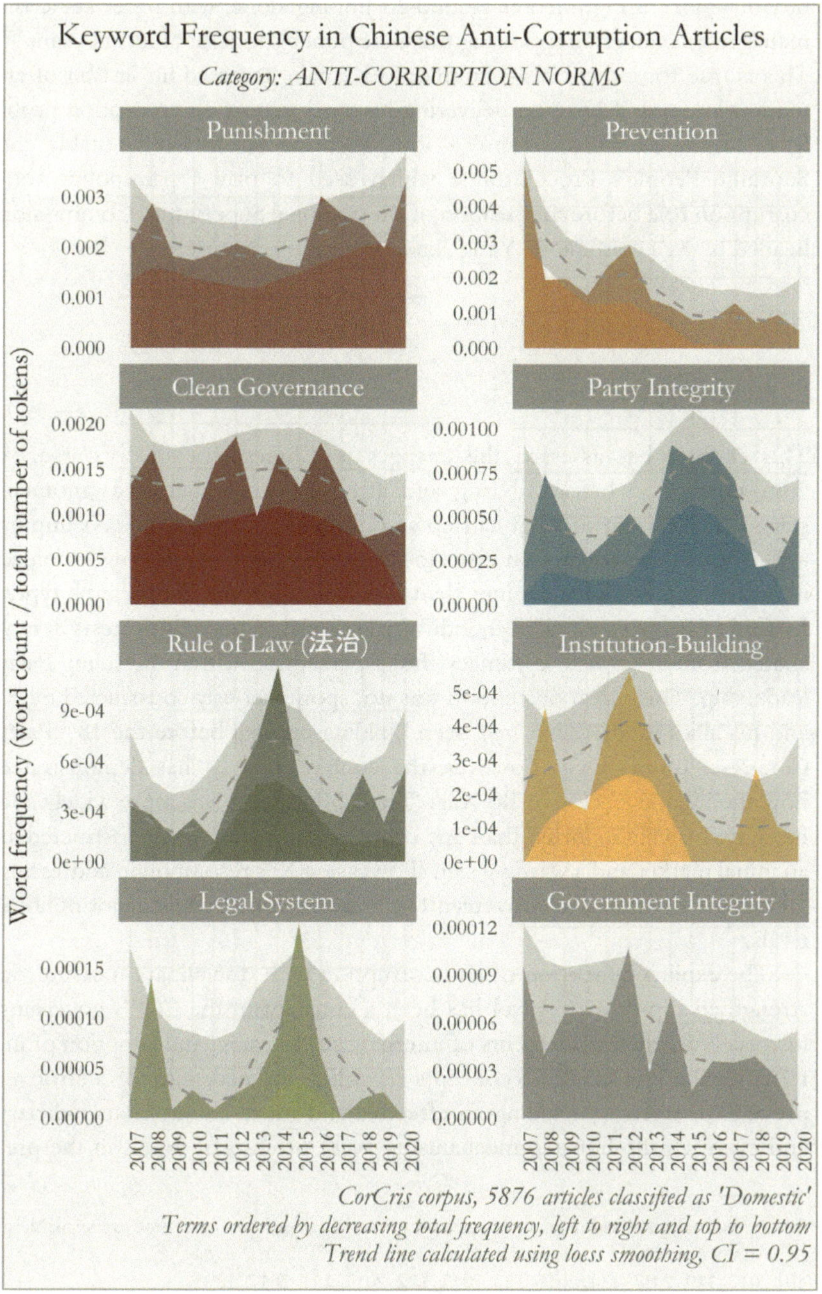

Finally, corruption-related articles—just like China's media discourse more broadly—increasingly center around Xi Jinping alone, with other key crisis management actors disappearing from the public spotlight in recent years.[100] This is true for individuals—Premier Li Keqiang received his last bit of attention in April 2017 upon delivering his work report on corruption problems in the financial system[101]—but also for institutions, notably the Supreme People's Procuratorate which used to play a paramount anti-corruption role before the creation of the National Supervisory Commission headed by Xi's confidante, Yang Xiaodu.

Concluding Discussion

This chapter has assessed the changes in Chinese media discourse on (anti-)corruption before, during and after the existential crisis moment staged at the dawn of what can now confidently be called the "Xi Jinping era". Clearly, the corruption crisis in China's authoritarian setting unfolded in an entirely different manner than it usually does in other regime types: Instead of being sparked by an individual scandal or popular protests, it emanated from a growing legitimacy threat perception within the ruling Party leadership. This threat perception was not spontaneously constructed by Xi and his allies in 2012, but had been building up well before the 18th Party Congress. Interestingly, however, the content analysis has demonstrated how the high-level case of Bo Xilai (Topic 30), which was more widely and more exclusively reported than any other investigation, was constructed as an initial marker and a warning sign showcasing Xi's resolution in addressing "the crisis"—while also conveniently eliminating one of Xi's major political rivals.

The explicit conflation of anti-corruption with disciplinary measures to strengthen top-down control has been a constant in the CCP's governing history. Nonetheless, elements of international learning, and adoption of international anti-corruption concepts regarding the necessity for a stronger prevention system, including an effective and more autonomous judiciary and even whistle-blowing mechanisms, were prominent topics in the pre-

100 Additional graphical displays of relevant keyword frequencies over time are available in Annex 4 on OSF.

101 2017_119, 2017_134, 2017_123, 2017_122, 2017_121, 2017_120

crisis and—albeit to a lesser extent—the crisis era. Notably, the "institutionalization" of anti-corruption, i.e., a departure from the ineffectual campaign-style efforts of Xi's predecessors, was a lofty promise and a great hope among China's progressive intellectual elite during the crisis era. However, both the topic model and the targeted keyword analysis confirmed that the idea of fighting corruption based on institutional reform, strengthened rule-of-law (in the liberal sense of *fazhi* 法治) and a prevention system following international best practices, intensively discussed in Chinese mainstream media between 2012 and 2014, largely vanished from public discourse afterwards. The authoritarian penchant of Xi's anti-corruption drive thus becomes increasingly obvious as we move from the immediate crisis period—where contingency and openness regarding the future trajectory still left room for relatively diverse opinions about necessary anti-corruption measures—to the post-crisis period. In retrospect, the moment of crisis actually proved to be one of relative openness, where even critical proposals for reform were openly voiced in mainstream media and the direction of future anti-corruption efforts still appeared open for debate.

This finding is crucial in understanding the discursive spaces for talking about corruption in Xi's "new era": Whereas this "post-crisis" period is indeed significantly different (thus confirming my basic hypothesis), the expected shift to an all-out victory framing I had expected based on Xi's speeches did not materialize in the wider media landscape. Instead, the most notable change is the sharp decline in the corruption topic's overall salience, not only compared to the crisis, but also to the pre-crisis period. The prevalence of success vocabulary has increased sharply since 2016, but this is mainly due to Xi's personal speeches and their re-publication and affirmative interpretation in various outlets. Beyond these abstract political declarations, there are almost no stories detailing how the situation on the ground has changed in terms of corruption control. Again, this is notably different from the crisis era, when Party and private media outlets repeatedly ran stories about investigative citizen journalists and bloggers hunting down corrupt local cadres (Topic 24). Instead, the post-crisis discourse is dominated by articles about the top leadership's unrelenting, "brave" struggle for Party discipline, reports about anti-corruption TV series or integrity education activities, as well as non-political tabloid stories.

Regarding broader questions relating to the management of crises in authoritarian systems, this chapter's main contribution has been to direct attention beyond the discursive *con*struction of crises and towards a regime's need to eventually transition from crisis mode into a post-crisis phase, in which the existential danger previously claimed has somehow disappeared. The case of the CCP's fight against anti-corruption shows that this *de*construction of a crisis is far more complicated than its rhetorical construction, particularly since there is no dearth of egregious bribery and embezzlement cases which might show that corruption remains a major systemic problem even in the "new era". Thus, reports about unceasing high-level corruption investigations are becoming a double-edged sword from the perspective of ruling Party legitimacy: On the one hand, they are used to convince the public of the top leadership's "unswerving resolution" (坚定不移...的决心)[102] to counter corruption and work in the public's interest; on the other, they are constant reminders that corruption continues to be widespread even in the Party-state's highest echelons, thereby contradicting Xi's claims of a "crushing victory" since 2018. Put differently, the same factual media reports about cases of blatant cadre corruption that were welcomed as a legitimating basis for Xi's all-out campaign during the crisis era are turning into threats to the legitimacy of Xi as the Party's "core" and his image as an upright, resolute and successful corruption fighter.

Hence, ever tighter media control is an inevitable feature of the post-crisis enactment: First, to ensure that all reports about instances of corruption are directly linked to references to the Party leadership's successful anti-corruption fight (i.e., no problem reporting without showing the correct solution); and second, to mete out the sort of systemic reflections (strengthening asset disclosure of Party cadres, empowering citizens through internet whistle-blowing, or encouraging investigative journalism at least at the local level) that were prominent in the crisis era. Instead, post-crisis framing strategies rely on diversion, moral elevation of Party members and the public, and assertions of unswerving top-level resolution.

In methodological terms, this chapter has helped to systematize and generalize insights into the official framing, as well as the varying range of opinions and topics in Chinese (anti-)corruption discourses over time, based on a much larger and more diverse corpus than used in previous analyses, and thanks to a combination of quantitative text mining tools and computer-assisted qualitative content analysis. Admittedly, the content analysis methods applied here also have inherent limitations. Since all articles in the corpus are given equal weight, I cannot account for their prominence in the

102 2016_103.

original newspapers, let alone audience reach or the influence of media frames on readers' beliefs and perceptions. For reasons of space, I have also stopped short of a comparison of different media outlets, which would certainly be important in tracing aspects like discourse diversity more systematically over time. Since the chapter is explicitly limited to the analysis of anti-corruption discourses, I remain cautious regarding the campaign's impact on actual levels of corruption or the CCP regime's longer-term legitimacy. However, this analysis has clearly demonstrated both the usefulness of anti-corruption crisis discourses for incoming leaders to rally a broad range of political and societal actors behind a noble goal, and the challenges related to the "resolution" of such a crisis without demonstrable evidence that the problem itself has actually vanished. One important question that cannot be answered by using the present approach concerns the impact of the uncovered "post-crisis" corruption narratives on different audiences. While crucial from the perspective of authoritarian regime legitimation, this question is, however, methodologically challenging to address in China today.

The following annexes are made available at the Center for Open Science's OSF repository (https://osf.io/7ymfp/):

Annex 1: Dictionary for Keyword Analysis
Annex 2: Explanation of Content Analysis Methodology
Annex 3: Corpus Original References
Annex 4: Additional Figures
Annex 5: Replication Code

Authoritarian (Dis-)Advantages: A Comparative Study of the Handling of the SARS and Covid-19 Crises in China

Carolin Kautz

Introduction

When the government of the People's Republic of China (PRC) imposed a comprehensive lockdown in the city of Wuhan, where the novel corona virus causing the respiratory disease Covid-19 was spreading, it was not clear at that time that this virus was going to cause a global pandemic and health crisis. After a much-criticized delay in initial reaction, the Chinese Party-state imposed far-reaching measures to control the virus and, despite repeated smaller outbreaks, claims to have the situation largely under control. This appears to point to an "authoritarian advantage"[1] in crisis management, suggesting that China was able to swiftly implement strict measures to contain the virus and lock down entire cities—measures that in democratic countries are more difficult to implement and lead to significant political debate.

The crisis that unfolded after the initial outbreak of Covid-19 exists in at least three different spheres. Firstly, it is a health crisis, challenging the ability of the Chinese medical system to cope with a sudden large number of patients and provide appropriate care to those in need of it. Secondly, the crisis played out on the political field, raising questions regarding the ability of the Chinese government to rapidly understand an emergency situation and implement appropriate measures to deal with it. Thirdly, the crisis has an international dimension, impacting the international reputation of the People's Republic of China (PRC) and involving discussions over the origin of the virus as well as mask and, more recently, vaccine diplomacy.

This chapter focuses on the second aspect of the crisis, the political reaction of the Chinese Party-state to the outbreak. The Chinese Communist Party (CCP) is firmly in charge of the political and legal system and, despite

1 Jonathan Schwartz, "Compensating for the 'Authoritarian Advantage' in Crisis Response: A Comparative Study of SARS Pandemic Responses in China and Taiwan," *Journal of Chinese Political Science* 17, no. 3 (2012): 313–331.

Party-internal control mechanisms, it is not subject to any external checks of its power. Therefore, one could expect that the Party-state is in an advantageous position to deal with the outbreak because it can implement measures in a top-down manner, without taking individual rights and freedoms into consideration. However, based on a comparison with a very similar crisis—the first SARS crisis of 2003—I argue that the CCP is in a contradictory position. On the one hand, it can make use of an authoritarian advantage in some areas of crisis management. On the other hand, it also faces an authoritarian disadvantage, particularly in the early stages of a crisis outbreak. This is due to the fragmented authority of the Party-state, and incentive and cadre management issues that are difficult to remedy. In the following chapter, I present leadership challenges and the Party-state's performance in both the SARS and the Covid-19 crises to argue that authoritarian crisis management for the CCP is a double-edged sword.

The Fragmentation of Authority and Challenges in Crisis Management

The Chinese Party-state is a one-party system with the CCP as the single ruling party, governing the PRC in an authoritarian manner. The CCP has a tight grip on personnel management of Party and state cadres, and exercises control over high-ranking personnel in a centralized manner.[2] Additionally, it is in charge of the legal system and has turned itself into the supreme interpreting authority on legal matters.[3] In its relations with Chinese society, it subjects the press to ultimate Party control,[4] limits the space for public

2 John P. Burns, "The Chinese Communist Party's Nomenklatura System as a Leadership Selection Mechanism: An Evaluation," in *The Chinese Communist Party in Reform*, ed. Kjeld Erik Brodsgaard and Yongniang Zheng (London, New York: Routledge, 2006), 33–58; Lance L. P. Gore, "Managing Human Resources to Sustain the One-Party Rule," in *The Chinese Communist Party in Action: Consolidating Party Rule*, ed. Yongnian Zheng and Lance L. P. Gore (London, New York: Routledge, 2020), 51–80.

3 Heike Holbig, "Making China Great Again – Xi Jinpings Abschied von der Reformära," *GIGA Focus Asien* 2 (April 2018).

4 Pinghui Zhuang, "China's Top Party Mouthpieces Pledge 'Absolute Loyalty' as President Makes Rare Visits to Newsrooms," *South China Morning Post*, accessed August 31, 2020, https://www.scmp.com/news/china/policies-politics/article/1914136/chinas-top-party-mouthpieces-pledge-absolute-loyalty.

debate[5] and, more recently, has begun to roll out a system of supervision and social management, relying on technical surveillance and artificial intelligence.[6] Thus, the Chinese Party-state appears well-equipped in terms of authoritarian control tools to deal with a health crisis of the magnitude of Covid-19, and limiting and controlling the behavior of its citizens.

However, authority in China does not only function in a centralized manner. The central Party-state cannot simply rely on authoritarian tools of control implemented in a top-down manner leading to stringent control of the entire political system. On the contrary, economic reforms in particular have led to processes of decentralization, and scholars frequently use the model of "fragmented authoritarianism" when analyzing the Chinese Party-state. Lieberthal argues that "authority below the very peak of the Chinese political system is fragmented and disjointed", since bureaucratic entities have to engage in bargaining processes with each other.[7] Decentralization in decision making has a number of advantages, and Heilmann and Perry hold that it is particularly localized adaptive decision making and policy experimentation that has contributed to the success of China's economic reforms.[8] However, Sorace argues in favor of seeing the fragmentation of authority as a dialectic process, where the advantages of the CCP's governing model at the same time contribute to the rise of new problems which undermine the Party's authority.[9] In his view, fragmented authoritarianism is both a blessing and a curse for the CCP because it supports successful reform policies while also creating major problems for the Party-state.

---

5 Carolin Kautz and Heike Holbig, "Bürgerrechte und Zivilgesellschaft in China: Diskursive Rechtfertigungsstrategien im Schatten parteistaatlicher Hegemonie," *ASIEN – The German Journal on Contemporary Asia* 137 (October 2015): 77–89.

6 Rogier Creemers, "China's Social Credit System: An Evolving Practice of Control," accessed September 5, 2018 (Available at SSRN), https://ssrn.com/abstract=3175792; Claire Seungeun Lee, "Datafication, Dataveillance, and the Social Credit System as China's New Normal," *Online Information Review* 43, no. 6 (2019): 952–970.

7 Kenneth Lieberthal, "Introduction: The 'Fragmented Authoritarianism' Model and Its Limitations," in *Bureaucracy, Politics, and Decision Making in Post-Mao China*, ed. Kenneth G. Lieberthal and David M. Lampton (Berkeley et. al: University of California Press, 1992), 8.

8 Sebastian Heilmann and Elizabeth Perry, "Embracing Uncertainty: Guerrilla Policy Style and Adaptive Governance in China," in *Mao's Invisible Hand: The Political Foundations of Adaptive Governance in China*, ed. Sebastian Heilmann and Elizabeth Perry (Cambridge et al.: Harvard University Press, 2011), 1–29.

9 Christian Sorace, "'When One Place is in Trouble, Help Comes from All Sides': Fragmented Authoritarianism in Post-Disaster Reconstruction," in *Chinese Politics as Fragmented Authoritarianism*, ed. Kjeld Erik Brødsgaard (Abingdon, New York: Routledge, 2017), 135–155.

Crisis management by the Party-state follows a similar dialectic model. The CCP can rely on centralized authority, mobilization capacities and media control when it comes to implementing measures to counter a crisis. At the same time, however, it is hampered by the fragmentation of authority and contradictory incentives for political leaders. Although fragmentation can be a strength when it comes to economic reforms and experimental policy making, it is a disadvantage for rapid crisis reaction. Building on Boin et al.'s[10] identification of leadership challenges in crisis management—crisis perception, decision making, meaning making, terminating and learning—I thus argue that some features of the Chinese Party-state allow for an authoritarian advantage in crisis reaction while others hold the Party-state back in mounting a rapid response. As can be seen with the SARS and Covid-19 crises, it is the challenge of crisis perception in particular that the Party-state is not well equipped to deal with. The authoritarian system is hence both a strength and a weakness when it comes to dealing with crises such as the ones discussed here.

Two Structurally Similar Crises: The SARS Outbreak in 2003 and the COVID-19 Outbreak in 2020

Although the Chinese government denied similarities in the outbreak of Covid-19 (*SARS-CoV-2*) with the first SARS crisis in 2003 (*SARS-CoV-1*),[11] the two crises have remarkable structural similarities. In both cases, the Chinese government was faced with the outbreak of a respiratory virus that is presumably zoonotic in nature and spreads between humans.[12] Additionally, in both cases, the viruses were discovered for the first time in China, thus providing a compelling basis for a case study on how the Chinese Party-state reacts to crises within its own territory. On a medical level, however, the two outbreaks are not entirely similar as the two viruses can be differentiated by infectiousness and fatality rates. It appears that the original SARS

10 Arjen Boin et al., *The Politics of Crisis Management: Public Leadership under Pressure* (Cambridge et al.: Cambridge University Press, 2005).

11 "Vigilance Needed on Novel Pneumonia," *Global Times*, accessed April 12, 2021, https://www.globaltimes.cn/content/1177480.shtml.

12 Kerry Brown and Congjiang Wang, "Politics and Science: The Case of China and the Coronavirus," *Asian Affairs* 51, no. 2 (2020): 247–264.

virus was less contagious than the virus causing Covid-19 with asymptomatic people not spreading it[13] and the case fatality ratios of SARS being higher.[14] Thus, it appears that SARS was less contagious but more deadly, thereby creating more favorable conditions to contain the spread of the disease.

In spite of these differences, the crisis reactions in the cases of SARS and Covid-19 were also similar in their development. In both cases, the Chinese government was accused of reacting too slowly and of covering up information about the outbreak of the respective diseases. Although the Chinese Party-state reacted significantly faster in the case of Covid-19 than in the case of SARS,15 there was still a marked delay between the discovery of the first cases and an official reaction by the Party-state.16 This delay is also visible in the reporting on SARS and Covid-19 respectively in the People's Daily, the mouthpiece of the Chinese Communist Party (see figures1 and 2).

Figure 1: Number of articles per month in the People's Daily containing the keywords "feidian" or "feidianxingfeiyan" (both referring to SARS) in the full body of the article

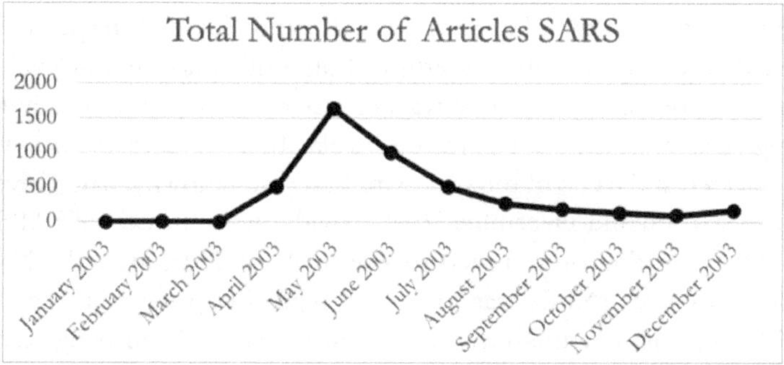

Source: Assembled by the author based on *Renmin ribao dianziban* (accessed via Crossasia)

---

13 United States Centers for Disease Control and Prevention, "Frequently Asked Questions About SARS," accessed May 14, 2021, https://www.cdc.gov/sars/about/faq.html.

14 Brown and Wang, "Politics and Science."

15 For timelines see: Susan M. Puska, "SARS 2002-2003: A Case Study in Crisis Management," in*Chinese National Security Decisionmaking under Stress* (Strategic Studies Institute, US Army War College, 2005), 85–133 (for SARS); and Susan V. Lawrence, "Covid-19 and China: A Chronology of Events (December 2019-January 2020)," accessed April 24, 2021, https://crsreports.congress.gov/product/pdf/R/R46354/3 (for Covid-19). Official timeline of Chinese government: The State Council of the People's Republic of China, "Fighting Covid-19: China in Action," accessed April 24, 2021,http://english.www.gov.cn/news/topnews/202006/07/content_WS5edc559ac6d066592a449030.html.

16 John Dotson, "The State Response to a Mystery Viral Outbreak in Central China," *China Brief* 20, no. 1 (17.01.2020): 1–5.

Figure 2: Number of articles per month in the People's Daily containing the keywords "buming yuanyin feiyan", "bingduxing feiyan", "xinguan" or "xinxingguanzhuangbingdu"[17] *in the full body of the article*

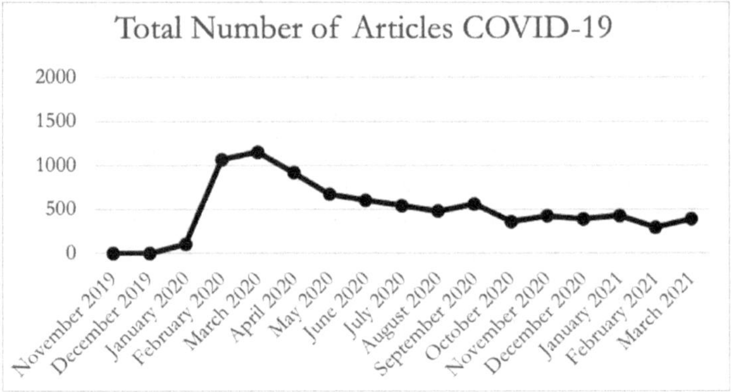

Source: Assembled by the author based on *Renmin Ribao tuwen shujuku* (accessed via Crossasia)

Comparing the number of articles on SARS and Covid-19 respectively, we can see that during the initial months of both outbreaks, central level media communication on the diseases was almost non-existent and only kicked into high gear at a later stage in the outbreaks. In both cases, the new viruses were detected at the end of the year, with first cases known in late November 2002 (SARS) and mid-December 2019 (Covid-19). In the case of SARS, central media reporting only started to rise in April 2003, after the National People's Congress (NPC) was over, and reporting peaked in May. When SARS broke out, a central-level leadership transition from Jiang Zemin to Hu Jintao was taking place, which, it can be assumed, should not have been overshadowed by negative news.[18] Regarding Covid-19, central media reporting reached a prominent level in February and peaked in March 2020. Thus, the time between the first cases and significant media coverage is shorter than in the case of SARS.

17 At different times of the outbreak, different terms were used to refer SARS Cov-2. At the beginning, particularly (*buming yuanyin feiyan*, pneumonia of unclear origin), (*bingduxing feiyan*, viral pneumonia) were used to refer to the disease. After the virus was sequenced, (*xinguan*) or (*xinxingguanzhuangbingdu*) became more prominent to refer to the novel coronavirus (see: Lawrence, "Covid-19 and China").

18 Joseph Fewsmith, "China and the Politics of SARS," *Current History* 102, no. 665 (2003): 250–255.

However, during the later stages of both the SARS and the Covid-19 crises, the Party-state reacted strongly and implemented far-reaching measures to contain the diseases. This is particularly interesting because the slow reaction to the outbreak of a virus that was discovered for the first time in China differs markedly from the Chinese government's reaction to viral outbreaks of diseases that were detected for the first time outside China. As Huang and Smith point out, the Chinese government did indeed react rapidly and vigorously to other viral outbreaks, such as swine flu in 2009.[19] Thus, the comparison of the cases of SARS and Covid-19 provides for a better understanding of how the Chinese Party-state is equipped to deal with crises, because it offers a comparative case for all stages of crisis management, such as understanding a crisis, decision making to counter a crisis, constructing a crisis narrative and drawing lessons from it. Additionally, due to the similarity of the two crises, it offers a unique opportunity to understand what the Chinese government learned from the first SARS crisis.

Why It Could Have Worked: Lessons from SARS

After the trauma of the first SARS crisis, the Chinese Party-state engaged in a number of legal and political reforms. Because one major problem with initially containing the spread of SARS was the slow reaction by the authorities and the fragmented nature of the Chinese Party-state,[20] these reforms were designed to control Party and government cadres more effectively and ensure a faster reaction to public health emergencies. The Party-state reformed the legal system governing public health emergencies, set up a new national emergency management system, and extended the hold-to-account system to punish cadres who fail to perform well in their roles.

The first lesson drawn following the SARS outbreak was to reform the legal system governing public health emergencies. As Keith and Lin argue, the legal basis enshrined in the 1989 Law on the Prevention and Treatment

19 Yanzhong Huang and Christopher J. Smith, "China's Response to Pandemics: From Inaction to Overreaction," *Eurasian Geography and Economics* 51, no. 2 (2010): 162–183.

20 Patricia Thornton, "Crisis and Governance: SARS and the Resilience of the Chinese Body Politic," *The China Journal* 61 (January 2009): 23–48.

of Infectious Diseases was insufficient in handling the SARS outbreak.[21] Thus, the law has been amended twice since then and expanded from 41 articles in the 1989 version to 80 articles.[22] It now includes detailed provisions on preventing, reporting on, and containing infectious diseases, as well as legal responsibilities. Additionally, the Regulation on Contingent Public Health Emergencies[23] was amended and a National Contingency Plan for Public Health Crises[24] was passed as part of the new national emergency management system.[25]

The new legal and regulatory setup prescribes in detail the reporting requirements and the scope of action for local governments in case of public health emergencies. For example, the amended version of the Regulation on Contingent Public Health Emergencies requires that, upon receiving a report on an outbreak or potential outbreak of an infectious disease, governments at the provincial level are required to report to the responsible department of the State Council within one hour.[26] All other governments at lower administrative levels are required to report to the next higher government or responsible agency within two hours (Article 20). Furthermore, the Law on the Prevention and Treatment of Infectious Diseases stipulates that governments at all levels are in charge of dealing with the outbreak of an infectious disease and grants them the right to set up local committees to react to it (Article 5). Thus, on a legal level, it appears that lessons from SARS were learned and that tools were in place for a rapid reaction to the Covid-19 outbreak.[27]

21 Ronald Keith and Zhiqiu Lin, "SARS in Chinese Politics and Law," *China Information* 21, no. 3 (2007): 403–424.

22 For the 2013 version of the law, see: Quanguo Renmin Daibiao Dahui Changwuweiyuanhui, "中华人民共和国传染病防治法" (Law of the People's Republic of China on the Prevention and Treatment of Infectious Diseases), accessed October 29, 2021, http://www.npc.gov.cn/wxzl/gongbao/2013-10/22/content_1811005.htm.

23 Zhonghua Renmin Gongheguo Guowuyuan, "突发公共卫生事件应急条例" (Regulation on Contingent Public Health Emergencies), accessed October 29, 2021, http://www.gov.cn/gongbao/content/2011/content_1860801.

24 Zhonghua Renmin Gongheguo Zhongyang Renmin Zhengfu, "国家突发公共卫生事件应急预案" (National Contingency Plan for Public Health Crises), accessed March 27, 2021, http://www.gov.cn/yjgl/2006-02/26/content_211654.htm.

25 Xiaoli Lu and Lan Xue, "Managing the Unexpected: Sense-Making in the Chinese Emergency Management System," *Public Administration* 94, no. 2 (2016): 414–429.

26 Zhonghua Renmin Gongheguo Guowuyuan, Contingent Public Health Emergencies.

27 Xiang Gao and Jianxing Yu, "Public Governance Mechanism in the Prevention and Control of the COVID-19: Information, Decision-Making and Execution," *Journal of Chinese Governance* 5, no. 2 (2020): 178–197.

Secondly, the Party-state more widely implemented the hold-to-account system to discipline cadres. This system "involves immediate, public and harsh sanctions against leading officials for negative policy outcomes resulting from the exercise of discretion over specific policy issues."[28] In other words, it allows the Party-state to punish cadres for allowing bad or undesirable things to happen on their watch. In the case of SARS, it resulted in the removal of the Mayor of Beijing, Meng Xuenong, and the Minister of Health, Zhang Wenkang, for concealing information and their sub-par performance in handling SARS.[29] Additionally, a significant number of cadres at lower levels were also dismissed for their poor performance in dealing with the outbreak.[30] Following its implementation during the SARS crisis, the Party-state had a tool at its disposal to punish cadres for inefficient performance in dealing with a public health emergency, for example. Thus, it appears that the Party-state learned lessons from the SARS crisis and established a system of crisis reaction for future crises. However, despite these reforms, the reaction to Covid-19 was no less delayed and time was lost before taking decisive action to deal with the crisis. The formal legal instruments were clearly not strong enough to overcome other structures embedded in the Party-state, such as adverse incentives and information asymmetries.

What Did Not Work: Understanding the Crisis

The initial leadership challenge of dealing with a crisis is understanding the crisis, i.e., grasping what is going on. This is not a straightforward process because, at the beginning of a crisis, it is not obvious that a crisis is developing since crises are phenomena of *ex-post* perception. In the case of China making sense of a local situation—let alone a crisis—the Chinese Party-state and its top-level leaders rely on rapid and accurate reports from local leaders to make sense of the situation on the ground. This information asymmetry has existed throughout the entire history of the PRC and worsened such disastrous events as the great famine of the early 1960s following the Great

28 Ciqi Mei and Margaret M. Pearson, "Killing a Chicken to Scare the Monkeys? Deterrence Failure and Local Defiance In China," *The China Journal* 72 (July 2014): 75–97.

29 Thornton, "Crisis and Governance."

30 Fewsmith, "China and the Politics of SARS."

Leap Forward.[31] Issues of information asymmetry, fragmented structures of governing and problematic incentive structures for local leaders also led to difficulties in making sense of the crises in the cases of both SARS and Covid-19.[32]

In the outbreaks of both SARS and Covid-19, other countries accused China of reacting too slowly to contain the respective viruses within China's borders and preventing them from spreading to other countries. It took the Chinese government about four months from the discovery of the first cases of SARS to the implementation of strict containment measures. During this time period, it appears that some government organs, as well as the military hospitals that were treating SARS patients, had at least some understanding of the developing crisis, but information was not passed on, or at least no decisive action at either the local or central level followed.[33] Additionally, Chinese researchers' research results were initially suppressed and the government officially held on to the theory that the cause of SARS was the chlamydia bacterium.[34]

The initial sense making of the Covid-19 crisis was hampered by similar information issues. Although the reaction time was not nearly as long as in the case of SARS, and the cause of Covid-19—the SARS-Cov-2 virus—was identified quickly, the initial process of making sense of the crisis and implementing decisive containment measures was also characterized by unclear chains of information and crisis communication. Initial cases of Covid-19 were detected at least as early as mid-December, but Wuhan health authorities only published an official statement warning of the health threat at the end of December. Additionally, Wuhan authorities at the beginning of January investigated eight doctors for "spreading rumors" related to the outbreak of a new virus[35] and they denied the possibility of human-to-human transmission of the virus.[36] Furthermore, although the CCP claims that a

31 For a detailed discussion of the Great Leap Forward, see, for example: Frank Dikötter, *Mao's Great Famine: The History of China's Most Devastating Catastrophe, 1958–1962* (New York: Walker & Co., 2010).

32 For similar issues in the case of Russia, see the contribution of Alexander Libman in this volume.

33 Fewsmith, "China and the Politics of SARS."

34 Puska, "SARS 2002–2003."

35 Wuhanshi Gong'anju, "散布谣言，8人被查处" (Eight People Investigated for Spreading Rumors), accessed, April 25, 2021, https://baijiahao.baidu.com/s?id=1654582380950520889&wfr=spider&for=pc.

36 Fang Fang, *Wuhan Diary: Dispatches from a Quarantined City*, trans. Michael Berry (New York: HarperVia, 2020).

Politburo Standing Committee discussed the epidemic situation in a meeting as early as January 7, 2020,[37] this certainly did not lead to the conclusion that China was facing a severe crisis and that immediate action was required. Thus, in the case of both SARS and Covid-19, the initial phase of perceiving the crisis was characterized by unclear information and chaotic crisis communication before the Party-state eventually took swift action.

There are multiple reasons why the Chinese Party-state struggled so much with initially grasping the crises and reaching the stage of taking action. The first one is information asymmetry, both between the center and the localities, and also between different bureaucratic entities. In the case of SARS, information up-sharing to the Party-state center was hampered, and information was only passed on slowly from the local level to the center.[38] For example, Beijing city officials and also officials in the Ministry of Health appear not to have shared information with the top central leadership around Hu Jintao and Wen Jiabao.[39] Additionally, there was insufficient information sharing between military hospitals and civilian institutions,[40] eventually leading to military doctor Jiang Yanyong drafting a letter to major press outlets and blowing the whistle on the real numbers of SARS cases in hospitals in Beijing.[41] Similar issues arose in the case of Covid-19. Although the Chinese Center for Disease Control later reported that the first cases of a new lung disease had been discovered in mid-December at the latest,[42] Wuhan health authorities only issued an official statement at the end of

37 "中央战'疫'日志" (Daily Record of the Center in the Fight against the "Epidemic"), *Zhongguo Gongchandang xinwenwang*, accessed March 14, 2021, http://cpc.people.com.cn/n1/2020/0203/c164113-31568437.html.

38 Hongyi Lai, "Local Management of SARS in China: Guangdong and Beijing," in *The SARS Epidemic: Challenges to China's Crisis Management*, ed. John Wong and Yongnian Zheng (New York et al.: World Scientific, 2004), 77–97.

39 John Pomfret, "China's Crisis Has A Political Edge," *Washington Post*, accessed April 24, 2021, https://www.washingtonpost.com/archive/politics/2003/04/27/chinas-crisis-has-a-political-edge/008b29d9-8bd5-4fe7-94f4-0567aa8ac00e/.

40 John Wong and Yongnian Zheng, "Introduction: SARS and Governance in China," in *The SARS Epidemic: Challenges to China's Crisis Management*, ed. John Wong and Yongnian Zheng (New York et al.: World Scientific, 2004), 1–10.

41 "Feature: A Chinese Doctor's Extraordinary April in 2003," *People's Daily*, accessed April 24, 2021, http://en.people.cn/200306/13/eng20030613_118182.shtml.

42 Wenjie Tan et al., "Notes from the Field: A Novel Coronavirus Genome Identified in a Cluster of Pneumonia Cases—Wuhan, China 2019−2020," ed. Chinese Center for Disease Control and Prevention, *China CDC Weekly* 2, no. 4 (2020): 61–62.

December.[43] Furthermore, the original message relating to the virus was that it was "not contagious between people; It is controllable and preventable."[44] At this time, it is impossible to know with certainty how information was passed on during the early stages of the Covid-19 crisis and which political leader knew what at which point in time.[45] However, what did not work in the crisis perception stage of the Covid-19 crisis was the chain of reporting, command and action that the legal framework for controlling infectious diseases had set up in the wake of the SARS crisis. As Lu and Xue discuss more broadly, the Chinese emergency management system still suffers from too many institutional issues to effectively solve issues of information management in a crisis situation.[46]

Closely linked to information asymmetry is the second reason for challenged sense making—adverse incentives for local cadres to report bad news up the hierarchy. Because promotion incentives for cadres are tied to their performance, and performance indicators importantly include the generation of economic growth and the maintenance of social stability in their respective localities,[47] cadres have an incentive to foster these at all costs. Sounding the alarm bell early on a possible new disease and causing public panic is, thus, not in their interest. In the case of SARS, preventing public panic was considered one reason why the outbreak of an unknown disease was not reported earlier and publicly.[48] We can also assume a similar issue in the case of the Covid-19 crisis. In a study meeting of the Politburo on the topic of disaster management that took place on November 29, 2019, Xi Jinping explicitly stressed that, next to saving lives, upholding social

---

43 Xu Wen (许雯), "武汉疾控证实：当地现不明原因肺炎病人，发病数在统计" (Wuhan CDC Confirms: Cases of Pneumonia of Unknown Cause Have Emerged in Wuhan and the Number of Cases Is Being Followed), *Beijing News*, accessed April 26, 2021, http://www.bjnews.com.cn/news/2019/12/31/668430.html.

44 Fang, Wuhan Diary.

45 Tom Mitchell, "What Xi Knew: Pressure Builds on China's Leader," *Financial Times*, accessed April 24, 2021, https://www.ft.com/content/3a294233-6983-428c-b74b-3cc58c713eb8.

46 Lu and Xue, "Managing the Unexpected."

47 Pierre Landry, "Does Performance Matter? Evaluating Political Selection Along the Chinese Administrative Ladder," *Comparative Political Studies* Vol. 51, no. No. 8 (2018): 1074–1105.

48 Amy Freedman, "Sars and Regime Legitimacy in China," *Asian Affairs* 36, no. 2 (2005): 169–180.

stability is the core mission of the Party.[49] Although the official note on the study meeting does not contain a reference to disease outbreaks as a form of disaster to be managed, the message coming from the center is clear. Upholding social stability is a core element of managing any kind of disaster, and Party and state cadres should do their utmost to ensure the fulfilment of this goal in their localities.

Further hampering the ability of local cadres to react, the top-down reaction of the Party-state in the first weeks of the Covid-19 outbreak on how to react was far from clear. In terms of leaders' activities, the official CCP timeline mentions the Politburo meeting on January 7, but no further outbreak-related activities until January 20.[50] Another official timeline published in English by the news agency Xinhua outlines that, during these days, the Chinese Center for Disease Control, as well as the National Health Commission, were working with authorities in Wuhan to investigate the outbreak and sequence the genome of the virus.[51] However, in a political system with highly fragmented authority and where vague and ambiguous signaling is used as a means of—also social—control,[52] clear messages from the center are required for a massive and successful crisis reaction. The relative absence of Xi Jinping during the initial phase of the crisis did not help with sending such a clear message from the center to local actors.[53] In the case of SARS, there is even evidence that high-ranking leaders in the Party and the military engaged in actively covering up the outbreak of the disease.[54]

Overall, we have to conclude that structural factors handicap the effective handling of the leadership challenge of sense making when dealing with

---

49 "习近平在中央政治局第十九次集体学习时强调：充分发挥我国应急管理体系特色和优势；积极推进我国应急管理体系和能力现代化" (Xi Jinping Stresses During the 19th Study Session of the Politburo That We Have to Sufficiently Develop the Characteristics and Superiority of China's Emergency Management System and Actively Advance the Modernization of China's Emergency Management System and Skills), *Gongchandangyuanwang*, accessed March 23, 2021, http://www.12371.cn/2019/11/30/ARTI1575103627283730.shtml.

50 "Daily Record of the Center."

51 "China Publishes Timeline on COVID-19 Information Sharing, Int'l Cooperation," *Xinhua*, accessed May 14, 2021, http://www.xinhuanet.com/english/2020-04/06/c_138951662.htm.

52 Rachel E. Stern and Kevin J. O'Brien, "Politics at the Boundary: Mixed Signals and the Chinese State," *Modern China* 38, no. 2 (2012): 174–198.

53 Lily Kuo, "Taking Credit, Avoiding Blame? Xi Jinping's Absence From Coronavirus Frontline," *The Guardian*, accessed May 17, 2021, https://www.theguardian.com/world/2020/feb/04/blame-xi-jinping-absence-coronavirus-frontline-china-crisis.

54 Fewsmith, "China and the Politics of SARS."

a crisis in China. Both in the SARS crisis and the Covid-19 crisis, initial problems of information asymmetry and thus fragmented chains of command and action, as well as problematic incentivization of cadres, contributed to slowing down understanding of the crises. These are factors that the reforms following the SARS crisis did not sufficiently mitigate. Although the reaction to the Covid-19 crisis only took slightly less than two months instead of four, as was the case with SARS, it was still not as rapid as it should have been to deal with the arising health crisis quickly. This amounts to an "authoritarian disadvantage" embedded in the Chinese political system and it cannot be remedied easily because it would require far-reaching institutional reforms affecting core elements of the Party-state that have, in the past, contributed to its success. Nevertheless, once the initial challenge of sense making is dealt with successfully, the CCP can still rely on an "authoritarian advantage" in the tasks that follow—dealing with the immediate crisis and meaning making.

Playing Out the Authoritarian Advantage: Reacting to Crises

Once the Party-state had eventually perceived the particular challenge to be a (national) crisis, it was in a position to play out the strengths of its authoritarian system. In understanding what is going on, passing information through the political hierarchy and arriving at the state of ultimate decision, the Chinese Party-state suffers from an "authoritarian disadvantage". However, once the central level is involved and decision making takes place at the top, the Chinese Party-state can rely on the full toolkit of an authoritarian regime to deal with a crisis. This involves swift, centralized decision making that is implemented hierarchically without regard for individual rights or concerns, and a propaganda campaign to implement the official narrative of the crisis as the sole acceptable interpretation of it.

Dealing With the Immediate Crisis: Full-Fledged Mobilization

Centralization of Decision Making

In the case both of SARS and Covid-19, an initial phase of unclear responsibilities, fragmented communication, and a lack of decisive action that hampered a rapid reaction was followed by a centralization of decision-making efforts and crisis reaction. In the case of SARS, this occurred around mid-April 2003 when Premier Wen Jiabao made public speeches conveying the urgency of dealing with SARS, and the Politburo Standing Committee eventually established a task force to deal with the disease.[55] Shortly thereafter, the Minister of Health, Zhang Wenkang, and the Mayor of Beijing, Meng Xuenong, were dismissed from their posts.

In the case of the Covid-19 pandemic, the center seems to have taken over in the second half of January 2019, establishing institutional and command structures to guide the reaction to the pandemic.[56] This is reflected in Xi Jinping's "important instructions" on January 20, where Xinhua reports him to have said that all Party and government entities should "mobilize all forces to launch measures of containment and implement practical effective action."[57] A few days later, on January 26, Premier Li Keqiang chaired the initial meeting of a central leading small group to respond to the epidemic situation,[58] thus reflecting the centralization of decision-making power and the importance the center attached to the situation. The central prerogative is further underlined by repeated inspection visits by central leaders, mainly Vice-Premier Sun Chunlan, to regions affected by outbreaks of Covid-19. Additionally, the Party-state strictly requested local leaders to comply with

---

55 Yongnian Zheng and Lye Liang Fook, "SARS and China's Political System," in *The SARS Epidemic: Challenges to China's Crisis Management*, ed. John Wong and Yongnian Zheng (Singapore: World Scientific, 2004), 45–75.

56 Alex Jingwei He, Yuda Shi, and Hongdou Liu, "Crisis Governance, Chinese Style: Distinctive Features of China's Response to the Covid-19 Pandemic," *Policy Design and Practice* 3 (2020): 242–258.

57 "习近平对新型冠状病毒感染的肺炎疫情作出重要指示：强调要把人民群众生命安全和身体健康放在第一位；坚决遏制疫情蔓延势头；李克强作出批示" (Xi Jinping Gives Important Directive on the Epidemic Situation Caused by the Spread of the Novel Coronavirus: Stresses That the Health and Safety of the People Should Be Put First and the Spread of the Epidemic Has to Be Resolutely Contained; Li Keqiang Issues Comments), Xinhua, accessed April 14, 2021, http://www.xinhuanet.com/politics/leaders/2020-01/20/c_1125486561.htm.

58 "李克强主持召开中央应对新型冠状病毒感染肺炎疫情工作领导小组会议：贯彻习近平总书记重要讲话和中央政治局常委会会议精神；进一步部署疫情防控工作" (Li Keqiang Convenes Meeting of the Central Leading Small Group to Respond to the Epidemic Situation Caused by the Spread of the Novel Coronavirus: Implement the Important Speech of General Secretary Xi Jinping and the Spirit of the Meeting of the Politburo Standing Committee Further; Work on the Task of Preventing and Controlling the Epidemic), *Zhongguo Gongchandang Xinwenwang*, accessed April 14, 2021, http://cpc.people.com.cn/n1/2020/0127/c64094-31562956.html.

central directives and not change or adapt them in the implementation process.[59]

Campaign-style Mobilization

Following the centralization of decision-making power, the Party-state in both cases engaged in a campaign-style mobilization of resources to combat the spread of the respective diseases. Political campaigns have been applied throughout the history of China for such diverse purposes as implementing existing or introducing new policies, correcting deviation from norms and rectifying leadership malpractices.[60] Additionally, campaigns were also applied in Maoist China to fight the spread of diseases and improve public health and hygiene.[61] Far from disappearing from the governing toolkit of the CCP, Perry argues that, in an adapted form, "managed campaigns" still play an important role as the Party's governing tool in overcoming bureaucratic hurdles and inertia.[62] In other words, the task of campaign-style mobilization is to overcome resistance and slack work of the bureaucracy at all levels, thereby eliminating possible veto points in the system. Whereas, in the logic of fragmented authoritarianism, where vested local interests and bureaucratic frictions and bargaining play a significant role, campaign-style mobilization can overcome this problem.

Applying the campaign-like mobilization tool from their governance toolkit, the Party mobilized massive material and personnel resources to battle first SARS and later Covid-19. In the case of Covid-19, the Central Committee in a meeting on January 26, 2020, decided on the all-out mobilization of resources, including medical personnel and resources, hospitals and quarantine centers, and the delivery of personal protective equipment and

59 Caiyu Liu, "Spring Festival Travel Shadowed by Excessive Virus Prevention as Some Local Govts Add New Restrictions on Top of Central Policy," *Global Times*, accessed April 19, 2021, https://www.globaltimes.cn/page/202101/1214304.shtml.

60 Gordon Bennett, *Yundong: Mass Campaigns in Chinese Communist Leadership* (Berkeley: University of California Press, 1976).

61 E.g., Nianquan Yang, "Disease Prevention, Social Mobilization and Spatial Politics: The Anti-Germ Warfare Incident of 1952 and the 'Patriotic Health Campaign,'" *The Chinese Historical Review* 11, no. 2 (2004): 155–182.

62 Elizabeth Perry, "From Mass Campaigns to Managed Campaigns: 'Constructing a New Socialist Countryside,'" in *Mao's Invisible Hand: The Political Foundations of Adaptive Governance in China*, ed. Sebastian Heilmann and Elizabeth Perry (Cambridge, London: Harvard University Press, 2011), 30–61.

daily necessities for the people of Wuhan.[63] The directive also demanded that "[l]eading groups must be set up and leading officials must stand at the front line,"[64] ensuring that the whole Party-state bureaucracy works to contain the spread of the disease. In terms of the mobilization of personnel and medical resources in both cases, the Party-state also mobilized medical personnel from the military to take pressure off the healthcare system. In the case of SARS, according to the defense white paper of 2004, the People's Liberation Army (PLA) dispatched 37,000 men to support in the fight against SARS and, in total, sent 1,383 military medical personnel to treat SARS patients.[65] The same is true in the case of Covid-19, where the military was originally dispatched to Wuhan to support anti-Covid efforts in the early days of the outbreak in the city[66] and Chinese media portrayed the efforts of the military as a heroic fight for the interests and well-being of the Chinese people.[67]

In addition to the all-out mobilization of personnel resources, the Party-state also invested significant amounts of material resources in fighting both SARS and Covid-19. In both cases, makeshift hospitals were rapidly constructed to treat infected patients. During SARS, the Xiaotangshan hospital was built within seven days in Beijing and staffed with military medical personnel to offer a dedicated facility to treat SARS patients and provide additional hospital beds during a highly volatile situation.[68] Initially, in a major financial effort in April 2003, the State Council dedicated a fund of two billion yuan to fight SARS and to fund free medical care for the poor.[69]

63 "China to Extend Spring Festival Holiday to Contain Coronavirus Outbreak," *Xinhua*, accessed April 12, 2021, http://www.xinhuanet.com/english/2020-01/26/c_138735589.htm.

64 Ibid.

65 State Council of the People's Republic of China, "China's National Defense in 2004: VIII. The Armed Forces and the People," accessed April 24, 2021, http://en.people.cn/whitepaper/defense2004/defense2004(8).html.

66 "Military Medical Staff Dispatched to Support Wuhan's Coronavirus Fight," *Xinhua*, accessed April 12, 2021, http://www.xinhuanet.com/english/2020-02/03/c_138752149.htm.

67 Zhongguo Xinwenwang, "为了人民——人民军队支援地方疫情防控纪实" (For the People—Record of the People's Liberation Army Providing Assistance to Control a Local Epidemic Situation), accessed April 26, 2021, https://www.youtube.com/watch?v=c6EE92_By8g.

68 David Hsieh, "A Hospital up in 7 Days," *The Straits Times*, April 30, 2003.

69 John Pomfret, "Thousands Flee Beijing, Fearing SARS," *Washington Post*, accessed April 24, 2021, https://www.washingtonpost.com/archive/politics/2003/04/24/thousands-flee-beijing-fearing-sars/da04ce95-058d-408c-ad97-a8f2017e4058/.

Similarly, during the Covid-19 outbreak, the Party-state also invested massive resources to build two makeshift hospitals dedicated to treating Covid-19 patients: Huoshenshan and Leishenshan.[70] Additionally, during the handling of the Covid-19 outbreak, the Party-state also directed significant resources towards setting up quarantine and makeshift test centers[71] for mass testing for Covid-19 in entire cities. More precisely, central authorities demanded that local governments be able to test as many as five million people within two days, in order to be able to carry out mass testing in case of an outbreak.[72] In the case of Covid-19, this campaign-style, all-out mobilization of personnel and resources was maintained even after the original outbreaks were contained. In reaction to small outbreaks, for example in Beijing,[73] and in Heilongjiang province[74] (Northeast China), local authorities conducted mass testing of inhabitants of entire villages or districts and re-imposed strict lockdown measures in an attempt to control the spread of Covid-19.

The campaign-style mobilization also extended to the Chinese population at large. Implementing quite far-reaching measures of control and curbing of personal rights, the Party-state intended to involve every Chinese citizen in the overall efforts to combat both infectious diseases. During both the SARS crisis and the Covid-19 crisis, the respective leaders, Hu Jintao and Xi Jinping, called for a "people's war"[75] to combat the diseases. Travel within the country was restricted or suspended entirely during major national

70 Ni Zhang and Xi Chen, "Wuhan's Huoshenshan Hospital a Symbol of Chinese Spirit," *Global Times*, accessed April 25, 2021, https://www.globaltimes.cn/content/1183849.shtml; "1,600 Beds for Leishenshan Hospital to Be Delivered in Wuhan on Feb. 8," *Xinhua*, accessed April 25, 2021, http://www.xinhuanet.com/english/2020-02/07/c_138764454.htm.

71 "North China's Shijiazhuang Sets up 458 Quarantine Centers to Curb COVID-19," *Xinhua*, accessed April 25, 2021, http://www.xinhuanet.com/english/2021-01/21/c_139687460.htm.

72 "China Sets Rules on Test Capacity, Requires Cities to Cover 5m Residents in Two Days," *Global Times*, accessed April 25, 2021, https://www.globaltimes.cn/page/202101/1213486.shtml.

73 "Beijing Conducts Nucleic Acid Tests on around 356,000 People," *Xinhua*, accessed April 25, 2021, http://www.xinhuanet.com/english/2020-06/17/c_139146397.htm.

74 "NE China's Heilongjiang Reports 40 New Confirmed COVID-19 Cases and 50 Asymptomatic Infections," *Global Times*, accessed April 25, 2021, https://www.globaltimes.cn/page/202101/1212742.shtml.

75 James Lawson and Feng Xu, "SARS in Canada and China: Two Approaches to Emergency Health Policy," *Governance: An International Journal of Policy, Administration, and Institutions* 20, no. 2 (April 2007): 209–232; The State Council of the People's Republic of China, "Fighting Covid-19."

holidays, i.e., the May 1st holiday in 2003[76] and the travel activities during China's most important family holiday, the lunar new year celebrations, during a renewed, albeit smaller, outbreak of Covid-19 at the beginning of 2021.[77] Additionally, and quite famously, the Chinese government implemented mass quarantine measures, such as locking down the entire city of Wuhan during the initial stage of the Covid-19 outbreak, thereby strictly limiting the freedom of movement of its citizens. Furthermore, religious gatherings were restricted at a local level in reaction to a Covid-19 outbreak that was allegedly caused by religious worshippers.[78] Thus, the Party-state did not hesitate to implement measures restricting basic rights and freedoms that democratic states might struggle with.

The overall success of this campaign-style mobilization is clearly visible in the rapid reaction that followed once clear signals emerged from the center and authority was centralized. The Party-state quickly mobilized resources and implemented far-reaching measures, such as, for example, the full lockdown of Wuhan. The massive reaction is even more impressive in light of the fact that no significant measures to control the diseases had been taken beforehand in either case. Thus, such strong mobilizational measures of personnel and resources required a central interference that can be implemented in an authoritarian manner, without having to take into consideration any veto players in the system. The rapid decline in case numbers and the return to a relatively normal life also testify to the success of the strong reaction by the Party-state. On June 24, 2003—about three months after the Party-state started reacting to the crisis—the World Health Organization lifted its travel advisory for Beijing,[79] thus indicating that the SARS crisis was under control there. Similarly, China managed to officially contain the spread of Covid-19 much faster than many democratic countries.

In terms of reacting to a crisis and implementing far-reaching measures, the Chinese Party-state is thus in a position to fully play out its "authoritarian advantage". It can centralize authority and decision making in line with the principle of democratic centralism that underpins the entire Party

76 Puska, "SARS 2002–2003."

77 "China Beefs up COVID-19 Defenses in Rural Areas during Festival Travel Rush," *Xinhua*, accessed April 26, 2021, http://www.xinhuanet.com/english/2021-01/21/c_139687292.htm.

78 Shan Jie, "Some COVID-19 Confirmed Patients in N. China's Shijiazhuang Outbreak Attended Recent Religious Activities: Media," *Global Times*, accessed April 11, 2021, https://www.globaltimes.cn/page/202101/1212203.shtml.

79 Puska, "SARS 2002–2003."

organization. Furthermore, it can rely on its campaign-style mobilization toolkit that dates back to Maoist China and has been adapted to fit the demands of reform-era China. Finally, it can implement far-reaching containment measures without paying attention to individual basic rights and freedoms. The same "authoritarian advantage" is also evident in the Party-state's approach to dealing with the leadership challenge of meaning making.

Meaning Making: The Official Narrative and Cracking Down on Alternative Voices

Meaning making, as a leadership challenge in a crisis situation, is about how a crisis in the eyes of the public is to be "labeled, understood, and evaluated".[80] Its core element for a government is, therefore, creating a narrative and communicating what is happening, how it should be understood, and how the results of government intervention should be perceived. Meaning making is a particularly crucial leadership challenge for an authoritarian regime because it has to influence and control how its citizens interpret a crisis in order to prevent open challenges to its rulership.

In the case of China, meaning making of a crisis takes place with the help of the official propaganda and censorship system. The PRC has an extensive propaganda system with a large bureaucracy responsible for controlling information.[81] Although the times of Maoist totalitarian "thought work"[82] are over, the CCP still engages in far-reaching information management, propaganda and media control.[83] This is also the case in the management of online content and social media.[84] Therefore, in the case of a crisis, the CCP is in a more advantageous position to spread its own interpretation of the crisis and government coping strategies. This advantage is also reflected in the meaning-making strategies that the CCP applies.

80 Boin et al., *The Politics of Crisis Management*, 87.

81 David Shambaugh, "China's Propaganda System: Institutions, Processes and Efficacy," *The China Journal* 57 (January 2007): 25–58.

82 E.g., Fengyuan Ji, *Linguistic Engineering: Language and Politics in Mao's China* (Honolulu: University of Hawai'i Press, 2004).

83 Anne-Marie, "Mass Persuasion as a Means of Legitimation and China's Popular Authoritarianism," *American Behavioral Scientist* 53, no. 3 (2009): 434–457.

84 E.g., Rogier Creemers, "Cyber China: Upgrading Propaganda, Public Opinion Work and Social Management for the Twenty-First Century," *Journal of Contemporary China* 26, no. 103 (2017): 85–100.

Despite initial delayed reactions and a lack of clear official communication, the CCP engaged in significant efforts at meaning making during both the SARS and the Covid-19 crises. In both cases, these efforts consisted of three main areas. First came the creation of an official narrative on the crisis. The orthodox and officially endorsed way of understanding the crisis and government strategies was spread through official media and public utterances by leading politicians. The second aspect was the concerted crackdown on alternative voices and on anyone in a position to challenge the official narrative on the crisis. Finally, in both cases, the CCP attempted to engage in official blame shifting by attributing responsibility to local cadres, thus directing potential criticism away from the central leadership.

The Bright Side: Highlighting Central Leadership and Success

The official narrative of the crisis in the case of both SARS and Covid-19 is a tale of success following a hard and dedicated struggle and relentless efforts by the political leadership. After the centralization of decision making and the involvement of the central leadership, central leaders were portrayed in official crisis reporting as working relentlessly on dealing with the crisis. For example, the official timeline of anti-Covid work[85] mainly depicts the activities of the three central leaders, Xi Jinping, Li Keqiang, and Sun Chunlan. According to this timeline, their main activities consisted of conducting central-level meetings, inspection meetings and engagement with local actors, as well as international coordination. International coordination activities were largely the task of Xi Jinping in his role as President of the PRC. Xi was also the leader whose activities were listed most frequently (127 times compared to 72 for Li Keqiang and 33 for Sun Chunlan). Thus, in this official narrative, central leaders made significant ongoing efforts to deal with the Covid-19 crisis.

The same is true for the SARS crisis in 2003 when the Party center was also portrayed as being in charge and working hard to handle the crisis. Most of the articles in the *People's Daily*, the CCP's official mouthpiece, dealt with the activities and involvement of the central leadership. While this is natural for a national-level Party newspaper, at the same time, it underlines the importance that the Party attributed to portraying the central leadership as being in charge of the crisis. Additionally, it also emphasizes the leadership

85 "Daily Record of the Center."

role of the Party and the commitment and efforts of Party members in dealing with the crisis. For example, the *People's Daily* states that "on this extraordinary battlefield, Party members and cadres step forward bravely, take the lead and fulfil the function of a vanguard and model of behavior."[86] In the official narrative, therefore, the central leadership, but also the entire Party, are portrayed as fighting arduously to deal with the respective health crises. This fight in the official narrative is also represented in the repeated use of military language and it is depicted as a success. Hu Jintao declared the fight against SARS to be a "people's war" and, in various speeches and statements, Xi Jinping also officially refers to the handling of Covid-19 as a "people's war" (*renmin zhanzheng*).[87] Further military terminology, such as, for example, the depiction of the health crisis as a "battlefield" (*zhanchang*), "battlefront" (*zhanxian*), "prevailing over [an enemy]" (*zhansheng*) or "victory" (*shengli*) are used in official crisis communication during both crises, thus underlining the severity of the crisis and the Party's relentless struggle to handle it.

The struggle and work of the Party are also presented as a success. In the case of SARS, the *People's Daily* reports that the disease has been "effectively contained"[88] (*youxiao kongzhi*). Similarly, the Party also portrays its handling of the Covid-19 crisis as efficient and effective.[89] This is particularly obvious in the white paper on fighting Covid-19[90] that mainly portrays the Party's successful efforts in containing the virus, rather than giving room to debates over its origins or the early mishandling of the crisis.[91]

---

86 Bai Jianfeng (白剑峰),"白衣战士；最可爱的人；记北京非典型肺炎防治一线的医务人员" (Warriors in White; Most Adorable People; Reporting on Beijing's Medical Personnel at the Frontline of Preventing and Curing SARS), *Renmin Ribao*, April 13, 2003.

87 Xi Jinping (习近平), "习近平在湖北省考察新冠肺炎疫情防控工作时的讲话" (Speech of Xi Jinping at the Occasion of Investigating the Situation of Controlling the Novel Coronavirus in Hubei Province), *Qiushi*, accessed April 26, 2021, http://jhsjk.people.cn/article/31655994.

88 Zhang Wenkang (张文康), "国务院新闻办公室举行记者招待会：卫生部长张文康就非典型肺炎防治情况答记者问" (The State Council Information Office of the PRC Holds a Press Conference: Minister of Health Zhang Wenkang Answers Questions of Journalists Regarding the Situation of Controlling the SARS Epidemic), *Renmin Ribao*, May 4, 2003.

89 Sheng Zhong, "Arduous Anti-Epidemic Efforts Manifest Great Strength of China," *People's Daily*, accessed April 26, 2021, http://en.people.cn/n3/2020/0610/c90000-9699211.html.

90 The State Council of the People's Republic of China, "Fighting Covid-19."

91 April Herlevi, "Fighting the Battle for the Narrative: The PRC White Paper on Its COVID-19 Response," *China Brief* 20, no. 11 (June 24, 2020): 6–11.

The Dark Side: Suppressing Alternative Narratives and Blame Shifting

The CCP's strategy of meaning making in a crisis situation also involves suppressing dissenting voices and fending off alternative narratives. To suppress alternative understandings of a crisis situation or the spread of information that casts doubt on the official narrative, the Party-state relies on methods that are only available to an authoritarian regime. For example, in the case of SARS, the Chinese government barred whistleblower Jiang Yanyong from speaking to reporters following the outbreak, although he was publicly praised as an anti-SARS hero.[92] While this is still a relatively benign reaction by an authoritarian regime, a significantly more pronounced and widespread reaction followed the outbreak of Covid-19. According to media reporting, during the year 2020, at least 17,000 people were investigated for "compiling and spreading false information on the epidemic situation".[93] While the charges were not detailed any further, this is a common accusation against online activists for spreading information that the Party-state would not like to be publicly discussed.

In addition to this broad crackdown, the Chinese Party-state has gone to great lengths to silence critics and citizen journalists who had reported on the Internet during the early stages of the outbreak in Wuhan. For example, influential entrepreneur, Ren Zhiqiang, was sentenced to eighteen years in prison, officially for graft, after having published an essay critical of the handling of the Covid outbreak on the Internet and calling Xi Jinping a "clown stripped of his clothes who still insisted on being emperor."[94] Additionally, lawyer and activist, Zhang Zhan, was sentenced to four years in prison after publishing photos and video footage from Wuhan during the early days of the pandemic. She was charged with the crime of "picking quarrels and provoking trouble,"[95] another common accusation against activists

92 Joe McDonald, "Chinese Release Hero Doctor; Jiang Exposed Scope of SARS; Hailed '89 Protests as Patriotic," *Associated Press*, July 21, 2004.

93 Wang Jun (王俊), "去年查处1. 7万余名编造、传播涉疫情虚假信息等违法犯罪人员" (Last Year More than 17,000 Criminals Were Investigated Who Compiled and Spread False Information on the Epidemic Situation), *Sohu.com*, accessed April 14, 2021, https://www.sohu.com/a/443604858_114988.

94 Chris Buckley, "China's 'Big Cannon' Blasted Xi. Now He's Been Jailed for 18 Years," *New York Times*, accessed April 12, 2021, https://www.nytimes.com/2020/09/22/world/asia/china-ren-zhiqiang-tycoon.html.

95 Christian Shepherd and Tom Mitchell, "Chinese Citizen Journalist Jailed after Accusing Officials of Covid Cover-up Zhang Zhan Sentenced to 4 Years as Beijing Reasserts

not falling into line with the official Party narrative. Furthermore, the work of the well-known Chinese author, Fang Fang, whose blogposts during the Wuhan lockdown were published as the *Wuhan Diary*,[96] were also censored by Chinese authorities after the *Wuhan Diary* was translated into English and published internationally.[97] Thus, discrediting information and interpretations that diverge from the official narrative is an important strategy for meaning making in a crisis situation.

A further attempt at meaning making that the Chinese government employed during both crises is the sacking of lower-level Party cadres and thus the shifting of responsibility further down the hierarchy. As Mei and Pearson point out, the hold-to-account system designed to punish cadres for policy mistakes and negligence was created as a reaction to the SARS crisis.[98] The creation of this system implies that the Party considered it important to be able to hold local cadres accountable for undesirable events and disasters in their jurisdictions. For example, in the case of SARS, already in the early stages of the Party-state's reaction to the SARS crisis, the Mayor of Beijing, Meng Xuenong, and the Minister of Health, Zhang Wenkang, were dismissed over their roles in handling SARS. Additionally, a significant number of lower-ranking cadres were punished for dereliction of duty and their insufficient handling of the SARS outbreak.[99] The same is true of the Covid-19 pandemic. On February 13, 2020, Xinhua announced that both the provincial Party Secretary of Hubei province, Jiang Chaoliang, and the Party Secretary of Wuhan, Ma Guoqiang, had been dismissed from their posts.[100] Although the Xinhua notice still awarded them the title "comrade" and thus did not indicate a full fall from grace, it appears that Jiang and Ma had to assume responsibility for the delayed response to the outbreak of Covid-19 in Wuhan. Particularly in light of Ma's comment in a TV interview

Official Narrative of Outbreak Handling," *Financial Times*, accessed April 12, 2021, https://www.ft.com/content/79ab1413-6eb9-49b5-a34a-36bc257c07cd.

96 Fang, Wuhan Diary.

97 Fan Wang and Grace Tsoi, "Fang Fang: Author Vilified for Wuhan Diary Speaks Out a Year On," *BBC News*, accessed April 14, 2021, https://www.bbc.com/news/world-asia-54987675.

98 Mei and Pearson, "Killing a Chicken to Scare the Monkeys?"

99 "Central China's Henan Province Punishes 800 Officials and Others over SARS," *Agence France Presse*, May 24, 2003.

100 "湖北省委主要负责同志职务调整：应勇任湖北省委书记" (Personnel Shuffle among Hubei's Leading Comrades: Ying Yong Appointed as Hubei Provincial Party Secretary), *Xinhua*, accessed April 14, 2021, http://www.xinhuanet.com/politics/2020-02/13/c_1125568253.htm.

regarding the delayed reaction by Wuhan authorities, it appears plausible that the CCP attempted to shift responsibility to Party cadres below the center and thus deflect blame from the Party-state as a whole.

The CCP's efforts at meaning making have been reasonably successful. Although public opinion surveys from authoritarian regimes always have to be taken with a grain of salt, research suggests that, overall, the Chinese public views the efforts of the Party-state at containing the spread of Covid-19 in a positive light. Results from surveys, for example by Wu et al., suggest high levels of trust in the government, particularly at the national level, and a favorable view of government performance during the pandemic.[101]

Conclusion

A comparative study of how the CCP reacted to the SARS crisis in 2003 and to the Covid-19 outbreak in 2020 gives us an insight into how the Party-state is equipped to deal with leadership challenges in crisis situations, and its ability to learn from past crises and challenges. The comparison reveals two main conclusions on crisis management by the Chinese Party-state, and potentially for authoritarian systems more generally.

Firstly, with regard to some leadership challenges, the CCP is equipped with an authoritarian advantage. When it comes to dealing with an immediate crisis and implementing far-reaching measures that infringe upon basic rights and freedoms, it can implement these in a top-down manner. Furthermore, it can engage in campaign-style mobilization of the entire population to deal with threats, such as the ones posed by a virus. This campaign-style mobilization requires clear central directions and messaging to overcome veto players in the system. In the cases considered here, the reactions by the Party-state only took off after this was implemented, and both disease outbreaks were largely contained in a comparatively rapid manner once the authoritarian advantage was fully played out. The same is true of the challenge of meaning making. Here too, the CCP can rely on authoritarian methods of propaganda and oppression to advance an official narrative, discredit and suppress alternative understandings, and shift blame away from the Party-state and onto individuals.

101 Cary Wu et al., "Chinese Citizen Satisfaction with Government Performance during COVID-19," *Journal of Contemporary China*, 2021.

Secondly, however, when it comes to the initial leadership challenge of perceiving a crisis situation, the CCP is faced with an authoritarian disadvantage. During both the SARS and the Covid-19 crises, the Party-state struggled to understand and make sense of the crisis in order to be able to react in a rapid and encompassing manner. This is due to issues of information asymmetry, fragmented governing structures, and adverse incentivization structures for Party cadres. Furthermore, it would require clearer governing structures top-down, less reliance on ambiguous signaling from the center and, overall, a more open political system primarily committed to best governance solutions instead of the interests of the Party. Fixing these problems would require far-reaching political reforms that would change promotion incentives for Party cadres, increase transparency, and make cadres more accountable to the public and public well-being, rather than to the immediate interests of the Party. Although after the SARS crisis the Party-state tried to improve its ability to deal with health crises and significantly expanded the legal basis for this, it cannot fundamentally reform its structures to avoid similar management issues in future health (and other) crises. The dilemma of the authoritarian (dis-)advantage in crisis management is ingrained in how the Chinese authoritarian system functions.

II. (Dis-)Continuity of Crisis— The Interwar Period

To Hold and to Let Go: The Political Discourse of the Committee of Union and Progress in the Ottoman Empire, 1908–1923

Duygu Coşkuntuna

The Committee of Union and Progress (CUP) perceived the Anglo-Russian talks on Macedonia (1908)[1] as the final nail in the Empire's coffin and decided to rebel against Abdülhamid II, assassinating intelligence suppliers to the Sultan and converting the soldiers, who were sent to subdue them, to their own political creed. Lacking crucial information about the state of rebellion and unable to deal a decisive blow to his own army, Abdülhamid II removed the suspension of the constitution on July 23, 1908, and announced elections for a new parliament. Thus, the Committee's stance on the issue was a conservative revolutionism: They believed the Ottoman Empire to be in a state of decline, but their preferred option to save it dictated that it must stay in one piece, under the Sultan and the constitution.

The acute suppression of the opposition to Abdülhamid II exacerbated the lack of public political discussion and other grievances, mostly economic in nature, into a full-blown crisis of political representation. Not only was the Sultan's authoritarian rule blocking political debate in the public sphere, but his surveillance network also started to seek and destroy the prospective debaters. The Revolution of 1908 was the organized and armed reaction to that crisis. This chapter captures how the CUP imagined and then remembered a post-Hamidian[2] Ottoman Empire.

Using their memoirs as gateways to their mindsets, I will argue that an intellectual, who was above all against the Hamidian regime and was well-versed in new concepts such as the nation, was supposed to save the country,

1 King Edward VII and Tsar Nicolas II met in Reval (today's Talinn) to forge an alliance against the rise of Germany. They also discussed the fate of Macedonia, basically proposing a European mandate over it to be ruled only nominally by the Sultan. They did not agree on a plan to break the entire Empire into pieces, that was only a rumor. See Erik J. Zürcher, *Turkey: A Modern History* (London, New York: I.B. Tauris, 2004), 90.

2 The regime of Sultan Abdülhamid II is often also called "Hamidian".

in implicit contradiction to the bureaucrat and Sultan combination of the *Tanzimat*[3] era. This perception of the intellectual on its own widened the political field considerably, as anyone with the right political ideas could join the movement, unlike the rather *clique*-like bureaucratic circles. The Unionist mindset dictated that the "potential" accumulation of knowledge had to turn into "kinetic" action and the propeller behind this change would be a kind of zeal, *hamiyet*, coupled with hope to raise morale. This idea of hope found its ultimate expression in the 1908 Revolution, bringing about a brief respite of intercommunal peace and celebration. The constitutional liberties were welcome as long as they were not used against the Unionists; thus, they talked about "good" and "bad" ways of employing freedom. The savior would also adhere to a "brigand" mentality, where a negotiation between the ideal (democratic and parliamentary) and practical (non-democratic and oligarchic) ways of governmental rule would take place. The perception of liberties not as ideals but malleable political carrots to be dangled in front of the "nation" and political debate becoming optional paved the way for the later authoritarianism of the CUP.

Analyzing memoirs is a way of getting a glimpse into the minds of the members of the CUP, who pinpoint certain ideas as the propeller behind their actions including, but not limited to, the Revolution of 1908. What the Unionists built and tore down is apparent in a number of publications—what they *thought*, less so. Smith and Watson understand autobiographic truth-telling as "an intersubjective mode" standing "outside a logical or juridical model of truth and falsehood".[4] Thus, memoirs reveal fewer "truths" than ways of truth-telling, i.e., memoirists' perceptions of the world around them and how they posited alternatives to it. These views are also time-bound, as memories are affected by the present context of record. The primary sources consulted fall into two periods: 1908–1923, when the Ottoman constitution was re-declared, the Empire fought and lost a world war. These earlier memoirs are written mainly to keep track of the events that immediately preceded them. Enver Paşa's memoirs on the events of 1908 is such an example. The second important period is 1923–1938, covering the declaration of the Turkish Republic and the presidency of Mustafa Kemal Atatürk. These memoirs are mainly written during the retirement days of their authors, who wished to leave a trace of their lives, Kazım Karabekir's

3 Tanzimat is the name of a reform period in the Ottoman Empire.

4 Sidonie Smith and Julia Watson, *Reading Autobiography: A Guide for Interpreting Life Narratives* (Minneapolis, London: University of Minnesota Press, 2001), 13.

Hayatım being an example. The accumulation in the first period may be attributed to the immediacy of the events and to a "defensive" stance in penning one's memoirs. Unionists wished to "enlighten" the Turkish reading public by providing their point of view, sometimes with an eye to swaying public opinion to their side. Generally, only history enthusiasts noticed these books, but a couple of them attracted the occasional ire of the government.[5]

A State of Crisis

The history of the Ottoman Empire after 1876 is mainly a history of painful modernization, where the bureaucrats took on the task of improving the army, balancing the budget and making state institutions more efficient under the auspices of the Sultan. Starting in 1839 with an Imperial Rescript prepared by a bureaucrat, the Sultan guaranteed to secure the Empire's subjects' lives, honor and dignity, promised equal justice to Muslims as well as non-Muslims and widened the legislative body, whose laws he promised to uphold. Later, the legislative body came to include an appointed Council of State to oversee judicial harmony. Young Ottomans, literati who found these measures insufficient, advocated publicly for a constitution since they opposed what they perceived to be single-handed rule by the bureaucrats. The tables turned against the bureaucrats as the court attempted to centralize power, pushing the statesmen to ally with the constitutionalists.[6] Drafted by Midhat Paşa, the constitution was approved by Sultan Abdülhamid II in 1876, granting the right to elect an electoral college to all tax-paying males over the age of 25 in the Ottoman Empire. The first parliament of the Ottoman Empire consisted of a Senate appointed by the Sultan and these elected representatives formed an assembly with quotas for fair representation of non-Muslim populations.[7] This brief parliamentary interlude came to an end with the conclusion of the Russo-Ottoman War of 1878, as Abdülhamid II blamed parliament for the disastrous results and, using his

5 Two examples would be Kazım Karabekir's notes on the National Struggle period (1919–1923), which were burned before their publication in 1933, and Rıza Nur's memoirs, which included serious allegations against Mustafa Kemal Atatürk and were banned.

6 M. Şükrü Hanioğlu, *A Brief History of the Ottoman Empire* (Princeton and Oxford: Princeton University Press, 2008), 111–114.

7 Ibid., 119.

constitutional rights, prorogued it. The rest of Sultan Abdülhamid II's reign was a series of authoritarian and modernizing vignettes: Bureaucratic power reverted to the Palace, more specifically to the Sultan and his immediate entourage; thus, the legitimization of the sovereign's power was emphasized as a divine right rather than for the will or the benefit of the nation. In addition to that centralization of power, the press was widely censored, and the Sultan's surveillance network monitored more aspects of daily life. Aware of the need to modernize his Empire to face European challenges in particular, an awareness he inherited from the *Tanzimat* reformers, the Sultan placed great value on building infrastructure, such as railroads, keeping up with the growing debts of the Empire, and improving the education system.[8]

The future opponents of Abdülhamid II, later known as the Young Turks, graduated from school with at least one foreign language under their belt. During their education and beyond, they became acquainted with various currents of thought, such as materialism and nationalism. Much influenced by the constitutionalist Young Ottomans, this younger generation of opposition became part of the "professional classes"—lawyers, teachers, doctors and, most importantly, officers. Their numbers surpassed the tightly knit circle of Young Ottomans, and they represented a wider political spectrum. What they did not yet have was the political knowledge and experience to step into any kind of possible power vacuum in the Ottoman Empire.[9] Their political demands could only be voiced in journals published abroad or circulated underground; as the parliament was still closed, no elections were held. Still, their underground organization in Thessaloniki managed to merge with the circles of previously exiled Ottoman intellectuals in Europe, bringing about the CUP in 1907. This was not a regular political party with a definitive agenda, but a collective of individuals that opposed the Sultan from various points of view and proposed different methods to deal with what they perceived as oppressive policies. The elements that made them into a collective body were their fierce constitutionalism, willingness to work with the Armenian committees at that point in time, and their Ottomanist tenor.

8 Ibid., 122–124.

9 Feroz Ahmad, *The Young Turks: The Committee of Union and Progress in Turkish Politics 1908–1914* (Oxford: Clarendon Press, 1969), 16–17. Hanioğlu adds that some *ulema*, Ottoman religious and legal scholars, chose to join the Young Turk movement as well (see 144–145).

From the vantage point of the members of the CUP, the domestic affairs of the Ottoman Empire were not in good order: Nationalist aspirations of various communities threatened the territorial integrity of the Empire, which was also having economic difficulties. Macedonia, home to a number of ethnicities, was brewing with unrest since some of its inhabitants advocated for national causes, wanted to use the Orthodox Church for their aims, or wished for autonomy.[10] The armed conflicts between these groups and the state were the first posts for many officers within the CUP, a case of nationalism in action. The Armenians in eastern provinces started to organize along nationalist lines as well, asking for reform and notably occupying the Ottoman Bank in Istanbul in 1896. The establishment of irregular Kurdish troops led to the brutal suppression of an Armenian rebellion in today's Batman[11] in 1894.[12] In the economic field too, the Empire's credit was so bad that, in 1881, Abdülhamid II had to allow European lenders to collect certain revenues in the name of the Ottoman state. Especially in the public sector, wages were usually late and rarely paid in full, impacting bureaucrats and officers directly. For the educated strata of Ottoman society, this mix of authoritarian rule, occasional state brutality, and economic instability did not bode well. The CUP meant to put an end to it by taking to the Macedonian mountains in 1908.

A Committee Called Union and Progress

The memoirists usually refrain from giving a detailed description of how they perceived themselves; certain aspects of their self-assigned identity, however, can be dwelled on. For the Unionist, Muhittin Birgen, the early Committee of Union and Progress stood for "good emotions" (*iyi hisler*) and the prospect of coming into a position of power intimidated them.[13] In this case, Birgen knew that the Committee of Union and Progress was not exactly a political success and was trying to explain its circumstances. He knew

10 Zürcher, *Turkey*, 82.

11 Also called Sasun in Armenian and Qabilcewz in Kurdish, Batman is in the southeastern Anatolia region of Turkey.

12 Zürcher, *Turkey*, 83.

13 Muhiddin Birgen, *İttihat ve Terakki'de On Sene*, Vol. 1 (İstanbul: Kitap Yayınevi, 2006), 71.

the group did not have a "national" (*milli*) or a class-related (*sınıfi*) agenda.[14] According to him, the CUP was something that was unable to execute its plans properly and that eventually turned into the authoritarian rule it sought to avoid.[15] The exploitation of power and the lack of a plan seep through his narrative, which is otherwise pro-Unionist. In another passage, Birgen claims that the Committee of Union and Progress was the "Turkish *komite*" in answer to other Balkan *komite*s of the time.[16] Birgen employs the term to show a relationship between the armed groups of the time. Vartkes Efendi,[17] representative of Erzurum in the Assembly, once elaborated on the "revolutionary" (*ihtilalci*) aspect of the scene. Upon receiving a threat by *Halaskar Zabitan*, the military branch of the Freedom and Accord Party, Birgen proceeded to give a speech: "[t]he lowly revolutionaries who lack the courage to sign their writings cannot frighten the revolutionaries here. Gentlemen, when we were revolutionaries, we let such crooks be murdered."[18] The oppositional stance provided a common thread binding various agendas, bringing the former Armenian revolutionary to the assembly and making an ally of Turkish revolutionaries.

Later, the great promise of this thread unraveled but remained a point of reference. Ahmed Rıza Bey[19] reflects on the impression that the Committee of Union and Progress made at the time of its establishment: "Union and Progress would fix everything, make it rain, and make the homeland into a better place." When this failed to happen immediately, disappointment followed.[20] Hüseyin Kazım Kadri thinks that if it were not for the later National Struggle (1918–1923), everybody would still pledge allegiance to the Unionist agenda.[21] Considering the fact that many of the former Unionists, including Mustafa Kemal Bey, helped to establish a new order, it is true that the Unionist influences did not stop immediately with the foundation of the Turkish Republic.

14 Birgen, *İttihat ve Terakki'de On Sene*, 74.

15 Ibid., 111.

16 Ibid., 245.

17 Efendi is an Ottoman honorific.

18 Celal Bayar, *Ben de Yazdım*, Vol. 2 (İstanbul: Baha Matbaası, 1966), 543.

19 Bey is an Ottoman honorific.

20 Ahmed Rıza, *Meclis-i Mebusan ve Ayan Reisi Ahmed Rıza Bey'in Anıları* (İstanbul: Arba Yayınları, 1988), 41.

21 Hüseyin Kâzım Kadri, *Meşrutiyetten Cumhuriyete Hatıralarım: İstanbul/Trabzon/Selanik/Suriye* (İstanbul: Dergâh Yayınları, 2000), 15.

While the discourse about the nature of the Committee of Union and Progress revealed a preference for a flexible organization that included only elusive aims beyond the declaration of the constitution, it was sometimes useful to equate the Committee of Union and Progress with the nation itself. It goes without saying that the connotations of the word "nation" were also left blank. Azmi Bey, former Governor of Beirut, was to take over the post of the Chief of Police after the Babıali Coup of 1913. Celal Bayar reports that, according to Azmi Bey's recollections, when Azmi Bey told the current Chief of Police that the Unionists, who had overthrown the government in the name of the nation, had ordered him to become Chief of Police, the officer complied.[22] The context suggests that the nation is possibly the Ottoman nation or even the CUP itself.

The CUP defined itself rather vaguely, allowing it to stretch its self-perception to imply the embodiment of an entire nation. This definition was a significant departure from the "men of *Tanzimat*", who were essentially Mehmet Reşit, Ali and Fuad Paşas,[23] later aided by Ahmet Cevdet and Midhat Paşas. These men were a close-knit, elite group of statesmen: Well-educated, and familiar with diplomacy and bureaucracy, these men had intricate plans of their own to modernize the Ottoman state structurally.[24] While striving for a more efficient Empire, the likes of which could be found in Europe, they made no efforts to derive legitimacy from the "nation", in direct juxtaposition to the CUP.

The Role of the "Savior"

In the eyes of the members of the CUP, intellectuals equated to possible liberators.[25] An intellectual for them could be a literary figure with high political aims in mind (such as Namık Kemal) or simply a person who was educated and wanted the state to be saved. Kazım Nami Duru records a possible reason for such a perception in his memoirs. According to him, the

22 Celal Bayar, *Ben de Yazdım*, Vol. 4 (İstanbul: Baha Matbaası, 1967), 1111.

23 Paşa is an Ottoman rank.

24 For their rise and fall, see Stanford J. Shaw and Ezel Kural Shaw, *History of the Ottoman Empire and Modern Turkey*, Vol. 2 (Cambridge: Cambridge University Press, 1977), 61–69.

25 Not all of the educated figures portrayed as "intellectuals" here earned a living through intellectual work. However, they perceived themselves as "intellectuals".

theory of *Tuba* tree, which postulated the diffusion of knowledge from top to bottom, influenced many intellectuals of the time.[26] A very literal interpretation of this theory would suggest that the reigning power was automatically a disseminator of culture, thus the intellectual was the one with a valid claim to power. İbrahim Temo puts the earlier Young Turks in this group, stating that they saw the terrible situation in the state and continued "opening high schools of medicine and military" to bring about enlightenment. The second wave of graduates from these schools came after Midhat Paşa and his generation.[27] Temo himself tried to "wake up" his younger fellow students in the same vein.[28] It is worth noting that the process is still imagined as an automatic one; once the schools had been opened and the people had been "touched" with the right ideas, it would progress of its own accord. Moreover, there is no mention of the religion-based education of the old days, which still continued to exist.

Another aspect of this enlightenment would be its reactionary character. Many of the students of the time felt oppressed by the strict Hamidian regime and sought a way out. Halil Halid, an earlier example of a Young Turk, claims that while the rest of the population was unable to recognize the true nature of Sultan Abdülhamid II's rule, he was "enlightened enough" to see through and hate his tyrannical ways.[29] His efforts went on even through the cholera epidemic,[30] displaying the urgency of the case at hand. Kazım Karabekir's perception put the "enlightened" Young Ottomans, such as Namık Kemal or Ziya Paşa, in direct opposition to the Hamidian regime.[31]

These intellectuals were supposed to take up the role of the pioneering teacher within society. One could also further the argument: The teaching of correct political vocabulary would lead to the demand for correct concepts, so that a better future would ensue. The *münevver* (literally, enlightened one) needed to instigate this process. Şevket Süreyya Aydemir complains about his soldiers (and the public by implication) "who are ignorant even of their own identity."[32] He even robs this silent mass of its own voice when

---

26 Kazım Nami Duru, *"İttihat ve Terakki" Hatıralarım* (İstanbul: Sucuoğlu Matbaası, 1957), 57.

27 İbrahim Temo, *İttihad ve Terakki Cemiyetinin Teşekkülü ve Hıdematı Vataniye ve Inkılâbı Millîye Dair Hatıratım* (Mecidiye: n.p., 1939), 3–4.

28 Ibid., 12.

29 Halil Halid, *The Diary of a Turk* (London: Adam & Charles Black, 1903), 257–258.

30 Temo, *İttihad ve Terakki*, 40.

31 Kazım Karabekir, *İttihat ve Terakki Cemiyeti Neden Kuruldu? Nasıl Kuruldu? Nasıl İdare Olundu?* (İstanbul: n.p., 1982), 28.

32 Şevket Süreyya Aydemir, *Suyu Arayan Adam* (Ankara: Öz Yayınları, 1959), 116.

he says that its ignorance is to be blamed on the intellectuals who should have known better and explained it to the public better, even if the issues were not yet very clear to them.[33] Here, one must note that the intellectual, who was supposed to inspire love for the sublime ideals of freedom and equality, is now also charged with teaching a national identity that had not yet fully developed. Aydemir's ideal was to "[...] become idealists, awakeners, leaders and multiply."[34] Again, the ideal was not very clear; the leaders were leading what they perceived as a clueless folk and the whole enterprise seemed to depend on numbers.

All the lip service paid to the value of the intellectual aside, we cannot answer this simple question yet: Was it possible for somebody to be an intellectual and to believe that the homeland did not need rescuing? Or, to ask it in another way, was pressing forth the need for liberation from the evil yoke of the Sultan enough for one to be counted as "enlightened"? The examples above show that the CUP members would like to harness the power of being enlightened for their own purposes. Thus, being educated came to mean more than a diploma; it also denoted a will towards an action with a fixed aim.

Hamiyet was seen as the fuel that would propel the enlightened youth forward. *Hamiyet* roughly translates as "honor" or "zeal" in English. The famed dictionary *Kamus-ı Türki* by Şemseddin Sami clearly shows that the word was infused with more than zeal; it was defined as "one's ambition to protect one's family, children and homeland from attacks and insults"[35] thus reflecting, besides an emphasis on family, a political tenor. Enver Bey, right after the Revolution of 1908, boldly stated that this zeal was so powerful that one could not withstand it.[36] Refik Nevzat Bey, whose voice we hear through his correspondence with Bahaeddin Şakir Bey and who later became a staunch socialist, states that this particular zeal was exactly the emotion of "the doctor" towards the "sick nation."[37] In a particularly poetic parallelism, Midhat Şükrü Bey discusses nation, morals and *hamiyet* in relation to each other: "The morals were pulled to the skies, the nation has sunk deep into

33 Ibid., 117. By presenting the issue as such, Aydemir denies agency to his "ignorant" soldiers.

34 Ibid., 145.

35 Ş. Sami, *Kamus-i Türki* (Dersaadet: İkdam Matbaası, 1899), 559.

36 Enver Paşa, *Enver Paşa'nın Anıları 1881–1908* (İstanbul: Türkiye İş Bankası Kültür Yayınları, 2010), 72.

37 Bahaeddin Şakir, *Bahaeddin Şakir Bey'in Bıraktığı Vesikalara Göre İttihat ve Terakki* (Ankara: Alternatif Yayınları, 2004), 54.

the ground, and *hamiyet* is between the heavens and the earth."[38] The youth, enlightened by an anti-Hamidian light, would find its energy in patriotic zeal—and ideally start looking for ways to change the present order.

The Hope in Brigandage

The suggestion that one was enlightened enough to take the initiative for the improvement of political, social and economic conditions with a considerable degree of zeal brought other implications with it. Once the cause had been set and the determination to reach it had been expressed, there was no room for pessimism or withdrawal. For many members of the Committee of Union and Progress, saving the state was urgent and gaining more than the necessary education was only an obstacle to the grand cause. For Rıza Tevfik, who later parted ways with the CUP, the Unionist mind was filled with an "effort arising from the will to dominate" and with a hope that, like the many other hurdles they had overcome, "this too shall pass."[39] It may seem too fatalistic but, within the context described by Rıza Tevfik Bey, it was more of a point of perseverance. Mehmed Reşid Bey may be considered an early appearance of such a state of mind. While he was being held prisoner in 1897 in Taşkışla, one of his guards approached him and accused him of spying for the benefit of the Greeks. Vehemently denying this, he concluded:

> "We saw these, learned about those who caused the situation, and declared war against the tyrants, the ones who live in luxury, the traitors; to alleviate these harms, to feed the hungry peasant and to save them from misery. We are sure we will triumph. [...] But we shall not be sad, because we know that sooner or later, we will triumph, will save the nation and the homeland from this gang of bandits, and will conduct festivities in our country which is now in grief. We are sure that you too will understand the reason behind your hardships and will rebel with us against the cruel ones who demolish your homes, snatch away your earnings and suck your blood."[40]

---

38 As quoted from a letter by Midhat Şükrü [Bleda] to Tunalı Hilmi, Ahmet Bedevî Kuran, *Osmanlı İmparatorluğunda ve Türkiye Cumhuriyetinde İnkılap Hareketleri* (İstanbul: Çeltüt Matbaası, 1959), 227.

39 Rıza Tevfik, *Biraz da Ben Konuşayım* (İstanbul: İletişim Yayınları, 2008), 190.

40 Mehmed Reşid, *Dr. Mehmed Reşid Şahingiray'ın Hayatı ve Hâtıraları: İttihâd ve Terakki Dönemi ve Ermeni Meselesi* (İzmir: Akademi Kitabevi, 1997), 61.

Muhittin Birgen seems to have agreed on the point about hope when he states that "[…] it was forbidden to be pessimistic back then!" about the future within close CUP circles. He speculates that it was perhaps this sort of hope that led to victory after defeat in World War I, but it was exaggerated to a fault back then.[41] Hüseyin Cahit Yalçın likens the Unionist state of mind to "a mystical power."[42] Eşref Kuşçubaşı reportedly comments on his memoirs as such:

> "We had nothing to lose. We believed that our cause was a just one… We were engaging in an effort to ignore that we would not win in the end. We thought we could gain at least some little victories before the world around us fell to pieces…"[43]

Here, hope is not tied to a better future but gains its power from the unavailability of such a bright prospect.

Apart from the prerequisite of hope getting in their way, there is another concept that eludes the attempt of a strict definition. It is the "*komitacı*," *mot-à-mot* translated as "brigand". As with *hamiyet*, the literal translation is misleading, since the Turkish term is used to denote not only rebels, but the specific mindset that these brigands supposedly had. Kazım Karabekir tries to define a *komita*. For him, the men who took up their arms and took to the mountains were just the tip of the iceberg. The real organization was within the centers; Manastır's consulates and churches, etc., provided support to these groups. The smaller towns and villages also had their back-up organizations, sometimes even supplying manpower to a fighting *komita*.[44] A small group of men in the mountains may have looked like a minor incident, but they had back-up from their local networks, which also meant that the action could possibly have spread to the villages and small towns at any time.

Not very surprisingly for readers of Karen Barkey's *Bandits and Bureaucrats*,[45] the lines between a lawful soldier of the Ottoman Empire and the brigands in the mountains could be blurry at times, as one could switch from one side to the other. Another story of brigandage is thus told by Halil Paşa, with perhaps a degree of exaggeration. According to him, he negotiated with the Greek brigands to wipe out the Bulgarian brigands. Since such

41 Birgen, *İttihat ve Terakki'de On Sene*, 399.

42 Hüseyin Cahit Yalçın, *Siyasal Anılar* (İstanbul: Türkiye İş Bankası Kültür Yayınları, 1976), 51.

43 Eşref Kuşçubaşı, *Hayber'de Türk Cengi* (İstanbul: Arba Yayınları, 1997), 209.

44 Kazım Karabekir, *Hayatım* (İstanbul: Yapı Kredi Yayınları, 2011), 265.

45 Karen Barkey, *Bandits and Bureaucrats: The Ottoman Route to State Centralization* (Ithaca: Cornell University Press, 1994).

an action could not occur under the Ottoman banner, he would dress up as a Greek brigand. The Greeks agreed, they gave him ammunition and Greek brigands, and even a seal with the name "*Kaptan Aetos*" so that he could make himself known. In this manner, he claims to have disbanded many a Bulgarian brigand and eventually received orders as Halil Bey to chase *Kaptan Aetos*, so he ended the ruse.[46]

Halil Paşa once officially suggested that a non-military staff was needed and was put in charge of a brigand-like group.[47] While he was fighting in Tripoli, he asked for a feat of courage from a man who used to be a "*şaki*" (bandit). The man accepted the challenge and blew up a half-built castle, injuring himself in the process. He managed to come back and told Halil Paşa that he who had been living as a *şaki* for sixteen years was now dying as a *şehit* (martyr), thanks to Halil Paşa. Halil Paşa then reflected: "I was crying now in front of this man who the Sultanate, not thinking of the people, had let loose in the mountains as *şaki* and who was actually pure-hearted and loved his country…"[48] Halil Paşa's language makes the reader empathize with the person who would otherwise be seen as a lawbreaker. He understands the brigand's predicament as one caused by the system, and not by the man himself, which meant that if the system changed, the man could have come back to his village as a law-abiding citizen.

In summary, the brigand state of mind dictated that the leaders take drastic decisions for the sake of "the cause", which was not very clearly stated. There was little attention paid to the sustainability of policies or even their concordance with each other. This pragmatism of the Committee of Union and Progress has drawn many comments and is seen as a defining feature of the group. Whatever one may attribute to a *komitacı* state of mind, it seems that it was a time-stamped concept which would become useless in due course.[49] Tunaya claims that its obsolescence was grasped after the Balkan Wars, as *komitacılık* had ripped the lands apart.[50]

46 Halil Paşa, *Bitmeyen Savaş: Anılarım ve Belgelerle* (İstanbul: 7 Gün Yayınları, 1972), 40–42.

47 Ibid., 123.

48 Ibid., 105–107, quote: 106–107.

49 Ahmet Refik Altınay, *İki Komite İki Kıtal: Kafkas Yollarında* (İstanbul: Tarih Vakfı Yurt Yayınları, 2010), 67.

50 Tarık Zafer Tunaya, *Türkiye'de Siyasal Partiler: İttihat ve Terakki*, Vol. 3 (İstanbul: Hürriyet Vakfı Yayınları, 1989), 463.

Cami Baykurt summarizes this ambiguous state of mind brilliantly:

"Sometimes we were bragging about the glorious nation which built a state out of 400 tents, but sometimes, looking at the material superiority of today's Europeans, who were vanquished yesterday, made us question our racial capability and the ancient civilization of the East. While we were dreaming desperately of a great Islamic union to resist the European imperialism which, using the policies of reform as a double-edged sword, was tearing our country apart; we were also trying to imitate the decadent French ways of the Levantine mass in an effort to be like Europe. The mentality, which was left to us as a legacy of Tanzimat, was simplifying the reasons for European material grandeur and without even looking for the real motives, the reason behind Eastern backwardness only to the racial superiority of the Europeans."[51]

For Baykurt, the difference between the European civilization and "the East" was clear cut. Although the aspiration for the East was to become like Europe, according to Baykurt, imperialist policies of the West still threatened the territorial integrity of the Ottoman Empire. The answer for him was twofold: One was to bring together a Muslim union against western encroachment; the other was to westernize the Empire more rapidly. These two solutions can be read as entirely contradictory, as the Islamic union indicates an essential alliance among the Empire's Turks, Kurds, Circassians and Arabs and possibly building spheres of influence to the east of the Ottoman borders. The second solution would be westernization, which, for Baykurt implies more successful mimicry of western ways, giving the lead in modernization to the Rums, Armenians and Jews of the Empire. These two solutions together give the brigand state of mind a wide repertoire of actions: They could press for Muslim brotherhood while gathering funds for the army at war, or they could praise the French Revolution for conferring equal treatment on all citizens. In 1908, the revolutionaries placed their bet on both. Their motto was "liberty, equality, brotherhood, justice"—while holding the ideals of the French Revolution in high regard, they also added a foundational element of the Ottoman Empire: Justice. Baykurt adds that his generation saw the constitution of 1876 as "the sole talisman"—when redeclared, it would cure all the ills of the Empire spontaneously.[52] The cause for him then becomes clear, making deliberation unnecessary.

51 Cami Baykurt, *Son Osmanlı Afrikası'nda Hayat* (İstanbul: Türkiye İş Bankası Yayınları, 2009), 33.

52 Ibid., 35.

It is worth noting here that the *Tanzimat* reforms were mainly changes in legislative and especially provincial administrative branches of the state. Lawmaking activities, such as writing a new civil code for the Empire, required an extensive knowledge of Islamic law as well as a debate on the concepts of French law.[53] For the provincial administration, the bureaucrats installed new councils—primarily to rally the allegiance of local notables, definitely not for political representation at the center of the Empire.[54] Their institutional aims were moving slowly, giving weight to the complaints of the Young Ottomans that no real change was happening. Sultan Abdülhamid II continued in the vein of *Tanzimat* reforms, counting on the bureaucrats for the smooth sailing of the Empire, sponsoring new schools, and linking the provinces to the capital with a new technology called the telegraph.[55] The Young Turks' insistence on flexibility and swiftness at the expense of proper deliberation can thus be read as an overcorrection of what they perceived to be old regime's tardiness, which resulted in an obstacle to political representation in their minds.

This feature of action without deliberation is affirmed later. One of the most important insights here belongs to Ahmet Bedevi Kuran, who stated that "[…] our revolutionaries, too, had to act according to this principle of creating a revolution: The ends justify the means."[56] For him, the aforementioned ends were "without sense" and there was a certain amount of ill will against the "minorities".[57] A very late example of this sort comes from Gazi Mustafa Kemal Atatürk, founder of the Turkish Republic, in 1931. In a dictated note, he claimed that men of their age, experience and learning shall no more read to gain inspiration, but instead display their own reasoning and produce something out of that knowledge. If one failed to do so, "[…] one should humbly abandon the place of being a *rolör* in the area of mankind."[58] The foundations of the Turkish Republic are thus tinged with this sense of urgency and this perception of too much theoretical knowledge getting in the way of true change.

53 Hanioğlu, *A Brief History of the Ottoman Empire*, 74–75.

54 Ibid., 76.

55 Ibid., 125.

56 Kuran, *Osmanlı İmparatorluğunda ve Türkiye Cumhuriyetinde İnkılap Hareketleri*, 320.

57 Ibid., 538.

58 Esat Sagay, *"Hocam": Maarif Vekili Esat Sagay'ın Hatıraları* (İstanbul: Yapı Kredi Yayınları, 2012), 63–64, quote: 64. *Rolör* means an actor here.

Liberties

For many of the Unionists who looked up to the ideals of the French Revolution, freedom was a pillar of political life and a legitimate political demand. As with any Unionists' ideal, it was not a very clear concept. According to Ahmet Bedevi Kuran, there were people who had entertained "visions of freedom and reform" since the times of Sultan Abdülmecid (reign: 1839–1861).[59] The members of the CUP inherited a narrative of what to do against oppressive sultans; they learned that replacing them with another member of the royal family might work. A change of regime was not yet in the cards. We may read Kuran's elaboration on the subject as trying to prove the movement's authenticity: "Freedom" was not a foreign concept; it was perceived as a "native" aim that people could pledge allegiance to.

Mevlânzade Rıfat talks about a freedom that had to be taught to the people so that they could shake off their previous ways of governance and get used to a more democratic lifestyle.[60] The feeling of being free also depended on proximity to the center. Cami Baykurt dwells on "a relative freedom" which one could enjoy at the outposts of the Ottoman Empire, such as Tripoli.[61] Freedom could also be used in a provocative manner, as a watchword. This is what İbrahim Temo did during Damad Mahmud Celaleddin Paşa's funeral. He shouted, "Long live freedom, down with despotism!" The attendees apparently became a bit uncomfortable.[62]

In many cases, we see that the concept of liberty was tightly linked to the redeclaration of the constitution. When freedom was "declared" again in 1908, Temo immediately attributes it to one specific group of people, that is, the self-sacrificing Turks.[63] Temo attributes the exact words to a crowd which came to his house after the declaration of the constitution, but his eloquent way of stating it, as well the narration of the story in an approving tone of voice, shows us that the idea of crediting the Turks with the granting of freedom belongs to Temo. Mithat Şükrü Bleda also comments on the joy around the declaration of freedom, stating that even those who had no idea

59 Kuran, *Osmanlı İmparatorluğunda ve Türkiye Cumhuriyetinde İnkılap Hareketleri*, 61.

60 Mevlanzade Rıfat, *Mevlânzade Rıfat'ın Anıları* (İstanbul: Arma Yayınları, 1992), 25.

61 Baykurt, *Son Osmanlı Afrikası'nda Hayat*, 11.

62 Temo, *İttihad ve Terakki*, 17.

63 Ibid., 207.

what liberty was joined the general atmosphere of enthusiasm.[64] For Lütfü Simavi Bey, himself a staff member at the Yıldız Palace, the freedom was taken by manipulating the cowardly Sultan, meaning that it had no real support, save for some Albanians and young soldiers.[65]

Although much eulogized, freedom was also a dangerous concept, since it could easily become uncontrollable. The CUP anticipated an overcorrection, where the "others" in their own community—women, workers, non-Turks and non-Muslims—would fail to value this precious asset and the political tables would turn against the CUP. The inherent power of the concept of liberty had to be contained and possibly channeled to other outlets. Cemal Paşa claims that freedom has been misunderstood,[66] while Şerif Paşa warns about the "good," "limited" use of freedom.[67] For Celal Bayar too, unlimited freedom of press carried negative connotations.[68] For Temo, freedom is a sweet drink which could get you intoxicated.[69] Mustafa Ragıp, speaking through Temo's memoirs, warns that this drink may also turn into poison.[70] Anxiety over a possible loss of control became a feature of the Unionist mindset. Also, they posited themselves as pioneers of freedom, who could either provide it to the masses or withdraw it from the public altogether.

Continuation of the State

The memoirists usually pinpoint a certain moment where they perceived that the Ottoman Empire was inevitably disintegrating. The concept also features in Mizancı Murad Bey's memoirs, where he stated that when the Bulgarian army was in Eastern Rumelia, he anticipated that the general trend was not

64 Mithat Şükrü Bleda, *İmparatorluğun Çöküşü* (İstanbul: Remzi Kitabevi, 1979), 50.

65 Lütfü Simavi, *Osmanlı Sarayı'nın Son Günleri* (İstanbul: Hürriyet Yayınları, [197–?]), 196–197.

66 Cemal Paşa, *Hatıralar* (İstanbul: Türkiye İş Bankası Kültür Yayınları, 2008), 379.

67 Şerif Paşa, *Bir Muhalifin Hatıraları: İttihat ve Terakkiye Muhalefet* (İstanbul: Nehir Yayınları, 1990), 19–20.

68 Celal Bayar, *Ben de Yazdım*, Vol. 1 (İstanbul: Baha Matbaası, 1965), 185. He is quoting a text, but approves the ideas nevertheless.

69 Temo, *İttihad ve Terakki*, 212.

70 Ibid., 219.

towards perpetuity, but towards disintegration.[71] İsmail Kemal Bey also remembers the years 1900–1908 with a sense of urgency, stating that the possible ways of avoiding imminent doom seemed to diverge into two: One was violent and recommended revolution (*ihtilâl*), while the other was more cautious and focused on getting European support. İsmail Kemal Bey leaned towards the latter.[72] Later, he changed his point of view due to bad management by the capital and riots in Macedonia, and he then focused on rescuing Albania.[73] A loss of hope regarding the fortunes of the Empire forced him to take the next best option, which was holding on to what he was sure he could save.

Others wished to keep the state in its entirety and attempted to take measures to that end. According to Bahaeddin Şakir, the CUP was a place where every idea could be defended, as long as it was aimed at the continuation of the state and the exalted Sultanate.[74] The same idea of continuum was a default in both the CUP and the Freedom and Accord Party, reports Celal Bayar.[75] For Muhittin Birgen, the Committee saw the declaration of the constitution as an end in itself; its continuation was the essential duty. The ministers of the Hamidian regime, on the other hand, represented the state.[76]

Some of the members chose to employ the CUP's political vocabulary to justify their secessionism. In İsmail Kemal Bey's example, we see that his definition of the Albanian community rests on "fidelity to their word of honor and the religion of patriotism, with which goes the love of independence."[77] However, these values did not contradict Ottoman rule over the Albanians since, in their opinion, they had to yield in order to exist. İsmail Kemal Bey states that they were loyal to the Ottoman Empire until it betrayed them, thereby absolving them of their ties of obligation.[78] Ironically enough, the next page displays a more pragmatic turn of events as İsmail Kemal Bey describes the independence of Albania as one would describe

71 Mizancı Mehmed Murad, *Meskenet Mazeret Teşkil Eder mi?* (İstanbul: Şehir Yayınları, 2005), 78.

72 İsmail Kemal, *İsmail Kemal Bey'in Hatıratı* (İstanbul: Tarih Vakfı Yurt Yayınları, 2009), 220.

73 Ibid., 224.

74 Şakir, *Bahaeddin Şakir*, 142.

75 Bayar, *Ben de Yazdım*, Vol. 2, 450.

76 Birgen, *İttihat ve Terakki'de On Sene*, 75–76.

77 İsmail Kemal, *The Memoirs of İsmail Kemal Bey* (London: Constable & Co., 1920), 360.

78 İsmail Kemal, *İsmail Kemal Bey'in Hatıratı* (İstanbul: Tarih Vakfı Yurt Yayınları, 2009), 258.

breaking away from a group of people who decided to commit suicide.[79] Therefore, benefits assigned to the "survival" of one specific *patrie* (homeland) could outweigh the benefits assigned to the continuity of the Ottoman Empire. Although an isolated example, İsmail Kemal Bey's argumentation shows that words such as *patrie* and freedom could be employed as empty signifiers and lent themselves to the justification of a variety of motivations.

"Yok Kanun, Yap Kanun"

The famous adage "*Yok kanun, yap kanun*" (There is no law, then make law) is attributed to Enver Paşa. Even if it were not true, the pithy phrase is useful since it reflects a peculiarly Unionist frame of mind. Hüseyin Cahit Yalçın's recollections about Enver Paşa include such a statement. Yalçın writes:

> "Perhaps he was imagining the Assembly as an unnecessary machine, a cogwheel turning in vain. When it was pointed out that some of his thoughts were out of line with the law, he would say with calm scorn: There is [supposedly] no law! Make law, then there is law!"[80]

This is a prime example of how the very same people who fought for a constitution later came to see it as a tool to enforce their will, eschewing the due process of political debate. Another example would be the attitude of Fuat Balkan, who had to recruit soldiers around Drama and did not have proper guidelines for recruitment or management. So, he narrates, he started to use his own common sense to make everything (laws, hats for soldiers) pretty much from scratch. He goes on, stating that "[…] there was no other way. My government, appreciating this, gave me unlimited authority in this respect."[81] Commenting on the spontaneous nature of the Babıali Coup in 1913, after which the CUP used political power directly, Kazım Nami Duru conveys a general Unionist state of mind:

> "We, the Unionists, were always under the pressure of sudden requirements in our collective actions. The actions, which had to be taken in the name of the country

---

79 Ibid., 259, see also 261 for another telling of this complicated relationship.

80 Hüseyin Cahit Yalçın, *Tanıdıklarım* (İstanbul: Yapı Kredi Yayınları, 2001), 24–25.

81 Fuat Balkan, *İlk Türk Komitacısı Fuat Balkan'ın Hatıraları* (İstanbul: Arma Yayınları, 1998), 34.

and the nation, were often decided upon in a few hours and put into action immediately."[82]

There is another story told by Halil Paşa which bears witness to the persistence of the practice. In 1918, while he was fighting the British around Süleymaniye, Iraq, he was cut off from possible sources of help and thought of a solution:[83]

"Amongst the Kurdish tribes, who had to make a living by means of plunder, there was this ağa [local notable], Şeyh Mahmut, who I used to know and who was smart, also commanding a leadership quality [...]. What I was going to do was to grant him full independence. Since the land he was living on was Ottoman land and was still counted as Ottoman territory, I could give him his independence."[84]

He then proceeds to send Şeyh Mahmut a telegram declaring him the "irremovable emir of Süleymaniye and its environs."[85] Şeyh Mahmut provided a contact for the Ottoman soldiers to get them out of Süleymaniye and, according to Halil Paşa, the action prevented a tribal rebellion.[86] Halil Paşa's "innovation" in creating a new *emirlik* around Süleymaniye seems to have fulfilled its *raison d'être* in that moment. Going through complex circumstances, the memoirists tried to rise to this chaotic challenge by manipulating what they could. It was not just a mindless act to save the day; it was also an attempt to sort out a modern situation. Regarding the last example, the *ancien régime* of the Ottoman Empire had a place for a minor sheikh like Şeyh Mahmut and the military had its own ways of finding subsistence. This state of affairs was shaken when the Ottoman army found itself facing the more modernized British army, and the fluid boundaries of the Ottoman map seem to have enabled Halil Paşa to take an inflated administrative initiative. Even if the whole story is not true and there never was a Şeyh Mahmut, in 1972, Halil Paşa was able to imagine that independence was now something he could bribe people with, a tool to get his way; the modern allure of the nation-state was starting to be felt.

Indeed, Tunaya found out that between 1908–1918, the Committee of Union and Progress managed to pass over a thousand temporary laws.[87] He understood this to be an attempt at authoritarianism and at "governing

82 Duru, *"İttihat ve Terakki"*, 54.

83 Halil Paşa, *Bitmeyen Savaş*, 214–215.

84 Ibid., 215–216.

85 Ibid., 216.

86 Ibid., 216–217.

87 Tunaya, *Türkiye'de Siyasal Partiler: İttihat ve Terakki,* Vol. 3, 385.

without assembly."[88] Thus, the crisis of political representation only seemed to be resolved: There were elections, but the CUP managed to rig them in 1912; there was media, such as newspapers, for political debate but the CUP heavily influenced the news. The stories narrated by the memoirists display a negotiation between the ideal modern and the practical present: While they felt the need for a more legitimate way of governing than the Sultan's way, they also felt pressured by the circumstances and by their lack of experience in managing the affairs of a state. The temporary laws, as well as several other tools, served to maintain the illusion of a functioning, modern, representative system and solved some important immediate problems, albeit in a non-official way. Another feature of this negotiation was the obscuring of the decision-making process. Government decisions still carried authentic signatures, but fewer statesmen were involved in the debate process. As such, the accountability of parliament and the army ended up as the accountability of a few individuals.

Conclusion

The rule of the CUP in the Ottoman lands did not go unchallenged. In 1909, an unlikely coalition of forces (mainly Islamists, liberals, and supporters of the Sultan) swayed some of the military forces in Istanbul to rebel against the government. The CUP retaliated by sending special forces from Macedonia, tightening their measures around labor activism, and controlling the press more tightly.[89] This armed insurrection of 1909 was also a convenient excuse for the CUP to replace Abdülhamid II with his brother, Mehmed V, who did not have high political ambitions.[90] From 1909 onwards, the Committee ruled only indirectly, gradually filling up important positions with their own men until 1913, when they blamed the government for the failure in the Balkan War and staged a coup (also called the Babıali Coup), taking power directly into their own hands. During World War I, the triumvirate leading the CUP ruled the empire as Commander-in-Chief Enver Paşa planned the war, Cemal Paşa was Minister of the Navy and also commanded the Fourth Army in Syria, and Talat Paşa was Minister of the

88 Ibid., 387.
89 Hanioğlu, *A Brief History of the Ottoman Empire*, 153–155.
90 Ibid., 162.

Interior. Hamidian features of governing continued and, in some cases, were amplified, especially in the case of Abdülhamid's playing Kurds against Armenians resulting in forced displacement and genocide in 1915.

In 1908, the CUP posited itself as reactionaries facing a crisis of political representation, seeking to reestablish the constitution as the guarantor of liberty and equality for all Ottoman citizens and ending what they perceived to be the Sultan's oppressive regime with no room for political opinion. By 1918, they had already conducted a rigged election, established the passing of temporary laws as a mean of legislation while eschewing parliamentary debate, censored the press, buttressed their paramilitary operations, and attempted to eradicate the voice of the Armenian population, first by sending their notables into exile, and then by instigating their murder as a precursor to genocide. Rather than striving for true and equal political representation for all, they claimed to embody the will of the Ottoman people themselves. Since this will was supposed to be infallible, they also managed to evade due responsibility for their rash actions.

Here, I looked at the mindset behind this clenched fist to see how it curled up. Firstly, I investigated who was legitimately entitled to a sense of duty. Following the clues gained from the memoirs, I depicted a group of literati, who were above all against the suppression of political life and were well-versed in various new concepts, such as the nation or freedom. They pressed for a constitution that would represent the will of all citizens of the Empire and the reopening of an elected assembly. The memoirists' narrative painted *hamiyet*, patriotic zeal, as the machine that turned knowledge of political oppression into revolutionary performance. Moving on, I dwell on the importance of hope, which was mainly used to inspire better morale. After the redeclaration of the constitution in 1908, the memoirists found it useful to evaluate the meaning of freedom too: If they drew the boundaries, liberties were "good", otherwise they were "bad". Their belief was that the naïve public should be taught how to use these new ideas. The CUP started to present themselves as political enlighteners who knew what was best for the people before the people had had a chance to deliberate. In this sense, they perceived liberties as political bargaining chips to be granted to people at their behest.

This monopoly of liberties became a feature of their later authoritarian rule, where they curbed labor movements and censored the press. This brigand state of mind, as exemplified by the adage "*yok kanun, yap kanun*" (There is no law, then make law) resulted in the weighing of proper procedure against practical concerns. Governmental decision making, according to the memoirists, had to be swift and resourceful and lengthy deliberations would only be an obstacle. Perhaps it goes without saying but the practical version won out most of the time. With this move, the CUP also appeared to disentangle the puzzle of political representation: While elections and a parliament gave the illusion of due political representation, the cabinet had taken over the legislative process with temporary laws.[91] We come full circle when we remember that the CUP's arch-nemesis, Abdülhamid II, allegedly shut down parliament over similar concerns in 1878. The CUP went one step further here and brought in the army as the protector of their new order in 1909 and again in 1913. Edhem Eldem states that Sultan Abdülhamid's reign left "room for an unaccountable and uncontrolled 'core' that will guarantee the survival of the state."[92] The CUP made this unaccountable, unrepresentative core into a strong fortress that took center stage in the Turkish political scene for decades to come.

91 Cf. Ibid., 163.

92 Edhem Eldem, "Sultan Abdulhamid II: Founding Father of the Turkish State?" *Journal of the Ottoman and Turkish Studies Association* 5, no. 2 (2018), 25–46, quote: 44.

A Permanent State of Exception? Managing Crises in Late Imperial Germany and the Early Weimar Republic, 1917–1923

Amerigo Caruso

Looking at crucial periods in the history of early twentieth-century Germany, this chapter investigates how the governing apparatus responded to social unrest and political protest.[1] It focuses on the legal framework under which emergency powers operated and the "mentality" behind the use and abuse of exceptional powers in the late Wilhelmine and early Weimar period.[2] In doing so, the chapter draws attention to the short-term continuities between the semi-authoritarian German Empire, especially after the declaration of the state of siege in 1914, and the construction of Weimar democracy in a near civil war situation after the November Revolution. Both regimes were confronted with a sense of political crisis, which reached its full expression after 1917 and was exacerbated by fears of Bolshevism and the shock of military defeat.[3] The chapter also looks at the long-term patterns and discontinuities in the conception and implementation of emergency powers in the period between the Bismarck era and the collapse of the Weimar Republic.

The German Empire, created in 1871, was an authoritarian monarchy, with influential political and social milieus that were openly against

1 This chapter is part of a broader project examining the practice and theory of emergency powers in nineteenth- and twentieth-century Europe. The author would like to thank James Retallack for his comments on a previous version of this chapter.

2 I refer here to the concept of "Mentalität des Ausnahmezustands," which historian Martin H. Geyer uses to describe the politics of crisis management as well as the emotions, experiences and expectations linked with the sense of permanent crisis in the late Kaiserreich and the Weimar Republic. Cf. Martin H. Geyer, "Grenzüberschreitungen: Vom Belagerungszustand zum Ausnahmezustand," in *Erster Weltkrieg. Kulturwissenschaftliches Handbuch*, ed. Stefan Kaufmann (Stuttgart: Metzler, 2014), 341–384, here: 341. On the long-term consequences of the "mentality" and practices of the emergency state, see also Martin H. Geyer, "What Crisis? Speculation, Corruption, and the State of Emergency during the Great Depression," *Bulletin of the GHI Washington* 55 (2014): 9–35.

3 For a general overview, see, among others, Robert Gerwarth, *The Vanquished: Why the First World War Failed to End, 1917–1923* (London: Penguin, 2016).

democracy and the parliamentary system of government. The public sphere and the labor movement, however, emerged as the main agents for democratization in the late nineteenth century, and parliamentary power increased slightly.[4] I will thus refer to the Kaiserreich using the notion of "semi-authoritarian", which underlines the overlapping of authoritarianism, monarchical principle, and the persistence of a hierarchical society on the one hand, and a functioning Rechtsstaat (legal state) and the rise of democratic participation on the other. This concept reflects the ambiguity in the process of democratization in modern Germany and marks a clear distinction between the Kaiserreich, the rise of Weimar democracy, and totalitarian forms of dictatorship such as the Third Reich.

The chapter is divided into three sections that analyze the transition between war and post-revolutionary democracy, with a special focus on the Kingdom—later Free State—of Saxony. "Red Saxony" was a stronghold of the Social Democratic Party, where the early development of industrialization and rapid urbanization made social and political conflicts particularly visible and polarizing. As noted by James Retallack, Saxony "has represented, at various points in its history, a worst-case scenario and the best of all possible worlds," which is one of the main reasons why the territorial focus on this German region provides a good vehicle for drawing comparisons and reconsidering wider problems.[5] The three sections of this chapter will explore the dynamics of the emergency state in the last months of the war, in spring 1919, and in summer 1919. In the second section, I will give a brief overview of legal articulations of emergency powers and on the change in meaning and use of concepts such as "state of siege" and "state of exception". Each section will shed light on the short-term contingencies, adaptability, turning points, and long-term transformations of the politics of crisis management and emergency powers.

---

4 Margaret Lavinia Anderson, *Practicing Democracy. Elections and Political Culture in Imperial Germany* (Princeton: Princeton University Press, 2000).

5 James Retallack, "Locating Saxony in the Landscape of German Regional History," in *Saxony in German History: Culture, Society, and Politics, 1830–1933*, ed. James Retallack (Ann Arbor: The University of Michigan Press, 2000), 1–31, here: 3. On polarization and continuity in early twentieth century Saxony, see also James Retallack, "Rotes Königreich oder Hort des Konservatismus? Sachsen im späten Kaiserreich," in *Der gespaltene Freistaat. Neue Perspektiven auf die sächsische Geschichte 1918 bis 1933* (Dresden: Sächsische Landeszentrale für politische Bildung, 2019), 27–41.

October 1918: "We Are Right in the Middle of a Revolution"

Given the early rise of a broad Social Democratic *milieu* in Saxony, it is not surprising that there was widespread anti-war sentiment in July 1914, especially among the working class. Large anti-war rallies and demonstrations took place in Chemnitz, Dresden, and especially in Leipzig, where left-wing socialism already held a dominant position before the founding of the Independent Social Democratic Party of Germany in 1917 (USPD, in opposition to the Majority Social Democratic Party, MSPD).[6] Even after Social Democratic members of the Reichstag had voted in favor of war credits and supported the so-called *Burgfrieden* (party truce), the patriotic "spirit of August 1914" proved to be even more vulnerable, contradictory and short-lived in Saxony than elsewhere in Germany.[7] The *Burgfrieden*, along with SPD unity, had already begun to collapse during the first year of the war. In June 1915, for example, left-wing socialists Karl Kautsky, Eduard Bernstein and Hugo Haase published a sensational appeal for peace without territorial gain in the *Leipziger Volkszeitung*.[8]

Deeply rooted and quite radical Social Democratic traditions were, however, not the only reason the *Burgfrieden* in Saxony was threatened at an early stage. The Kingdom was one of the most industrialized and urbanized regions in Germany and was, therefore, particularly affected by the British naval blockade of the Kaiserreich, the breakdown in international trade, and the catastrophic food crisis, which reached its first peak during the so-called Turnip Winter of 1916. Following the anti-war demonstrations of 1914, protests against food shortages were already taking place in 1915. Social unrest culminated in a major strike in Leipzig in April 1916 involving thousands of workers, mostly women. During the course of the war, it became increasingly evident that "the authoritarian state failed to meet the demands of total

6 Sean Dobson, *Authority and Upheaval in Leipzig, 1910–1920. The Story of a Relationship* (New York: Columbia University Press, 2001). On solidarity and political divisions within the proletarian *milieu* in Wilhelmine and Weimar Germany, see also David E. Barclay and Eric D. Weitz, *Between Reform and Revolution. German Socialism and Communism from 1840 to 1990* (New York: Berghahn, 1998).

7 For a critical reassessment of the "spirit of 1914" and the myth of war enthusiasm, see Jeffrey Verhey, *The Spirit of 1914: Militarism, Myth, and Mobilization in Germany* (Cambridge: Cambridge University Press, 2000).

8 *Leipziger Volkszeitung*, June 19, 1915, 1–2.

war at home".[9] Initially, peace and hunger relief were the main issues of concern although, throughout 1918, political issues became of key importance. A second major wave of strikes began in early 1918 and, during the summer, the revolutionary threat gained intensity as it became clear that neither the civil government nor the military administration was able to deal with the dramatic food shortages and the deteriorating living conditions on the home front. Mounting social protest and calls for democratic reforms generated a sense of urgency among the political elites and the military commanders, who had gained control over normal civil functions after the proclamation of the state of siege in summer 1914.

Historians John Deak and Jonathan E. Gumz have shown how the permanent state of exception and the assumption of political-juridical authority by the army during World War I led to a fundamental crisis in state legitimacy and subverted the rule of law in the Habsburg Empire.[10] These observations are also largely true for other European belligerents, such as Germany or Italy. However, although the party truce had already begun to disintegrate in 1916, there is consensus among historians that German public opinion, despite growing numbers of strikes and protests, still largely supported the "defensive" war effort promoted by the official propaganda, albeit rather passively and without enthusiasm. The persistence of the *Burgfrieden*, which was based on a mixture of coercive methods and nationalist mobilization, broke down decisively in late summer 1918. After General Erich Ludendorff called for armistice negotiations, and a new liberal government under Max von Baden was installed, the shock of military defeat jeopardized not only the war effort, but also the entire political system of the Kaiserreich.[11] With the prospect of an imminent collapse of the western front and a desperate push for democratic reforms in Berlin, disaffection with the regime and the specter of revolution became clear and imminent. In Saxony, an MSPD-organized demonstration against food shortages took place in Dresden in September 1918, while the USPD's attempt to mobilize

9 James Retallack, *Red Saxony. Elections Battles and the Spectre of Democracy in Germany 1860–1918* (Oxford: Oxford University Press, 2017), 594.

10 John Deak and Jonathan Gumz, "How to Break a State: The Habsburg Monarchy's Internal War," *American Historical Review* 122, no. 4 (2017): 1105–1136.

11 Cf. Roger Chickering, *Imperial Germany and the Great War, 1914–1918* (Cambridge: Cambridge University Press, 2000), 180–186.

for a general strike was largely unsuccessful.[12] As the crisis of confidence in the state intensified, a radically uncertain future was unfolding.[13]

In his studies on the collapse of Imperial Germany, Lothar Machtan argues that it was almost impossible to organize the politics of crisis management in late 1918—not only because civilian authorities and the monarchy had fallen into discredit, but also, and more importantly, because their decision-making power was largely limited since the army had assumed semi-dictatorial powers, especially after Paul von Hindenburg and Erich Ludendorff had taken control of the Supreme Army Command in 1916.[14] These observations are only partly true for Saxony, where the regional army commanders acted in a more consultative and less authoritarian manner than elsewhere in Germany and were more open to cooperation with civilian authorities,[15] so that the Saxon Interior Ministry still played a key role in securing the home front.

The minutes of a special meeting held at the Saxon Interior Ministry on October 14, 1918, approximately one month before the revolution, is a key document that illustrates how the crisis was perceived and the strategies that were adopted to deal with it. High-ranking military officers attended the meeting, along with Interior and War Ministry officials, including Walter Koch, who would be nominated Interior Minister two days later. The Chief of Dresden Police, Paul Köttig, who remained in charge after the revolution

12 See Christoph Nonn, "Saxon Politics during the First World War: Modernization, National Liberal Style," in *Saxony in German History: Culture, Society, and Politics, 1830–1933*, ed. James Retallack (Ann Arbor: The University of Michigan Press, 2000), 309–321. On Saxony during WWI, see also Konstantin Hermann and Matthias Rogg, *Sachsen im Ersten Weltkrieg. Politik und Gesellschaft eines deutschen Mittelstaates 1914 bis 1918* (Stuttgart: Steiner, 2018).

13 Jörn Leonhard, *Der überforderte Frieden. Versailles und die Welt 1918–1923* (Munich: Beck, 2018), 249.

14 Lothar Machtan, *Kaisersturz. Vom Scheitern im Herzen der Macht* (Darmstadt: Theiss, 2018), 9. For a general overview of civilian and military powers during WWI, and the growing influence of Germany's military leadership after the accession of the new Army Command under Hindenburg and Ludendorff in 1916, see Lukas Grawe, "Civilian and Military Power (Germany)," in *1914–1918-online. International Encyclopedia of the First World War*, ed. Ute Daniel, issued by Freie Universität Berlin (Berlin, 2020). On the "silent dictatorship" under Hindenburg and Ludendorff, see also Wolfram Pyta, *Hindenburg. Herrschaft zwischen Hohenzollern und Hitler* (Berlin: Siedler, 2009); Manfred Nebelin, *Ludendorff. Diktator im Ersten Weltkrieg* (Berlin: Siedler, 2011).

15 Cf. Peter Mertens, *Zivil-militärische Zusammenarbeit während des Ersten Weltkrieges. Die Nebenregierungen der Militärbefehlshaber im Königreich Sachsen* (Leipzig: Leipziger Universitätsverlag, 2004).

until September 1919, was also present at the meeting. Deputy Interior Minister Koch opened the meeting by acknowledging the extreme seriousness of the situation: "We are right in the middle of a revolution."[16] He warned that all state organs and officials should be prepared for the worst-case scenario, and that the USPD was responsible for the spread of revolutionary ideas. This last statement is important because, while the USPD's political activities were systematically repressed, Saxon civil authorities had been trying to integrate the moderate SDP into the regime and the imagined "*Volksgemeinschaft*" (people's community) since the outbreak of the war.[17] This strategy was largely successful: On the one hand, the MSPD still reluctantly supported the *Burgfrieden* until late summer 1918 while, on the other hand, censorship, arrests of political leaders, "protective custody" (the most prominent case was the incarceration of Karl Liebknecht in 1916), and bans on assemblies managed to silence the USPD opposition.[18] By contrast, the MSPD's political activities and their newspapers were largely tolerated. Koch and his colleagues were therefore convinced that if the Majority Socialists "maintained control over the masses", then a revolution could be prevented.[19] A similar perception had already emerged in 1905, when mass

16 This and the following quotes are from the Sächsisches Staatsarchiv (SäStA), 10736 Ministerium des Innern, no. 11074, 1.

17 Gustav Stresemann, future Chancellor and Foreign Minister of Weimar Germany, was one of the most prominent supporters of this strategy and his use of the term "*Volksgemeinschaft*" helped its spread. Cf. Karl Heinrich Pohl, *Gustav Stresemann. Biografie eines Grenzgängers* (Göttingen: Vandenhoeck & Ruprecht, 2015), 197 and 202. On the concept of "*Volksgemeinschaft*", or "*Kriegsvolksgemeinschaft*" during World War I, see Steffen Bruendel, *Volksgemeinschaft oder Volksstaat. Die "Ideen von 1914" und die Neuordnung Deutschlands im Ersten Weltkrieg* (Berlin: Akademie Verlag, 2003). In the 1930s, the concept of "*Volksgemeinschaft*" became a key propaganda slogan of the Nazi regime. See Martina Steber and Bernhard Gotto, *Visions of Community in Nazi Germany: Social Engineering and Private Lives* (Oxford: Oxford University Press, 2014).

18 At least 5,000 people were placed under "protective custody" during the war in Germany. After the strike in January 1918, for example, the secretary to the USPD's Central Committee, Wilhelm Dittmann, was charged with "attempted treason" and sentenced to five years in prison by court martial. See André Keil and Matthew Stibbe, "Ein Laboratorium des Ausnahmezustands. Schutzhaft Während des Ersten Weltkriegs und in den Anfangsjahren der Weimarer Republik – Preußen und Bayern 1914 bis 1923," *Vierteljahrshefte für Zeitgeschichte* 68, no. 4 (2020): 535–572, here: 550.

19 SäStA, 10736 Ministerium des Innern, no. 11074, 4.

demonstrations in support of universal suffrage took place in Dresden and Leipzig.[20]

However, as Koch frankly admitted during the meeting, left-wing socialist propaganda was not the only reason for the crisis of confidence in the semi-authoritarian regime. He mentioned one further issue, which is crucial to understanding how government officials perceived the crisis on the eve of the November Revolution. This issue was the food supply crisis, especially the soldiers' and workers' dissatisfaction with the unfair distribution of food. An internal report by the Ministry of the Interior dated April 7, 1917, had already cited the acute food and fuel shortages as being a major problem, and warned that "what is needed now is not mere declarations or promises, but action."[21] This report, once again, proposed cooperation with representatives of the moderate unions and the MSPD to deal with the food crisis. Fearing major outbreaks of strikes in spring 1917, Minister of the Interior, Count Vitzthum, devised a plan to bring the MSPD into a coalition government to preserve domestic unity.[22]

By 1917, the Saxon civil authorities recognized that it was crucial not only to consult the Majority Socialists but also to allow workers' councils to participate in the coordination of food distribution in order to keep the crisis under control. Although some tentative steps in this direction were made by the Ministry of the Interior,[23] the strategy to give the workers' movement greater institutionalized involvement in the politics of crisis management failed due to firm opposition from the Imperial German Government. The Saxon envoy in Berlin reported to Dresden on April 17, 1917, that Reich Chancellor Theobald von Bethmann Hollweg had refused to consult the workers' delegations and had ordered the workers' councils to be firmly repressed.[24] A few days later, these cautious attempts to democratize the politics of crisis management failed definitively after the publication of an article written by Bethmann Hollweg, in which he portrayed strikes and popular protest as acts of treason, and advocated ruthless repression of those deemed to be "outside the *Volksgemeinschaft*".[25]

20 See Amerigo Caruso, *"Blut und Eisen auch im Innern." Soziale Konflikte, Massenpolitik und Gewalt in Deutschland vor 1914* (Frankfurt: Campus, 2021), 57–102.

21 SäStA, 10736 Ministerium des Innern, no. 11071, 10.

22 Retallack, *Red Saxony*, 595.

23 *Dresdner Neueste Nachrichten*, April 15, 1917, 3.

24 SäStA, 10736 Ministerium des Innern, no. 11071, 142.

25 *Dresdner Anzeiger*, April 26, 1917.

However, despite the harsh rhetoric, the authorities in both Berlin and Dresden were aware that violent repression was a risky strategy, especially in light of the participation of large numbers of women and children in the popular protests. In early 1918, a report by the Saxon envoy in Berlin described this dilemma clearly:

"Of course, if we persist in our passive attitude towards popular protests, the revolutionary movement will spread [...]. However, violent repression [of peaceful demonstrations] should also be critically considered. It involves great danger. This dilemma will become the most crucial question for Germany's future."[26]

These considerations illustrate very well the challenges in dealing with revolutionary threats in modern political systems based on consensus. Although the dilemma between repression and "passivity" had already emerged in the late nineteenth century, it acquired special importance in the period between 1917–23, when it destabilized both the late Kaiserreich and the early Weimar democracy. However, while in Wilhelmine Germany repressive violence had been kept within limits, it reached unprecedented levels during the early Weimar years.

As mentioned above, a key strategy employed by the Saxonian government to avoid both far-reaching political reforms and the outbreak of popular protest was to cooperate with the Majority Socialists. This strategy was still active in late October 1918 when a new Saxon government was formed under liberal Rudolf Heinze with two MSPD ministers.[27] Even after Berlin adamantly refused to support their plans to cooperate with the workers' councils in 1917, the Saxon authorities maintained their strategy of cooperation—more symbolic than effective—with the moderate Social Democrats. In late January 1918, for example, Minister of the Interior Vitzthum received a delegation of Social Democratic workers and promised to at least preserve current food rations. Ministry officials wrote a detailed report on the meeting between Vitzthum and the MSPD and sent it to the major newspapers with

26 SäStA, 10736 Ministerium des Innern, no. 11071, 30. Original quote: "Natürlich liegt bei dieser mehr passiven Haltung die Gefahr der weiteren Ausbreitung, insbesondere in der Provinz, nahe, während andererseits scharfes Zufassen ebenfalls die größten Bedenken in sich birgt. So kann diese schwere Frage leicht zur Schicksalsfrage auch für Deutschland werden."

27 Ministers without portfolio Max Heldt and Julius Fräßdorf.

the order to publish it.[28] During the meeting, the Majority Socialists declared that if the authorities heeded their demands, the MSPD would "be able to help defend the threatened order".[29]

Similar negotiations also took place on an informal level. On February 6, 1918, for example, Gustav Noske (later Minister of Defense in Scheidemann's first democratically elected government in the Weimar Republic) and a high-ranking police advisor met casually on a tram in Chemnitz. Noske made it clear that the MSPD still wanted to prevent "foolish things" (a revolution).[30] A similar situation had occurred after the April 1917 strike in Leipzig when MSPD leaders intervened to curb disturbances and, in return, the Saxon authorities promised to improve working conditions and preserve existing food rations.[31] Furthermore, since 1917, four MSPD politicians had been part of a special parliamentary committee set up to consider constitutional reforms.[32]

To sum up, cooperation between the conservative authorities and the moderate SPD in Saxony intensified after the outbreak of World War I, especially after the founding of the USPD, the escalation of social unrest, and the rise of anti-Bolshevism in 1917. Although the role played by the MSPD in the politics of crisis management during the war was far more symbolic than effective, the strategy to include the Majority Socialists among the "parties of order" was successful in delaying the collapse of the *Burgfrieden*. Furthermore, the moderate SPD's commitment to combating revolutionary socialism, which was still controversial before 1914,[33] became firmly established during World War I, especially after 1917. The "SPD of the twentieth century" emerged as a consequence of the separation of more radical forces and the support of state and parliamentary democracy in the period 1917–23.[34] This had a decisive impact on the November Revolution and on the defense of Weimar democracy in the civil war-like situation of 1919.

28 All the major Saxon newspapers did indeed publish the report on February 2, 1918, two days after the meeting. See, for example, *Leipziger Zeitung*, February 2, 1918, 253; *Sächsische Staatszeitung*, February 2, 1918, 4; *Dresdner Anzeiger*, February 3, 1918, 5.

29 SäStA, 10736 Ministerium des Innern, no. 11073, Teil 1, 36.

30 SäStA, 10736 Ministerium des Innern, no. 11073, Teil 2, 142.

31 Retallack, *Red Saxony*, 596.

32 Besides the four MSPD members, there was also one USPD member (Hermann Fleißner).

33 See Jens-Uwe Guettel, "Reform, Revolution, and the 'Original Catastrophe': Political Change in Prussia and Germany on the Eve of the First World War," *The Journal of Modern History* 91 (2019): 311–340.

34 Bernd Faulenbach, *Geschichte der SPD: von den Anfängen bis zur Gegenwart* (Munich: Beck, 2012), 37.

In Saxony, the effects of the politics of crisis management in delaying the collapse of the Kaiserreich and shaping post-revolutionary Germany were particularly evident. The repression of the USPD's anti-war position, and the cooperation between the MSPD and the state, contribute to explaining the population's acquiescence. Given the widespread anti-war sentiment, the rise of popular protests as early as 1915, and the strong radical left *milieu* in Leipzig, it is remarkable that "Red Saxony" was not a hotspot in the German Revolution. Even in early 1919, after the January Uprising and the escalation of political violence in Berlin, the situation in Saxony remained relatively quiet compared with other parts of the country.

Alongside its middle-term consequences for post-revolutionary Germany, what is remarkable about the crisis in October 1918 is the clear perception the state authorities had of the causes of the social and political disintegration. This is well illustrated by the mid-October meeting held at the Ministry of the Interior. Despite having clearly discerned the crisis, the monarchical state showed itself incapable of dealing with the critical issues raised during the meeting—political modernization, food scarcity, the housing crisis, and unemployment (following demobilization). These problems remained largely unaddressed, and they escalated in the early Weimar years. It was therefore not a lack of perception of the causes of the crisis that affected the politics of crisis management during the late Kaiserreich, but rather a lack of political will and decision-making power. This was as much due to the army's semi-dictatorship as to the Reich government's exclusive authority in the field of foreign politics, which limited the Saxon authorities' decision-making power.

The Saxon government was well aware that political modernization was the "most effective weapon" against the revolutionary threat—at the end of the mid-October meeting all participants agreed on this point[35]—yet both the civilian and military authorities were reluctant to democratize the monarchy. These contradictions were also evident when it came to policing the protests. On the one hand, the Saxon authorities recognized that violent repression could provoke revolutionary uprisings and exacerbate the social and political conflicts. On the other hand, they instigated repressive measures that foreshadowed the escalation of political violence in 1919. In October 1918, for instance, police authorities and the Interior Ministry requested the army to form rapid response units equipped with machine guns,

35 SäStA, 10736 Ministerium des Innern, no. 11074, 8.

armored cars, and even military aircraft to counter revolutionary insurgency. In addition, they urged the formation of vigilante groups and the distribution of arms to "well-disposed citizens".[36] These repressive measures—the deployment of paramilitary *Freikorps* alongside fully-armed government soldiers against revolutionary uprisings—were enacted in 1919.

April 1919: Post-Revolutionary States of Emergency

The regime change in November 1918 was largely bloodless and limited in scope since the Majority Socialists had managed to take control of the revolutionary workers' and soldiers' councils which, in part, had a more radical, left-wing, socialist agenda.[37] Despite deep internal divisions, the MSPD and USPD agreed to form a provisional coalition government. However, in late December 1918, and definitively after the January 1919 uprising, violent clashes between the revolutionaries and the provisional government brought the initially peaceful phase of the German Revolution to an end. The USPD withdrew from government and a long struggle for authority began in Weimar Germany. Faced with enormous challenges, such as the demobilization of millions of soldiers, severe food scarcity, and the "war in peace" in Central and Eastern Europe, the new Weimar state was threatened not only by the radical left that was trying to "complete" the November movement, but also by militant right-wing forces pushing for an authoritarian comeback.[38] Social unrest and political conflicts radicalized in early 1919, initially in Berlin, and then in Saxony and Bavaria in the spring of that year. Until 1923, Weimar Germany was in a state of almost permanent turmoil.

Democratization, the expansion of welfare benefits, and a series of labor reforms, such as the eight-hour workday, were the main achievements of the new regime. However, the November Revolution remained limited since there were no major changes in the structure of industrial capitalism or land ownership, nor in the civil service, the army, or the justice system. This

36 SäStA, 10736 Ministerium des Innern, no. 11074, 6.

37 For a general overview, see Robert Gerwarth, *November 1918: The German Revolution* (Oxford: Oxford University Press, 2020).

38 On political extremism and the escalation of violence, see Andreas Wirsching, *Vom Weltkrieg zum Bürgerkrieg? Politischer Extremismus in Deutschland und Frankreich 1918–1933/39 Berlin und Paris im Vergleich* (Munich: Odenbourg, 1999).

limited nature of the regime change was a necessary precondition for the resilience of Weimar during the general crisis of 1919–23 and its relative stability in the 1920s. At the same time, however, the idea of an unfinished revolution was a source of permanent political conflict and led to the "negative integration" of the radical left into the first German democracy.

The paradigm of Weimar as a "failed state" had already entered the political discourse in the 1920s, especially among the Republic's enemies. This negative perception shaped retrospective views of Weimar in Nazi Germany and after 1945.[39] The way in which German authorities perceived and dealt with the crisis of 1919 shows that, on the contrary, the Republic was not a failed or doomed state, but rather a "threatened order" in which the contingencies of the "war in peace" after 1918 coexisted with continuities with the past and multiple possible futures.[40] This raises a twofold question that concerns 1) the implications of the limited revolution of 1918 for the uncertain future of Weimar democracy, and 2) the continuities in German history, i.e., the issue of authority and authoritarianism in Wilhelmine and Weimar Germany.[41] This section, which examines the legal framework and the political debates on the state of emergency in the early Weimar years, is underpinned by the assumption that the focus on emergency powers can help shed more light on controversial aspects of German history, such as the issue of historical continuities between the late Kaiserreich and the Weimar Republic.

Recent studies on Imperial Germany, the Habsburg Empire, and on neutral countries such as Switzerland, have shown that the unprecedented expansion of emergency powers after 1914 also had a major impact on postwar societies.[42] This includes not only the legal articulations and mentalities linked with the prolonged state of siege during World War I, but also the rise of the politics of state intervention in almost every area of social, cultural, and economic life. Most parts of the decrees and orders issued under

---

39 This negative paradigm has been convincingly reassessed by recent research. See, among others, Rüdiger Graf, *Die Zukunft der Weimarer Republik: Krisen und Zukunftsaneignungen, 1918–1933* (Munich: Odenbourg, 2008).

40 On "threatened order" as an analytical category, see Ewald Frie and Mischa Meier, *Aufruhr – Katastrophe – Konkurrenz – Zerfall. Bedrohte Ordnungen als Thema der Kulturwissenschaften* (Tübingen: Mohr Siebeck, 2014).

41 Cf. Anthony McElligott, *Rethinking the Weimar Republic: Authority and Authoritarianism, 1916–1936* (London: Bloomsbury, 2013).

42 See Geyer, "Grenzüberschreitungen"; Deak and Gumz, "How to Break a State"; Oliver Schneider, *Die Schweiz im Ausnahmezustand. Expansion und Grenzen von Staatlichkeit im Vollmachtenregime des Ersten Weltkriegs, 1914–1919* (Zurich: Chronos, 2019).

the state of siege since 1914 were not related to censorship or surveillance, but to the supply of food, clothes and war materials. In Bavaria, for example, a total of 35 decrees concerning transportation, trade and maximal prices of apples, pears and dried fruit were issued during the war.[43] Military intervention and overregulation in almost all spheres of everyday life gradually undermined public confidence in the authorities. In the following section, I will analyze these issues further, with reference to the specific dynamics of the emergency powers in the Free State of Saxony in 1919.

In early November 1918, mass demonstrations in Leipzig, Dresden and Chemnitz resulted in the abdication of Frederick Augustus III and the collapse of the Saxon monarchy. Only a few hours after the proclamation of the Republic in Berlin, the revolutionary movement also gained the upper hand in Saxony. There, the monarchy was replaced by the Free State of Saxony—a federal state within the Weimar Republic. The new democratic regime was initially based on revolutionary workers' and soldiers' councils, whose members had been elected at the local level. At the central level in Dresden, the political upheaval took place on November 10, 1918, when a newly constituted United Council of Revolutionary Workers and Soldiers asserted itself as the leading force within the revolutionary movement. In the following days, analogous to the situation in Berlin, the moderate SPD managed to convince the USPD to join a new united council that constituted the first government of revolutionary Saxony. After the USPD pulled out of the council in Berlin in late December and conflicts escalated during the January Uprising, the socialist coalition of the MSPD and USPD in Saxony also collapsed. Following the elections to the new Saxon parliament (*Volkskammer*) on February 2, 1919, the USPD rejected a coalition with the MSPD and the DDP (German Democratic Party).[44] As a result, Georg Gradnauer, who was the head of the provisional government, established an MSPD minority government and became the first elected Prime Minister of democratic Saxony. The new "Red Saxony," as noted by James Retallack, "fooled many contemporaries into believing it had been born overnight."[45]

43 Thomas Blanck, "A Revolutionary State of Exception: Munich, 1918/1919," *Zeitschrift für Politikwissenschaft* 28 (2018): 453–467, here: 457.

44 See Benjamin Lapp, *Revolution from the Right: Politics, Class and the Rise of Nazism in Saxony* (Boston: Humanities Press, 1997), 28. In the February election, the two socialist parties gained almost 58 percent of the vote, the moderate SPD 41.6 percent, and the USPD 16.3 percent.

45 Retallack, *Red Saxony*, 613.

Indeed, the history of emergency powers demonstrates that the revolutionary foundations of the Free State showed elements of historical continuity.

In Saxony, the first formally regulated state of emergency after the November Revolution was declared in the late afternoon of April 12, 1919, as a consequence of the death of Minister of War, Gustav Neuring, who was murdered "in a bestial manner" in Dresden.[46] The shocking scene made the front pages of newspapers around the world. *The New York Times*, for example, reported it as follows:

> "Wounded patients in the Dresden hospitals, says a Dresden dispatch, collected in the morning in the Theater Square to protest against an order issued by Herr Neuring to the effect that the wounded in the future should receive only peace time pay. Five or six hundred men then formed a procession to the War Ministry and sent a deputation to see the Minister, who, it was alleged, refused to receive them. […] An excited crowd meanwhile had thronged the square, and machine guns posted at various points were firing on the Ministry. At 4 o'clock in the afternoon, the demonstrators forced their way into the main building, followed the War Minister to the upper story, where he had fled, and dragged him out into the street. After the Minister had been severely maltreated by the crowd he was hurled from the bridge into the river. When he tried to swim to the bank the demonstrators fired at him, and within a few minutes he disappeared under the water. […] A state of siege has been proclaimed in Dresden."[47]

Much scholarly attention has been dedicated to the constitutional mechanisms for emergency powers under Article 48 of the Weimar constitution, which were not in force at the time of Neuring's murder, as the new constitution only came into force in August 1919. The proclamation of the state of emergency in April 1919 was based on a Saxon law from 1851. The legal context of the emergency powers and the "mentality" underlying them in Weimar Germany are linked, on the one hand, to the legislation and the discourse on the state of emergency that emerged in the nineteenth century and, on the other, to the unprecedented intensification of emergency powers during World War I. This is particularly true for the early Weimar crisis between 1919 and 1923.

The concept of emergency powers and their first modern legal articulations emerged after the French Revolution of 1789 and spread throughout Europe after the revolutionary wave of 1848–49.[48] One common crucial

46 *Dresdner Neueste Nachrichten*, April 13, 1919, 1.

47 *The New York Times*, April 14, 1919, 1.

48 See Hans Boldt, "Ausnahmezustand: necessita publica, Belagerungszustand, Kriegszustand, Staatsnotstand, Staatsnotrecht," in *Geschichtliche Grundbegriffe. Historisches Lexikon zur*

aspect of "modern" states of emergency was the suspension or limitation of constitutional rights and the imposition of martial law, which were applied not only in the case of war but also in the case of revolutionary upheavals and other internal threats to national security. The term "state of siege" (*Belagerungszustand*), which prevailed during the nineteenth century, was not a widespread concept in political discussions, but rather a technical term used to indicate the emergency measures that legitimized the use of the army for domestic repression. By contrast, the term "state of exception" (*Ausnahmezustand*), which became widespread in the first half of the twentieth century, shaped the public debates and the legal framework in the Weimar years. The superordinate concept "state of emergency" refers to both the *Belagerungszustand* during the war and the new *Ausnahmezustand* introduced by the Weimar constitution.

Despite the change in meaning and use of the concept, "state of siege" in the nineteenth century and "state of exception" after 1919 were not entirely dissimilar from a legal point of view. Both measures allowed for the suspension of constitutional rights and the use of military force to restore law and order. However, while *Belagerungszustand* applied to both internal and international security, the legal articulation and use of the term *Ausnahmezustand* in public debates was almost exclusively linked with internal threats and political conflicts. An example illustrates this point well: While Article 68 of the 1871 Reich constitution, which was based on the Prussian state of siege law of 1851, stated that both the external and internal dimensions of potential emergencies were regulated by law, Article 48 of the Weimar constitution only applied to internal matters (§ 1 on subversion of a single federal state, § 2 more generally on internal threats to national security). Both in Imperial and Weimar Germany, it was the head of the state (the Kaiser and the President of Germany, respectively) that declared the state of emergency. Parliamentary control over emergency legislation was, however, much more pronounced after the reorganization of *Ausnahmezustand* in the Weimar constitution. Furthermore, while under *Belagerungszustand* the army assumed almost unlimited power, the new legal and administrative articulation of the state of exception after 1919 facilitated a more effective control by civilian authorities.

After World War I, the legal theory and the philosophical foundations of emergency powers became increasingly controversial. The two opposite

politisch-sozialen Sprache in Deutschland, ed. Otto Brunner et al. (Stuttgart: Klett, 1972), Vol. 1, 343–376.

conceptions are well represented in the Kelsen-Schmitt debate. While the Austrian left-liberal jurist Hans Kelsen supported a strict, positivist concept of law and thus of emergency legislation, Carl Schmitt advocated a metaphysical, anti-positivist view of emergency powers.[49] Conceiving the *Ausnahmezustand* as a measure of authoritarian regeneration of parliamentary democracy, Schmitt radicalized his anti-socialist and anti-democratic position during the 1920s and became one of the most influential intellectuals of the German right. Remarkably, both Schmitt and Kelsen were involved in practical terms in the implementation of emergency politics during World War I. They advised the German and Austrian military administrations, respectively. After the collapse of the Habsburg Empire, Kelsen was the author of the liberal Austrian Constitution of 1920, and became a judge in the Constitutional Court until he left Vienna in 1930 in opposition to Austrian conservatives and fascists. By contrast, Schmitt advised conservative Chancellor Franz von Papen when the Reich government decided to use emergency powers to seize control of the SPD-led Prussian government in 1932, and later was actively involved in the Nazi regime.

Besides these theoretical and political disputes on the justification and scope of emergency powers, what is remarkable for the immediate post-war period is that the spread of notions such as "emergency" and "crisis" in public discourse contributed to perpetuating the "intellectual climate of exceptional thinking" that emerged during the war.[50] Continuities in the practices of the state of emergency are indeed evident, at least between the late Kaiserreich and the early Weimar Republic—even though one of the first measures announced by the provisional government in Berlin on November 12, 1918, was the suppression of the state of siege proclaimed in 1914.[51] Although the state of siege was abolished, the old *Belagerungszustand* legal framework remained in place. As mentioned above, the proclamation of a new state of siege on April 13, 1919, issued by the SPD-led cabinet in

49 On the contrasts between Schmitt and Kelsen, see Dieter Grimm, *Recht oder Politik? Die Kelsen-Schmitt-Kontroverse zur Verfassungsgerichtsbarkeit und die heutige Lage* (Berlin: Duncker & Humblot, 2020).

50 Blanck, "Revolutionary State of Exception," 461.

51 The immediate end of martial law was controversial among the Majority Socialists. In the Saxon *Landtag*, for instance, they rejected a USPD motion against martial law in late October 1918 because they shared the view of the "*bourgeois*" parties that social movements were spinning out of control. See Retallack, *Red Saxony*, 611.

Dresden was based on the Kingdom of Saxony's Internal Security Act of 1851.[52] Moreover, in late April, when Reich President Ebert upheld the state of siege in Saxony, he was applying Article 68 of the Reich constitution of 1871, which remained in place until the Weimar constitution came into effect in August 1919. In Bavaria, continuities were even more evident, as the state of siege proclaimed in 1914 was not suppressed after the revolution and lasted until 1921. Thus, the acute crisis of the Weimar Republic between January and May 1919 was shaped by the mentality and practices of the emergency state that emerged during World War I on the one hand, and by Wilhelmine Germany's *Belagerungszustand* legislation on the other.

In May 1919, a report by the Ministry of Justice sent to Reich President Ebert made it clear that Article 68 of the 1871 constitution had not been abolished. The report also explicitly stated that the authority of the Kaiser concerning the state of emergency was now transferred to the Reich President.[53] As a result, state of siege decrees under Article 68 of the Bismarckian constitution, i.e., the Prussian state of siege law of 1851, were applied more than 50 times in the first half of 1919, as Ebert almost systematically used emergency powers against popular protest and revolutionary upheavals.[54] The practice of "protective custody" (*Schutzhaft*)—arrest and indefinite detention without charge or trial—was also extensively used under the state of siege in times of war and with even more frequency and "brutality" by the Weimar authorities until 1923 (and again under the Nazi regime).[55]

Even after the Weimar constitution was promulgated, some of the preexisting emergency measures remained without major transformations, for example, the state of siege in Saxony after Neuring's murder, which was extended until March 1920. In the early 1920s, emergency powers based on pre-war legislation overlapped with the emergency measures under Article 48 of the Weimar constitution, such as the proclamation of a state of emergency after a violent mob gathered outside the Reichstag in January 1920, which was then extended to Saxony by Reich President Ebert in late

52 Cf. *Gesetz und Verordnungsblatt für den Freistaat Sachsen vom Jahre 1919* (Dresden: Meinhold, 1919), 94.

53 See Report of the Ministry of Justice of May 5, 1919 (Akten der Reichskanzlei), http://www.bundesarchiv.de/aktenreichskanzlei1919-1933.

54 Geyer, "Grenzüberschreitungen," 360.

55 See Keil and Stibbe, "Ein Laboratorium des Ausnahmezustands."

January,[56] or the Decrees for the Protection of the Republic (*Verordnungen zum Schutze der Republik*), which were issued in 1921 and 1922 after major political assassinations, most prominently the murders of former Minister of Finance, Matthias Erzberger, and of Foreign Minister, Walther Rathenau. Article 48 was used in 135 cases not only against "political extremism" and "revolutionary upheavals", but also for politics of crisis management in the economic, financial and social fields, especially after 1923.[57]

It is clear that the transfer of practices, mentalities and legal articulations from the pre-revolutionary emergency state to the early Weimar Republic shaped not only the immediate post-war period but also the early 1920s. There is, however, a great deal of discontinuity between the extensive, but constitutionally-bound use of emergency powers in the early Weimar Republic and the authoritarian methods of the emergency state in the 1930s that went in the anti-liberal direction advocated by Carl Schmitt. According to Eberhard Kolb,

> "the application of Article 48, as practiced by Ebert, is sharply contrasted with the use of emergency decrees under Hindenburg. [...] Under Ebert, the measures relating to Article 48 were based on extensive agreement between the government, the President and the parliamentary majority; in nearly all cases, the application of Article 48 took place at a formal sitting of a Reichstag which was basically in a position to take action—quite the contrary to the situation in the years from 1930 onwards."[58]

On the one hand, these observations on the discontinuity between the dynamics of emergency powers under Ebert and under Hindenburg are fully defensible. On the other hand, the crucial role played by emergency powers in the early Weimar years brought the practices and mentalities of the late Kaiserreich's state of emergency into the first German democracy and paved the way for the authoritarian abuse of Article 48 to become one of Weimar's possible futures. I will return to the intricacies of continuity and change in the use of emergency measures later in this chapter.

---

56 Cf. SäStA, 10736 Min. des Innern, no. 11062, 170. It was the same process to legitimize emergency powers which Ebert had already adopted in April 1919 when he upheld the Saxon state of siege.

57 Peter Blomeyer, *Der Notstand in den letzten Jahren von Weimar. Die Bedeutung von Recht, Lehre und Praxis der Notstandsgewalt für den Untergang der Weimarer Republik und die Machtübernahme durch die Nationalsozialisten. Eine Studie zum Verhältnis von Macht und Recht* (Berlin: Duncker & Humblot, 1999), 81.

58 Eberhard Kolb, *The Weimar Republic* (London: Routledge, 2005), 163.

Along with the legal framework, the political legitimacy of emergency powers is also of special importance in understanding the interplay of historical continuity and change after the German Revolution of 1918. In Wilhelmine Germany, a large part of public opinion and of the well-established political parties, such as the SPD, left-wing liberal parties, and the Catholic Centre Party, were skeptical of emergency powers. They were against the extension of the anti-Socialist laws and, with them, the so-called minor state of siege (*kleine Belagerungszustand*) in 1890;[59] they also opposed—to differing extents—the proclamation of emergency measures during the mass suffrage demonstrations of 1905, and during the political unrest in Alsace-Lorraine in late 1913 (the "Zabern Affair"). This widespread criticism of emergency powers changed radically after the outbreak of World War I. In fact, centrist forces, liberal intellectuals and the Majority Socialists supported, or at least tolerated, the Supreme Army Command's emergency powers until at least late September 1918.

After the revolution, there was little change in the broad support for emergency powers and in their largely positive connotation. In nearly all cases, at least until the Reich's intervention against the socialist-communist coalition in Saxony in 1923, emergency decrees were supported by the Weimar Coalition parties (MSPD, German Democratic Party and Centre Party) as being necessary measures in upholding democratic achievements and in warding off Bolshevism. Conservative parties and radical right movements also had a largely positive view of emergency powers—not only as a bulwark against communism but also as a potential strategy to effect an authoritarian transformation of Weimar. Thus, after the outbreak of World War I, and without major changes during the early Weimar years, only a minority of left-wing forces opposed emergency measures. As a consequence, it became much easier than in late Imperial Germany to implement the practices of the emergency state. This was one of the main factors that led to unprecedented episodes of violence and state-sponsored authoritarian repression between 1919 and 1923.[60] The escalation of political violence was facilitated by a more positive conception of emergency powers, which in the

59 Under the anti-Socialist laws, the concept of "state of siege" became more and more a political concept, since the "minor state of siege" was used to banish Socialist activists and anarchists from major German cities such as Berlin, Leipzig, Frankfurt and Hamburg in the 1870s and 1880s. See Heinz-Gerhard Haupt, *Den Staat Herausfordern: Attentate in Europa im Späten 19. Jahrhundert* (Frankfurt: Campus, 2019), 97–100.

60 Cf. Mark Jones, *Founding Weimar. Violence and the German Revolution of 1918–1919* (Cambridge: Cambridge University Press, 2016).

eyes of the Weimar Coalition parties were a means of providing security and ensuring freedom in the face of left-wing and right-wing extremism. This is clearly explained in a statement by Saxon Prime Minister Georg Gradnauer, in which he defended the state of emergency in April 1919 and endorsed the emergency powers as necessary to defend "freedom not only in economic activities but also in political life, which is threatened by the criminal and terrorist activities of small but unscrupulous minorities."[61] This "democratic" conception of the emergency state predominated during the first acute political crisis of Weimar (1919–23) while, during the second disruptive crisis in the early 1930s, a new authoritarian conception of emergency powers prevailed, which led to the collapse of democracy.

Summer 1919: The "Intensified State of Emergency"

This section will further examine the mosaic of emergency constructions in the early Weimar years. It focuses on the proclamation of a *verschärfter Belagerungszustand* ("intensified state of siege") after a violent riot in August 1919 in Chemnitz. The "intensification" of the state of siege as well as the "intensified state of exception" after 1919 (*verschärfter Ausnahmezustand*) were not formally regulated measures. The term "intensified" was used to indicate a comprehensive state of emergency that included the use of military courts and the suspension of constitutional rights. Like the state of siege declared four months earlier following Neuring's murder, the "intensified" state of emergency of August 1919 was the consequence of a disruptive event that drew attention to the escalation of violent confrontations and generated a new sense of urgency among centrist and moderate left-wing forces. On August 9, 1919, once again after Neuring's murder, shocking scenes in Saxony made the front pages of both regional and international newspapers. *The New York Times*, emphasizing the "Bolshevist threat", reported that:

"Fifty persons were killed in disturbances yesterday near Chemnitz, Saxony. Troops were overpowered and disarmed by a mob. The soldiers' horses were slaughtered and the flesh was distributed to the crowd. [...] The riots are due to the shortage of food. Spartacide [sic] agitators persuaded a mob to storm the railway station. The

61 *Dresdner Anzeiger*, April 18, 1919, 1. Original quote: "[der Belagerungszustand] soll die Freiheit des politischen und wirtschaftlichen Lebens gegen verbrecherische terroristische Vergewaltigung durch kleine, aber skrupellose Minderheiten schützen."

mob dispersed the Government troops sent against it and then stormed the prison and released several Communists. Telegrams have been sent to Dresden demanding the lifting of martial law, the withdrawal of the troops and better food."[62]

During the riot, the army used machine guns and hand grenades, receiving explicit praise from Social Democrat Prime Minister Gradnauer for its reaction.[63] The acute food crisis, anti-Bolshevism, and fears of social disintegration emerged as common features in the perception of the crisis immediately before and after the collapse of Imperial Germany. This fits very well with recent studies on World War I, that point to the crisis of empires and the intensification of anti-Socialist fears after the October Revolution as representing a turning point that led to unprecedented levels of political extremism and violence after the formal end of the war.[64]

As a consequence of the violent protest in the early afternoon of August 8 in Chemnitz, a *verschärfter Belagerungszustand* was proclaimed by the local military commando.[65] Even if the Weimar government tried to demilitarize the state of emergency (for example, civilian commissioners were appointed by the Reich Interior Ministry in regions placed under a state of siege), the role played by military authorities was another element of continuity between Wilhelmine and Weimar Germany. Both regimes were polycratic with a multiplicity of power and policy structures, which were closely related to German federalist traditions. Thus, besides the role played by the army, the conflicts between regional states and central government were of special importance in implementing the politics of crisis management and the use of emergency powers between 1917 and 1923. These conflicts increased exponentially when the regional governments' political line clashed with Berlin's. The political battles between central government and the federal states were more virulent in the Weimar democracy than in the pre-1914 period when there was, all in all, less disparity between the central and regional government forces.

What is remarkable, looking at the various reactions in the aftermath of the "Chemnitz bloodbath" of 1919, is that not only the left-wing but also the centrist newspapers criticized the overly extensive use of emergency powers.[66] As a result, the *verschärfter Belagerungszustand* proclaimed by the

62 *New York Times*, August 9, 1919, 1.
63 *Dresdner Neueste Nachrichten*, August 14, 1919, 4.
64 See, among others, Gerwarth, *The Vanquished*; Leonhard, *Der überforderte Frieden.*
65 *Dresdner Neueste Nachrichten*, August 9, 1919, 3.
66 *Leipziger Volkszeitung*, April 9, 1919, 1; *Dresdner Neueste Nachrichten*, August 10, 1919, 1.

military commando in Chemnitz on August 8, 1919, was revoked just four days later. By contrast, the state of emergency proclaimed by the civilian authorities in spring 1919 would continue until March 1920. This highlights once again the overlap between the different legal articulations and conceptions of emergency powers in the early Weimar years: 1) The state of siege of April 1919 in "Red Saxony", which was based on the Security Act of 1851; 2) the more than 50 emergency decrees signed by Reich President Ebert in the first half of 1919 under Article 68 of the 1871 constitution (*Belagerungszustand*); 3) the short-lived military state of siege of August 1919; and 4) the emergency decree of January 1920 under Article 48 of the Weimar constitution, as well as the several other emergency measures under Article 48 that followed, for example, in September 1923 under Stresemann.

In 1923, when Stresemann's Great Coalition cabinet proclaimed a national state of emergency in response to the Bavarian-Reich conflict, the government in Munich reacted by declaring a regional state of emergency.[67] This represents an element of discontinuity between the general crisis of 1917–23 and the early 1930s, when the federal system and—to a certain extent—also the role of the army was less important. The crisis of the regional states and the enforcement of Berlin's emergency powers, which first emerged in 1923 during the Reich's intervention against Saxony,[68] became evident after the takeover of the Free State of Prussia by Papen's government using emergency powers in 1932, and eventually after the Nazi's seizure of power. Even if Papen used emergency legislation with authoritarian means in order to dismantle parliamentary democracy, it was only after the emergency decree of February 28, 1933 ("Reichstag Fire Decree"), and the infamous *Ermächtigungsgesetz* ("Enabling Act") of March 23, 1933, that state-led terror and arbitrary use of power became part of everyday life in Germany.[69] The unprecedented political repression and the escalation of anti-Jewish violence transformed the realities of everyday life in Nazi Germany

67 Cf. Dirk Schumann, *Political Violence in the Weimar Republic, 1918–1933* (New York: Berghahn, 2009), 128.

68 See Donald B. Pryce, "The Reich Government versus Saxony 1923. The Decision to Intervene," *Central European History* 10, no. 2 (1977): 112–147.

69 On the authoritarian abuse of Article 48 during the Brüning and Papen governments, and the emergency legislation of February 1933 as the basis of "legal" terror in Nazi Germany, see Michael Wildt, "Gewalt als Partizipation. Der Nationalsozialismus als Ermächtigungsregime," in *Staats-Gewalt. Ausnahmezustand und Sicherheitsregimes. Historische Perspektiven*, ed. Alf Lüdtke and Michael Wildt (Göttingen: Wallstein, 2008), 215–240.

and, with them, the general perception of the (permanent) state of emergency.

Concluding Remarks

The normalization of emergency powers after 1914 generated a fundamental crisis of liberal constitutionalism and state legitimacy. Claims of necessity and emergency became a crucial part of political discourses and practices in belligerent states, their global empires and even in neutral or non-belligerent countries. As shown by John Deak and Jonathan E. Gumz in the Habsburg Monarchy and reaffirmed in this chapter in the case of Germany, the use and abuse of emergency legislation had major effects not only on the internal disintegration of pre-war regimes but also on the fragility of post-war democracies.

Emergency powers are a lens through which we can look afresh at the intricacy of patterns of continuity and discontinuity in German history. Continuity prevailed if we compare the extensive use of emergency powers in late Imperial Germany and the early Weimar years, while discontinuity prevailed between the technical-administrative emergency measures of the Bismarck era and the unprecedented expansion of emergency powers during and after World War I. The notion of technical-administrative refers more to the limited use of emergency powers than to their supposed "unpolitical" character before 1914. Indeed, under the anti-Socialist laws the concept of "state of siege" became more and more a political concept since the so-called minor state of siege was used to banish Socialist activists from major German cities such as Berlin, Leipzig, Frankfurt and Hamburg in the 1870s and 1880s. However, the use of emergency powers remained limited if compared with the post-1914 era. Discontinuity prevailed also between the "democratic" stance of the emergency state in the early Weimar years and the authoritarian state of emergency in the late Weimar period that culminated in the construction of Hitler's "prerogative state", which operated outside the traditional legal system (normative state).[70]

70 On Ernst Fraenkel's definition of the Third Reich as a "dual state" (normative vs prerogative state) and its limits, see Alan E. Steinweis and Robert D. Rachlin, "The Law in Nazi Germany and the Holocaust," in *The Law in Nazi Germany. Ideology, Opportunism, and the*

This chapter has also shed light on those long-term consequences of politics of crisis management that go beyond legal frameworks of emergency powers such as, for example, an authoritarian conceptualization of public opinion. This idea, based on the assumption that the masses were pliable and needed to be led, emerged as a key part of propaganda campaigns during the war and continued to have major impact after 1918.[71] As shown in the first section, the politics of crisis management during the war and the fact that state intervention (and emergency decrees) was extended to almost every area of social and economic life also had a major impact on the construction of the post-revolutionary order. Both the semi-authoritarian Kaiserreich and Weimar democracy faced a dilemma between violent repression and "passivity" towards popular protest and political extremism. This also explains how the practices and mentality of the emergency state that emerged in late Imperial Germany came to be conveyed into the new Weimar democracy.

Continuity in the structure of the civil service, the army, and the justice system provides another explanation of the persistence in the practices and mentality of the emergency state—as Otto Mayer, a German jurist, coined in 1924: "*Verfassung vergeht, Verwaltung besteht*" (while the constitutional order changes, the state administration persists).[72] Another factor that explains the continuity of emergency regimes is the adaptability of crisis discourses. In the era of the anti-Socialist laws, these discourses were directed against the SPD and its calls for democracy; after 1918, they were redirected by the SPD and the centrist parties against left-wing extremism, in order to defend the democratic achievements of the November Revolution. The change in the meaning and dominant perception of emergency powers, which were seen as a reactionary instrument under the Kaiser and became a bulwark against extremism under Ebert, is crucial to understanding the politics of crisis management in the early Weimar years. In the 1930s, once again, a different view of emergency powers prevailed—and this reveals an important aspect of discontinuity. Emergency decrees under Hindenburg in the early 1930s, and especially the extraordinary measures that led to Hitler taking power in 1933, were clearly intended to bring about an authoritarian transformation of

---

Perversion of Justice, ed. Alan E. Steinweis and Robert D. Rachlin (New York: Berghahn, 2013), 1–14.

71 See Corey Ross, *Media and the Making of Modern Germany: Mass Communications, Society, and Politics from the Empire to the Third Reich* (Oxford: Oxford University Press, 2008), 206.

72 Cf. Frieder Günther, "Verfassung vergeht, Verwaltung besteht? Die vier deutschen Innenministerien 1919 bis 1970," *Vierteljahrshefte für Zeitgeschichte* 68, no. 2 (2020), 217–247.

Weimar democracy. This represents a fundamental difference not only with the early Weimar years but also with the conception and implementation of state of siege in Imperial Germany. The idea of using emergency powers to impose authoritarian rule and suppress alleged "internal enemies" had already been circulating among radical nationalist groups such as the Pan-German League before 1914 but remained politically marginal.[73]

Another issue related to the former point is the transformability of the concept of state of emergency/state of siege and its political legitimacy. Over the course of the nineteenth century, state of siege was a technical-administrative concept, but became more of a political concept as a result of the anti-Socialist legislation in the late 1870s, and especially during World War I, as well as in the early Weimar years. Furthermore, the concept gained positive connotations in the 1920s: In the eyes of the Weimar coalition's centrist parties, emergency powers were necessary to secure the democratic achievements of November 1918. However, conservative opponents of the Republic and the radical right also saw emergency powers in a positive light—as a strategy to forge an authoritarian comeback. In both cases, for the Weimar coalition and for its opponents, it was the total crisis experienced during World War I and the rise of political extremism after 1917 that explained the transformation of the concept and its enactment. Long-term transformations were also involved: During the nineteenth century and increasingly so in the early twentieth century, concepts such as "state of emergency" and "crisis" began to have a decisive impact on a plurality of different fields (initially medicine, then the economy, politics, culture, and ecology).[74] This increased usage and qualitative transformation of concepts such as crisis and emergency can be explained by the need to justify controversial political decisions, and to indicate the way to a crisis-free future, which became a crucial political metanarrative after the ordeal of the World War and the near civil war situation in the aftermath of the November Revolution. It was this new, positive, almost messianic connotation of the emergency state (with democratic or authoritarian means) that led to the extensive use of emergency powers in the period 1917–23, and to authoritarian abuse of them in the 1930s.

73 Geyer, "Grenzüberschreitungen," 346.

74 See Rüdiger Graf, "Zwischen Handlungsmotivation und Ohnmachtserfahrung—Der Wandel des Krisenbegriffs im 20. Jahrhundert," in *Handbuch Krisenforschung*, ed. Frank Bösch (Wiesbaden: Springer, 2020), 17–38.

Triple Threat: Resource Interdependence and the Interwar Authoritarian Crises

Rob Konkel

Introduction: The Interwar Raw Materials Problem

In 1919, Charles Leith travelled to France as part of Woodrow Wilson's team of advisors at the Paris Peace Conference. A young geology professor at the University of Wisconsin, Leith would spend the rest of his career raising public awareness of resource interdependence and the impossibility of autarky. "No country," Leith argued again and again, "is entirely self-sustaining in its mineral requirements."[1] But in Paris, nation-statism dominated the proceedings. Slicing imperial territories into political entities of singular nationality would, the peacemakers argued, be the building blocks of peace. Leith had other ideas. "Needless loss and friction," Leith wrote, "might have been avoided if the distribution of raw materials and the industries based upon them had been taken into account when the terms of peace were settled."[2]

Leith was describing the essence of the interwar raw materials problem—the uneven distribution of, and access to, resources needed for both modern industrial life and modern warfare. Some territories were relatively rich in raw materials, others were relatively poor, dividing the world into "have" and "have not" countries.[3] The "haves" included those with access to raw materials and markets, either domestically or via colonial or mandatory territories: Britain, the United States, France, the Netherlands, and to a lesser

---

1 C.K. Leith, "International Control of Minerals," in *Mineral Resources of the United States, 1917: Part I, Metals* (Washington: Government Printing Office, 1921), 7A–16A, here: 7A.

2 C. K. Leith, *World Minerals and World Politics: A Factual Study of Minerals in Their Political and International Relations* (New York: Whittlesey House, 1931), 59.

3 This language was a common shorthand to refer to specific countries, and it was widespread—the terms "haves" and "have nots" were used in international forums, publications, and speeches all over the world. The "have"/"have not" terminology was contested, often appearing in scare quotes, which I have replicated here. See Norman Angell, *This Have and Have-Not Business: Political Fantasy and Economic Fact* (London: H. Hamilton, 1936).

degree, the Soviet Union. The "have nots" were those either without colonial territories or those perceived to be lacking in raw materials, and generally referred to Japan, Germany, and Italy. These "have nots" insisted that they needed colonies not only for resources, but as markets for their manufactured goods and outlets for excess population. The "haves," along with internationalist economic experts, tended to see the problem in terms of trade and exchange restrictions—liberalized multilateralism and the Open Door, they suggested, could solve the problem of raw materials. But depending on access to foreign-controlled resources was, for some, an intolerable and dangerous condition. States looked to carve out spheres of influence in pursuit of autarky while industrialists stockpiled key inputs, integrated their operations, and harnessed the power of the state to protect their foreign and domestic interests. Instead of international cooperation, resource interdependence spurred economic nationalism and autarkic policies. Amid currency instability, reparations and war debts, throttled international credit, and intractable resource interdependence, internationalist cooperation disintegrated, and the world splintered into hostile blocs.

The raw materials problem pervaded matters of international relations between the wars. Interdependence created vulnerabilities and anxieties on the one hand, while facilitating intervisibility, shaping strategic calculations, and motivating geopolitical ambitions on the other.[4] This was true for both the "have not" and "have" regimes.[5] And it was especially true for mineral resources—particularly ferro-alloying minerals used to make steel, like manganese, tungsten, nickel, and chrome. Modern industry required steady supplies of these metals, but none of the industrialized powers possessed sufficient domestic deposits. Indeed, no state or empire was entirely self-sufficient.[6] These minerals were processed and consumed far from the sites of extraction, rendering every industrial power irrevocably dependent on imports for their military and productive strength. Without steady, secure

4 Stephen Kotkin, "Modern Times: The Soviet Union and the Interwar Conjuncture," *Kritika: Explorations in Russian and Eurasian History* 2, no. 1 (2001): 111–164.

5 Isaiah Bowman, *The New World: Problems in Political Geography*, 4th ed. (Chicago: World Book Company, 1928), 12–14.

6 A ferro-alloy is an alloy of iron containing a substantial proportion of another element. These alloys are mostly used to impart desirable qualities to steel, such as ductility, strength, or corrosive resistance. G. A. Roush, *Strategic Mineral Supplies* (New York: McGraw-Hill Book Company, 1939), 1; Leith, *World Minerals and World Politics*, 11–12; Lauri Holappa, "Basics of Ferroalloys," in *Handbook of Ferroalloys: Theory and Technology*, ed. Michael Gasik (Waltham, MA: Butterworth-Heinemann, 2013), 9–28.

access to these ores, a country could not have a functioning industrial sector, let alone wage a war. Importantly, up to 80 percent of these mineral deposits were under British or American political or commercial control.[7] Although minerals were not the only raw materials sought by the "have nots," they were "the spearpoint" of their demands for territory and other concessions.[8]

Japan, Italy, and Germany did not begin the interwar period as authoritarian regimes, and their fascist authoritarianisms took different forms.[9] In each instance, however, the Great Depression catalyzed and radicalized authoritarian responses to resource interdependence. Amid the economic crisis, the "have nots" took "sharp fascist turns," relying on authoritarian state control to realize imperial ambitions and turn themselves into "haves."[10] As Reto Hofmann has argued, fascist regimes subsumed and "selectively appropriated" the strategies, ideas, and ideals of imperialism to address the problems of interwar mass society, the crises of liberal capitalism, and the failures of the international order ushered in by the Treaty of Versailles.[11] As depression set in, the non-authoritarian "haves" began closing the doors to trade, erecting tariffs, and turning trade inward. The liberal world order was failing, and the "have not" states of Japan, Italy, and Germany sought to open up different possibilities—forging self-sufficiency through imperial state action.

These quests for autarky and autonomy were the authoritarian regimes' response to a three-headed crisis: access to raw materials, looming American

7 Commercial control could take several different forms—owning direct concessionary rights over a parcel of land, or indirect ownership through control over smelters, refineries, transportation lines, cartels, or selling agencies. Leith, *World Minerals and World Politics*, 15. The British Empire still had perhaps the world's strongest mineral position. The most important producers in the Empire were the United Kingdom itself (almost exclusively coal), South Africa, Canada, Australia, India, and the Federated Malay States. "Canadian Mining Problems in their Inter-Imperial Aspects," 1932, Library and Archives Canada, Ottawa, RG20/361/22.

8 C. K. Leith, "Mineral Resources and Peace," *Foreign Affairs* 16, no. 3 (1938): 515–524, here: 515.

9 Juan J. Linz, *Totalitarian and Authoritarian Regimes* (Boulder, CO: Lynne Rienner Publishers, 2000).

10 Louise Young, "When Fascism Met Empire in Japanese-Occupied Manchuria," *Journal of Global History* 12, no. 2 (2017): 274–296, here: 280. Young argues that "radical statism" formed a crucial part of Japanese fascism—that is, the notion that the state could be the key agent in radically changing the *status quo*.

11 Reto Hofmann, "The Fascist New–Old Order," *Journal of Global History* 12, no. 2 (2017): 166–183, here: 174.

power, and the Great Depression.[12] Consolidating a self-contained bloc was how the "have nots" hoped to escape the limits and constraints of resource interdependence, economic interdependence, and American world dominance. Doing so required emulating the United States—promulgating new Monroe Doctrines for East Asia, Eastern Europe, and the Mediterranean, in which resource-rich peripheries fed a hungry industrial heartland.[13] Minerals offer one way to understand why a regionalist world, or a world ordered by Great Power blocs, was a compelling vision. Mineral resources were a source of industrial and military power, but mineral consumption was a zero-sum game. So too was the territory in which the minerals were embedded. Indeed, the unequal distribution of certain mineral resources around the world was widely regarded as a latent source of conflict. But not only did World War I fail to resolve these tensions, the Treaty of Versailles exacerbated them.

The Seeds of Resource Interdependence: Steel, Imperialism, and World War I

Global interdependence was driven by a fusion of technological, economic, and geopolitical interests. The nineteenth-century world system of trade and finance was built from London and radiated outward to integrate the world—violently and unevenly. New steelmaking techniques in the late-nineteenth century—the Bessemer Process and open-hearth methods—helped to inaugurate a new era of globalization by making steel production much cheaper and faster.[14] Robert Hadfield's discovery of manganese steel

12 Adam Tooze, *The Deluge: The Great War and the Remaking of Global Order, 1916–1931* (New York: Penguin, 2014); Sven Beckert, *Empire of Cotton: A Global History* (New York: Alfred A. Knopf, 2014); Stefan J. Link, *Forging Global Fordism: Nazi Germany, Soviet Russia, and the Contest over the Industrial Order* (Princeton: Princeton University Press, 2020).

13 Sven Beckert, "American Danger: United States Empire, Eurafrica, and the Territorialization of Industrial Capitalism, 1870–1950," *The American Historical Review* 122, no. 4 (2017): 1137–1170.

14 David S. Landes, *The Unbound Prometheus: Technological Change and Industrial Development in Western Europe from 1750 to the Present* (Cambridge: Cambridge University Press, 1969), 249–276. When Henry Bessemer blew air into molten pig iron, he decarburized the metal about 70 times faster than simply applying heat. This made steel economically competitive with wrought iron.

in 1882 kicked off the "age of alloy steels," and was quickly followed by applications of other ferro-alloying minerals to steelmaking, like chromium, nickel, and tungsten.[15] Manganese became a standard, essential ingredient in steelmaking almost overnight. Tungsten-tipped machine tools, similarly, quickly became indispensable to modern engineering industries for their cutting speed, efficiency, and durability.[16] These metallurgical innovations stimulated a global search for alloying steel inputs, intensifying that scramble in at least two ways. Firstly, through the very infrastructure it created, most notably rail lines penetrating deeper into global hinterlands. Secondly, through the pre-1914 arms race, as armaments increasingly depended on specialty steels alloyed with minerals like manganese, tungsten, nickel, and chrome.[17]

Industrialists quickly learned that these essential minerals were scattered around the world and concentrated in remote locations. Manganese was sourced chiefly from the Central Provinces of India, the Caucasus (Tchiaturi, present-day Georgia), and the province of Minas Gerais in Brazil.[18] Tungsten ore was even more concentrated, found overwhelmingly in East and Southeast Asia—over half of the world's tungsten was mined by hand in southern China.[19] Chrome ore came from Rhodesia, India, New Caledonia, and Turkey. British Malaya, Bolivia, and the Dutch East Indies produced about three-quarters of the world's tin. Over 90 percent of the world's nickel supply came from Sudbury, Ontario, with the only other significant deposits located in Finland and New Caledonia. Peru had a virtual monopoly on vanadium.[20] In short, there were truly only a few nodal points in the world

---

15 Geoffrey Tweedale, "Sir Robert Abbott Hadfield F.R.S. (1858–1940), and the Discovery of Manganese Steel," *Notes and Records of the Royal Society of London* 40, no. 1 (1985): 63–74, here: 63; Alfred E. Eckes, *The United States and the Global Struggle for Minerals* (Austin: University of Texas Press, 1979), 11.

16 Robert C. Deale, "What a Shop Executive Should Know about Cutting-Tool Materials," *Machinery* 40, no. 12 (1934): 729–730.

17 David Stevenson, *Armaments and the Coming of War: Europe, 1904–1914* (New York: Clarendon Press, 1996).

18 Over the interwar years, a few more lines of manganese would open up, most notably in Gold Coast and South Africa.

19 G. A. Roush, "Strategic Mineral Supplies: 5. Tungsten," *The Military Engineer* 27, no. 154 (1935): 280–285. Other significant tungsten deposits could be found in Burma, Malaya, and Bolivia. The only tungsten in Europe was on the Iberian Peninsula, mostly in Portugal, and mostly low-grade. Similarly, the United States possessed some small, low-grade tungsten deposits, but they were costly to mine and inadequate for the country's needs.

20 Josiah Edward Spurr, "The Commercial Control of the Mineral Resources of the World: Its Political Significance," *The Scientific Monthly* 9, no. 1 (1919): 73–82; Josiah Edward Spurr,

mineral situation, which were relatively fixed for the future due to some measure of path dependence. Minerals like these could become "pawns in a diplomatic game rather than mere commodities."[21]

By 1914, ferro-alloying minerals were well-known to metallurgists and steelmakers, but virtually unknown to politicians. World War I, however, quickly alerted government bureaucrats to the critical importance of mineral resources to national survival. To their horror, British officials discovered that although the British Empire produced around 40 percent of the world's tungsten ore, domestic steel producers depended entirely on Germany for the refined product, ferro-tungsten.[22] Indeed, before World War I, German metal trading companies gained notoriety as "the octopus" by tightening their grips on metal markets through globe-spanning integration.[23] For example, German metal traders amassed commercial control over key mineral deposits in Australia, New Caledonia, Malaya, and Bolivia, and integrated those concerns with European refining facilities. Although the United States mined or processed somewhere between 50 and 70 percent of the world's copper prior to 1914, German metal trading companies controlled the distribution, coordination, and price setting for the global copper market.[24] Trade experience also helped spur metallurgical advances, with German conglomerates like *Metallgesellschaft* and *Krupp* on the leading edge. This integrative business and industrial strategy depended on being deeply embedded in global networks and dynamics of commerce, industry, and finance. These networks, which were a source of German industrial strength before 1914,

---

Political and Commercial Geology and the World's Mineral Resources (New York: McGraw-Hill, 1920); C. K. Leith, "The Political Control of Mineral Resources," *Foreign Affairs* 3, no. 4 (1925): 541–555; Josiah Edward Spurr, "Steel-Making Minerals," *Foreign Affairs* 4, no. 4 (1926): 601–612; Leith, *World Minerals and World Politics.*

21 C. K. Leith, H. Foster Bain, and S. M. Marshall, eds., *Elements of a National Mineral Policy* (New York, 1933), 61.

22 Eleanora Bliss Knopf, "Some Problems of International Readjustment of Mineral Supplies as Indicated in Recent Foreign Literature," *Economic Geology* 14, no. 2 (1919): 147–171; Thomas H. Holland, "Proposed Review of the Mineral Resources and Industries of the Empire, and the Conditions Affecting Their Development," *Transactions of the Institution of Mining and Metallurgy* 36 (1927): 399–435, here: 402.

23 Nathan Delaney, "Copper Capitalism: The Making of a Transatlantic Market in Metals, 1870–1930" (PhD diss., Case Western Reserve University, 2018), 141; Susan Becker, "The German Metal Traders before 1914," in *The Multinational Traders*, ed. Geoffrey Jones (New York: Routledge, 1998), 77; Simon Ball, "The German Octopus: The British Metal Corporation and the Next War, 1914–1939," *Enterprise & Society* 5, no. 3 (2004): 451–489.

24 Nathan Delaney, "The Great War and the Transformation of the Atlantic Copper Trade," *Scandinavian Economic History Review* 65, no. 3 (2017): 263–278.

were quickly weaponized by the Allies against Germany during World War I, contributing directly to its defeat.[25]

From the very beginning of the war, Germany was deficient in a number of critically important minerals. In preparation, Germany had ratcheted up its purchases of Russian manganese ore, and imported as much tungsten as it could source.[26] Although domestic mines and those captured in Belgium and France produced more than enough coal and iron ore, Germany remained deficient in all ferro-alloying minerals.[27] On top of the blockade, the Allies pursued preclusive purchases of neutral countries' goods to prevent Germany from acquiring raw materials via the neutrals.[28] Germany depended on imports for its food and industrial raw materials, and the world quickly saw how vulnerable states like Germany were. Britain's superior navy meant that long-distance trade routes and an increasingly specialized global division of labor could be weaponized against potential usurpers.[29] Without control over the oceans and its sea lanes, interdependence posed a threat to Germany's very survival.

From the Paris Peace Conference onward, the raw materials problem plagued state and market actors alike, and vexed internationalist efforts to restore an idealized vision of nineteenth-century free trade, stable exchange rates, and capital movements. Imperial competition over global raw materials was a popular causal explanation for World War I, and accordingly, there were a host of efforts to resolve the conflict after 1918. At the Paris Peace Conference, Bernard Baruch insisted in his capacity as Chairman of the US War Industries Board, that "a just and continuing peace should include a just

25 Henry Farrell and Abraham Newman's concept of "weaponized interdependence" is a useful analytic for understanding the dynamics of resource interdependence during this period. Britain, with its naval primacy and extensive empire, controlled the key nodes of the world's mineral trade. Henry Farrell and Abraham L. Newman, "Weaponized Interdependence: How Global Economic Networks Shape State Coercion," *International Security* 44, no. 1 (2019): 42–79.

26 Roy MacLeod, "'The Mineral Sanction': The Great War and the Strategic Role of Natural Resources," in *Environmental Histories of the First World War*, ed. Richard P. Tucker et al. (New York: Cambridge University Press, 2018), 99–116, here: 101–102; Ronald H. Limbaugh, *Tungsten in Peace and War, 1918–1946* (Reno: University of Nevada Press, 2010), 24.

27 Frank Pentland Chambers, *The War behind the War, 1914–1918: A History of the Political and Civilian Fronts* (New York: Harcourt, Brace, 1939), 144.

28 Marjorie M. Farrar, "Preclusive Purchases: Politics and Economic Warfare in France during the First World War," *The Economic History Review* 26, no. 1 (1973): 117–133.

29 Farrell and Newman, "Weaponized Interdependence."

and equal access to the raw materials and manufacturing facilities of the world."[30] Other delegates harbored hopes of subjecting raw materials to supranational control.[31] The Italian draft for the League of Nations covenant, for example, pointed to the necessity for international control over foodstuffs and raw materials such that every country could secure what was necessary.[32] The Italians also brought up the question at the League's first Assembly—after all, imperial competition over raw materials was, the delegate argued, one cause of the war.[33] In response to a League Council resolution in October 1920, Italian economist Corrado Gini led a team of experts to tackle the raw materials problem, to understand the extent and causes of the difficulties countries were having importing raw materials.[34] The issue of equalizing access to raw materials was also raised by the International Congress of Miners in Geneva in 1920; the International Chamber of Commerce in 1921; the Economic and Financial Committee of the League in 1922; the World Economic Conference in 1927; the Diplomatic Conference of the League in 1927; the Raw Materials Committee in 1937; and in many other monographs, studies, and speeches.[35]

---

30 Quoted in Jordan A Schwarz, *The Speculator: Bernard M. Baruch in Washington, 1917–1965* (Chapel Hill: University of North Carolina Press, 1981), 132.

31 Adam Tooze and Ted Fertik, "The World Economy and the Great War," *Geschichte und Gesellschaft* 40, no. 2 (2014): 214–238, here: 230; MacLeod, "'The Mineral Sanction.'"

32 Royal Institute of International Affairs, *Raw Materials and Colonies* (London: The Royal Institute of International Affairs, 1936), 55.

33 Leith, *World Minerals and World Politics: A Factual Study of Minerals in Their Political and International Relations*, 59.

34 Gini, *Report on the Problem of Raw Materials and Foodstuffs*, 8–10. In Gini's opinion, most of the difficulties for countries in obtaining raw materials stemmed from the post-war disequilibrium and exchange rate fluctuation.

35 The following is only an indicative list: Gini, *Report on the Problem of Raw Materials and Foodstuffs*; William S. Culbertson, "Raw Materials and Foodstuffs in the Commercial Policies of Nations," *The Annals of the American Academy of Political and Social Science* 112, no. 1 (1924): 1–147; James Wilson Furness and Lucy Marshall Jones, *Mineral Raw Materials: Survey of Commerce and Sources in Major Industrial Countries* (Washington: United States Government Printing Office, 1929); Benjamin Bruce Wallace and Lynn Ramsay Edminster, *International Control of Raw Materials* (Washington, D.C.: The Brookings Institution, 1930); Leith, Bain, and Marshall, *Elements of a National Mineral Policy*; Brooks Emeny, *The Strategy of Raw Materials: A Study of America in Peace and War*, ed. J. Edward Ely (New York: Macmillan, 1934); Thomas H. Holland, *The Mineral Sanction as an Aid to International Security* (London: Oliver and Boyd, 1935); Harold R.G. Greaves, *Raw Materials and International Control* (London: Methuen & Co., 1936); League of Nations, *Report of the Committee for the Study of the Problem of Raw Materials* (Geneva: League of Nations, 1937); Hubert Douglas Henderson, *Colonies and Raw Materials*, Pamphlets on World Affairs 7 (New York: Farrar & Rinehart, 1939);

For internationalists clustered around the institutions of interwar Geneva, resurrecting free trade was the favored solution to the raw materials problem. Networks of economic experts working through the League of Nations' Economic and Financial Organization gathered statistics, promoted trade policy harmonization, and tried to convince states to dismantle trade barriers.[36] The economy should be global, they insisted, because an interlacing of shared interests was the best promoter of peace and prosperity. The reality they ultimately faced, however, was a world splintering into blocs. Internationalist mechanisms to address the raw materials problem, like those initiated by the pre-fascist Italian state, largely failed. Fascist Italy, and the other "have nots," would dispense with international cooperation in favor of imperial bloc-building.

Bloc-Thinking: "American Danger" and the Proliferation of Monroe Doctrines

The need to enumerate and marshal raw materials on an unprecedented scale during World War I created new bureaucracies and management techniques on the one hand, and anxieties about shortfalls on the other.[37] In Britain, several mineralogists set about examining the mineral resources of the Empire, in the hope "of finding the Empire to be self-contained."[38] "It is absolutely *essential*," wrote British economic geologist Thomas Holland, "to be sure that we can get access to supplies of the necessary ores." But prior to the war, "who thought it necessary to provide for the smelting of an

---

Eugene Staley, *Raw Materials in Peace and War* (New York: Council on Foreign Relations, 1937); C. K. Leith, *Minerals in the Peace Settlement* (New York: The Geological Society of America, 1940), 3; Eugene Staley and K. E. Knorr, *Raw Material Problems and Policies* (Geneva: League of Nations, 1946).

36 Louis Pauly, "The League of Nations and the Foreshadowing of the International Monetary Fund," SSRN Scholarly Paper (Rochester, NY: Social Science Research Network, December 1, 1996); Patricia Clavin, *Securing the World Economy: The Reinvention of the League of Nations, 1920–1946* (New York: Oxford University Press, 2013).

37 Mark Mazower, *Governing the World: The History of an Idea* (New York: Penguin, 2012), 144–145.

38 Thomas H. Holland, "International Movement of Mineral Products in Peace and War," *Journal of the Royal Society of Arts* 78, no. 4030 (1930): 373–392, here: 375.

inconspicuous metal like tungsten, either in Britain or in British territory?"[39] The scale and scope of mechanized warfare and industrial developments over the course of the war only widened the array of resources needed by modern industry—in both peacetime and wartime.[40] Resource interdependence was going to intensify, not abate, in the interwar years.

Resource interdependence exhibited continuity over these years, but the geopolitical dynamics of the world were transformed by World War I. The United States had, by 1918, reached an apex of its power. A future of American dominance threatened to upend the prevailing international order and foreclose possibilities of great power aspirations, launching extremist reactions in Fascist Italy, Nazi Germany, and Imperial Japan.[41] The American threat, coupled with the experiences of wartime material difficulties, drove, intensified, and amplified the attractiveness of "bloc-thinking"—the strategies dreamed up to create self-sufficient, self-contained blocs of territory and trade networks to circumvent the potentially disastrous consequences of global interdependence on the one hand, and stabilize world order on the other.[42]

By far the most compelling solutions to the raw materials problem revolved around the consolidation or expansion of territory. Political power was associated with territorial bigness, an obsession which came in part from the fear of American power. Around the world, industrialists, economists, and state officials looked at the United States as a model for success and object of competition.[43] In the imaginaries of anxious state officials, the United States seemed to possess boundless resources. Indeed, the questions and debates around the relationship between raw material access and national autonomy (both political and economic) occurred against the backdrop of geopolitical rivalry with the United States.[44] The American threat lent new urgency not only to the idea of "living space," but also economic

---

39 Holland, "Proposed Review of the Mineral Resources and Industries of the Empire, and the Conditions Affecting Their Development," 402–403. Emphasis in original.

40 Eckes, *The United States and the Global Struggle for Minerals*, 25.

41 Tooze, *The Deluge*, 6–16. Tooze suggests that the end of World War I was more akin to the post-Cold War unipolar moment than the divided world of 1945.

42 Bloc-thinking preceded World War I, as did anxieties about rising American power. See Beckert, "American Danger."

43 Beckert, "American Danger."

44 Joseph Bohling, "Colonial or Continental Power? The Debate over Economic Expansion in Interwar France, 1925–1932," *Contemporary European History; Cambridge* 26, no. 2 (2017): 217–241.

space.[45] Embodied in the articulation of "great spaces" was a critique of, and alternative to, the prevailing liberal international order.[46] Similarly, embodied in the pan-ideological discourses of Pan-Europe or Pan-Asia was the possibility of material self-sufficiency and political-economic autonomy. World War I catalyzed these ideas. The war showed European state officials just how dependent they had become on the United States for raw materials, economic resources, and armaments.[47] Emulation was a form of competition, and the stakes were nothing less than national security and survival.

In Europe, the American threat pushed many intellectuals and officials to cast their eyes to the African continent.[48] The idea that Africa held a vast, untapped, almost inexhaustible supply of resources for European exploitation was indeed popular.[49] "Eurafrica," the idea of fusing together Africa and Europe into a massive economic unit, was developed by the Pan-European Union during the 1920s, and named in a 1929 article by its founder, the Austrian-Japanese intellectual Richard Coudenhove-Kalergi. Eurafrica became ubiquitous in European public political discourse.[50] Coudenhove-Kalergi published a programmatic book, *Pan-Europa*, in 1923, in which he set out the details and benefits of a Eurafrican bloc. By 1926, the book had been translated into every European language except Russian and Italian, and had sold over 16,000 copies, placing it among the best-selling books of those years.[51] Africa's vast territory was low in population

45 Willeke Sandler, "'Here Too Lies Our Lebensraum': Colonial Space as German Space," in *Heimat, Region, and Empire: Spatial Identities under National Socialism*, ed. Claus-Christian W. Szejnmann and Maiken Umbach (New York: Palgrave Macmillan, 2012), 148–165; Adam Tooze has also argued convincingly that "America should provide the pivot for our understanding of the Third Reich," in Adam Tooze, *The Wages of Destruction: The Making and Breaking of the Nazi Economy* (New York: Allen Lane, 2006), 10.

46 Joshua Derman, "Prophet of a Partitioned World: Ferdinand Fried, 'Great Spaces,' and the Dialectics of Deglobalization, 1929–1950," *Modern Intellectual History* 18, no. 3 (2021): 757–781.

47 Beckert, "American Danger."

48 Charles-Robert Ageron, "L'idée d'Eurafrique et Le Débat Colonial Franco-Allemand de l'entre-Deux-Guerres," *Revue d'histoire Moderne et Contemporaine* 22, no. 3 (1975): 446–475.

49 Beckert, "American Danger."

50 Benjamin J. Thorpe, "Eurafrica: A Pan-European Vehicle for Central European Colonialism (1923–1939)," *European Review* 26, no. 3 (2018): 503–513; the Pan-European Union was founded by Coudenhove-Kalergi and launched in 1923 with the publication of his book, which was essentially a program for the movement: Richard Coudenhove-Kalergi, *Pan-Europe* (New York: A. A. Knopf, 1926).

51 Anita Prettenhaler-Ziegerhofer, "Richard Nikolaus Coudenhove-Kalergi, Founder of the Pan-European Union, and the Birth of a 'New' Europe," in *Europe in Crisis: Intellectuals and*

density, but full of potential. There were rich deposits of copper and cobalt in the Belgian Congo, chrome in Rhodesia, and manganese in the Gold Coast, not to mention the gold and diamonds in the Union of South Africa. With further exploration and surveying, more could be found. For Coudenhove-Kalergi, Africa held out promise for smaller Central European countries to maintain a semblance of power balance among large, continental blocs.[52] Depending on others for raw materials or markets was a recipe for disaster in terms of national security. In the age of blockades and economic sanctions, forging a new Eurafrican bloc promised protection against American economic imperialism from the west, rising Bolshevism from the east, or a new, brewing war from within.[53]

Into the 1930s, memories of the blockades remained vivid, and military and business strategists wrote their plans with the threat of material shortage front of mind. In Japan, for example, the experience of trench warfare and efforts to achieve wartime autarky among the combatants convinced Japanese military personnel that battlefield success depended on resource self-sufficiency. This thinking prompted a shift in strategic thinking among the General Staff, which prioritized the control of resource-rich territories such as Manchuria and parts of mainland China. As early as 1918, Section Chief Ugaki Kazushige argued that the lesson of World War I was the need for "self-sufficiency." Japanese military and political success would depend, he argued, on creating "a self-sufficient economic sphere that extends to the continent and in particular to China." It would be imperative to merge "China and Japan into a single economic unit."[54] If Japan hoped to confront or defend itself from Western powers, access to the raw materials and labor power of China would be imperative.[55] The idea of a "Greater Japan," with a resource-rich periphery and industrializing core won favor among policy-making elites, and later evolved into a new vision of world order—the "Greater East Asian Co-Prosperity Sphere," a Japanese-dominated Asian bloc extending through China, the Korean peninsula, Taiwan, Manchuria,

the European Idea, 1917–1957, ed. Mark Hewitson and Matthew D'Auria (New York: Berghahn Books, 2012), 89–110, here: 107.

52 Coudenhove-Kalergi, *Pan-Europe*; Thorpe, "Eurafrica."

53 Prettenhaler-Ziegerhofer, "Richard Nikolaus Coudenhove-Kalergi, Founder of the Pan-European Union, and the Birth of a 'New' Europe."

54 Quoted in Jeremy A. Yellen, *The Greater East Asia Co-Prosperity Sphere: When Total Empire Met Total War* (Ithaca, NY: Cornell University Press, 2019), 12.

55 Gordon M. Berger, "The Three-Dimensional Empire: Japanese Attitudes and the New Order in Asia, 1937–1945," *The Japan Interpreter* 12, no. 3–4 (1978): 355–382.

French Indochina, and the Dutch East Indies.[56] Indeed, like the advocates of Eurafrica or Pan-Europe, the Greater East Asian Co-Prosperity Sphere envisioned an industrialized Japanese center with an expansive, integrated, resource-rich periphery.[57] Japanese intellectuals and political leaders saw liberal capitalism failing, crumbling Anglo-American power, and a new opportunity. They pushed for the creation of a "new order," imagining "a regional political-economic bloc over which Japan reigned supreme." By building a counter to "the white race bloc," peoples of East and Southeast Asia might be liberated from the Anglo-American sphere.[58] The vision for an East Asian sphere deliberately paralleled the British Empire's imperial bloc, or the Pan-American bloc in the Western Hemisphere.[59]

The Co-Prosperity Sphere would offer Japan a way to address its limited resource base, by integrating resource-rich territories producing minerals, rubber, rice, soybeans, and oil. In short, the Co-Prosperity could make Japan a "have" country. Before the Paris Peace Conference, future Prime Minister Konoe Fumimaro, then a young member of the Japanese House of Peers, recognized Japanese resource dependence as an existential matter. The "haves," such as Britain and the United States, possessed networks of colonies, territories, or resources that far outstripped those of "have nots" like Germany, Italy, and Japan. Without equal access to markets and resources, Konoe suggested that Japan might be compelled to "overthrow the *status quo* as Germany did before the war."[60] Japan was, for example, generally deficient in minerals.[61] Indeed, its steel industry was "almost completely

56 Some imagined that the Co-Prosperity Sphere might eventually include Australia and India. See Peter Duus, "The Greater East Asian Co-Prosperity Sphere: Dream and Reality," *The Journal of Northeast Asian History* 5, no. 1 (2008): 143–154; Yellen, *The Greater East Asia Co-Prosperity Sphere*. The Co-Prosperity Sphere was not only about economic self-sufficiency and great power status for Asian peoples. The concept of a Greater East Asian sphere included convivial elements of mutuality, cooperation, solidarity, co-existence, and of course, co-prosperity. The commonalities of Asian cultures, languages, and experiences of oppression at western hands helped drive the concept.

57 L. H. Gann, "Reflections on the Japanese and German Empires of World War II," in *The Japanese Wartime Empire, 1931–1945*, ed. Peter Duus et al. (Princeton: Princeton University Press, 1996), 335–362.

58 Yellen, *The Greater East Asia Co-Prosperity Sphere*, 4.

59 Duus, "The Greater East Asian Co-Prosperity Sphere: Dream and Reality."

60 Quoted in Yellen, *The Greater East Asia Co-Prosperity Sphere*, 14.

61 Catherine Porter, "Mineral Deficiency Versus Self-Sufficiency in Japan," *Far Eastern Survey* 5, no. 2 (1936): 9–14; Harry Foster Bain, *Ores and Industry in the Far East: The Influence of Key Mineral Resources on the Development of Oriental Civilization* (New York: Council on Foreign

dependent upon water-borne imports," and a Japanese war economy would be highly vulnerable to blockade measures.[62] The Greater East Asian Co-Prosperity Sphere was an ideational articulation of Japan's perceived needs to challenge and subvert the prevailing world order—not only for its own economic and political security, but to take its rightful place in world affairs.[63] After acquiring its first colonies, the imperial division of labor intensified over the ensuing decades—Japan relied increasingly on its peripheries for raw material inputs and as markets for its manufactured goods.[64]

Tellingly, these regionalist responses to the American threat were often framed in terms of the Monroe Doctrine, which famously reserved the Americas for the United States. The Greater East Asian Co-Prosperity Sphere, for example, articulated (among other things) the notion of an "Asian Monroe Doctrine," and embodied the belief that Japan could become a great power as the leader of an Asian sphere.[65] Coudenhove-Kalergi similarly believed that the best response to American power was to proclaim a Monroe Doctrine for the Continent: "Europe for the Europeans!"[66] Nazi jurist Carl Schmitt would similarly advocate replacing the liberal international order with "great spaces," based on the non-interventionist principles of the Monroe Doctrine.[67] For Britain and France, both of which already possessed expansive colonial empires, the Monroe Doctrine was the metaphor mobilized to advocate for imperial blocs. Leopold Amery, a conservative British imperialist and staunch advocate of tariff reform, advocated for

Relations, 1927); United States Strategic Bombing Survey, *Coals and Metals in Japan's War Economy* (Washington: Basic Materials Division, 1947).

62 United States Strategic Bombing Survey, *Coals and Metals in Japan's War Economy*, 63.

63 Berger, "The Three-Dimensional Empire," 555–557.

64 Manchuria would become Japan's storehouse. Korea was similarly used as a source of raw materials and cheap labor—it also happened to be relatively rich in tungsten. Chad Denton, "More Valuable than Gold: Korean Tungsten and the Japanese War Economy, 1910 to 1945," *Seoul Journal of Korean Studies* 26, no. 2 (2014): 361–395; Michael A. Barnhart, *Japan Prepares for Total War: The Search for Economic Security, 1919–1941* (Ithaca: Cornell University Press, 1987).

65 George H. Blakeslee, "The Japanese Monroe Doctrine," *Foreign Affairs* 11, no. 4 (1933): 671–681; Sven Saaler, "The Construction of Regionalism in Modern Japan: Kodera Kenkichi and His 'Treatise on Greater Asianism' (1916)," *Modern Asian Studies* 41, no. 6 (2007): 1261–1294.

66 Coudenhove-Kalergi, *Pan-Europe.*

67 Carl Schmitt, "The Grossraum Concept of International Law with a Ban on Intervention for Spatially Foreign Powers: A Contribution to the Concept of *Reich* in International Law," in *Writings on War*, trans. Timothy Nunan (Malden, MA: Polity, 2011), 75–124; Derman, "Prophet of a Partitioned World."

a "British Monroe Doctrine," marrying together the raw material wealth of the Empire with the skill and industry of British manufacturers.[68] Amery believed that the global balance of power—and Britain's geopolitical pre-eminence—would be best-secured through the creation of large economic blocs.[69] Speaking to the British Imperial Council of Commerce in 1925, Amery contrasted the development of the United States' territories with those of the British Empire. The United States had developed "wealth exceeding anything the world has ever seen before," while the British Empire had failed to keep up despite having "far greater and far richer territories."[70] Within the Empire, Amery promoted white settlement schemes and preferential tariffs. Outside the Empire, he supported Japan's position in Manchuria, Italy's in Ethiopia, and Germany as the leader of a Central European bloc. Nation-statism was economically inefficient, he argued, given the scale and market needs of modern industry.[71] In France, Minister of the Colonies Albert Sarraut argued that the development of colonies went hand in hand not only with national security, but also with national prosperity and competitiveness. He had been championing French economic autarky for a long time, and colonies were central to his plans. Sarraut reorganized the Conseil supérieur des colonies, empowering it to create plans for investment in public works and commercial diversification. This investment, he suggested, would help unlock colonial potential and ensure political stability.[72] For empire boosters like Sarraut, "The immense treasure of commodities and raw materials that our colonial domains possess will alone be able to free us from the foreign markets that fleece us."[73]

---

68 L. S. Amery, *My Political Life*, vol. II: War and Peace, 1914–1929 (London: Hutchinson, 1953), 162; Max Beloff, *Imperial Sunset: Dream of Commonwealth, 1921–42* (Macmillan, 1989), chapter 6; see also "The Commonwealth and the League," *The Round Table* 26, no. 104 (1936): 655–674.

69 Richard S. Grayson, "Leo Amery's Imperialist Alternative to Appeasement in the 1930s," *Twentieth Century British History* 17, no. 4 (2006): 489–515.

70 Leopold Amery, "Inter-Imperial Trade," speech delivered at the annual luncheon of the British Imperial Council of Commerce, June 10, 1925, Churchill Archives Center, Churchill College, Cambridge University, papers of Leopold Amery, 1/4/12.

71 L. S. Amery, "The British Empire and the Pan-European Idea," *Journal of the Royal Institute of International Affairs* 9, no. 1 (1930): 1–22, here: 3.

72 Albert Sarraut, *La mise en valeur des colonies françaises, avec onze cartes en noir et en couleurs*, Bibliothèque politique et économique (Paris: Payot & cie, 1923); Martin Thomas, "Albert Sarraut, French Colonial Development, and the Communist Threat, 1919–1930," *The Journal of Modern History* 77, no. 4 (2005): 917–955, here: 930–931.

73 Albert Sarraut, "Nationalisons l'idée Coloniale," *Europe Nouvelle*, no. 428 (May 1, 1926): 579–581, here: 580; quoted in Bohling, "Colonial or Continental Power?," 218.

The Great Depression: Autonomy, Autarky, and Acquisition

At the same time Sarraut was laying plans for colonial development and Britain turned to its Empire, Germany, Italy, and Japan complained that they needed colonies to source scarce raw materials and provide outlets for their manufactured goods. In 1926, President of the German *Reichsbank* (and future Nazi Minister of Economy) Hjalmar Schacht stated: "The fight for raw materials plays the most important part in world politics, an even greater role than before the war […] Germany's only solution is her acquisition of colonies."[74]

Global raw material prices had been falling leading up to 1929 but fell catastrophically thereafter. The immediate reaction to the general price fall was a general rise in tariffs. One by one, countries worked through partial, successive, or wholesale changes to their tariffs to prevent the import of foreign goods and protect their national markets.[75] After the collapse of the gold standard, trade became increasingly oriented around rival currency blocs, centered on Britain, the United States, Germany, Japan, and France.[76] In a world of floating exchange rates, acquiring goods from abroad required foreign exchange. Countries like Germany and Italy, which struggled to export goods into certain markets, had difficulties earning sufficient foreign exchange, and endured chronic balance of payments problems. Unable to acquire the necessary foreign exchange to purchase raw materials in sufficient quantities, the "have nots" restricted their imports, searched for substitutes, or exploited raw materials uneconomically.[77] They also made plans to acquire resource-rich territories.

Although short on colonial territory, Italy and Germany began ambitious autarkic projects. As historian Nicholas Mulder describes it, countries like Germany, Italy, and Japan pursued an expansionist autarky, in which they sought to eliminate their dependence on foreign imports of industrial raw

74 "Says Germany Needs Colonies to Pay Allies: Reichsbank Head Holds Dawes Plan Obligations Cannot Be Met Without Them," *New York Times*, May 26, 1926.

75 League of Nations Economic Committee, *Report to the Council on the Work of the Forty-first Session* (Geneva, 1934), 7–8.

76 France remained on gold until 1936. It formed a "gold bloc" along with other countries sticking to the gold standard—Belgium, Luxembourg, the Netherlands, Poland, Italy, and Switzerland.

77 International Consultative Group, "Some notes and reflections concerning the problem of raw materials," May 5, 1937, League of Nations Archives, Geneva (henceforth LON) R4433/10A/22798/25880.

materials, foodstuffs, and manufactured goods. They did this by investing in synthetics research, developing low-grade ore deposits, gaining technology transfers, or through territorial expansion.[78] There were, however, real limits to what the "have nots" could achieve. Italy, for example, had virtually no petroleum, produced only 20 percent of its iron ore, and had to import all of its coking coal. As it turned out, Italy could not reduce its dependence on foreign sources of iron ore, coal, copper, crude oil, chromite, nickel, tin, tungsten, or manganese.[79] Autarkic policies put greater pressure on Italy's foreign exchange, which made it even more difficult to procure industrial raw materials. Autarky was far from being economically efficient. Both countries spent lavishly on developing internal resources—synthetic fuels, agricultural products, and low-grade mineral deposits.[80] But certain raw materials existed only in foreign territories. Without commercial or political control, or without a shared currency, acquiring these materials would be tricky. In the wake of the Great Depression, and especially after the failed League sanctions against Italy during the Abyssinian crisis in 1935, these autarkic strategies were radicalized.

Similarly in Germany, pursuing self-sufficiency required an increasingly centrally directed and managed economy.[81] Short on mineral inputs for its steelworks and foreign exchange with which to purchase them, Germany consolidated a *Reichsmark* bloc through a series of bilateral clearing arrangements with smaller countries in southeastern Europe.[82] Germany was in a

78 Nicholas Mulder, "The Economic Weapon: Interwar Internationalism and the Rise of Sanctions, 1914–1945," (PhD diss., Columbia University, 2019), 531–532.

79 Leith, "Mineral Resources and Peace," 519–520.

80 Jeffrey A. Frieden, *Global Capitalism: Its Fall and Rise in the Twentieth Century* (New York: W.W. Norton & Company, 2006), see chapter 9, "The Turn to Autarky," 195–228.

81 There were continuities across Weimar and Nazi market regulations, and the Nazi regime was never a full-fledged command economy. But the Nazi Four Year Plan and rearmament program required tighter control over foreign exchange and raw material purchases and distribution. Dieter Ziegler, "'A Regulated Market Economy': New Perspectives on the Nature of the Economic Order of the Third Reich, 1933–1939," in *Business in the Age of Extremes*, ed. Hartmut Berghoff, Jurgen Kocka, and Dieter Ziegler (New York: Cambridge University Press, 2012), 139–152.

82 David S. Jacks and Dennis Novy, "Trade Blocs and Trade Wars during the Interwar Period," *Asian Economic Policy Review* 15, no. 1 (2020): 119–136; Stephen G. Gross, *Export Empire: German Soft Power in Southeastern Europe, 1890–1945* (New York: Cambridge University Press, 2015). Bilateral trade involves the direct balancing of trade between two countries. Multilateralism, on the other hand, means that a country can import from one country, export to another, and thereby balance its payments among its various trading

much-weakened mineral position after World War I—the Treaty of Versailles stripped Germany of its colonies and its mineral-rich territories in Europe. During the interwar period, Germany imported practically 100 percent of its chrome and tungsten ore requirements.[83] Moreover, Germany was almost wholly reliant on Russia for its manganese ore—indeed, manganese was one reason among many that Russia figured so prominently in Nazi conceptualizations of *Lebensraum*.[84] Although German capital owned zinc mines in Poland, chrome ore mines in Turkey, and bauxite in Greece and Yugoslavia, it still needed to acquire foreign exchange to procure their outputs. As such, the German economy depended fundamentally on these bilateral agreements in which countries accepted German manufactures in lieu of currency.[85] Forging this sphere of influence was one German response to its deficiencies and ambitions.

Pressure was mounting, not only on the German economy, but externally, to resolve the raw materials problem peacefully. In January 1931, Joseph Goebbels declared to the Berlin Branch of the National Socialist Party that it would be dangerous for the world not to concede colonial demands, "because some day the bomb will explode."[86] Japan installed a puppet regime in Manchuria in 1932, and Italy invaded and annexed Abyssinia in 1935–36. If Japan got Manchuria and Italy got Abyssinia, what, Schacht asked, does Germany get? The "have" powers, Schacht added, had retreated into economic nationalism, placing their raw materials behind tariff and currency barriers. Germany, he insisted, must have raw materials within its own territories, and these colonial territories must be part of Germany's monetary system.[87] Raw materials were diplomatic leverage—an economic weapon to be wielded by the "haves." Whether or not the weapon was ever used was beside the point, so long as the threat persisted. Freedom to buy today, the "have nots" argued, did not mean freedom to buy tomorrow.

---

partners. See Solomos Solomou, "Trade Protection in the 1930s," in *The Interwar Depression in an International Context*, ed. Harold James and Elisabeth Müller-Luckner (Munich: R. Oldenbourg, 2002), 139–158, here: 151.

83 James Rubinfeld, "Chrom und Chromerz im Welthandel. Deutschland als Chromverbraucher," *Metallwirtschaft* 39 (1928): 1045–1046.

84 A.H. Curtis, *Manganese Ores* (London: J. Murray, 1919), 74.

85 Leith, "Mineral Resources and Peace," 519.

86 Quoted in Royal Institute of International Affairs, *Raw Materials and Colonies*, 58.

87 Hjalmar Schacht, "Germany's Colonial Demands," *Foreign Affairs* 15, no. 2 (1937): 223–234.

There was certainly substance to their complaints. Cross-border trade flows fell dramatically during and after the Great Depression. But the trade policies of the 1930s—whether tariffs, quotas, or exchange controls—might not have been the most important factor reducing trade flows during the period. Instead, as economic historian Kevin O'Rourke has recently argued, these policies had major effects on the *direction* of those flows.[88] Britain, France, Japan, and the Netherlands turned increasingly toward their empires for trade. Britain sought insulation through Imperial Preference, which was extended through the Ottawa Agreements of 1932. Meanwhile, France cobbled together a commercial policy aimed at self-sufficiency within its empire.[89] France maintained close trade ties with its colonies, and after the Colonial Customs Act of April 13, 1928, the "assimilated areas" (including Indochina, Madagascar, Guadeloupe, French Guiana, Martinique, and Reunion) enjoyed free trade with France, but maintained tariffs for others. New Caledonia and other territories also had tariffs which strongly favored France.[90] These shifting tariff policies turned imperial trade increasingly inward. As a percentage of total French imports, the colonies averaged nearly 12 percent between 1925 and 1929. By 1932, the colonial share of imports was nearly 21 percent and reached 28.5 percent by 1936. A similar trend can be seen with the colonial percentage of exports, more than doubling from an average 16.3 percent between 1925 and 1929 to 33.4 percent in 1936.[91]

The Japanese case was even more extreme. Japanese possessions (except the leased territory of Kwantung) belonged to a customs union with Japan, imposing the same import duties.[92] By 1937, 83.3 percent of Taiwan's imports came from Japan and 92.5 percent of its exports were sent to Japan. For Korea, those figures were 85 percent and 87.4 percent, respectively. Japan's share of Manchuria's imports leapt from 52.8 percent to 75.1 percent in the single year between 1937 and 1938.[93] To be sure, Japan's inward turn

88 Kevin Hjortshøj O'Rourke, "Two Great Trade Collapses: The Interwar Period and Great Recession Compared," *IMF Economic Review* 66, no. 3 (2018): 418–439.

89 France Annual Report, Economic (A), 1936, United Kingdom National Archives, Kew (henceforth UKNA), Treasury: Papers of Sir Frederick Leith Ross, T 188/167.

90 Royal Institute of International Affairs, 37–43.

91 Conseil National Economique: Enquêtes, "La protection et les Encouragements à Donner par les Pouvoirs Publics aux Diverses Branches de l'Economie Nationale," 18 juillet 1936, Tableau V, Archives National, Pierrefitte, 20110147 Box 18; France Annual Report, Economic (A), 1936, UKNA, Treasury: Papers of Sir Frederick Leith Ross, T 188/167.

92 Royal Institute of International Affairs, *Raw Materials and Colonies*, 45.

93 Yellen, *The Greater East Asia Co-Prosperity Sphere*, 18.

and dependence upon its empire was also spurred by the mobilization of resources required by the onset of the Sino-Japanese War.

Japan had managed to contain the economic crisis by allowing the yen to depreciate, stimulating its exports—especially cotton textiles. Devaluation for Germany, on the other hand, would have entailed a heavier burden of foreign debt service, not to mention added expense to raw material imports.[94] After following Britain off gold in 1931, the Japanese economy turned upward. New Finance Minister Korekiyo Takahashi set out on an expansionary policy—he created policies through which the Bank of Japan would purchase government bonds, expanding the money supply and initiating public spending. 1933 was the nadir of the Great Depression for most of Europe and the United States, but in Japan, growth rates topped 10 percent. In 1934, the economy grew 8.7 percent. The devaluation of the yen undercut international competition and strengthened Japan's own competitiveness in foreign markets.[95] But as trade increasingly turned inward on currency blocs, Japan had greater difficulty purchasing from the sterling or dollar areas. Moreover, Japan's manufactures found greater resistance in a world of heightened tariffs and protectionism—not to mention racism—and the collapse in the price of silk made foreign exchange even harder to come by. Looking to East Asia, Japan adopted autarkic industrial policies and set out to free itself of import dependence.

The eventual full-scale war in China can indeed be thought of as the first shots of World War II. But it also consolidated for Japan an economic bloc centered on northeast Asia. Looking south, Japan's "Southward advance" became a pillar of its foreign policy from around 1936, and once the Netherlands and the French were defeated by Germany in mainland Europe, Japan's action was swift. Japanese troops swept into Southeast Asia, replacing European colonial overlords.[96] Southeast Asia possessed rich mineral deposits which could mostly satisfy Japanese consumption—the

94 Draft Section for Raw Materials Committee, Frederick Leith-Ross, July 19, 1937, LON R4433/10A/22798/27805; "General Aspects of the Problem as Brought out by the Principal Statements made and Publications since September 1935," February 24, 1937, UKNA, Treasury: Registered Files: Finance Files, T 160/859/2.

95 Hideaki Miyajima, "Japanese Industrial Policy during the Interwar Period: Strategies for International and Domestic Competition," *Business and Economic History* 21 (1992): 270–279.

96 Mark R. Peattie, "Nanshin: The 'Southward Advance,' 1931–1941, as a Prelude to the Japanese Occupation of Southeast Asia," in *The Japanese Wartime Empire, 1931–1945*, ed. Peter Duus et al. (Princeton: Princeton University Press, 1996), 189–242.

Philippines, Borneo, the Dutch East Indies, Malaya, and even New Caledonia could be developed for tungsten, manganese, chrome, bauxite, nickel, and petroleum. Indochina and Thailand, together with Manchuria, would be vital sources of foodstuffs.[97] In an era of total war, consolidating an autarkic regional bloc took precedence over the creation of an "Asian community."[98]

The onset of global depression exacerbated the crisis facing interwar authoritarian regimes. As one study on the raw materials problem put it in 1937, the world appeared to be locked in a "vicious circle," in which:

> "[T]he fear of war prevents progress towards a system of freer trade and migration, while the restrictions on trade and migration, and the consequent immobilization of raw materials and credit, powerfully increases the danger—and hence the fear—of war."[99]

Economic measures were not sufficient to break the circle. There was an undeniable pervasiveness to the belief that a direct relationship existed between political control over sources of raw materials (including colonial territories) and economic well-being.[100] The notion of "security" had grown to encompass military and economic dimensions.[101] In any case, the concerns of the "have nots" were never going to be settled by some commercial agreement, since commercial access was only one aspect of their anxieties. If blocs were a form of national security, then they were also a means toward industrial self-sufficiency, which set the stage for a prolonged global war.[102]

---

97 Yellen, *The Greater East Asia Co-Prosperity Sphere*, 80–81.

98 Sven Saaler, "The Construction of Regionalism in Modern Japan: Kodera Kenkichi and His 'Treatise on Greater Asianism' (1916)," *Modern Asian Studies* 41, no. 6 (2007): 1261–1294; Duus, "The Greater East Asian Co-Prosperity Sphere: Dream and Reality," 150.

99 International Consultative Group, "Some notes and reflections concerning the problem of raw materials," May 5, 1937, LON, R4433/10A/22798/25880.

100 Ibid.

101 Joseph A. Maiolo, "Armaments and International Instability between the Two World Wars," in *Disarmament and Arms Control in the History of International Politics: From the Nineteenth Century to the Present*, ed. Tamara Enomoto (Tokyo: Nihon Keizai Hyouronsha, 2017), 71–90.

102 Shumpei Takemori, "Comment on 'Trade Blocks and Trade Wars During the Interwar Period,'" *Asian Economic Policy Review* 15, no. 1 (2020): 139–140.

Conclusion

After angrily leaving France in 1919, Charles Leith devoted himself to the problem of mineral interdependence. His proposals ranged from the restoration of nineteenth-century *laissez-faire* commerce, to national stockpiling programs, to supranational control over the world's scarce mineral resources.[103] Arthur Salter, the longtime Director of the Economic and Financial Section of the League of Nations, suggested that the Great Depression presented an opportunity to eliminate resource competition as a cause of war. The crisis, he suggested, could prompt new, much needed cooperation among states to devise international rules to make raw materials freely available on equal terms.[104] The Depression certainly marked a turning point, but not the sort that Salter had envisioned. Instead, the economic crisis exacerbated an existential crisis for the authoritarian states. The Depression collided with pre-existing tensions over mineral access and the newer threat of American global dominance. Instead of international cooperation, the triple-threat crisis drove illiberal modes of governance, economic nationalism, and bids by authoritarian regimes to extricate themselves from webs of globality and interdependence—and prevent future crises.

All powers in the interwar period faced similar global challenges, confronted the same global structures, and inhabited an increasingly intervisible world.[105] But they operated under different constraints and possibilities. For the three-headed crisis facing authoritarian regimes—resource access, ascendent American power, and global depression—territorial expansion represented a blanket solution. Global thinking in terms of blocs—as mechanisms to protect against resource denial—helped drive expansionist autarkic ambitions and quests for autonomy by the "have nots," but also attempts to wall off political and economic space by the "haves." Indeed, the vulnerabilities engendered by mineral interdependence played an important role in the inward turns taken by the British Empire, the French Empire, and the United States, and the outward turns taken by Japan, Italy, and Germany. Continued resource weakness during the trans-war period can

103 Leith, "International Control of Minerals," 8A.

104 Mats Ingulstad, "Regulating the Regulators: The League of Nations and the Problem of Raw Materials," in *The Political Economy of Resource Regulation: An International and Comparative History, 1850–2015*, ed. Andreas R. D. Sanders, Pål Thonstad Sandvik, and Espen Storli (Toronto: UBC Press, 2019), 231–258; Arthur Salter, *The Causes of War: Economic, Industrial, Racial, Religious, Scientific, and Political* (New York: The Macmillan Company, 1932).

105 Kotkin, "Modern Times," 114.

even help explain the authoritarian turns taken in the domestic politics of each "have not" state. An aggressively expansionist, nationalistic, and illiberal mode of governance promised to throw off the economic burdens and political limitations of the Versailles world order. Rather than live at the mercy of foreign powers, authoritarian regimes carved out spheres of influence that could be self-contained and independent.

The conditions for the hostile trading and currency blocs of the 1930s were created by globalized resource interdependence and World War I. On the one hand, the nodes of mineral production and consumption were relatively set from the turn of the century. On the other hand, World War I was a critical juncture—both ideologically and materially—in which the imperial tensions of the late-nineteenth and early-twentieth centuries were accelerated and then built into the Versailles world order. In some ways, the blocs were already in place by 1919, awaiting a catalyst. Certainly, the experience of the blockades, and the sudden realization that industrial production depended on formerly obscure, distant minerals like manganese and tungsten, pushed officials to consider the potential virtues of self-sufficiency. The dangers of nineteenth-century globalization and interdependence were exposed by total war, which also rewarded states' abilities to organize a war economy on a hitherto unseen scale, harnessing expertise and knowledge to coordinate global supplies of munitions, food, labor, soldiers, and resources. The organizational prowess exhibited during the war also pushed policymakers to entertain the continuation of centralization and rationalization. This not only spurred liberal fantasies like supranational governance through the League of Nations, but also regionalist world-ordering into Great Power blocs, or other visions of illiberal, anti-global world order.

Territorial space was not necessarily intrinsic to power—but the raw material and agricultural wealth embedded in the territories were. If minerals were sources of power and security, then subduing and controlling a large economic bloc was an attractive solution. Braiding together the problems of mineral interdependence, the "American danger," and the Great Depression, we can see how authoritarian regimes sought resolution by looking outward, while the "haves" could turn inward. If steel was the foundation of national prosperity and security, then secure access to these far-flung minerals was a matter of life and death—economically, industrially, and militarily. Access to these minerals, or their refined products, was an existential matter. Lack of access was a structural problem. Authoritarian expansion was the only escape from the intolerable constraints of Versailles and the three-headed crises faced down by the "have nots." For a moment during World War II, it looked as though the Axis powers might succeed. Then, remarkably, the defeated authoritarian regimes were rehabilitated and incorporated into the post-1945 US sphere of influence—largely resolving their longstanding raw material problems.

III. Identities and Ideologies of Crisis

Towards Native "Fascism From Above": Crisis of Legitimacy, "Legal Revolution", and the Reshaping of Polish Politics in the Mid-1930s

Grzegorz Krzywiec

Introduction[1]

The short-lived experience of a constitutional regime, modelled on the system of the Third French Republic in the 1920s, had struck many Poles as something tantamount to anarchy, given the corruption of parliamentary politicians and the rabid social, economic, and ethnic conflicts. The newly reborn state faced multiple dire challenges. Firstly, it had to unite three markedly distinct lands, separated from each other for the previous 123 years, during which time they had functioned under different administrative, legal, and social systems. Secondly, it had to build new infrastructure for the new nation-state. Thirdly, it had to secure its borders and win their international recognition. As such, the new Poland was reborn after bitter wars with six out of seven neighbors, of which the conflict with Soviet Russia (1919–1921) was the most pregnant with meaning as a multinational state with about 60 percent ethnic Poles, the majority of whom were of peasant origins,[2] the rest Ukrainians, Germans, Jews and other smaller groups.[3] Sooner or later, the Polish political elites had to face these challenges.[4] The actual base of this

---

1 I would like at this point to thank very much Stefan Schubert and the editing team for their critical comments which made this text clearer. The article was prepared during my scholarship funded by the Alexander von Humboldt-Stiftung.

2 Dietmar Müller, *Bodeneigentum und Nation. Rumänien, Jugoslawien und Polen im europäischen Vergleich, 1918–1948*, (Göttingen: Wallstein Verlag, 2020), 291–296.

3 See Mieczysław B.B. Biskupski, "The Second Republic. The geopolitics of failure," in *Interwar East Central Europe, 1918–1914. The Failure of Democracy-building, the Fate of Minorities*, ed. Sabrina R. Ramet (London and New York: Routledge, Taylor & Francis Group, 2020), 35–74, here 43.

4 For a thought-provoking overview of these dilemmas, see Jochen Böhler, *Civil War in Central Europe, 1918–1921. The Reconstruction of Poland* (Oxford: Oxford University Press,

constitutional period was narrow at its outset and did not widen as many had expected. The general opinion was that the parliamentary regime (and consequently liberal democracy) represented the political class itself.[5] As political scientist Sabrina Ramet notes: "corruption and financial scandals were rife in these years".[6] Polish national politics in those days "seemed to be spiraling out of control".[7] The first years of liberal democracy in Poland were dominated by parties and groups of the nationalist right, and it was therefore these circles that symbolized the crisis in the democratic system.

The *Sanacja* as an Authoritarian Regime: Definition and Controversies

In this regard, Marshal Józef Piłsudski (1867–1935) as a prominent Polish leader, ex-socialist militant and, first and foremost, the charismatic figurehead of Poland's re-established independence, seemed perfectly suited to be head of state and the leader of a new political regime.[8] From the early 1920s on, Piłsudski gathered around him a large part of the pro-independence intelligentsia, as well as military men of the Polish Legions—a military formation led by him during World War I. In mid-May 1926, along with a group of his most loyal officers, he staged a bloody coup (with some 400 deaths), leading to the resignation of the government and the democratically elected president.[9] Until the end of his life, Piłsudski remained the most important person in the state, holding the posts of Minister for Military Affairs,

---

2018) and Klaus Richter, *Fragmentation in East Central Europe, Poland and the Baltics, 1915–1929* (Oxford: Oxford University Press, 2020), 89–101, 108–131.

5 For a synthesis of this period, see Brian Porter-Szücs, *Poland in the Modern World: Beyond Martyrdom* (Chichester, Wiley Blackwell, 2014), 91–95. Piotr Wandycz, "The Second Republic," *Polish Review*, 54, no.2 (2009), 159–171, here 165–167.

6 Sabrina Ramet, "An Introduction," in *Interwar East Central Europa, 1918–1941*, 1–34, here: 16.

7 Biskupski, "The Polish Second Republic," 45.

8 Paul Brykczyński, *Primed for Violence: Murder, Antisemitism, and Democratic Politics in Interwar Poland* (Madison: WI: University of Wisconsin Press, 2016). In general, see also Joseph Rothschild, *Piłsudski's Coup d'Etat*, (New York: Columbia University Press, 1966), 284–286. For a more regional context for the coup, see Richter, *Fragmentation in East Central Europe*, 303–305.

9 For a synthetic description of the last days of the Polish parliamentary system, as well as the course of the coup itself, see Ramet, "An Introduction," 15–16.

General Inspector of the Armed Forces (a position created especially for him) and Head of the War Council. In this sense, politically, the May coup was directed against liberal democracy as the political system that made possible the rule and *de facto* hegemony of the well-organized nationalist right.

Therefore, the Piłsudski military coup was widely supported by the liberal intelligentsia, socialists, and even communists at first —and by a large majority of Jews. Initially, the new regime often heeded the various demands placed on it by these sections of society. Piłsudski's regime owed its stability to the openly enjoyed state patriotism or even state nationalism that characterized many Poles of the time. An important point of reference for the new regime was anti-Bolshevism, which admittedly did not take militant forms, but fundamentally defined the conservative social face of the political system.[10]

From the very beginning, both Piłsudski himself and his supporters saw the post-1926 regime as an alternative to liberal democracy, disregarding and even ostentatiously rejecting all doctrine, obtuse ideas, and dogmas. The term *Sanacja* (Latin: *Sanatio*—healing, curing) signified the intention to repair the system that was constituted under liberal democracy (1921–1926). In the democratic-liberal system, Piłsudski's supporters challenged the power of political parties (i.e., party cronyism/*partyjniactwo*) as the greatest ailment. Therefore, the role of parliament was essentially limited to controlling—though the military and police were excluded—the functioning of the state, as well as representing currents of thought in society.[11]

Shortly after the military coup in 1926, Piłsudski pursued a rather moderate course, sometimes dubbed a "semi-constitutional guided democracy".[12] By creating a government party, the Nonpartisan Bloc for

10 Stephan Lehnstaedt, *Der Vergessene Polnisch-Sowjetische Krieg 1919–1921 und die Entstehung des modernen Osteuropa* (München: C.H. Beck, 2019). For a different perspective, see also, Jerzy Borzęcki, *The Soviet-Polish Peace of 1921 and the Creation of Interwar Europe*, (New Haven: Yale University Press, 2008).

11 Waldemar Paruch, "Parlament w państwie autorytarnym," in *Józef Piłsudski a parlamentaryzm Polski*, ed. Arkadiusz Adamczyk (Warszawa: Instytut Piłsudskiego w Warszawie, 2009), 15–39.

12 See Antony Polonsky, "The Second Republic in Contemporary Perspective," in *Poland between Wars 1918–1939*, ed. Timothy Wiles, (Bloomington: Indiana Polish Studies Center, 1989), 2–4; Polonsky, *Politics in Independent Poland, 1921–1939. The Crisis of Constitutional Government* (Oxford: Oxford University Press, 1972), VII. For better contextualization of the early *Sanacja* regime, see also António Costa Pinto, *Fascism, Corporatism and the Crafting of Authoritarian Institutions in Inter-War European Dictatorships*, in *Rethinking Fascism and Dictatorship in Europe*, ed. António Costa Pinto and Aristotle Kallis, (New York: Palgrave

Cooperation with the Government (*Bezpartyjny Blok Współpracy z Rządem, BBWR*), that embraced a broad coalition of groups, Piłsudski and his supporters hoped to keep parliament and a large part of public opinion under their control.[13]

The Piłsudski-ites' vagueness on various issues was, however, significant. Combined with the dynamic rhetorical invocation of "imponderables", moral cleansing, and a strong state,[14] it gained considerable support in public opinion and had four intrinsic features: 1) A very heterogeneous internal structure; 2) a low level of institutionalization; 3) numerous external affiliated organizations and 4) the volatility of its political camp. Nevertheless, this statism (*pro-państwowość*) promoted by the ruling camp had elements of a multicultural approach to nation-building, including the rights of ethnic minorities and women, hints of secularism and, above all, a new concept of national identity, one more inclusive than the ethno-religious, integral nationalism cherished by the right.[15]

One of the best manifestations of this was the establishment in 1927 of a pro-governmental organization based on county representatives (*starostwa*), the aforementioned *BBWR*. It was created from above to bring together local social and political elites, but not to organize or mobilize the social masses. In this regard, the *BBWR*'s emphasis was placed on non-ideological support for Piłsudski and his ruling group. The group gathered supporters from the extreme left (including syndicalists), from the Christian Democrats and social peasant circles, conservatives and even monarchists.[16]

The need for a common ideology, or rather legitimacy for the new authority, was often replaced by the will of the dictator himself or pure

---

Macmillan, 2014), 87–117, here 103–104. Biskupski called the Piłsudski regime "a virtual military dictatorship," 44. Borodziej characterized the regime as "extra-constitutional," see Włodzimierz Borodziej, *Geschichte Polens in 20. Jahrhundert*, (München, C.H. Beck, 2010), 162–164.

13 Andrzej Chojnowski, *Piłsudczycy u władzy: Dzieje Bezpartyjnego Bloku Współpracy z Rządem* (Wrocław: Ossolineum, 1986).

14 On the rhetoric of the *Sanacja* in the first years after the May coup, see Eva Plach, *The Clash of Moral Nations: Cultural politics in Piłsudski's Poland* (Athens: Ohio University Press, 2006), 6–7, 15–16.

15 On the nationalist right in the early 1920s, see Paul Brykczyński, *Primed for Violence*, 10–25. See also Grzegorz Krzywiec, "Catholic authoritarians or fascists as such? The Polish rightist subculture turns fascist, 1919–1939," in *Conservatives and right radicals in interwar Europe*, ed. Marco Bresciani (London, New York: Routledge, 2021), 143–166, here 143–146.

16 Chojnowski, *Piłsudczycy u władzy*, 98.

improvisation. The first important tightening of the regime's course towards authoritarian rule after 1929 therefore, resulted not so much from some ideological project but from a response to the challenges of the time, such as the economic crisis or the consolidation of the political opposition. This combination of factors gave rise to a peculiar cult of the state and the pro-state ideology embodied by Piłsudski himself. The role of Piłsudski as a bonding figure for the *Sanacja* is key to understanding the authoritarian regime's evolution after 1926: The dictator was not only seen as the true father of Polish independence, the undisputed leader of the Polish army, and the victor over Soviet Russia (1920), but was also considered the main guarantor of Polish sovereignty.[17]

The cult of the state, which was organically mixed with the cult of personality, often took peculiar, even caricatured forms (e.g., Piłsudski's name day was an unofficial state holiday) and corresponded quite well with the conviction of many Piłsudski-ites that they, as actual participants in the struggle for the liberation of Poland, were the elite of Polish independence. The emphasis on the state was important because the state, as opposed to the nation, which was commonly understood ethno-linguistically, could integrate all groups living on Polish territory.[18] After the May coup, an important and growing role in the country was played by both the military pedigree of Piłsudski's main supporters and the social background of the ruling camp in the army.[19] A side effect of the army's growing influence each year, and also of officers in public life, was the constant and widening brutalization of political culture, but also the systematic barbarization of language and political customs. Everyday manifestations of these practices were not only political and administrative repressions against opponents of the *Sanacja* (including the demonstration trial in Brest, 1930, and even the first concentration camp in Bereza Kartuska, 1934), but also ordinary political corruption.

17 See Heidi Hein-Kircher, *Der Piłsudski-Kult und seine Bedeutung für den polnischen Staat 1926–1939, Materialien und Studien zur Ostmitteleuropa-Forschung*, Band 9 (Marburg: Verlag Herder-Institut, 2002).

18 Brykczyński, "Reconsidernig Piłsudski-ite nationalism," *Nationalism Papers* 42, no. 5, (2014), 771–790.

19 Joseph Rothschild, "The Ideological, Political, and Economic Background of Piłsudski's Coup d'Etat," *Political Science Quarterly* 78, no. 2 (June 1963), 224–244, here 231–234; Andrzej Wojtaszak, "Generalicja Wojska Polskiego przed przewrotem majowym i jej udział w zamachu," in *Zamach stanu Józefa Piłsudskiego 1926r*, ed. Marek Sioma, (Lublin: Wydawnictwo Uniwersytetu Marii-Curie Skłodowskiej, 2007), 30–44.

The *Sanacja* authorities thus defined themselves at the outset primarily as an alternative to the liberal order. Significantly, therefore, the main *Sanacja* ideologists after 1926 (such as Stanislaw Car, Tadeusz Hołówko, Wacław Makowski, and Wojciech Stpiczyński) justified their position as a "supplement" to or even "enrichment" of democracy, often declaring themselves defenders of democratic values against external (the Soviet Union) or internal threats (party cronyism).[20] This approach to Piłsudski's rule was no different from the way it was perceived by the political opposition and most contemporary observers.[21] For example, Christian Democracy criticized the *coup d'état* and the illegal seizure of power but, like the whole right side of the political scene, was fascinated by Mussolini's fascism.[22] Likewise, the peasant parties, especially their right-wing faction, were already very strong and were determined to give the parliamentary system a "muzzle and moral whip" (Wincenty Witos).[23] The left, opposed to Piłsudski, was split between the supporters of the Polish Socialist Party (*Polska Partia Socjalistyczna, PPS*), who initially saw the 1926 coup as a response to native fascism, and the approach of the communists for whom it was the *Sanacja* that was the local version of global fascism.[24]

The most comprehensive approach in this regard can be seen within the National Democracy (*Narodowa Demokracja, ND* or *Endeks*), dominant on the right. Though the success of Pilsudski's coup shocked the nationalist movement, its leader, Roman Dmowski, did not consider the situation hopeless; on the contrary, he saw it as the dawn of a "new era". In his famous letter to Enrico Corradini, a prominent Italian nationalist then fascist, he described the coup as the beginning of a constitutional crisis that would eventually elevate the *Endeks* to full power. After the final victory, the nationalist party would impose a system based on limited political representation, a homogeneous vision of the national community, and one fully

20 See Jarosław Tomasiewicz, *Naprawa czy zniszczenie demokracji? Tendencje autorytarne i profaszystowskie w polskiej myśli politycznej 1921–1935,* (Katowice: Wydawnictwo Uniwersytetu Śląskiego, 2012), 240–249.

21 See *Zamach stanu Józefa Piłsudskiego i jego konsekwencje w interpretacjach polskiej myśli politycznej XX wieku*, ed. Zbigniew Karpus, Grzegorz Radomski, Wojciech Wojdyła, (Toruń: Wydawnictwo Adama Marszałek, 2008).

22 Bożena Krzywobłocka, *Chadecja 1918–1937,* (Warszawa: Książka i Wiedza, 1968), 117.

23 Andrzej Zakrzewski, *Wincenty Witos- chłopski polityk i mąż stanu*, (Warszawa: Książka i Wiedza, 1978), 172.

24 Tomasiewicz, *Naprawa czy zniszczenie demokracji?* 333–345.

controlled by "true patriotic" forces based on a native fascist model.[25] On December 4, 1926, Dmowski set up a new organization, modelled on Italian fascism—the Camp of Great Poland (*Obóz Wielkiej Polski, OWP*). Although the *OWP* was originally conceived as a broad anti-*Sanacja* front, open to the Polish Peasant Party and the Christian Democrats, it quickly began to transform itself into Poland's first mass fascist movement.[26]

As a matter of fact, the authoritarian core had been a dominant undercurrent of the *ND* movement since the turn of the century. In this regard, democracy, or rather democratic rhetoric, led to the most effective means of controlling the masses.[27]

From its very inception, Piłsudski's regime included some borrowings from Mussolini's model, especially in rhetoric.[28] As Ramet noted: "After May 1926, the flawed parliamentarism of the first half dozen years was replaced by a system in which Piłsudski had the final word."[29] Thus, on the one hand, under Piłsudski's own semi-authoritarian dictatorship, the chances of the nationalist opposition taking power were very slim. On the other hand, the tell-tale nationalistic climate that predominated, especially in the early 1930s, favored the growth of genuine fascist-style movements.

How to Get Out of the Crisis? Domestic and Foreign Sources

In order to understand the ideological sources of the right-wing transition that took place within the *Sanacja* regime in the mid-1930s, it is necessary to take a closer look at the composition of the groups that supported Józef Piłsudski's coup. While within left-wing circles there were mainly

25 *Roman Dmowski to Enrico Corradini*, VIII 1926, quoted in Jerzy W. Borejsza, *Mussolini był pierwszy* (Warszawa: Czytelnik, 1979), 232.

26 Antony Polonsky, "Roman Dmowski and Italian Fascism," in *Ideas Into Politics. Aspects of European History 1880–1950*, ed. Roger Bullen, Hartmunt Pogge von Strandmann, Antony Polonsky, (London: Sydney Barnes & Noble Books, 1984), 130–146, here 142–144.

27 See Porter-Szücs, "Democracy and Discipline In Late Nineteenth Century Poland," *Journal of Modern History* 71, no. 1 (June 1993), 346–393.

28 See Borejsza, "East European Perceptions of Italian Fascism," in *Who Were the Fascists? Social Roots of European Fascism*, eds. Stein Ugelvik Larsen et al., (Bergen-Oslo-Tromsø: Universitetsforlaget, 1980), 354–366. See also Henryk Wereszycki, "Fascism in Poland," in *Native fascism in the Successor States*, ed. Peter F. Sugar, (Santa Barbara Calif.: ABC-Clio, 1971), 85–91, here 85–86.

29 Ramet, "An Introduction," 20.

syndicalists and various groups of cooperatives, the "militarized left" (e.g., members of which were most often active soldiers in the Polish Army), as well as split groups among the largest grouping of the Polish left wing of the *PPS*, it was the right wing of the *Sanacja* that represented a wide spectrum of groups. Two groups in particular deserve special attention.

As early as 1928, the One Hundred Group (*Zespół Stu*), a circle of Lviv activists in the *ND*, who from early 1923 promoted the native version of fascism, joined the Piłsudski camp. The *Zespół Stu*, which took over the largest daily nationalist newspaper in western Galicia (circa 50,000 circulation), proposed not so much the further "disciplining" and "purifying" of democracy, slogans which Piłsudski and his supporters created, but of building a new "reborn" ethnic Polish community. Within the framework of the "national consolidation", the group governed the accelerated radical assimilation of all Slavic minorities, and the Germans and Jews were to be systematically marginalized and then removed from public life. The *Zespół Stu* did not so much want to restrict the liberal-democratic system or to amend it in any way, but rather to build a new one based on a "national oligarchy", a "governing group" produced within itself through "national selection". The conclusion drawn from this was that "society is completely organized within the State and does not exist outside the State." The aim of such a "reborn national community", subordinate to the state, was to be a state governing all citizens, because "society is strictly organized within the state and outside the state it does not exist."[30]

In this vision, nothing has been left out of the control of the state; the group postulated far-reaching control of all churches and religious associations. An alternative to the representative system could be seen in the Italian corporate system; only in this way could the interests of the individual be organically harmonized with that of the nation-state. Interestingly, the publications by the *Zespół Stu* immediately included a vision of foreign policy in which the Polish hegemon was to be the axis for the whole of Central and Eastern Europe: It was to liberate the region from the economic supremacy of Germany and the "hegemonies of Jewish finance". Although the *Zespół Stu* was the extreme wing of the *Sanacja*, it was famous for its steady criticism

30 All terms taken from the manifesto of the *Zespół Stu* quoted in Aleksander Domaszewicz, *Oblicze polityczne "Zespołu Stu"* (Lwów: "Zespół Stu," 1928). For a synthetic discussion around the ideology, place and activity of the *Zespół Stu* within the *Sanacja* regime, see Tomasiewicz, *Naprawa czy zniszczenie demokracji?* 206–211.

of the *BBWR*'s lack of consistency and leniency towards the regime's opposition, and its role grew with each year it was active.

In the right wing of the Piłsudski camp, there was the League for Poland's Powerful Development (*Liga Mocarstwowego Rozwoju Polski, LMRP*), whose main publication was the weekly *Nowa Kadrowa*—the seat of the magazine was in the headquarters of the State Police in Warsaw—which was supported by Minister of the Interior, Felicjan Sławoj-Składkowski.[31] The group was distinguished by radicalism in its proclamation of an open, full-fledged authoritarian vision: Militant intransigence towards the political opposition, as well as parliament as a whole, the need to replace all representative bodies with institutions created personally by Józef Piłsudski, and an elitist vision of society, which was personally bound to the Marshal. All the League's writings were characterized by the idolatrous cult of Piłsudski. As Polish historian Piotr Dubaniewicz wrote, the group wanted to subject Poland "without reservation to the command of the Chief of the Nation".[32] Under the command of the "Chief of the Nation", Poland was to become a regional superpower that, on the one hand, heralded "the Slavic era", e.g., *Nowa Kadrowa* recognized claims not only to the historic lands of the First Republic, but also to eastern Germany as far as Magdeburg. On the other hand, it was to be able to oppose and actively confront the Soviet Union. The corporate example, which is characteristic of all economic solutions, was explicitly referring to "the fascist system as the life-giving sun of the Italian system".[33]

Polish historian, Jarosław Tomasiewicz, identified a dozen similar groups that were on the right of the Piłsudski camp.[34] All of them were advocating the need for a radical approach, and the majority of them cherished a homogeneous nation-state which needed to be militarized. The new state had to create a new "citizen soldier". Without such a radical transformation, it would not have been possible to move on to the next stage of the nation-state: The building of a regional empire that would dominate Central and Eastern Europe. In retrospect, all these groups represented a fusion of the

31 Felicjan Sławoj-Składowski was the last Prime Minister of the Polish government in the years 1936–1939.

32 Piotr Dubaniewicz, "Nowa Kadrowa - tygodnik "zorganizowanej demokracji" (1930–1931)," *Niepodległość i Pamięć*, no.4 (1998), 159–172.

33 N-or, "Moskwa czy Rzym," *Nowa Kadrowa*, no 6–7, 1930 quoted in Tomasiewicz, *Naprawa czy zniszczenie demokracji*, 262.

34 Tomasiewicz, *Naprawa czy zniszczenie demokracji*, 259–313.

right wing of the *Sanacja*, and extreme paramilitary forms of the National Democracy.

Facing the Crises: The Great Depression, the Death of Piłsudski, and the Polarization of the *Sanacja* Establishment

Though the new political offensive at the very beginning of the 1930s, both from the left and the right, saw the country facing a civil war, the *Sanacja* regime successfully stifled such political mobilization. Specifically, a repeat of Hitler's nationalist revolution, which had made a great impression on Polish nationalists of different ilks, never got off the ground.[35] This concerns the tactic of dividing public opinion and presenting the ruling elite (and Piłsudski, in particular) as, above all, the guardian of the Jewish population in order to eliminate political enemies. At the beginning of 1933, the largest fascist party (*OWP*, circa 200,000 members) was banned; 1934 saw the outlawing of its most radical terrorist wing, the National Radical Camp (*Obóz Radykalno-Narodowy, ONR*). Most of the leaders of the latter group ended up in the Bereza Kartuska concentration camp. Along with the suppression of the center-left opposition (the *Centrolew* in 1929–1930), extensive legislation restricting the autonomy of universities, local authorities, and the judiciary system (1932–1934), as well as the adoption of a new constitution (1935), this period of "colonel governments" (*rządy pułkowników*) seems to be the culmination of archetypal authoritarian rule in interwar Poland.[36]

However, all these measures failed to bring stability to the government. From this point on, the regime found itself in deep crisis—but what was the crisis of the *Sanacja* regime? The crisis of authoritarian formation in Poland should actually be understood on multiple levels. It was largely due to the failure to effectively deal with the economic crisis that broke out around the world in the late 1920s, which was harsher and more severe than among the industrialized and developed countries of Western and Central Europe. Apart from economic stagnation, above all, it meant huge unemployment

35 See Arnd Bauernkämper, "Transnational Fascism: Cross-Border Relations between Regimes and Movements in Europe, 1922–1933," *East Central Europe* 37, no. 2–3 (2010), 240–246.

36 For a synthesis, see Waldemar Paruch, "Podstawy i uzasadnienie tożsamości politycznej obozu piłsudczyków," *Annales UMCS*, sec. k, Vol. 4, (1997), 40–45.

(reaching over 40 percent and, in some parts of the country, over 60 percent of the working-age population), and a radical deterioration in living conditions, both in cities and especially in the countryside.[37]

The army of unemployed youth, primarily male and estimated in 1935 to number around one million, the so-called "redundant people" who joined extreme groups, grew with each passing year.[38] For all these problems, the authorities had conventional solutions which essentially amounted to police brutality, austerity policies and local eradication of conflicts.

Above all, however, the *Sanacja* crisis from within resulted from both the lack of a sufficient social base and the failure of the regime to take mass root in society. Apart from the army, the only other social group that the government could count on were civil servants and the state apparatus dependent on the budget (approximately five percent of the total population). What had seemed to be an asset only a few years before, in a situation of extreme polarization strengthened by the economic and social crisis of the early 1930s, turned out to be a serious burden. The regime suffered its most spectacular defeat among the youth and in the universities, which in the 1930s became the natural breeding ground for radical nationalism or, conversely but on a much smaller scale, for militant Communism. All in all, there was little room for socially conservative, heterogeneous visions around a state that was neutral towards religion and nationality.

Hitler's rise to power and the subsequent rapid takeover by the NSDAP created an enormous impression on, and a challenge for, the Polish elite. While throughout the first decade Italian fascism was the most important reference point for the native right wing,[39] the successes of the Nazis were, however, received ambivalently. Nazism was treated as a peculiarly German product, and racism in particular was presented in this optic as an anti-Catholic position.[40] Not without significance was the hostility of public

37 For a brief characterization of the Great Depression in Poland in 1930, see Porter-Szücs, *Poland in the Modern World*, 119–123. One of the most famous journalistic accounts of the crisis was published by a supporter of *Sanacja*, Konrad Wrzos, *Oko z oko z kryzysem. Reportaż z podróży po Polsce* (Warszawa: Rój, 1933).

38 Stefan Czarnowski, "Redundant People in the Service of Violence," trans. Tristian Korecki, *Acta Poloniae Historica*, no. 114 (2016), 297–306.

39 Krzywiec, "Czekając na polskiego Mussoliniego. Pojęcia i konteksty 'faszyzmu' we wczesnym dyskursie politycznym polskiej prawicy. Rekonesans (1922–1926)," in *Z dziejów pojęć społeczno-politycznych w Polsce XVIII-XX wieku*, ed. Maciej Janowski (Warszawa: Instytut Historii PAN, 2020), 187–222.

40 See Michał Musielak, *Nazizm w interpretacjach polskiej myśli politycznej okresu międzywojennego* (Poznań: Wydawnictwo Poznańskie, 1997).

opinion which remained actively anti-German, and not only in the former parts of the Prussian partition. This did not change the fact that the Nazis' success in domestic policy (e.g., eliminating political opposition, eradication of Jews from public life) and their elaborate social and economic policies were held up by many as benchmarks.[41] This pick-and-choose attitude towards Nazism was not only dominant among the *Endeks*, with their self-proclaimed mandate to transform Poland into a country free of Jews, but also among the Marshal's supporters who looked to "totalism from the West"; copycat movements remained marginal on the Polish scene.[42] Until the end of the Second Republic, the two dominant groups on the right (namely the *Endeks* and the rightist Piłsudski-ites) played the anti-German card by deftly mobilizing patriotic opinion, particularly in the period after Munich.

After Piłsudski's death, a sense of decline and crisis became widespread and was shared by the main political parties. There was growing frustration, not only among opposition groups and national and ethnic minorities, but also, for example, among the army, whose representatives perceived the anachronism of the previous era. This general "end of an era" climate was given credence by the Piłsudski-ites. However, while for many Polish Jews Piłsudski's death heralded only the end of relative social peace and a deterioration in security, many educated Polish people expected rapid and radical changes. Naftali Saleschütz, a Jewish inhabitant of Galician Kolbuszowa, remembered those moments as a solemn time, the only time in his life when Poles and Jews manifestly shared a public space:

> "In 1935, the death of [...] Piłsudski, the nation's greatest hero, caused grief throughout the country. Mourning processions were held in cities across Poland, and Kolbuszowa was no exception [...] It was the only event I remember when Jews and Poles participated as equal partners in an event of national importance."[43]

Zygmunt Klukowski, a left-wing liberal and supporter of Piłsudski from the Lublin region, who opposed the right wing and their militant anti-Semitism, regarded Piłsudski's death as the end of an era of anachronism and stagnation.[44]

---

41 See e.g., Żądamy polskiego "hitleryzmu," *Polityka* 4, (February 25, 1939), 1.

42 See Jarosław Tomasiewicz, *W kierunku nacjokracji. Tendencje autorytarne, totalistyczne i profaszystowskie w polskiej myśli politycznej (1933–1939): narodowcy- narodowi socjaliści- narodowi radykałowie* (Katowice: Wydawnictwo Uniwersytetu Śląskiego, 2019).

43 Naftali Saleschütz, "Sztetl Kolbuszowa," *Karta* 70 (2012), 25.

44 Zygmunt Klukowski, *Zamojszczyzna*, 1918–1959 (Warszawa: Karta, 2017), 111–112.

The Piłsudski funeral ceremonies, which lasted several days, seemed to end the apparent peace among the ruling establishment. As the historian Władysław Pobóg-Malinowski later wrote: "The death of the Marshal was becoming like the cracking of a magic hoop." Violent power struggles among former Piłsudski supporters that broke out shortly after the funeral led to a dramatic sharpening and radicalization of the idea of crisis of legitimization of power. Paradoxically, after Piłsudski's death in 1935, the *Sanacja* regime began a new course to the right. Among the ruling establishment, the belief surged that, in order to survive as a political force, one had to ally somehow with the new anti-Semitic young generation.[45] In this regard, the *Sanacja* camp, as such, began to lose legitimacy and disintegrated.

To many observers at the time, the single common denominator in all the diversified, frequently warring groups of interest seemed to be self-preservation. The ruling elite had no strategy to respond to the situation in the country. By this point, too, the local elite of *Sanacja* seemed to be in deep trouble. Meanwhile, the international position of Poland continued to deteriorate. As a diplomatic historian stated: "By 1936, Poland's position was in a downward spiral."[46] The dilemma from the inception of independence returned with even greater force among the elite: How to create a Poland capable of surviving?[47] This conviction went hand in hand with a message that Piłsudski himself had espoused at one time: To survive, Poland is doomed to greatness.

Even more interestingly, many former members of the outlawed *OWP* somehow slipped into the governmental camp. Some of them (officially as members of the Association of Young Nationalists—*Związek Młodych Narodowców, ZMN*) began to cooperate with the regime from 1934; many others did so on a more unofficial basis. The ardent, radical, anti-Semitism of all these groups was but one constant feature. By radically diminishing "Jewish influence", they postulated the birth of a radically new society with new people, the "new Poles" (*nowi Polacy)*, inhabiting it free from the social and cultural ills that were spawned by false modernity—in its pathological version largely a "Jewish creation".

45 See Andrzej Micewski, "Polish youth in the thirties," *Journal of Contemporary History* 4, no. 3 (July 1967), 155–167.

46 Biskupski, "The Polish Second Republic," 62.

47 Biskupski, 34.

"Polonism" and the Transformation into a Totalitarian Utopia (1936–1939)

The death of Józef Piłsudski (May 12, 1935) was a great shock to the entire *Sanacja* camp: Not only did it reveal the internal deepening tensions in the governmental camp, the importance of charismatic leadership, and the role of personal cult binding it together, it also showed the real shortcomings of authoritarian, and therefore elitist, mobilization in society. In the face of the Great Depression and its far-reaching and long-lasting consequences, the increasing polarization of political life, police and administrative solutions, corruption and the intimidation of opponents, which still seemed to be effective solutions in the early 1930s proved to be insufficient.[48]

Significant impulses towards the fascistization of social and political life were provided by the tense international situation: Restoration of universal military service in Germany and the re-militarization of the Rhineland[49] and, in turn, the aggressive international policy of the Nazi regime in that region, the advances of fascist Italy in Africa, as well as, most paradoxically, the Spanish Civil War. The German incursion into the Rhineland and the lack of a political and military response from France was perceived in late *Sanacja* circles as a complete fiasco and proof of the internal weakness of Poland's greatest ally. The victories of the left and the creation of the Popular Front afterwards was, in turn, received as a symbolic progressive degeneration of the French political system, and even as a "Bolshevization" of the political scene.[50] Similarly, Mussolini's victories in Ethiopia, his brash rhetoric on the international stage, and the lack of response from the League of Nations as guarantor and symbol of the Versailles order were a blow to democratic values.

---

48 For a comprehensive account of the significance of the Great Depression for Poland and the *Sanacja* regime specifically, see Piotr Cichoracki, Joanna Dufrat, and Janusz Mierzwa, *Oblicza buntu społecznego w II Rzeczpospolitej doby Wielkiego Kryzysu (1930–1935). Uwarunkowanie, skala, konsekwencje.* (Kraków: Towarzystwo Wydawnicze "Historia Iagiellonica," 2019), 29–113. For a synthesis, see Porter - Szücs, *Poland in the Modern World*, 119–123.

49 See Paul Jankowski, *All Against All. The Long Winter of 1933 and the Origins of the Second World War*, (New York: Harper, 2020), in particular chap. "Warsaw and Budapest," 150–181. For Poland's weakening international position beginning in 1936, see Mark Mazower, *Dark Continent. Europe's Twentieth Century*, (London: Penguin Books, 1999), 67.

50 Michał Czajka, "Polska opinia publiczna wobec wojny domowej w Hiszpanii," *Przegląd Historyczny*, no. 71/72, (1980), 253–275. On the evolution and perception of the conflict in Spain by *Sanacja* circles cf., see in particular 268–270.

In this spirit, the outbreak of civil war in Spain was interpreted as a harbinger of a new time: The progressive collapse of the European *status quo* and, at the same time, the emergence of the foundations of new "national" systems. The acts of aggression against representatives of the Spanish Catholic Church by Republican forces were understood by the whole Polish right, including the *Sanacja* right, as the consolidation of a new type of left wing. As a result, the entire Polish right-wing press, as well as the Catholic media—the largest media of the time with a circulation of more than one million—conducted one of the largest campaigns of moral panic in the interwar period. Here, it is difficult to overlook the fact that the very tactic of creating people's fronts, i.e., alliances of the moderate left and the Communists, was not so much seen among the *Sanacja* establishment as putting up a barricade against the new right but, conversely, as a malicious new tool of the Stalinist Soviet Union. Poland, as a state, did not take an unequivocal stance towards the conflict on the Iberian Peninsula, but that time was marked by close cooperation with the Nazi security services in combating Communists.

This combination of various events contributed enormously to the weakening of democratic and liberal values and the rapid invasion of a new authoritarian and fascist mentality within the ruling establishment. What is more, the Versailles system, of which Poland as a state seemed to have been one of the greatest beneficiaries in the previous decade, began to collapse, and the Polish elite, or at least the dominant, right-wing part of it, saw this as the impetus for comprehensive, far-reaching change.

At first glance, the Camp of National Unity (*Obóz Zjednoczenia Narodowego, OZN*) was similar to efforts by other authoritarian, in most cases military-based, regimes to create government parties or mass organizations in Eastern and Southern Europe in the late 1930s. The conservative elite, largely of military origin, advocated organic nationalism, referred to ideology or at least fascist rhetoric, and embraced vague corporatism and paramilitarism. In the longer run, however, they competed with the local nationalist or fascist movement. In more practical terms, the *OZN* seemed to be a byproduct of the struggles between Piłsudski's heirs: President Ignacy Mościcki, with his more center-liberal supporters, and General Rydz-Śmigły, with his paramilitary faction in the *Sanacja* establishment. The first symbolic victim of these games was Walery Sławek, the informal leader of the "colonels" and the actual creator of the *BBWR* and the April constitution of 1935.[51] All groups

51 W. Sławek (1873–1939), widely considered to be the "right hand" of Piłsudski (e.g., three-time Prime Minister, Speaker of the *Sejm)*, was presented as the Marshal's successor forced

invoked the will of the late "Commandant". The new Marshal (November 1936) promoted himself as a leader capable of continuing Piłsudski's tradition and bridging the gap between the government in a strict sense, and its social and political basis in society. His intention was to build a movement beyond the *Sanacja,* one that would consolidate power in his hands.[52] On May 24, 1936, in his famous address to the Union of Polish Legionnaires, the Piłsudski-ite veterans' organization, Rydz-Śmigły announced that the security of Poland, trapped between the Soviet Union and Nazi Germany, depended on national unity and consolidation, and he called for the creation of a new mass organization.[53]

On the rise of Rydz-Śmigły, one can see the similarities, but above all the differences, between the cult of personality in the authoritarian but socially conservative regime, which symbolized Piłsudski as such, and the new leadership of the "Fascist-Era dictatorship".[54] Piłsudski, a borderland ("*Kresy*") nobleman almost never appeared in public, avoided mass gatherings, and communicated with the public mainly through press interviews. Power was held by a narrow, unbeknownst to the public, group of his most loyal associates. Rydz-Śmigly, a peasant by origin, was in this respect as much a product of mass propaganda (his cult spread not only in the mass media controlled by the authorities, but also in the nascent radio and film industry), as he was presented as an active participant in current politics. Propaganda emphasized not only his role as a close associate of Piłsudski, a hero of the wars of independence, but also as an attractive man in the prime of his life. In this context, he was completely within the optics of the totalitarian

---

to resign from high state positions. Sławek's departure meant the actual disintegration of the group of authoritarian "colonels". He committed suicide in April 1939.

52 On the short-term political horizon, the emergence of the new *Sanacja* formula was a reaction to a massive wave of political protest (over two million in the early spring of 1936) and attempts to unite the Socialist and Communist left, see Turlejska, *Rok przed klęska,* 39–44.

53 Edward D. Wynot Jr., *Polish Politics in Transition. The Camp of National Unity and the Struggle for Power, 1935–1935*, (Athens: University of Georgia Press, 1974), 21–69. For an analysis of the socio-political thoughts of the *OZN*, see Jacek Majchrowski, *Silni-Zwarci-Gotowi. Myśl polityczna Obozu Zjednoczenia Narodowego,* (Warszawa: Państwowe Wydawnictwo Naukowe, 1985).

54 See Costa Pinto, "Ruling Elites, Political Institutions and Decision-Making in Fascist-Era Dictatorships: Comparative Perspectives," in *Rethinking the Nature of Fascism. Comparative Perspectives*, ed. António Costa Pinto (Basingstoke: Palgrave Macmillan, 2011), 197–226.

imaginaire as a dictator "of the masses, for the masses, and by the masses."[55] Until the last months before the outbreak of World War II, the image of Rydz Śmigły as a supreme military commander, but also a new type of charismatic leader, was to dominate Polish politics.

However, as a typical Eastern European power-party, the *OZN* has not attracted particular attention from historians of fascism or radical right-wing movements.[56] The grouping, considered to be a continuation of the *BBWR* and, at the same time, a failed attempt to consolidate the power of the governing camp, is usually quoted as an unfortunate, i.e., doomed, example of fascism "from above".[57] Moreover, researchers accustomed to treating the 1930s in Poland and the *Sanacja* as an ideological and social entity, have focused on personal changes in the circles of the highest authorities[58] and consistently overlooked the fundamental transformation that Polish politics underwent in this period.[59] The program of the *OZN* advocated national unity above party and class divisions ("a movement to galvanize the nation") and praised the army as a uniting force, while paying nominal respect to the Catholic Church.

Although its declaration promised land reform, it failed to spell out how this redistribution would take place. The *OZN*'s leaders, such as Adam Koc, Stanisław Skwarczyński and Zygmunt Wenda, also declared that state

---

55 Roger Griffin, "Mass Dictatorship and the 'Modernist State,'" in *Mass Dictatorship and Modernity*, eds. Michael Kim, Michael Schoenhals, and Yong-Woo Kim, (Basingstoke: Palgrave Macmillan, 2013), 33–54, here 37.

56 "As a final effort to create a national ideology based on Polish history, its failure was truly a pity," see Biskupski, 53. See also Wolfgang Wippermann, *Faschismus: Eine Weltgeschichte vom 19. Jahrhundert bis Heute*, (Darmstadt: Primus Verlag, 2009), 139–140.

57 On the concept of fascism "from above" as a reaction by authoritarian regimes against grassroots nationalist mobilization, see Aristotle Kallis, The "Fascist Effect": On the Dynamic of Political Hybridization in Inter-War Europe, in *Rethinking Fascism and Dictatorship in Europe*, 13–41, here 28–31.

58 Characteristic here is the position of the eminent historian Maria Turlejska, who describes Polish politics after 1935 as "an accelerated march towards defeat," Maria Turlejska, *Rok przed klęską, 1 września 1938- 1 września 1939* (Warszawa: Wiedza Powszechna, 1969), 69. Others describe this period as "Poland without Piłsudski," see Polonsky, *The Little Dictators. The History of Eastern Europe since 1918* (London and Boston: Routledge & Kegan Paul, 1975), 41–43; Władysław Pobóg Malinowski, *Najnowsza Historia Polityczna Polski 1864–1945*, T.2. Chapt. 1 (London: Gryf Printers, 1956), 576–665.

59 See e.g., Timothy Synder, *Black Earth. The Holocaust as History and Warning* (New York: Tim Duggan Books, 2015), 29–57. See also the monumental synthesis by John Connelly, *From People into Nations. A History of Eastern Europe* (Princeton & Oxford: Princeton University Press, 2019), 419 and the following.

regulation of the economy would increase through closer supervision of private enterprises.[60] More revealing was its muted but ever-radicalizing anti-Semitism: While denouncing anti-Jewish violence coming from the nationalist opposition, the *OZN* also called for the need for an ethnically homogenous Polish society to defend its culture and seek economic self-sufficiency from the Jews. Starting in 1936, official anti-Semitism with the aim of removing about 80 percent of the Polish Jewish population from Poland became one of the government's priorities.[61]

Even larger transitions took place outside the top level of power. In fact, the new formula marked the regime's rapid conversion from a "guided" controlled authoritarian regime to the vision of a "nationalizing state" (Roger Brubaker) already advocated by the paramilitary, fascist *Endecja*.[62] This formula championed not only the interests of ethnic Poles, but sought the radical assimilation ("polonization") of Slavic minorities (e.g., Ukrainians and Belarusians, and the dissimilation and eventual forced purging of Jews and Germans.[63] In a famous radio address, the Chief of Staff of the *OZN*, Zygmunt Wenda, announced that the official policy of the government was a policy of "Polonism", which was to be an energizing interaction of "national" and "pro-state themes".[64] From the second half of 1936, Poland began to make colonial claims to various territories in Africa internationally as compensation for partition, but primarily to "get rid of demographic

60 Mark Mazower describes the Polish Investment Plan of 1936 as "one of the most important ventures in centralized planning to take place outside the Soviet Union," see Mazower, *Dark Continent*, 141.

61 Edward D. Jr. Wynot, "'Necessary Cruelty': The Emergence of Official Anti-Semitism in Poland, 1936–1939," *American Historical Review* 76, no. 4 (October 1971), 1035–1058. Since mid-1936, all "Jewish affairs" in government policy were dealt with by the Foreign Ministry, and the Jews were recognized as potential immigrants. E.g., one of the leading ideologists of *Sanacja* after 1936, Bolesław Miedziński, announced that the Polish state could "adopt" for its own sake ca. fifty thousand Polish Jews, see Miedziński, *Uwagi o sprawie żydowskiej* (Warszawa: Gazeta Polska, 1938), V.

62 Biskupski, 51. See Roger Brubaker, "National Minorities, Nationalizing States, and External National Homelands in the New Europe," *Dedalus* 124, no.2, 107–132.

63 For a synthesis of the late *Sanacja* policy towards the German minority, see Albert Kotowski, *Polens Politik gegenüber seiner deutschen Minderheit 1919–1939* (Wiesbaden: Harrassowitz Verlag, 1998), in particular 348–349.

64 Z. Wenda was, for example, the co-author of project of racial civil rights acts. The case was piloted by the Minister of Justice, Dr Witold Grabowski (e.g., a member of the fascist group *Klub 11 Listopada*, supporter of the alliance with the Third Reich). The racial laws did not come into force before the outbreak of WWII, but the introduction of racial legislation was only a matter of time. See Majchrowski, *Silni-Zwarci-Gotowi*, 137.

surpluses."[65] All these moves were accompanied by an aggressive foreign policy.

The flow of "young" politicians and nationalist activists also upended the late *Sanacja*'s politics.[66] There were various levels of this engagement by the regime in radical rightist and eliminatory *per se* politics. In particular, the second half of 1936 witnessed several major transformations in Polish political culture. The most important and meaningful are: The rapidly growing role and position of Edward Rydz-Śmigły and his inner circle in the political establishment, and the cooperation of different segments of the nationalist political scene with the regime.[67] In turn, the leading ideologist of the *ZMN*, Zdzisław Stahl, referring to the April constitution of 1935 announced that the "legal revolution" had already taken place, only now it needed to be filled with "national content".[68] It was above all the *milieu* of the "national statehooder" who wanted to carry out an "anthropological revolution"[69] by "legal" means, that is, through parliament or by presidential decrees, to remove the Jews, militarize society and raise a "new man/Pole" to regenerate the nation.

Most spectacular in this process that unfolded up until the outbreak of World War II seems to be the creation of the youth branch of the *OZN*, the

65 Zofia Trębacz, *Nie tylko Palestyna. Polskie plany emigracyjne wobec Żydów 1935–1939* (Warszawa: Żydowski Instytut Historyczny, 2018); Wojciech Skóra, "Auswärtige Nationalitätenpolitik. Der konsularische Dienst Polens und die nationalen Minderheiten (1918–1939)," *Zeitschrift für Ostmitteleuropa-Forschung* 62, no. 2 (2013), 206–232.

66 See Mikołaj S. Kunicki, *Between the Brown and the Red. Nationalism, Catholicism, and Communism in Twentieth-Century Poland: The Politics of Bolesław Piasecki* (Athens: Ohio University Press, 2012) 40–46; Wynot, *Polish Politics in Transition*, 153–154.

67 For the best introduction to Rydz-Śmigły's ideological and political background, see Tomasz Sikorski, *Żelazny krok potężnych zdyscyplinowanych szeregów… Oblicze ideowo-politycznej środowiska "Zaczynu" (1936–1939). Studium z dziejów myśli politycznej piłsudczyków* (Warszawa: Wydawnictwo Von Borowiecky, 2014), 23–40.

68 Zdzisław Stahl, "Wobec nowej Konstytucji," in *W stronę autorytaryzmu. Nacjonalizm integralny Związku Młodych Narodowców*, 1934–1939, ed. Maciej Marszał (Kraków: Ośrodek Myśli Politycznej, 2009), 361–365. Stahl was the first head of the Youth Movement of the *OWP* and one of the leaders of the fascist faction in the nationalist right (e.g., a member of the *SN*, 1930–1935); after switching to the *Sanacja*, he became one of the ideologists of the *OZN* (e.g., Deputy Editor-in-Chief of the *Sanacja* official organ *Gazeta Polska*). He was the first Minister of Propaganda in the Polish government (August 1939).

69 Griffin, "Mass Dictatorship and the 'Modernist State,'" 37. See also Jie-Hyun Lim, "Mapping Mass Dictatorship: Towards a Transnational History of Twentieth-Century Dictatorship," in *Gender Politics and Mass Dictatorship. Global Perspective,* eds. Jie-Hyun Lim, and Karen Petrone (Basingstoke: Palgrave Macmillan, 2011), 8.

Union of Young Poland (*Związek Młodej Polski—ZMP*) and the appointment of Jerzy Rutkowski, the *OWP* former activist and later Bolesław Piasecki's close associate in the *ONR-Falanga*, as its head.[70] In a radio speech on June 22, 1937, Rutkowski outlined the goals of his organization: The implementation of a "breakthrough", a kind of national revolution—the mobilization of the people's energy for national creativity, and the struggle against communists, Freemasons, and conservatives. The "Jewish problem", as the background to most social and political problems, was to be solved through forced emigration. In Rutkowski's own words, responsibility for the "new Poland" was to be taken by "citizen soldiers", veterans of the independence movement and, last but not least, the young nationalist generation. These groups ought to form an alliance of "pro-state nationalist forces" *(siły narodowo-państwowe)* set on crushing the left once and for all, which Rutkowski in his own words called the *Folksfront*.[71]

Publications by the new organization demanded that responsibility for the "new Poland" be taken by the soldiers and, above all, by the young generation.[72] Despite numerous obstacles and setbacks (some of the *OZN* officials tried to undermine the *ONR-Falanga* activists' influences), the *ZMP* grew in size, claiming 40,000 members in the fall of 1937, and over 60,000 by the spring of 1938. Nonetheless, Rutkowski and his circle's accession to the leadership of the *ZMP* triggered many pro-government activists to walk out. Some negative responses came from the *Sanacja* left-nationalist faction groups (e.g., *Naprawa*), which had rather intended to use the broad forum of the *OZN* to cooperate with the socialists and the peasants. All these groups criticized the *ZMP* for its openly fascist tendencies, fearing that the link between the military and the fascists could push the Polish state toward further political extremism. At that time, right-wing extremists began to

70 The *ONR-Falanga* (1935) was an openly totalitarian branch of the *ONR*, which emerged after the de-legalization of the group in 1934. Until WWII, it was under the leadership of Boleslaw Piasecki. See Kunicki, *Between the Brown and the Red*, 34–40. For a comprehensive approach, see Rudnicki, *Falanga. Ruch Narodowo-Radykalny* (Warszawa: Towarzystwo Naukowe Warszawskie, Instytut Historyczny Uniwersytetu Warszawskiego, 2018).

71 The term "*Folksfront*", very popular among the Polish right wing, was an anti-Semitic slogan indicating that the coalition of left-wing groups trying to oppose the fascistization of social life in 1930s Poland was actually led by Jews. "Folks" in this sense was a reference to Yiddish. See (Jerzy Rutkowski) "Nasz radykalizm," *Młoda Polska*, no. 2 (September 1937), 1.

72 *Deklaracja ideowa Związku Młodej Polski* (Warszawa, 1937).

systematically take control of powerful social organizations under the influence of the government.[73]

Nonetheless, after weeks of internal tensions, Rydz-Śmigły ordered an end to cooperation with the national radicals and eventually even forced Koc to resign. The *OZN*'s new leader, General Stanisław Skwarczyński, advised the "young nationalists" to abandon their extremism in service of "an ill-defined revolutionary goal" or to leave the camp. On April 22, 1938, Rutkowski and some of his close associates left the *OZN*. To many researchers, this political defeat of the rightist radical illustrated a broader Eastern European tendency; the failure of East or Central-East European native fascists to acquire power in an environment dominated by socially conservative authoritarians. As in Horthy's Hungary in the 1930s and Antonescu's Romania, the *Sanacja* establishment emulated the fascists, adopting radical ethnonationalism, aggressive statism, vague corporatism, and mass organizations based on the leadership principle.

But how did matters look in the countryside? Interestingly enough, the *ZMP*, as the youth organization of the *OZN*, still growing by systematically recruiting new members, acquired its main influences here. Highly significantly, the ex-*ONR-Falanga* activists were exchanged for members of the Union of Young Nationalists (*ZMN*), another aforementioned fascist embryo that arose from the outlawing of the *OWP*.[74] The organization did not give up the intention to take on the trappings of the other fascist or para-fascist organizations in any way. The *ZMP* members still donned a paramilitary uniform and terrorized the streets by playing the role of ruling party militia, expecting a hierarchical form of leadership to be accepted. From the very beginning, the *ZMP* proceeded frenetically in its rivalry with the other radical rightist groups to win the hearts and minds of the younger generation, while having the organizational support of the state. Until the outbreak of World War II, the organization, still being the most popular youth organization connected with the *Sanacja* regime (circa 80,000 members), conducted the anti-Jewish boycott which deteriorated into small riots, and actively took part in state-sponsored acts of violence against other minorities (mostly against the Ukrainians and the Germans).

73 Rudnicki, *Obóz Narodowo-Radykalny*, 313–318.

74 Rudnicki, *Falanga*, 277.

Conclusion

The crisis of Piłsudski's authoritarian regime, particularly after the dictator disappeared from public life, seems to have been a permanent state. Since both the grounds for the legitimacy of power and the mechanisms for transferring power could not be systematically guaranteed, a situation of constant tensions and rivalries between the various pressure groups in the political arena seems to be, if not a constant, then certainly a protracted state of affairs. The stabilizing role of the dictator as a symbol of an independent state, the conqueror of the Soviet Union—in the interwar period, considered to be the greatest and, what is more, permanent enemy of Poland—but also a guarantor of public order, which not only limited the rivalry of the groups supporting him, but also quite effectively united their opposing interests, began to weaken with each passing year. In this regard, the late *Sanacja* regime could therefore be analyzed as a case study of crisis management in which individual interest groups, as well as political and social circles and ideological centers, continuously competed for more influence. From 1931 and Piłsudski's illness, and the steady personal withdrawal of the dictator from many political matters—apart from issues of state security—there was constant, often violent, rivalry between individual centers of power.

The case of the late *Sanacja* regime shows that an enduring state of crisis forced continuous attempts to expand the political base, and to seek allies, often even makeshift alliances. The natural foundations for such solutions were other authoritarian regimes in the region. From the end of the 1920s, the greatest significance and the furthest-reaching inspiration for the *Sanacja* authorities can be found in Italian fascism. Although Piłsudski distanced himself from the methods, goals and fascist ideology itself, Mussolini's Italy aroused keen interest among his numerous collaborators and aides (including Senate Marshal Bohdan Podoski, Prime Minister Leon Kozłowski, and most notably Minister of the Interior, Bronisław Pieracki). Significantly, fascist Italy remained a constant point of reference for Polish politics, even in the second half of the 1930s when Poland's security was under direct threat. As late as the spring of 1939, the *Sanacja* authorities tried to build a "Catholic" axis with Italy, in an attempt to overcome the tensions that had arisen between "Catholic" Rome and "pagan" Berlin.

However, from the mid-1930s, the greatest—although not always direct—challenge and source of inspiration was the Third Reich. Although the takeover of power by Hitler was initially criticized by the *Sanacja* authorities, also due to the intense relations within the state (after the non-aggression agreement of 1934), the significance of these influences grew steadily. While the place and role of liberal-democratic inspirations and values was declining, the significance of the Third Reich and Nazi modernity in virtually all sections of social policy increased systematically. Moreover, the policy of the west towards Germany was interpreted by the Polish elite as a "free hand" for Hitler in Central and Eastern Europe. Thus, the international situation in the mid-1930s, in which Poland's position began to weaken, widened the scope for totalitarian solutions. Significantly, Poland's location between the two totalitarian regimes in fact increased the need for holistic, comprehensive solutions. In this sense, in the view of the ruling elite at the outbreak of World War II, there seemed to be no alternative to a para-fascist or fascist system of government.

Reinventing Pétain: Crisis and Cults of Personality in Vichy France, 1940–1942

Stefan Schubert

Introduction

What are we talking about when we speak of a "crisis"?[1] According to Swiss cultural historian Jacob Burckhardt, a crisis is characterized primarily by the experience of massive acceleration.[2] This description certainly applies to World War II, in which entire states collapsed and political systems lost their legitimacy. Hence, it is not surprising that many French experienced the years between 1940 and 1944 as an ever more rapid succession of crises. Yet, every form of speed is subjective. The term "crisis" is thus closely associated with human perception.[3] Crises are not historical facts, rather they are a special form of experience that needs to be situated in world events as a process of ascribing meaning to the experience.[4]

From the perspective of experiential history, this situating of the experience is characterized by normal routines appearing to no longer function and previous conditions being deemed irretrievable. One outcome is contemporaries experiencing widespread loss of control. A crisis can be described accordingly as the intense experience of contingency that has an immediate impact on decision making. This is the premise of the following study on the cult of personality in the Vichy regime during World War II.

In 1942, wartime France faced multiple successive moments of crisis that threatened the political stability of the authoritarian *État français* (French State). Ostentatious collaboration with the Nazi regime, especially in rapidly

---

1 I would like to thank Daniel Hefflebower and the Collaborative Research Center 948 for the translation of this chapter.

2 Jacob Burckhardt, *Weltgeschichtliche Betrachtungen* (Essen: Magnus-Verlag, 1983), 158.

3 Reinhart Koselleck, "Krise," in *Geschichtliche Grundbegriffe, Vol. 3*, eds. Otto Brunner, Werner Conze, and Reinhart Koselleck (Stuttgart: Klett-Cotta, 1982), 617–650.

4 Moritz Föllmer, Rüdiger Graf, and Peter Leo, "Einleitung: Die Kultur der Krise," in *Die „Krise" der Weimarer Republik. Zur Kritik eines Deutungsmusters*, eds. Moritz Föllmer, and Rüdiger Graf (Frankfurt a. M.: Campus-Verlag, 2005), 9–41.

accelerating the deportation of the Jewish population,[5] and the public failure of the Riom show trial in the spring, in which high-ranking politicians of the Third Republic were blamed for the defeat, added to the challenges of a regime whose population was suffering from the unsettling experiences of war and occupation. In November, the landing of Anglo-American troops in northern Africa and the subsequent occupation of the entire country by the Germans and Italians threatened the existence of the authoritarian state. 1942 was a year of crisis that revealed the fragility of the political order.[6]

The overlapping developments of this year marked an end to the illusion that normality—of whatever kind—could be returned to by collaborating. They demonstrated clearly how little control the French could exert even over the unoccupied part of their state, their economic resources, and their everyday lives. On the one hand, this resulted in a loss of control and uncertainties being felt by a large part of the French populace which, on the other hand, needed to be reassured by the political decision makers and the regime's intellectual elites. But how was that to be achieved with the limited instruments of power of a state that, in many respects, was dependent on Berlin? An answer was found in the field of symbolic politics, which is examined in this chapter.

The Authoritarian Character of the Vichy Regime

In 1942, this field was by no means untilled.[7] From its very beginning, the *État français* was given a new ideological structure in the form of the tripartite motto *travail, familie, patrie* (work, family, fatherland), which had been modified to meet the requirements of the authoritarian regime. The motto was to render the French people emotionally loyal to the system and persuade them

5 Michael Marrus and Robert Paxton, *Vichy France and the Jews* (Stanford: Stanford University Press, 2019), 159–262.

6 Matthias Waechter, *Geschichte Frankreichs im 20. Jahrhundert* (Munich: Beck, 2019), 249–271.

7 Particularly noteworthy in this respect: the *Secrétariat particulier*, the *ministère de l'Information*, the *ministère de la Guerre* and the *Légion des Anciens Combattants*. The private secretariat was important in the early phase of the regime before the Ministry of Information in particular gained in importance until the *Milice*, a paramilitary organization founded in 1943, became influential in the last months of Vichy. Cf. Alexander Hanisch-Wolfram, *Pensez français, pensez Pétain! Diskursanalytische Studien zur Propaganda des Vichy-Regimes 1940–1944* (Vienna: Praesens Verlag, 2007), 145.

to give credence to the ideological principle of the national revolution, the so-called *révolution nationale*, as well as endorse collaboration with the occupying power. However, there was no consistent or uniform strategy. In Vichy, there was only one major ideological adhesive: Marshal Philippe Pétain. The political order was inseparably linked to the Head of State; the regime rested entirely upon *le culte du maréchal.* This cult of personality turned the Marshal into the myth upon which Vichy built its political, social, cultural and moral legitimacy. This was one of the central elements of the authoritarian character of the regime.

This character became manifest as early as July 1940 in the constitutional acts, by which the separation of powers and popular sovereignty were *de facto* abolished. Philippe Pétain was, thus, not only France's new Head of State and Government, he also dissolved the national assembly and, a few months later, conferred upon himself supreme judicial powers.[8] This facilitated the persecution of the opposition; the imprisonment of former members of the government, such as Léon Blum, Édouard Daladier and Paul Reynaud, and the expropriation and deportation of Jews.[9] In addition, from the summer of 1941 onwards, the authoritarian state no longer took aim solely at the declared enemies of the state, i.e., Jews, communists and Freemasons, but also turned against its own civil servants by legalizing political purges within the bureaucracy. All of this was accompanied by waves of political violence against any form of resistance to the regime.[10]

Vichy's authoritarian character could not be denied. Many who supported and profited from the regime even saw it as a necessity, since it seemed to be an auspicious political model in a time of ideological extremes. In light of the military success of the National Socialists, this notion was prevalent in intellectual civil society and in French military circles. Writers, such as Robert Brasillach and Pierre Drieu La Rochelle, high-ranking military personnel, such as François Darlan, and politicians like Marcel Déat and Pierre Laval, displayed a deep fascination with the NS regime and decisively

8 See the constitutional acts, numbers 1 to 3, of July 11, 1940.

9 Marc Olivier Baruch, *Das Vichy-Regime. Frankreich 1940–1944* (Stuttgart: Reclam, 1999), 33; Philippe Burrin, "Vichy," in *Les lieux de mémoire*, ed. Pierre Nora (Paris: Gallimard, 1992), 320–345; Michèle Cointet, *Nouvelle histoire de Vichy. (1940–1945)* (Paris: Fayard, 2011), 101–210.

10 Baruch, *Vichy-Regime*, 91–98; Heinrich August Winkler, *Die Zeit der Weltkriege. 1914–1945*, 3rd ed. (Munich: Beck, 2016), 1025.

contributed to sustaining Vichy's collaboration.[11] It was precisely for these groups of people that maintaining the cult of personality around Marshal Pétain was of such crucial importance in order to thereby secure their power basis in the new state. The motto of these groups can be expressed in the words of Bernard Ménétrel, the Head of State's *éminence grise*[12]: "To defend the Marshal is to defend France."[13]

Hence, the figure of the Marshal and the cult of personality maintained around him needed to be protected with all the means of an authoritarian state. In the following section, I understand cult of personality as the veneration of a leader figure that is a stabilizing component of the political culture of a community.[14] Such veneration exhibits parallels with processes of heroization. On an analytical level, these can be seen, for example, in that both a hero and a cultically venerated leader are attributed such characteristics as exceptionality, a high degree of agency, transgressive potential and great emotional affect.[15] I therefore argue in this study that the cult of personality maintained around Pétain was based, to a significant extent, on his heroization. Since heroizations combine positive notions of morality in a personified form, they are also enlightening as regards societal processes, as communities debate their framework of norms and values using *inter alia* individual heroic figures.[16]

11 Alya Aglan, Johann Chapoutot, and Jean-Michel Guieu, *L'heure des choix. 1933–1945* (Villeneuve d'Ascq: Septentrion, 2019), 78–88; Jean-Paul Cointet, *Les hommes de Vichy. L'illusion du pouvoir* (Paris: Perrin, 2017); Annie Lacroix-Riz, *Les élites françaises entre 1940 et 1944. De la collaboration avec l'Allemagne à l'alliance américaine* (Paris: Armand Colin, 2016).

12 Bénédicte Vergez-Chaignon, *Le docteur Ménétrel. Éminence grise et confident du maréchal Pétain* (Paris: Perrin, 2002).

13 AN 2 AG 79. Dossiers du Docteur Ménétrel. Dossier relatif aux questions d'information, de propagande, d'opinion. Les évènements et l'état d'esprit actuels montrent la nécessité d'une propagande relative à la personne et à la politique du Maréchal, undated, most likely 1941.

14 Hein-Kircher, "Führerkult und Führermythos. Theoretische Reflexionen zur Einführung," in *Der Führer im Europa des 20. Jahrhunderts*, eds. Benno Enker and Heidi Hein-Kircher (Marburg: Herder-Institut, 2010), 3–23; Frank Möller, "Zur Theorie des charismatischen Führers im modernen Nationalstaat," in *Charismatische Führer der deutschen Nation*, ed. Frank Möller (Munich: Oldenbourg, 2004), 1–18.

15 Tobias Schlechtriemen, "Der Held als Effekt. Boundary work in Heroisierungsprozessen," *Berliner Debatte Initial* 29 (2018): 106–119.

16 Bernhard Giesen, "Zur Phänomenologie der Ausnahme: Helden, Täter, Opfer," in *Zwischenlagen. Das Außerordentliche als Grund der sozialen Wirklichkeit*, ed. Bernhard Giesen (Weilerswist: Velbrück Wiss, 2010), 67–87; Schlechtriemen, Der Held als Effekt; Wolfgang Lipp, *Stigma und Charisma. Über soziales Grenzverhalten* (Würzburg: Ergon, 2010).

The study of heroizations, therefore, allows insightful conclusions to be made about societal value systems' contributors, media, and authorities. That is the basis for the guiding premise of this chapter: By analyzing the heroizing, system-stabilizing cult surrounding Philippe Pétain, inferences can be drawn about notions of socio-cultural and political order in the authoritarian Vichy regime, which were subject to change particularly in times of crisis.[17]

In 1942, however, this stabilizing cult was challenged by overlapping layers of crisis, which had a sustained socio-economic, an accelerated political, and a short-term military dimension. The *État français* coped with these challenges not only by restructuring the administration, appointing Pierre Laval as Head of Government and using paramilitary force,[18] but also by strategically shifting the discourse of Pétain's cult of personality. In exploring the meanings and effects of the redefined cult of personality, the aim of this chapter is to shed some light on how authoritarian regimes react to crises regarding their legitimacy by shifting fundamental political narratives, including the cults of personality they construct.

Pétain as "War Hero"—The Indispensable Heart of the Cult of Personality

World War I marked a seminal turning point in the life of Philippe Pétain, who was born in 1856.[19] The war led to Pétain's rapid promotion to the rank of General during the first few months of the conflict. This advancement was not only due to his abilities, but also to the noticeable lack of officers, especially in the higher ranks of the French army.[20] Promoted to Divisional General on February 26, 1916, he was responsible for the defense against the German attack during the Battle of Verdun. For a few months, he was one of the most famous war heroes in France. After the war, the newly

Cf. also the publications of the Collaborative Research Center 948 Heroes – Heroizations – Heroisms: https://www.sfb948.uni-freiburg.de/en.

17 Olmo Gölz, "The imaginary field of the heroic: on the contention between heroes, martyrs, victims and villains in collective memory," *helden. heroes. héros. E-Journal zu Kulturen des Heroischen* Special Issue 5 (2019): 27–38.

18 Michèle Cointet, *La milice française* (Paris: Fayard, 2013), 11–36.

19 Bénédicte Vergez-Chaignon, *Pétain* (Paris: Perrin, 2014), 19–67.

20 Ibid., 86.

appointed Marshal Pétain remained a person of public interest, not least because he continued to hold civil and high military offices during the post-war period. With that prominence, Pétain continued to be counted among the many war heroes in post-war France. What distinguished him from the others, however, was the close discursive connection with the highly emotionally-charged memory of the Battle of Verdun.[21]

It was another world war that would give Pétain's life a new turn. After the unexpectedly swift advances of the German armies in May 1940, the high losses suffered by the French defenders, the government's flight from Paris to Bordeaux, and the millions of refugees seeking to escape the German occupation, President Albert Lebrun entrusted the Marshal with the formation of a government on June 16, 1940.[22]

Although the armistice signed six days later put an end to the fighting, the war in no way came to an end. The experience of occupation and collaboration became part of the everyday lives of the French for the next four years. According to the constitutional amendment ratified by the Chamber of Deputies and declared by Pétain on July 10 and 11, as *chef d'État* (Head of State) he was able to control only the unoccupied south of France. There, however, he had almost dictatorial powers.[23]

This at least constitutional omnipotence was interwoven with a visual omnipresence by means of the state-controlled cult of personality. As Head of State, he symbolized notions of a fundamentally new societal and political order that was to amount to a *révolution nationale*, and lead to a kind of moral renewal of the nation through the values of work, family, and fatherland, at

---

21 In July 1919, he became a member of the *Académie des Sciences Morales et Politiques*; from January 1920, he was Vice-President of the *Conseil Supérieur de la Guerre* and from February 1922, he was Inspector General of the Army. In addition, in 1925, he briefly took over command in the Rif War against the Moroccan troops of Abd al-Karim. In 1931, he was appointed to the *Académie Française*, succeeding the late Ferdinand Foch. Gaston Doumergue offered him the post of Minister of War in 1934, which he held between February and November. See the biographies of Richard Griffiths, *Marshal Pétain* (London: Constable, 1970); Herbert Lottman, *Pétain* (Paris: Ed. du Seuil, 1984); Vergez-Chaignon, *Pétain*.

22 Jean-Pierre Azéma, *1940, l'année terrible* (Paris: Éd. du Seuil, 1990); Stefan Martens, "Frankreich und das Jahr 1940: 'L'année terrible,'" *Francia* 37 (2010), 317–334.

23 Constitutional acts 1 to 3 of July 11, 1940; Baruch, *Vichy-Regime*, 33; Cointet, *Nouvelle histoire*, 101–210.

least according to the aspirations of the political elite.[24] The Marshal was not only the head of the new state; as a role model and unifying figure, he was more the central source of legitimation of the *État français* that would be maintained by an extensive propaganda apparatus.[25]

"War Hero" Despite Defeat?

Although there were in no way 40 million Pétainists overnight,[26] a large portion of the French population felt a great degree of affection and admiration for the new Head of State in the summer of 1940. As the research on the Vichy regime has been able to show, the Marshal's political authority was based not least on his status as the "hero of Verdun".[27]

In the course of the surprisingly swift military defeat and Pétain's self-appointment as *chef d'État* on July 11, 1940, the interpretations of the past associated with the term Verdun that referred back to an imagined heroic defense of the French nation were updated. That was not difficult as the significance of the Battle of Verdun as an emotionally charged place of remembrance for the French nation had hardly waned over the post-war period.[28] The "savior of Verdun" would again become the savior of

24 Regarding the origins and the fundamental ideological features of the *révolution nationale*, cf. Debbie Lackerstein, *National regeneration in Vichy France. Ideas and policies, 1930–1944* (Farnham: Ashgate, 2012).

25 Rémi Dalisson, *Les fêtes du Maréchal. Propagande festive et imaginaire dans la France de Vichy* (Paris: Tallandier, 2007); Claude Lévy and Dominique Veillon, "Propagande et modelage des esprits," in *Le régime de Vichy et les Français*, eds. Jean-Pierre Azéma and François Bédarida (Paris: Fayard, 1992), 184–202; Dominique Rossignol, *Histoire de la propagande en France de 1940 à 1944. L'utopie Pétain* (Paris: Presses Univ. de France, 1991); Christian Delporte, "La propagande a joué un rôle décisif pendant la Seconde Guerre mondiale," in *Les mythes de la Seconde Guerre mondiale*, eds. Jean Lopez and Olivier Wieviorka (Paris: Perrin, 2017), 277–293.

26 Henri Amouroux, *Quarante millions de pétainistes. Juin 1940–juin 1941* (Paris: Laffont, 1977); Henry Rousso, *Frankreich und die "dunklen Jahre": Das Regime von Vichy in Geschichte und Gegenwart* (Göttingen: Wallstein, 2010).

27 Eric Alary, *Nouvelle histoire de l'Occupation* (Paris: Perrin, 2019), 136; Mason Norton, "Counter-Revolution? Resisting Vichy and the National Revolution," in *Vichy France and everyday life. Confronting the challenges of wartime, 1939–1945*, eds. Lindsey Dodd and David Lees (London: Bloomsbury, 2018), 197–211.

28 Serge Barcellini, "Mémoire et mémoires de Verdun 1916–1996," *Guerres mondiales et conflits contemporains* 182 (1996): 77–98; Antoine Prost, "Verdun," in *Les lieux de mémoire*, eds. Jean-

France—at least according to the early interpretation of journalistically active supporters of the Vichy regime. The Battle of Verdun was, thus, a central framework to the heroic figure Pétain and to the Vichy regime that invoked him.

For example, in his biography published in 1940 in occupied Paris, the author and journalist Georges Suarez created the image of a military leader and hero of the Great War. A committed pacifist, Suarez supported the new political system because the armistice agreement of June 22, 1940, had put an end to the fighting between France and Germany. He drew upon narratives and attributions that had their origins in World War I. Pétain's military achievements were at the center of a heroizing narrative. Suarez labeled him the only commander who could turn a catastrophe into a victory that is described as heroic. According to Suarez, thanks to his defensive doctrine, his influence on the troops, his perfect knowledge of the tactical conditions and his organizational talent, he was able to defend the threatened fatherland.[29] He was credited with saving a hopeless situation.[30] The author José Germain similarly heroized the "great soldier"[31] Pétain in his 1941 biography, in which the Battle of Verdun is narratively stylized as the Marshal's great heroic deed.[32] Germain also portrayed the Marshal in the tradition of a true war hero. Using this portrayal of the military commander, Pétain's credibility and competence as the national leader were to be reinforced in the initial years of World War II. He who had defied the German invaders once could do it a second time—this was the message of the hagiographers.

Such descriptions of Pétain's impact during the Great War did not just constitute a heroization of the Marshal; they can also be understood as the narrative parallelization of two layers of time. Suarez emphasized that the Marshal steadied not only the army in 1916, but also the fatherland as best he could. Germain underlined that Pétain taking over command had aroused great hope among the soldiers during the war. In 1941, General Émile Laure, a close confidante of the Marshal, published a biography on Pétain that was

---

Pierre Babelon and Pierre Nora (Paris: Gallimard, 1986), 111–141; Pierre Servent, *Le mythe Pétain. Verdun, ou, les tranchées de la mémoire* (Paris: Payot, 1992).

29 Georges Suarez, *Le Maréchal Pétain* (Paris: Plon, 1940), 26–27.

30 "Tout était à rétablir et à restaurer dans ses limites, ses attributions et ses devoirs." Ibid., 43.

31 José Germain, *Notre chef Pétain* (Paris: La Technique du Livre, 1941), 21–96.

32 "Mais c'est au cours de l'armée suivante que, défenseur de Verdun, il inscrira dans notre Histoire une page de gloire immortelle, s'égalant ainsi aux plus grands chefs que la France ait connus." Ibid., 27.

the decisive work about him for some time. That book also includes clear allusions that stylize the Marshal as the hope of occupied and defeated France.[33]

Although most biographies were written by supporters of the National Revolution or by those of the Marshal himself, Pétain and his personal cabinet were not able to control biographical publishing in all of France. The Head of State was by no means completely in control of his public image. The collaborationists in Paris used his image, his speeches, and his political decisions without consulting the political decision makers in Vichy. In unoccupied southern France, the Secretariat for Information and Propaganda distributed millions of documents, posters, brochures, and photographs of Pétain. However, the different directors—Paul Marion, Pierre Laval, and Philippe Henriot—successively pursued their own goals, which collided with the interests of Pétain and his private cabinet.[34]

In this cabinet, the Marshal had gathered close associates and friends, such as Bernard Ménétrel and Henry du Moulin de Labarthète,[35] who tried to control the public image of the Head of State according to Petain's wishes. This was primarily achieved through the French Legion of Combatants, a centralized veterans' organization loyal to the Marshal, and through decrees and laws. Thus, on July 18, 1941, a law determined that any picture of Pétain should highlight his blue eyes. Unwanted images and attributions were banned at Pétain's command, for example, those referring to him as an "elderly man". Instead, he was to be portrayed as an active and virile leader. While the staging of his political performance certainly did not reach the levels of Hitler or Mussolini, the Marshal did pay close attention to his public image.[36] However, he was never able to dictate each biography or every other means of propaganda.

Nevertheless, considering Pétain's commitment to the politics of history in the interwar period and his meticulous proofreading of drafts and

33 Émile Laure, *Pétain* (Paris: Berger-Levrault, 1941), 223: "Ce faisant, Pétain demeure fidèle à son plan du moment, comme nous venons de le dire, mais aussi et surtout à sa doctrine fondamentale: tenir d'abord, riposter ensuite."

34 Vergez-Chaignon, *Pétain*, 592–598.

35 Jérôme Cotillon, "Les entourages de Philippe Pétain, chef de l'Etat français, 1940–1942," *Histoire@Politique* 8, no. 2 (2009).

36 Vergez-Chaignon, *Pétain*, 592–598; Jan C. Behrends, "Drei Gesichter des Führerkults. Eine vergleichende Skizze zu Bolschewismus, Faschismus und Nationalsozialismus," in *Der Führer im Europa des 20. Jahrhunderts*, eds. Benno Ennker and Heidi Hein-Kircher (Marburg: Verlag Herder-Institut, 2010), 325–346.

speeches, it is very likely that he took a scrutinizing look at any publication he could get his hands on. The biography by Émile Laure in particular, who belonged to his inner circle and was one of his longtime ghostwriters, definitely had the approval of the Head of State.[37] It is rather difficult to draw reliable conclusions about the reception of any biographical works. Most likely, they were read primarily by supporters of Pétain. It is known that short hagiographic brochures published by the Secretariat of Information and Propaganda were distributed to functionaries and high-level officials—who in turn largely ignored them.[38] Biographies were only one medium of the cult of personality that developed around Pétain. However, they reflect an image of the Head of State that was drawn by intellectual supporters of the French State and, partially, by Philippe Pétain himself. Undoubtedly, the messages of such biographies could be conveyed more efficiently through other media, such as speeches or posters—a fact that was well known and used by the Legion or by Paul Marion. Both, in the early years of the regime, consistently referred to the Marshal as a hero of the Great War. Thus, they followed the narratives that were also spread by Émile Laure and other biographers.[39]

In that sense, the war hero Pétain served as the prefiguration of the Head of State.[40] Even 22 years after it ended, memories of the Great War structured what publicists, intellectuals and other parts of the French population expected from political decision makers. Although the impact of a number of such semi-official biographies remained greatly limited,[41] they nevertheless bespeak the state's attempts to establish the Marshal during the crisis of war and occupation as an integrating national figurehead, who was placed among the ranks of such French national heroes as Vercingetorix, Joan of

---

37 SHD GR 13 YD 1260. Fonds Laure. Relevé des notes. Notes particulière, September 5, 1931 and SHD GR 13 YD 1260. Fonds Laure. Relevé des notes. Notes de l'année courante, October 14, 1932. Bénédicte Vergez-Chaignon, "Présentation," in *La bataille de Verdun*, ed. Bénédicte Vergez-Chaignon (Paris: Perrin, 2015), 9–19. Lottman, *Pétain*, 189–194.

38 Michèle Cointet, *Pétain et les Français. 1940–1951* (Paris: Perrin, 2002), 110.

39 Denis Peschanski, "Encadrer ou contrôler," in *La propagande sous Vichy, 1940–1944*, eds. Laurent Gervereau and Denis Peschanksi (Nanterre: Bibliothèque de Documentation Internationale Contemporaine, 1990), 10–31, here: 39.

40 Hans Blumenberg, *Präfiguration. Arbeit am politischen Mythos* (Berlin: Suhrkamp, 2014).

41 Cointet, *Pétain et les Français*, 110; Pierre Laborie, *L'opinion française sous Vichy. Les Français et la crise d'identité nationale. 1936–1944*, 2nd ed. (Paris: Ed. du Seuil, 2012), 253–260.

Arc, and the Unknown Soldier.[42] In addition, the biographies, slogans, songs, pamphlets, books and posters in the early period of Vichy France depicting Pétain as a war hero were also meant to collapse space and time to present life in the authoritarian regime as one of "continued crisis and permanent resistance."[43]

In a time of military crisis and political transition, updating Pétain's war hero status fulfilled an identifying and mobilizing function in that the *chef d'État* was narratively established as the military hope in resisting the German invaders. Thus, a trust-building and thereby system-stabilizing function was attributed to him, which he could fulfil as long as the expectations made of him appeared justified in the eyes of his supporters. This evocation failed, however, because of the reality of a provisional state dependent upon the goodwill of the occupying power. Nevertheless, the political confidence placed in the Head of State was high at the start of the regime. This was one of the reasons why the cult of personality maintained around Pétain was initially met with great acceptance and found its counterpart in demonstrations of affection that were not organized by the state.[44]

However, even this approval could not prevent morale among the French people from sinking considerably in 1941. Given the precarious economic situation, unkept promises like the return of 1.5 million prisoners of war and the ever more vivid reality of the occupation in the north of the country, discontent was first seen mid-year in major public demonstrations like the miners' strike at the Pas-de-Calais in May 1941. As a result, Pétain had political gatherings banned, doubled police numbers, and went ahead with a series of politically motivated purges.[45] The authoritarian regime did not tolerate opposition of any kind.

The brutal acts of retaliation by the German occupiers against such forms of civil disobedience from the summer of 1941 onwards—including mass executions of hostages, the beginning of deportations, and an

---

42 An exemplary example: Jacques Reynaud, *De Vercingétorix à Pétain. Le don de soi-même* (o. O. 1942). Cf. Lackerstein, *National regeneration.*

43 The phenomenon can also still be observed today in authoritarian regimes, as Kevin Schwarz and Olmo Gölz have been able to show in the example of Iran, cf. Kevin L. Schwartz and Olmo Gölz, "Going to war with the Coronavirus and maintaining the state of resistance in Iran," *Middle East Report Online* (September 2020): https://merip.org/2020/09/going-to-war-with-the-coronavirus-and-maintaining-the-state-of-resistance-in-iran/.

44 Griffiths, *Pétain*, 249–255; Vergez-Chaignon, *Pétain*, 584–607.

45 Marc Ferro, *Pétain* (Paris: Fayard, 1987), 326–327; Winkler, *Zeit der Weltkriege*, 1025.

acceleration of the activities at military tribunals ending in numerous death penalties—dynamized the resistance movements and polarized public opinion.[46] At the same time, the Vichy regime made further concessions to Germany and a new phase of collaboration began, marked by the Paris Protocols signed in May 1941. Under that agreement, the Germans were pledged logistical support in Africa and the Middle East. In Syria, this resulted in a war between the French troops of the *État français* and the French units fighting on the side of the Anglo-Gaullist army. The latter emerged the victors in mid-July.[47]

In light of these experiences, the expectations of the French populace began to shift. The hopes of rebuilding France under Pétain's leadership or even expelling the German occupiers and re-establishing France in the European power system proved to be illusory. One consequence was an intensified experience of contingency, which is typical in perceived crisis situations. Neither renegotiations nor a peace treaty that might have reduced these uncertainties followed the extremely harsh conditions of the armistice. The politics of the *État français* clearly showed the people their dependence on the German occupiers.[48]

A Shift in Meaning Due to Crisis—Reactions of the Authoritarian Regime to War Hero Pétain's Loss of Legitimacy

Referencing Pétain's military prowess was becoming less and less an avenue for establishing the legitimacy of the Head of State and hence that of the Vichy regime. As the certainty grew that a counterattack comparable to Verdun was not forthcoming under Pétain, the narrative link between the

46 Sébastien Albertelli, Julien Blanc and Laurent Douzou, *La lutte clandestine en France. Une histoire de la Résistance, 1940–1944* (Paris: Seuil, 2019), 74–76.

47 Cointet, *Les hommes de Vichy*, 65–77; Lottman, *Pétain*, 378–383; Vergez-Chaignon, *Pétain*, 617–637.

48 Stefan Martens, "Vom Ersten Weltkrieg bis zum Ende des Vichy-Regimes (1914–1944)," in *Kleine Geschichte Frankreichs*, eds. Heinz-Gerhard Haupt and Ernst Hinrichs (Stuttgart: Reclam, 1997), 361–414, here: 406–407.

Marshal and the battle had to be redefined. As that happened, the war hero Pétain waned in significance in both state and journalistic propaganda.[49]

Repression was therefore not the regime's only option in responding to a critical development. While violence, arrests and deportations were means of reacting to the perceived increase in political resistance, the regime used other avenues to stem a perceived crisis in the representation of the Marshal. State control over public agencies, but primarily over the media, such as radio, pamphlets and books, proved to be considerably more comprehensive than in democratic systems; and this control needed to be implemented. Pierre Laval and the Marshal's entourage were informed, for example, by an intelligence report dated July 15, 1942, that 80 percent of the French resented the Germans and that this hostility extended to all those who were collaborating with the occupying forces. Therefore, the legitimacy of the regime was at stake. As the report pointed out, the unpopularity of the regime's political decisions was a fact: "This is the reality of the situation. It would be vain to deny it, ridiculous not to say it."[50]

Authoritarian systems such as the Vichy regime are characterized by the use of their interpretational authority to bind the populace ideologically to the new order. This allegiance was manufactured in France from 1940 to 1944 through the high degree of symbolic and narrative unambiguity typical of authoritarian systems. While democratic, pluralist states are characterized by at least allowing ambiguity in symbolic politics, authoritarian states attempt to obliterate alternative interpretations. This becomes particularly evident in the politics of memory and memory culture. For example, Pétain himself and his civil cabinet under Henry du Moulin de Labarthète aimed to have the post-revolutionary period forgotten through the politics of memory by attempting to cover over the tripartite motto of *liberté*, *égalité*, *fraternité* with the slogan *travail*, *familie*, *patrie* and by styling the republican tradition as a failed counter-model to the new France.[51]

Vichy had the unique characteristic that the state had comparably few instruments of power and was permanently in the exceptional state of war. Consequently, the political decision makers had a more limited arsenal at their disposal to respond to crises than other authoritarian states normally

49 Laure, *Pétain*, 267, 403–414. Similarly, the war hero had already begun to diminish in the works of Academy member Henry Bordeaux, cf. Henry Bordeaux, *Images du Maréchal Pétain* (Paris: Sequana, 1941).

50 Report by the *renseignement généraux* of July 15, 1942, quoted in: Laborie, *L'opinion*, 273.

51 Alya Aglan, *La France à l'envers. La guerre de Vichy, 1940–1945* (Paris: Gallimard, 2020).

do. In terms of censorship and propaganda, which was centrally managed by the Secretariat for Information and Propaganda under Paul Marion (1941–1942) and Pierre Laval (1942–1943), the regime was primarily able to influence regional and local decision makers through personally appointed Propaganda Delegates. Calls to order, travel restrictions and even dismissals were used as a means of exerting pressure. With the creation of the paramilitary *Milice* and the radicalization of the regime under Philippe Henriot and Marcel Déat, violence also became part of the authoritarian state's repertoire from 1943 onward, albeit with varying results. In the departments of the formally free south, the prefects in particular distrusted the envoys from the center, as they feared for their legal prerogatives and did not want to see their competences reduced. The dependency on regional and local cooperation was all too clear to the central decision makers of the French state.[52]

The Vichy regime therefore reveals ambivalences and overlooked ambiguities in authoritarian regimes. Attempts were made to compensate for the lack of political and military might through interpretational power spread on a regional level by its Propaganda Delegates. The efforts to maintain the cult of personality around Philippe Pétain through constant attestation and redefinition were an integral part of these attempts. The attempts to preserve the Pétain cult were influenced directly by the crisis experiences of Vichy's political and intellectual elite, as could be seen, for instance, in the works of René Benjamin, Henry Bordeaux, and Albert Paluel-Marmont, or in the endeavors of the propaganda departments under Bernard Ménétrel, and the long-serving Secretary General for Information and Propaganda, Paul Marion.[53]

Yet simultaneously, this type of state control, namely the interpretational authority over the regime's ideological foundation, was also fragile. In that moment in which the interpretation prescribed by the authoritarian state is no longer accepted, the state is compelled to compensate for the lost legitimacy by other means. In the case of Vichy, these other means came in the form of *la Milice*. Founded in 1943, this paramilitary troop and veterans'

52 Denis Peschanski, "Vichy au singulier, Vichy au pluriel. Une tentative avortée d'encadrement de la société (1941–1942)," *Annales* 43, no. 3 (1988): 639–661; Peschanski, "Encadrer ou contrôler?".

53 René Benjamin, *Le grand homme seul* (Paris: Plon, 1943); Bordeaux, *Images du Maréchal*; Albert Paluel-Marmont, *Pétain* (Paris: Libr. des Champs-Elysées, 1942). For the endeavors of the Secretary General for Information and Propaganda, see Robert Mencherini, "Étude départementale: la propagande dans les Bouches-du-Rhône," in *Le régime de Vichy et les Français*, eds. Jean-Pierre Azéma and François Bédarida (Paris: Fayard, 1992), 203–208.

organization brutally quashed acts of resistance.[54] The increase in violent oppression can also be seen as a sign that the claim asserted with the cult of personality around Pétain for the interpretational authority over the symbolic politics of the Vichy regime was being called into question more and more by the people.

The redefinition of the heroic figure of the Head of State—and with that the redefinition of the cult of personality—was thus a reaction to a transformation of the field of experience that was being driven by political realities. To most of the French populace and the political decision makers of Vichy, it was becoming ever clearer that nothing would change the reality of occupation without a change in political course. This intensified experience of contingency led to established patterns of thought and behavior being called into question. The uncertain moment of the crisis demanded action. This challenge culminated in the process of redefining Pétain's heroic figure, accelerating even further in the year of crisis—1942. The Head of State had to be reinvented.

The 1942 Crisis—From War Hero to Sacralized Savior

In 1942, the aforementioned crisis experiences became more dynamic and were augmented with ever newer layers of crisis to which the regime was compelled to respond. The attempts that were initiated by Darlan starting in February 1942 for more intensive collaboration did not lead to the desired successes. The return of the prisoners was still progressing sluggishly at best and there was hardly any easing of the conditions of the armistice.[55] Without either of these, any closer or overt cooperation with National Socialist Germany was unthinkable to a large portion of the population. Moreover, the foreseeable failure of the Riom show trial against former senior politicians of the Third Republic, such as Léon Blum, Édouard Daladier, Paul Reynaud, and Georges Mandel, was placing the political leadership of the Vichy regime under national and international pressure.

Begun on February 19, the trial was to lay the responsibility for the declaration of war against Germany on the government of the Third Republic, as was Hitler's will and in the Vichy regime's interests. The blame for the

54 Cointet, *La milice française*; Laborie, *L'opinion*, 287.

55 Waechter, *Geschichte Frankreichs*, 249–271.

defeat and the occupation was to thereby be placed on the Third Republic's leadership. However, the charges could not be proven against the defendants. On the contrary, the defendants used this international stage to incriminate the regime and Pétain. Foreign newspapers were present throughout the trial and especially Léon Blum's defense earned him great sympathy among the Americans. The French press, on the other hand, covered the trial less and less. As the accusers found themselves being accused, the Secretariat for Information and Propaganda issued very clear instructions for censorship, such as not to broadcast Édouard Daladier indicating that Pétain, during his time as Secretary of War in 1934, had decided not to fortify the Northern Front and the Ardennes. As a result, the trial had severely tarnished the Marshal's prestige and compromised the Vichy regime.[56] In light of these devastating effects, it was suspended on April 14 and officially abandoned the following year.[57]

Pétain responded to this political failure by recalling Pierre Laval on April 18, 1942, to again head the government in the newly created office of *chef du gouvernement*. This was far more than a change of political leadership. Pétain lost the authority he had had to govern unitarily as Head of State since July 1940. With this step, the Marshal finally distanced himself from the day-to-day business of politics, not least because he had proven to be inept at managing the governmental apparatus.[58]

It was this threefold development of sinking approval, a shifted power structure and the decision makers' intensified experience of a political crisis that led to Pétain being presented increasingly as a sacred symbolic figure and less as a capable war hero. The Head of State himself was a central actor in this shift. As in Fascist Italy, Nazi Germany or the Bolshevik Soviet Union, the cult of personality was staged through the repetitive use of short core messages, as well as through standardized iconography and public

56 Elisabeth Bokelmann, *Vichy contra Dritte Republik. Der Prozess von Riom 1942* (Paderborn: Schöningh, 2006), 138.

57 Ibid., 138–145; Alain Bancaud, "Le procès de Riom: instrumentalisation et renversement de la justice," in *Justice, politique et République. De l'affaire Dreyfus à la guerre d'Algérie*, eds. Marc Oliver Baruch and Vincent Duclert (Brussels: Complexe, 2002), 221–241; Stefan Grüner, "Vom Umgang mit der demokratischen Vergangenheit. Das Deutsche Reich, Vichy und das politische Führungspersonal der Dritten Republik 1940–1945," in *Frankreich und Deutschland im Krieg. (November 1942–Herbst 1944); Okkupation, Kollaboration, Résistance; Akten des deutsch-französischen Kolloquiums La France et l'Allemagne en Guerre (novembre 1942–automne 1944) Occupation, Collaboration, Résistance*, ed. Stefan Martens, (Bonn: Bouvier, 2000), 73–98.

58 Vergez-Chaignon, *Pétain*, 695.

performances. In the French State—as in Italy, Germany, and the Soviet Union—the goal was to bridge the distance between the leader and his followers. Celebrations and public rituals, such as the oath that Legionnaires and civil servants had to swear to Petain,[59] were an important aspect of the cult of personality. They implied a close link between the ruler and the ruled, and were, thus, a form of seemingly direct legitimation that responded to the legacy of a parliamentary democracy that had fallen into disrepute.[60]

Pétain reached people in the whole of France primarily through speeches, radio addresses and public appearances, which were written exactly as he wished and were later printed in newspapers and leaflets by selected publishing houses. Key messages were captured on posters and distributed by the Secretariat of Information and Propaganda and his personal cabinet.[61] Another way to bridge the gap between the people and the Head of State was deeply rooted in French political culture: The Head of State undertook several journeys through the unoccupied south of the country. Pétain passed through dozens of cities in the years of his rule. In Lyon, Marseille, Montpellier and Toulon, the Marshal was received with a staged choreography and celebrated by the citizens. He delivered his messages to the French public as a fatherly figure. The public appearances of Pétain were meticulously organized,[62] but they mostly lacked the martial mass staging that was cultivated under Fascism, National Socialism, or Bolshevism.[63] His personal cabinet did not only give strict instructions to the mayors and regional propaganda delegates in advance, but also sent materials: 6,000 posters and 200,000 leaflets were delivered to Lyon before Pétain's arrival on November 16, 1940.[64] Those journeys had a brief positive impact on

---

59 Rossignol, *Histoire de la Propagande*, 81–83.

60 Benno Ennecker, "Der Führer im Europa des 20. Jahrhunderts – eine Synthese," in *Der Führer im Europa des 20. Jahrhunderts*, eds. Benno Ennker and Heidi Hein-Kircher (Marburg: Verlag Herder-Institut, 2010), 347–378.

61 Vergez-Chaignon, *Pétain*, 592–598.

62 Rémi Dalisson, *Les fêtes du Maréchal.*

63 E. A. Rees, "Leader Cults: Varieties, Preconditions and Functions," in *The Leader Cult in Communist Dictatorships. Stalin and the Eastern Bloc,* eds. Balázs Apor, Jan C. Behrends, Polly Jones and E. A. Rees (Houndmills, Basingstoke, Hampshire: Palgrave Macmillan, 2004), 1–26, here: 16–17; Jan Plamper, *The Stalin Cult. A Study in the Alchemy of Power* (New Haven: Yale University Press, 2012); Ludolf Herbst, *Hitlers Charisma. Die Erfindung eines deutschen Messias* (Frankfurt a. M.: Fischer, 2010.)

64 Vergez-Chaignon, *Pétain,* 598–604.

morale and public opinion of the Head of State, at least until summer 1942, as reports by the intelligence service indicate.[65]

Not only did he disseminate political messages and the ideology of national renewal through his political instructions, public appearances and radio addresses, he also decisively shaped the image of his public figure with his journeys, as evidenced by his public appearances, for example, during the festivities associated with Joan of Arc Day on May 10, 1942, in Limousin.

As with similar occasions, the Marshal used the figure of the maid of Orléans to increase his credibility as the symbolic embodiment of national unity. He did this by framing the era of Joan of Arc as a historical foil to the year 1942:[66] At both times, French society had been internally torn, but the maid of Orléans had shown the French the way to salvation. Pétain goes on: In absolute love and devotion to her fatherland, she took on the suffering of all as her burden and sacrificed herself. By projecting these virtues onto Joan of Arc, Pétain claimed them for himself. He suggested to his audience that he, as an exemplary leader, should be admired and followed just like the heroine of the Hundred Years' War. He thereby constructed his exceptional and commendable role in the *État français*, from which he derived his political authority on May 10, 1942, by appealing to the inhabitants of Limousin:

> "to gather behind the Leader, and to abandon the chimeras of the Alien. One began to understand that a people can only expect its salvation from itself, that it must unite, discipline itself, stop arguing with its leaders. [...] France had been cured of its doubts, it now believed in God and in its leader. France was saved."[67]

This quote makes plain that the speech fulfilled several functions. It heroized Pétain by implicitly equating the Marshal to Joan of Arc and embedding him simultaneously in a savior narrative. The emphasis of the redeeming, yet

65 AN 2 AG 438. CC Dossiers Maréchal. Commission de Contrôle Postal. Synthèse spéciale sur la visite du Maréchal en Corrèze. Correspondance contrôlée du 4 au 10 juillet 1942.

66 Regarding the significance of Joan of Arc in the Vichy regime, cf. Eric Jennings, "'Reinventing Jeanne': The Iconology of Joan of Arc in Vichy Schoolbooks, 1940–44," *Journal of Contemporary History* 29 (1994), 711–734; Gerd Krumeich, *Jeanne d'Arc in der Geschichte. Historiographie - Politik - Kultur* (Sigmaringen: Thorbecke, 1989).

67 AN 3W/282. Dossier B. Faits de propagande écrite et parlée. III 1 B 39. Message du Maréchal Pétain, Chef de l'Etat à la population Limousin à l'occasion de l'inauguration de la statue de Jeanne d'Arc à Limoges le 10.5.1942: "[...] de se grouper derrière le chef, et d'abandonner les chimères de l'Etranger. On commençait à comprendre qu'un peuple ne peut attendre son salut que de lui-même, que pour cela il doit s'unir, se discipliner, cesser de discuter ses Chefs. [...] La France était guérie du doute, elle aussi désormais croyait en Dieu, et en son Chef. Elle était sauvée."

exceedingly difficult, path towards national unity suggested to the audience that the path being taken under Pétain's rule would ultimately also lead to salvation. Unlike other figures in the state's canon of heroes,[68] in the politics of memory propagated by the *État français* as detailed here, the maid of Orléans functioned as a prefiguration. That made her a call to action, but also a call to obedience when Pétain said: "Gather yourselves closely behind your Leader, hold nothing in your hearts but French thoughts."[69]

The religiously charged "savior" *topos* combined all the manifold heroic qualities attributed to the public figure of Philippe Pétain and constituted an essential narrative and symbolic pillar of his political rule. At the same time, as the French historian Pierre Servent emphasizes, it reflected the societal expectation of a new social and political beginning.[70]

While the state's institutionalized "savior" *topos*[71] pervaded the entirety of Pétainist biographical texts or in the unofficial state anthem *Maréchal, nous voila!* (Marshal, here we are!) of 1941[72], a shift towards a moral and religious message could increasingly be observed from 1942 onwards. Moral authority, leadership qualities and a willingness to make sacrifices comparable to Jesus and Joan of Arc were moved to the center of Pétain's heroization by the propaganda.[73] At the moment when war hero Pétain waned on account of the accelerated development of the crisis of 1942, the savior Pétain appeared in a new light. The Head of State became increasingly immersed in an aura of the sacred.

This is especially evident when looking at hagiographers loyal to the regime. In 1942, the journalist and writer, Albert Paluel-Marmont, wrote about the Head of State: "His name is Philippe PÉTAIN. And his name is blessed, because its double initial is also that of the word '*Patrie*' (fatherland),

68 Rossignol, *Histoire de la propagande*, 84–87.

69 Philippe Pétain, speech of May 10, 1942: "[…] groupez-vous étroitement derrière votre Chef, n'ayant plus dans vos cœurs que des pensées françaises."

70 Servent, *Le mythe Pétain*, 234.

71 Rossignol, *Histoire de la propagande*, 78.

72 Nathalie Dompnier, "Entre La Marseillaise et Maréchal, nous voilà! quel hymne pour le régime de Vichy?", in *La vie musicale sous Vichy*, eds. Josette Alviset and Myriam Chimènes (Brussels: Complexe, 2001), 69–88; Alary, *Nouvelle histoire*, 135.

73 An exemplary piece on the subject: D. Agostini-Milanta, *Pensées françaises, hommage au Maréchal Pétain qui fait resplendir dans la nuit sombre le soleil de son âme* (Niort: A. Nicols, 1942). Further examples: Benjamin, *Le grand homme seul*; Maurice Muret, *France héroïque* (Paris: A. Michel, 1942); Paluel-Marmont, *Il était une fois un Maréchal de France* (Paris: Editions et publications françaises, 1943); Lucien Romier, *Esquisse d'un Portrait moral de Philippe Pétain* (Paris: Impr. nationale, 1942).

the most beautiful name in our language after that of God."[74] In his illustrated biography, Pétain was depicted as a "light [that] reached the very depths of souls"[75] and his accession to power in the summer of 1940 was equated with the sacrifice of Jesus Christ.[76] A comparable tone was struck in the poetry collection of D. Agostini-Milanta, carrying the revealing title: "Thoughts from France, a tribute to Marshal Pétain who makes the sun of his soul shine in the dark night."[77] The light metaphor was meant to assure the reader that the Marshal was chosen by God. In writings like these, the martyrdom in the experience of occupation and war found its narrative and symbolic translation in the sacralized savior of Pétain.

The religious connotation of this self-interpretation of many French in no way represented an unquestioned consensus, however.[78] The interpretational authority over Pétain's cult of personality, which was clearly crumbling—especially from November 1942 onwards—came under more and more defamatory attacks from opponents of the Vichy regime.[79] The resistance against the regime coalesced not just around Charles de Gaulle in his London exile, but also formed at various levels and in different locations within France.[80] A repeated basic pattern in the argumentation of the deheroization and delegitimization processes was accusing Pétain of having committed treason against the French people. Parallel to the semi-official veneration of Pétain in the Vichy regime, an opposing discourse about the Head of State emerged that turned the "savior" into a "traitor".[81]

---

74 Paluel-Marmont, *Pétain,* 8: "Il s'appelle Philippe PÉTAIN. Et son nom est béni, car sa double initiale est celle, aussi, du mot Patrie, le plus beau nom de notre langue après celui de Dieu."

75 Ibid., 30: "L'horizon s'éclaircit et sa lumière pénétra jusqu'au plus profond des âmes. Les hésitants se sentirent soulevés d'ardeur, et les sceptiques convaincus de certitude."

76 Paluel-Marmont described it as an "ineffable moment when he walked towards his Calvary, redeemer of the Fatherland, apostle of our resurrection, martyr of his own offering." Ibid., 68: "Moment ineffable où il marcha vers son calvaire, rédempteur de la Patrie, apôtre de notre résurrection, martyre de sa propre offrande."

77 Agostini-Milanta, *Pensées françaises.*

78 Delporte, "Propagande," Laborie, *L'opinion*, 257–260.

79 Matthias Waechter, *Der Mythos des Gaullismus. Heldenkult, Geschichtspolitik und Ideologie 1940 bis 1958* (Göttingen: Wallstein, 2006), 49–51.

80 Albertelli, Blanc, Douzou, *La lutte clandestine*, 74–76, Nicolas Beaupré, *Les Grandes guerres. 1914–1945* (Paris: Belin, 2012), 944–961; Robert Gildea, *Fighters in the shadows. A new history of the French Resistance* (London: Faber & Faber, 2015).

81 Jörn Leonhard and Stefan Schubert, "Verrat," in *Compendium heroicum*, ed. Sonderforschungsbereich 948 "Heroes – Heroisations - Heroismens" (Freiburg, 2020): https://www.compendium-heroicum.de/lemma/verrat/.

Accordingly, the rhetoric of the sacred propagated under the *État français*, as illustrated above using Pétain's own equation with Joan of Arc, in no way went undisputed, even though it did reference potent sources of legitimation as regards the politics of memory. On the one hand, it drew on the monarchical tradition, which in France was additionally influenced by Bonapartism. On the other hand, the religious veneration of Pétain resembled the sacralization of the nation, which the Marshal embodied in the eyes of his supporters. To this extent, constructing Pétain into a sacred, heroic figure was based on traditional mechanisms of communication via which authority in France was established and solidified in different political orders. In the savior narrative tied to Pétain, several interpretations consequently overlaid one another that oscillated within a complex semantic field between rulership, sacrality and the heroic, legitimating the political order embodied by the Marshal in a variety of ways.

Furthermore, as the perceived traumatic loss lingered, the rhetoric of the sacred united a large part of the French population into a community of shared experience that increasingly considered itself to be a victimized community as the occupation persisted.[82] This collectively shared experience gave meaning to the rapidly overlapping crises and offered guidance and direction in times of uncertainty.[83] One of these was the sacralization of the Head of State, whose supposed self-sacrifice was to symbolize the martyrdom of the French people.

The sacralization of the *chef d'État* thus served to solidify the political order that was destabilized by the intensified crisis experience of 1942. Moreover, the sacred victim and savior message that became ever clearer in 1942, can be seen as a reaction to the French people's disappointed expectations and to an established reality of occupation and war. Pétain actively saving France no longer seemed possible to the majority of French people. The political elites had already realized that France could not resist, let alone liberate itself from the occupying power through its own efforts. This

---

82 Luc Capdevila, "La communauté de souffrance, l'identité nationale à travers l'image du 'bon Français' au lendemain de l'occupation l'exemple de la Bretagne," in *Frankreich und Deutschland im Krieg. (November 1942–Herbst 1944); Okkupation, Kollaboration, Résistance; Akten des deutsch-französischen Kolloquiums La France et l'Allemagne en Guerre (novembre 1942–automne 1944) Occupation, Collaboration, Résistance*, ed. Stefan Martens, (Bonn: Bouvier, 2000), 831–844.

83 Felix Heinzer, Jörn Leonhard, and Ralf von den Hoff, "Einleitung: Relationen zwischen Sakralisierungen und Heroisierungen," in *Sakralität und Heldentum*, eds. Felix Heinzer, Jörn Leonhard, and Ralf von den Hoff (Würzburg: Ergon, 2017), 9–18.

development reinforced a central characteristic of any crisis experience: During war and occupation, there is hardly anything resembling a normal routine. However, by no later than the occupation of the entire country in November 1942, it became immediately palpable that the pre-war *status quo* and the desired restoration of France was no longer possible.

From 1942 onwards, that religious layer of meaning overlaid other aspects of his cult of personality and defined the representation of the Head of State even after the Vichy regime ended.[84] This development was made possible by a transformation of the relationship between church and state in the preceding decades. The anticlerical and laicist tendencies of French politics during the young Third Republic eventually led to the separation of church and state. However, as a result of World War I, the anticlericalism of the turn of the century dissolved in the mid-1920s. By the 1930s, the image of French Catholicism had fundamentally changed: It was now no longer seen in terms of an elite clericalism, but as an integral part of French society. This revival was reflected not least in the importance that Christian symbolism regained. The cult of Joan of Arc, for example, a Catholic icon, became part of the republican commemorative culture, which was adopted and reinterpreted by the Vichy regime and by Philippe Pétain himself.[85] From 1940 onwards, the French State was to benefit from this development, as demonstrated by the church's support for the new regime, and religious practices that interpreted the defeat in a religious context.[86]

In this way, high-ranking catholic authorities gave credence to the sacred symbolism and religious exaltation of the Head of State. The religious French populace was thereby presented a guiding symbolic figure that was capable of seemingly embodying their suffering. In this regard, Pétain

84 Christiane Florin, *Philippe Pétain und Pierre Laval: Das Bild zweier Kollaborateure im französischen Gedächtnis; ein Beitrag zur Vergangenheitsbewältigung in Frankreich von 1945 bis 1995* (Frankfurt a. M.: Peter Lang, 1997); Jörn Leonhard, "Mythisierung und Mnesie: das Bild Philippe Pétains im Wandel der politisch-historischen Kultur Frankreichs seit 1945," in *Führer der extremen Rechten. Das schwierige Verhältnis der Nachkriegsgeschichtsschreibung zu „großen Männern" der eigenen Vergangenheit*, eds. Georg Christoph and Berger Waldenegg (Zurich: Chronos, 2006), 109–129.

85 Jacques Duquesne, *Les catholiques français sous l'occupation*, 2nd ed. (Paris: Grasset, 1986), 328–330; Jens Ivo Engels, *Kleine Geschichte der Dritten französischen Republik (1870–1940)* (Cologne, Weimar, Vienna: Böhlau, 2007), 182–185; Robert Paxton, *Vichy France: Old guard and new order, 1940–1944* (New York: Columbia University Press, 1982), 148–153; Rossignol, *Histoire de la propagande*, 87–89.

86 Michèle Cointet, *L'Église sous Vichy 1940–1945: La repentance en question* (Paris: Perrin, 1998).

benefited from a revisited form of monarchical legitimacy, adopting the fundamentals of Christian values and the support of the church, both of which were rejected by other authoritarian rulers such as Hitler, Stalin, and Mussolini. Albeit waning, the stability of the regime until the summer of 1944 cannot be explained without this redefinition of Pétain from a military to a sacral savior figure.

Reinventing Pétain: Crisis and Cults of Personality in Vichy France

The year 1942 proved to be a phase of particularly intense perceptions of crisis in the authoritarian Vichy regime. On the one hand, there were the French people, who in their prolonged social and increasingly economic plight were shown the impotence of the state through the failed Riom show trial, ostentatious collaboration with Germany, the transition to a new government under Pierre Laval and, finally, through the occupation of the entire country after November 8 by German and Italian troops. On the other hand, the ensuing delegitimization resulted in the regime's political elites sensing an accelerated decline of the *État français* political order, not least due to the increasing influence of the various resistance movements. A loss of control and many uncertainties were the consequences of these crisis experiences that reciprocally reinforced one other. One way in which the political leadership of the Vichy regime responded to this was violence. Another way, however, was with subtler methods in the realm of symbolic politics. Herein, I have attempted to show examples of the effects these mutually reinforcing, greatly intensified experiences of contingency had on the cult of personality maintained around Philippe Pétain.

Pro-regime depictions of the Head of State therefore referenced a contemporary leader discourse which, on its own, referenced the dominance of notions of a personalized political order in Europe owing to the domestic and foreign policy successes of authoritarian systems.[87] In the public depiction of the *chef d'État*, the short-term dominance of authoritarian leader concepts coalesced with long-established traditions of a *bon chef*, a good leader,

87 Walther L. Bernecker, *Europa zwischen den Weltkriegen. 1914–1944* (Stuttgart: Ulmer, 2002), 308–310; Lutz Raphael, *Imperiale Gewalt und mobilisierte Nation: Europa 1914–1945* (Munich: Beck, 2011), 186–230.

which were firmly rooted in the Third Republic and informed French expectations during World War II and beyond. As Yves Cohen was able to show in his study, the *siècle des chefs* (century of leaders) was marked by numerous hues[88] but, in the figure of Pétain, these two main lines of discourse in particular reinforced each other reciprocally and legitimized a singular form of personalized rulership in the *État français*.

This can be explained by the *État français* remaining inseparably linked to the heroized Marshal. In this context, the heroization of Pétain shifted within a few short years. The war hero deferred to the sacred savior. The experiences of collaboration and occupation and the widespread belief among the French of being a victimized community formed the basis for this reinterpretation of the Head of State. Thereafter, Pétain was seen by his community of admirers as a religiously connoted role model. As such, he was far better suited—at least to some extent—to maintaining French unity, compared to a war hero in a war hardly anyone believed could be won.

Examining the unifying and state-bearing figure of Pétain through the lens of his heroizations has shown the analytical value in positing a vast number of representations of the cult of personality around Pétain that overlaid and reciprocally influenced one another. In order to uncover the complexity of narratives, attributions, interpretations and meanings associated with the Marshal, I suggest regarding each of those layers on an analytical level as a unique form of the cult interwoven via time and space with its multiple counterparts. This analytical approach would offer the possibility to separately decode the meaning of each layer, allowing us to respect the singularity of the historical context. Moreover, the synchronic and diachronic interactions between these layers could be understood more accurately, thus enabling us to trace the causes and effects of changes in history.

Neglecting the various layers of the cult of personality would suggest an unambiguity, which was not consistent with contemporaries' world of experience. Especially not in times of accelerated perceptions of a crisis that seemed to make rapid reinterpretations in the realm of symbolic politics necessary. Regarding the different layers of the representation of the Head of State, as well as the evident crisis-driven shift of his public image, one could even speak of different cults of personality in 1940 and in 1942. If the layers of these cults of personality are deciphered individually, they reveal norm and value systems characterized by a particular dynamic in times of crisis.

88 Yves Cohen, *Le siècle des chefs. Une histoire transnationale du commandement et de l'autorité (1890–1940)* (Paris: Amsterdam, 2013).

Against this background, this study has attempted to show that the reinvention of Pétain reacted to the transforming world of experience of the contemporaries and the associated perceptions of crises. The various layers of the cult of Pétain show that even an authoritarian regime like Vichy, which had relatively few instruments of power, knew how to use the field of symbolic politics flexibly in order to maintain the political order.

Student Politics Between Imagination and Action: The National Students Federation and the Anti-Ayub Movement in Pakistan, 1956–1971

Meher Ali

When news of the assassination of Patrice Lumumba, the first democratically elected Prime Minister of the independent Democratic Republic of the Congo, broke in February 1961, protesters took to the streets from Accra to Belgrade. In New York, demonstrators stormed UN buildings; meanwhile, in Karachi, Pakistan, a group of left-wing students staged a *jaloos* (demonstration) against US imperialism and in solidarity with the Congolese people. The next day, a virulent editorial in the country's leading daily—*Dawn*—criticized the demonstrators for their selective sympathies. How, asked the writer, could they muster such concern for the Congo, but remain silent for their Muslim brethren across the border—where communal riots had recently affected the Indian state of Madhya Pradesh? In response to this provocation, the students organized a demonstration against the killing of Muslims in Jabalpur. The number of demonstrators and supporters multiplied. The spectacle of open defiance of martial law—one of the first such instances since Ayub Khan imposed military rule in 1958—drew a harsh government response. Police *lathi*-charged[1] the crowds, dozens of students were arrested, a handful of their leaders were tried in military courts and ultimately externed from the city. "They would command us: 'say *Ayub Khan Zindabad*' (long live Ayub Khan),"[2] recounted student leader Meraj Muhammad Khan. "We said no. They told us, 'say socialism *murdabad*' (death to socialism). But we said no."

Unbeknownst to the authorities, the banishment of these youth activists would provide the spark for student mobilizations that would ultimately spread across the country, playing an important role in bringing down Ayub Khan's authoritarian regime. Having seized power in a military coup in 1958,

1 Baton charge, a coordinated tactic for dispersing crowds.

2 Meraj Muhammad Khan, interview, Karachi, Pakistan, June 22, 2012.

Khan's decade of rule actualized the drift towards autocratic methods of governance that had been in motion since the nation's birth in 1947.[3] His development-oriented agenda included an ambitious program of rapid economic growth and social reform, operating through the centralization of state authority and the systematic depoliticization of Pakistani society. Upon taking power, the martial law regime suspended political parties and suppressed political opposition, conducting mass arrests and detentions of left-leaning activists and intellectuals, as well as instituting draconian press controls. Although martial law was formally replaced, in 1960, by a system of "controlled democracy",[4] any semblance of democratic process was undercut by deepening bureaucratic control, the suppression of civil liberties, and the denial of fundamental political rights. As Tahir Naqvi has argued, such authoritarian projects of political regulation rested, ultimately, on the dictatorial logic of emergency—couching the threat of coercion in the language of developmental citizenship and democratic tutelage.[5] Frustration with government policies, growing inequality, and mounting provincial and class-based grievances erupted, finally, in mass anti-government protests in November 1968. By March, amidst escalating labor strikes, mass demonstrations, and urban unrest, Ayub Khan was forced to resign.[6]

Students were at the forefront of these mobilizations, which brought unprecedented numbers of workers, intellectuals, and urban classes onto the streets in cities across the country. Foremost amongst them were radically minded youths spearheaded by the National Students Federation (NSF), a left-oriented student organization that had been building an opposition movement to the regime from the early days of military rule. The moment of social and political "crisis" constituted by the anti-Ayub movement manifested itself, first and foremost, as a mass uprising against an unpopular dictator. However, it was also the crystallization of a more meaningful challenge to the vision of citizenship and national life offered by state authoritarianism, an oppositional politics made acutely visible by students and their

3 Ayesha Jalal, *Democracy and Authoritarianism in South Asia* (Cambridge: Cambridge University Press, 1995), 55.

4 The Basic Democracies scheme, launched in 1960, was a hierarchical system of local government through limited adult franchise, see: Tahir Naqvi, "Nation, Space, and Exception: Pakistan's Basic Democracies Experiment," in *Comparative Studies of South Asia, Africa and the Middle East* 33, no. 3 (2013): 279–294.

5 Naqvi, "Nation, Space," 282.

6 For a classic overview of the Ayub Khan era, see: Lawrence Ziring, *The Ayub Khan Era: Politics in Pakistan, 1958–1969* (Syracuse: Syracuse University Press, 1971).

forms of resistance. Their role—not only in toppling a dictatorship, but within the wider social and political upheavals of the period—remains understudied in the historiography of this era, subsumed within more familiar narratives of the rise of populism and the People's Party of Pakistan (PPP).[7]

Progressive student activism thus remains underexplored as its *own* category of political activity, one which, if engaged critically, could help illuminate the frictions between existing and possible forms of political discourse and performance. This chapter, based on oral histories of the student leadership of the NSF, aims to revisit these distinctive modes of ideological contestation and action through the lens of youth subjectivity and memory. I argue that it was, in part, the unique liminality and inherent flexibility of student activism—temporary, aspirational, and in-between—that made it a powerful vehicle of contentious politics, existing between emerging modes of appeal and "resistance", agitational movements and organized parties, ideological commitments and embodied action.

After the prohibition of student unions in 1983 by General Zia-ul-Haq, and the effective end to progressive social movements in the country, student politics in Pakistan has increasingly degenerated into ethnic, religious, and sectarian-based violence—as typified by the rise of the *Muhajir Qaumi Movement*[8] and the dominance of the *Islami Jamiat-e Talaba*.[9] This devolution tracks easily into the twin trajectories—the demise of secular democracy, and the growing strength of ethno-separatism and Islamization—from which contemporary Pakistan is usually understood. Given the dominance of such frameworks; Pakistan as a hotbed for religious extremism, a democracy in crisis, and a state riddled with both internal and external security threats—histories of the left are often forced to operate as projects of

7 Standard accounts of this historical moment can be found in Ayesha Jalal, *Democracy and Authoritarianism in South Asia* (Cambridge: Cambridge University Press, 1995); Aqil Shah, *The Army and Democracy: Military Politics in Pakistan* (Cambridge, MA: Harvard University Press, 2014); and Riaz Ahmed Shaikh, "1968—Was it Really a Year of Social Change in Pakistan?" in *Sixties Radicalism and Social Movement Activism: Retreat or Resurgence?*, ed. Bryn Jones and Mike O'Donnell (London: Anthem Press, 2010), 73–88. The role of students has been addressed in Lal Khan, *Pakistan's Other Story: The 1968–69 Revolution* (Lahore: The Struggle Publications, 2008); and Iqbal Haider Butt, *Revisiting Student Politics in Pakistan* (Gujranwala: Bargad, 2009).

8 This political party finds its origins in the All Pakistan Muhajir Student Organization and remains deeply driven by student participation. See: Oskar Verkaaik, *Migrants and Militants: Fun and Urban Violence in Pakistan* (Princeton: Princeton University Press, 2004).

9 Laurent Gayer, *Karachi: Ordered Disorder and the Struggle for the City* (Oxford: Oxford University Press, 2014), 70.

recovery, suffused with either nostalgia or cynicism for an "alternative" vision for Pakistan that has long since been eclipsed.[10] As evaluative analyses, such narratives are ultimately unable to escape questions of success versus failure: Why these social movements were unable to succeed, why progressive politics never recovered, and what possible legacies we might garner from histories of the left.

My critique of this positioning is not that these histories were of little significance, but that the fixation on consequence—on how much or how little movements lived up to their purported ambitions—prevents us from seeing the wider contexts in which they emerged, as well as the productive ambiguities and tensions within their discourse. As a forum of the political left, the NSF provides a useful window into the very construction, imagination, and contestation of the category of "progressivism" at this critical juncture in Pakistani history, at a moment of global upheaval and revolt. As such, it also offers an opportunity to explore Pakistan's place within transnational frameworks of Third World internationalism and the "global sixties", not necessarily to answer whether or not Pakistan had its own "'68 moment", but in order to trace how internationalist ideas and rhetoric inflected local understandings of politics and struggle. More significantly, the NSF movement represents one view of the broader shift in political and social relations taking place in Pakistan at this time, a shift which fundamentally transformed the meaning and practice of mass politics.

This chapter is based primarily on 26 in-person oral history interviews conducted in Lahore and Karachi between 2012 and 2014. Given its limited scope, this study cannot claim to represent the thoughts and ideas of any "majority", nor to capture the total possible motivations and interests of participating groups.[11] As a product of oral history work, it is also tied up with the politics of narrative and memory—shaped by present perceptions

10 Recent important scholarship that addresses the history of the Pakistani left includes Saadia Toor, *The State of Islam: Culture and Cold War Politics in Pakistan* (London: Pluto Press, 2011); Kamran Asdar Ali, *Surkh Salam: Communist Politics and Class Activism in Pakistan, 1947–1972* (Karachi: Oxford University Press, 2015); Ali Raza, "An Unfulfilled Dream: The Left in Pakistan ca. 1947–50," *South Asian History and Culture* 4, Issue 4 (2013): 503–519; and Anushay Malik, "Alternative Politics and Dominant Narratives: Communists and the Pakistani State in the Early 1950s," *South Asian History and Culture* 4, Issue 4 (2013): 520–537.

11 It is also skewed by certain biases and omissions, most notably the absence of women's voices, as well as the geographic exclusion of smaller cities and the participation of East Pakistan, Balochistan, and the NWFP.

as much as past experiences. This provides an opportunity to interrogate not only the unfolding of remembered events, but also the multivalent *meanings* these memories hold for the participants themselves—to glimpse, as Alessandro Portelli once put it, not only what they *did*, but "what they wanted to do, what they believed they were doing, what they now think they did."[12] It is an opportunity, in other words, to explore student-hood "as a unique form of subjectivity",[13] as well as the ways this historical moment—as a turning point, a transformation, or even a "crisis"—has been remembered, memorialized, and narratively reconstructed. What I hope to offer, then, is an exploratory discussion around the ways political vocabularies, imaginaries, and discourses emerge and ultimately constitute themselves as identifiable practices, resistances, and movements—through, among other things, the interplay between rhetoric and activism, idealism and action, the global and the local.

Origin Stories: The DSF and Progressive Student Politics

"When Pakistan was created, students had a certain dream. A mindset that Pakistan will be beautiful, free, self-sufficient, prosperous. There will be no exploitation here. There will be no injustice here [...] but when students saw this [...] they saw that the system is the same landlordism and feudalism. The same forms of capitalist exploitation. People deprived of basic human necessities like food, shelter, and education. This is called the Islamic democracy of Pakistan, but there is no sign of democracy here [...] This was not the dream they had dreamed of."[14]

Meraj Muhammad Khan was only ten years old when his family migrated to Pakistan after Partition from their home in Uttar Pradesh, India. Like many of my other interviewees, he remembered the experience of migration and the promises of the new nation as fundamental to his politicization as a young student. The expectations of independence were arguably highest for those who gave up everything—uprooted their lives, abandoned ancestral homes—to pursue the promise of the new nation. These were not the

12 Alessandro Portelli, "The Peculiarities of Oral History," *History Workshop Journal* 12, Issue 1 (autumn 1981): 96–107, here: 100.

13 Dan Hodgkinson and Luke Melchiorre, "Introduction: Student Activism in an Era of Decolonization," *Africa* 89, no. S1 (2019): S1–S14, here: S1.

14 Khan, interview.

refugees of Punjab, forced across the border by brutal violence and communal massacres. They were the Urdu-speaking *muhajirs* (migrants) of Uttar Pradesh and Bombay, who migrated largely by choice and settled in urban Sindh. The sleepy colonial port city of Karachi transformed into a teeming megacity overnight; the population jumped from about 450,000 before Partition to over a million within four short years, drastically transforming not just the demographics but also the culture, politics, and physical landscape of the city.[15] The population of Sindhi-speaking and Urdu-speaking groups practically reversed (from 61 percent Sindhi and 6 percent Urdu in 1947, to 9 percent Sindhi and 50 percent Urdu by 1951), establishing a contentious dynamic between the two groups that reverberates to this day. This conflict first became visible in the controversy over the establishment of Karachi as the federal capital, a short-lived scheme that would nonetheless have massive repercussions for the city's urban development and the genesis of its political culture.

"I had never seen a port city," remembered Jamal Naqvi, about his arrival in Karachi in 1949. "I came from the plains of UP, where I had never even seen a hillock [...] yes, this city was very different. I went to the place we were living on a camel cart—all the way to PIB Colony where we lived."[16] The Urdu-speaking *muhajirs* that flooded into the city during Pakistan's earliest years occupied the open land and empty buildings left behind by fleeing Hindus, creating uniquely multi-class refugee settlements across Karachi and in the area around Saddar Bazaar.[17] This "downtown" area developed rapidly in response to its new population; the federal secretariat was constructed adjacent to the Bazaar, embassies sprung up nearby, and existing educational institutions expanded. In 1951, Karachi University was established in the vicinity, on the grounds of an old Hindu trust middle school—the first federal university[18] to be set up in West Pakistan in response to the demands for higher education in the new nation. The growing population of youth and students in the city were thus exposed to, among other things, an emerging "cosmopolitan" culture around Saddar city center—where politicians, diplomats, intellectuals, and working-class people frequented the same shared spaces. The recreational spaces of this downtown—such as popular

15 Arif Hasan, *Understanding Karachi: Planning and Reform for the Future* (Karachi: City Press, 2000), 24.

16 Jamal Naqvi, interview, Karachi, Pakistan, August 6, 2014.

17 Hasan, *Understanding Karachi,* 132.

18 Aside from the existing Punjab University in Lahore.

bookshops, cinemas, cafes, and bars—came to play an important role in the proliferation of progressive subcultures in the city and continue to loom large in elite nostalgia for the liberalism of bygone times. "Karachi was like an island,"[19] described Pakistani architect, Arif Hasan; a safe port for migrants amidst the raucous waves of independence, offering the chance of not only socio-economic mobility but rare inter-class encounters, a place where the borders of the political might open up to previously unforeseen possibilities and actors.

Like other newly independent Third World countries, Pakistan underwent an expansion of educational opportunities during the 1950s–1960s, extending to previously marginalized communities and thus making students an important link between those communities and the public political sphere.[20] In Karachi, the capital of Pakistan until 1959, schools and colleges—like many other institutions in the city—were not able to keep up with the rapid pace of growth, exacerbated by the influx of refugees after Partition. Students entering colleges and universities—many of them middle- and lower middle-class migrants, like Jamal and Meraj—found themselves facing a lack of basic amenities, run down facilities, and high tuition fees. Moreover, they found no effective avenues from which to address these issues, the only existing student organization, the Muslim Students Federation, being the student wing of the ruling party. It is from this context of displacement, upheaval, and economic hardship—a context inextricable from that of the *muhajir* experience and the emerging urban life of downtown Karachi—that student activism first emerged, with the formation of the Democratic Students Federation (DSF) at Dow Medical College. The DSF was unofficially affiliated with the local chapter of the Communist Party of Pakistan (CPP), which was struggling to recover its ranks after the departure of the city's non-Muslim intelligentsia.

According to Eric Rahim, the membership of the new Karachi party was "overwhelmingly young, urban, middle class, *muhajirs* whose families had been exposed to the Indian independence movement, and possibly to left

19 Arif Hasan, interview, Karachi, Pakistan, June 5, 2012.

20 Humeira Iqtidar, "Radical Times: Students in Political Mobilization During the 1960s and 1970s," in *At the Crossroads: South Asian Research, Policy, and Development in a Globalized World*, ed. Sustainable Development Policy Institute (Islamabad: Sustainable Development Policy Institute, 2005): 232–244, here: 236.

political influences."[21] The student front proved to be the local party's most active source of participation and activity—if not in official membership, then certainly through the influence of its most prominent leaders.[22] The DSF was soon sweeping college union elections across the city and, in 1953, they launched a coordinated urban agitation around student demands such as fee reductions, infrastructure provisions, and the establishment of a full-fledged university in Karachi.[23] The "Eighth January Movement", as it came to be known, garnered nationwide attention and support after police violence escalated the protests, and seven students were killed. Its unexpected escalation on the streets made it an emblematic flashpoint thereafter for any and all progressive student politics in the country, a reference point for activism for generations to come.

The way the DSF student movement has come to be memorialized—its unprecedented initiative notwithstanding—arises not only from what it *did* achieve as from what it *might* have, had it not been abruptly cut short amidst escalating state repression. In 1954, the DSF was banned along with the Communist Party of Pakistan, and the spark of student unrest was briefly diminished. The ban followed on the heels of Pakistan's entrance into formal military pacts with the United States, the first of many such alliances.[24] The Constituent Assembly was dissolved soon after and, by 1955, Governor General Ghulam Muhammad would use emergency powers to push through the controversial "One Unit" policy, delivering a massive blow to regional autonomy and exacerbating regional and ethnic unrest across the country.[25] Although military rule would not be imposed until 1958, it is this earlier

21 Eric Rahim, "Karachi Communists in the Early 1950s," *Criterion Quarterly* 14, no. 1 (January/March 2019), accessed May 31, 2021, https://criterion-quarterly.com/memoir-1950s-pakistan.

22 These included committed communist party members Mohammad Sarwar, Mir Rehman Ali Hashmi, Ayub Mirza, and Haroon Ahmed.

23 Until that point, Karachi University was merely a "non-teaching university", and its location in the congested and cramped heart of Saddar was not conducive to studies. Prime Minister Muhammad Ali Bogra promised student agitators a new campus in a better location—resulting in the shift to the current KU campus, 12 kilometers east of the city center (this relocation also suited the ruling powers, who aimed to contain student agitation by keeping students away from the political heart of the city center).

24 The Mutual Defence and Assistance Pact; see Ayesha Jalal, *The State of Martial Rule: The Origins of Pakistan's Political Economy of Defence* (Cambridge: Cambridge University Press, 1990), 190.

25 This national administrative program merged the different regional provinces of West Pakistan together to counterbalance the population domination of East Pakistan.

confluence of events that effectively marked the end of constitutional politics—and thus the first, hopeful chapter of democratic nation-building—in Pakistan's early history. It is also in this context that the progressive action mounted by DSF takes on its emblematic meaning becoming, for many of the leaders I interviewed, a point of origin in their stories that stretched beyond the boundaries of their own experience. "1954 was a turning point, you see,"[26] explained one interviewee—a moment which would direct the course of his activism although it predated his own politicization. By the time this new generation of students entered college, the template for progressive student politics had been created—one defined, not only (or even primarily) by ideological content, but by a position of inherent *opposition* to the repressive, anti-democratic character of the state.

"It was a Revolutionary Time": The Emergence of the NSF

The National Students Federation was originally founded as a pro-establishment organization in 1953, patronized by the government in order to counter the increasing influence of the DSF.[27] Soon after the latter was banned, however, independent left-minded students quietly joined the NSF leadership and began to change its ideological make-up from within. "We were *sherwani*-wearing folks, we looked more Muslim," laughed Hussain Naqi, remembering his election to the NSF executive body in 1955.[28] The following year, Naqi was one of the leaders who organized a demonstration in protest of the occupation of the Suez Canal. Prime Minister Suhrawardy's public support for the invasion, in line with the Baghdad Pact, was deeply unpopular with the general public, not least because it was seen as an offense against fellow Muslims.[29] "For other people it was only a Muslim issue, but for us it was a cause against imperial forces," Naqi remembered. The confluence of opinion provided the perfect opportunity for the NSF to launch

26 Abid Hasan Manto, interview, Lahore, Pakistan, July 6, 2012.

27 Nadeem Paracha, "Student Politics in Pakistan: A Celebration, Lament & History," *Dawn,* July 3, 2014, accessed May 31, 2021, https://www.dawn.com/news/1116782; and I.A. Rehman, interview, Lahore, Pakistan, August 1, 2014.

28 Hussain Naqi, interview, Lahore, Pakistan, July 7, 2012. "*Sherwani*" is a traditional garment for men worn in South Asia.

29 Tanvir Tahir, *Political Dynamics of Sindh, 1947–1977* (Karachi: Pakistan Study Centre, 2010), 397.

its new brand of activism, cementing its increasingly leftist and anti-establishment orientation with a massive public *jaloos*. From Jahangir Park in the heart of Saddar, the NSF led a public rally towards the Prime Minister's residence. Near Bolton Market, the students and their supporters—chanting anti-imperialist slogans ("Down with England, Israel, and France!")—were *lathi*-charged by the police. "From then on, its [NSF's] ideological leanings became very left," recounted Naqi. When Ayub Khan seized power in 1958, student unions were among the first targets of the martial law regime, banned alongside political parties and elections.

The 1958 coup was accompanied by mass arrests of leaders and active members of political organizations, of progressive journalists and writers, and members of workers, peasants, and youth movements throughout the country. Faiz Ahmed Faiz, the renowned progressive poet, was arrested in November upon his return from Moscow, where he had been attending the Afro-Asian Writers Conference.[30] During his subsequent stint in the infamous Lahore Fort, he penned one of his many famous revolutionary couplets: "*Nisar main teri galiyon ke ae watan ke jahan / chali hai rasm ke koi na sar utha ke chale*" (I dedicate myself to my country where / nobody can walk with their head held high).[31] In 1959, on the occasion of US President Eisenhower's visit to the country, further mass arrests were made, this time targeting student and youth leaders. "The accusation was that we wanted to stage a rally against Eisenhower. And we wanted to cause a rebellion in the country," remembered Khan. "They wanted to show the Americans—look at these students creating havoc, you know,"[32] recounted Sibghatullah Qadri, another student leader. As Ayub Khan moved to ensconce Pakistan firmly within the ambit of the American Cold War agenda, students were targeted as part of a larger scapegoating of "subversive" communist elements in the country. This itself was a largely fabricated threat—the actual political and organizational strength of the left having always been scattered and weak—but trumped up by the state to impress its new Cold War allies. The longstanding state strategy of framing the "left"—broadly defined—as interchangeably "anti-Islamic" and "anti-national" assumed both renewed

30 Toor, *State of Islam*, 81.

31 Faiz Ahmed Faiz, "Nisar main teri galiyon ke," quoted in Kamran Asdar Ali, Surkh Salam: Communist Politics and Class Activism in Pakistan, 1947–1972 (Karachi: Oxford University Press, 2015), 163.

32 Sibghatullah Qadri, interview, London, UK, May 29, 2012.

gusto and an increased scope, in which "student indiscipline" became an increasingly active category.[33]

In reality, of course, the Pakistani left was not only weak, it was also steeped in internal contradictions and, in some cases, not even unified in its opposition to the martial law regime. As Kamran Asdar Ali has discussed in his work, the early 1960s saw the fracturing of the underground communist movement from within, not only through the course of the international Sino-Soviet split but also via local debates around the nature of Ayub's regime. Some on the left believed, for example, that his "benevolent dictatorship" should be considered representative of the progressive (as opposed to comprador) *bourgeoisie*, and that the indirect election system he initiated (Basic Democracies) was similar to the Russian Soviets at the time of the October Revolution in 1917.[34] Student groups were not immune to these ideological debates and cleavages; by 1967, the NSF would itself split into pro-Moscow and pro-China camps. Yet despite the emergence of individual differences and loyalties, the overarching brand of "leftism" performed by most students in this era was nebulously defined. These young activists arrived at their association loosely and informally with communist-inspired ideologies, less through a rigorous indoctrination into party doctrine, and more through the culture and experiences of student life. After the loosening of martial law regulations in 1960—followed by the lifting of the ban on the NSF in 1962—campus life flourished, particularly in urban centers like Karachi. The National Students Federation was at the forefront of this burgeoning campus culture, sweeping union elections and eventually opening chapters across the rest of the country.

"There used to be regular elections and conventions, at Khatrak Hall in Saddar, or at Khaliq Dina Hall. All the students—girls and boys—would go to listen to the speakers,"[35] recounted Tipu Sultan, who was a student at Karachi's DJ Science College in the 1960s. Union elections and conventions supplemented a lively agenda of cultural programs and hugely popular intercollegiate debating. All of the "leading lights" of the NSF—prominent figures such as Meraj Muhammad Khan, Fatehyab Ali, Jauhar Hussain, and Hussain Naqi—were star debaters, drawing massive crowds to the

33 Sadia Bajwa, "Student Politics and National Education in West Pakistan: A Review Essay," *South Asia Chronicle* 9 (2019): 329–362, here: 333.

34 Kamran Asdar Ali, *Surkh Salam: Communist Politics and Class Activism in Pakistan (1947–1972)* (Karachi: Oxford University Press, 2015), 231.

35 Tipu Sultan, interview, Karachi, Pakistan, June 26, 2012.

renowned showdowns between Punjab and Sindh University. "We used to lift almost all the trophies," smiled Naqi, turning these students into minor celebrities across campuses beyond their hometowns. "It was a time of great political activity,"[36] explained Karamat Ali, who became an important trade union leader following his time in student politics. "On a daily basis there would be some issue or other on which people were debating, discussing, taking out rallies and pamphlets—and a lot was being written, that was a major source of our education."

The popular reading culture to which Ali was referring included a heady exposure to progressive writing and Soviet literature in translation—Tolstoy, Gorky, Marx—which was available at roadside book dealers and small presses (such as the People's Publishing House in Lahore). In the latter half of the decade, when relations between Pakistan and China grew closer, cheap Chinese literature became ubiquitous as well—such as CCP pamphlets and Mao's Little Red Book. The NSF leadership proactively organized study circles to educate and recruit new members, in which communist literature was discussed—including the works of Marx, Engels, Lenin, and Mao. But when asked to recall what they were reading—and what, in particular, might have contributed to their politicization—many interviewees admitted that it was not classic theory that enthralled them, but local progressive literature, criticism, and poetry. Small-circulation publishing flourished, with a plethora of literary organizations (such as the *Awami Adhoori Anjoon* in Karachi, or the *Halqa-e-Arbab-e-Zauq* in Punjab) all bringing out their own newsletters, publications, and literary magazines.[37] Despite state censorship of the left-wing press (epitomized by the government takeover of *Progressive Papers Limited),* literary forums remained a medium of critical dissent in the public sphere.[38] Between 1959 and 1964, new progressive magazines were launched which my interviewees remembered fondly: *Funun, Takhleeq, Lail-o-Nahar, Awami Jamhooriat.*[39] Radical poetry penned by Faiz Ahmed Faiz, Sindhi nationalist Sheikh Ayyaz, and—most memorably for the student movement—firebrand youth, Habib Jalib, was recited and chanted at protests. Amongst Jalib's most famous pieces was a response to

36 Karamat Ali, interview, Karachi, Pakistan, June 19, 2012.

37 Amin Mughal, interview, London, UK, July 15, 2014.

38 For a discussion of left-wing print culture during this period, see Irfan Waheed Usmani, "Print Culture and Left-Wing Radicalism in Lahore, Pakistan, c.1947–71," (PhD Dissertation, National University of Singapore, 2016).

39 Mughal, interview.

Ayub Khan's sham constitution, promulgated in 1962: "This bare-faced lie, this plunder of our intellect, I do not accept, I do not accept."[40] When the NSF students threw their support behind Fatimah Jinnah in the 1964 elections, Jalib—known as "the people's poet"—would address audiences at her rallies. "If most people went to see *Mohtarma* (madame) Jinnah, I would say about 40 percent were there to hear his poetry," remembered Jamil.

The youth and students mingled with the urban intelligentsia at these literary forums and *mushairas* (poetry readings), gathering at popular cafes, bars, and hotels. In Karachi, Empress Market and Regal Cinema, in the heart of Saddar, used to be the main meeting ground for political rallies. "There was a cafeteria opposite Regal Cinema, so people used to have their rallies in between these two, then go sit in the cafeteria, have chai,"[41] described Karamat Ali. Occasionally, these rallies would take the form of demonstrations in solidarity with global anti-imperialist causes, such as in the examples of Lumumba's assassination and the occupation of the Suez Canal. Awareness of global movements or uprisings could serve as powerful sources of inspiration, influencing how students came to construct themselves as activists. "Vietnam dominated, of course," said many of my interviewees, at the forefront of both the news and their discussions. The plight of Palestine was another issue of popular importance, drawing on Pan-Islamic sympathies as well as the influence of Palestinian exchange students who attended Punjab University in the mid-1960s.[42] In 1969, a film about an Arab woman who becomes a fighter in the Palestinian liberation movement, *Zarqa*, would become the hit of the decade, running for over 100 weeks and earning the status of Pakistan's first Diamond Jubilee film.[43] Habib Jalib, incidentally, wrote the film's song lyrics, as part of a long partnership with the director, Riaz Shahid (himself a prominent member of the leftist clique of Pakistani artists and intellectuals that congregated around Faiz Ahmed Faiz).

That the actual size and scope of this clique—and of progressive cultural production at large—was quite limited does not take away from the broader influence it exerted on newly politicized urban youth, who readily absorbed the rhetoric of socialism, liberation, and anti-imperialism. The picture that

---

40 Habib Jalib, "Dastoor," quoted in Saadia Toor, *State of Islam*, 91.

41 Ali, interview.

42 Azizuddin Ahmad, interview, Lahore, Pakistan, July 28, 2014.

43 Nate Rabe, "Sound of Lollywood: To Palestine, With Love," *Scroll.in*, March 18, 2017, accessed May 31, 2021, https://scroll.in/reel/832134/sound-of-lollywood-to-palestine-with-love-from-the-great-pakistani-star-neelo.

emerges from their descriptions and memories is that of a world in which campus life, progressive urban subcultures, and political activism were deeply intertwined, and in which student life was inseparable from a wider sense of political momentum and change. "It was a political time," as my interviewees commonly put it, "there was a revolutionary fervor."[44] As Imtiaz Alam described: "Those days were full of energy and romance. Everybody had a romance with revolution."[45] The vague nostalgia of such descriptions echoes a narrative thread one finds in oral testimonies of the radical 1960s worldwide: Of a revolutionary "spirit" that was all-encompassing, spontaneous, and inevitable.[46]

This emphasis on the intangible and the ambiguous—an overarching "revolutionary atmosphere" that suffused everything from campus debates to popular poetry, literary circles, coffeehouse culture and global media—is a narrative strategy worth considering. Among other things, it serves to endow student activism with moral purpose, emotional *telos*, and an agency that exceeds that of formal political processes (movements as merely orchestrated by parties, students as pawns or puppets, etc.). It also points to a mode of relating to progressive politics that could be widely inclusive, ideationally ambiguous, and even contradictory. The expression of diverse solidarities for example—from the war resistance in Vietnam, to the plight of the Congolese, to Muslims in Jabalpur—were not necessarily ideologically consistent.[47] In drawing connections between local, regional, and international sites of contention and power, it was a kind of political performance that operated closely through the collective identity of student-hood itself. Arguably, the inherent liminality of that identity—between childhood and adulthood, subordination and authority, expectation and disillusionment—helped foster the fluidity and openness that marked their orientation to politics.[48] The temporary suspension of social hierarchies afforded by the college space—of community, class, and linguistic difference—could prompt forms of egalitarian sociality, as well as heightened exposure and access to

44 Ali, interview; Jamil, interview; Ahmad, interview.

45 Imtiaz Alam, interview with Lal Khan, in Lal Khan, *Pakistan's Other Story: The 1968–69 Revolution* (Lahore: The Struggle Publications, 2008), 138.

46 Francesca Polletta, *It Was Like a Fever: Storytelling in Protest and Politics* (Chicago: University of Chicago Press, 2006), 34.

47 The expression of Pan-Islamic sympathies, for instance, sat uncomfortably with the secular or Marxist-atheist orientation of leftist ideologies.

48 Constantine Nakassis, *Doing Style: Youth and Mass Mediation in South India* (Chicago: University of Chicago Press, 2016), 15.

alternative collective imaginaries, identities, and subjectivities. Against the backdrop of the global sixties, the fluid revolutionary aspirations of "youth in revolt"[49] became one such currency in the performance of student activism and protest.

In highlighting the elements of fluidity and ambiguity, I do not mean to argue that students touted the rhetoric of the revolutionary left in a purely performative way, as nothing more than a fashionable coffeehouse trend. On an individual level, activists were motivated by, and invested in, specific and tangible aspirations and grievances, ranging from material concerns (i.e., employment opportunities at a time of economic hardship) to ethnic identity (the anti-One Unit movement). The point is not to evaluate whether their relationship to progressive causes was "authentic", but to note how their vocabularies—linking transnational youth movements, Afro-Asian solidarity, anti-imperialism, socialism, the global New Left, and more—enabled unique and productive modes of political imagining and *action*. How did this language of revolution—these Marxist ideals or transnational imaginaries—translate into a concrete experience of activism, or particular forms of resistance? Beyond campus politics and rallies of solidarity, what is significant is how students used these overlapping ideological frameworks to understand and oppose the specific injustices of the Ayub regime, organizing around the issues that directly impacted their lives.

From Imagination to Action: The Sharif Commission and Anti-Ayub Movement

In 1962, Ayub Khan's newly appointed Commission on National Education (the Sharif Commission) published its report. Amongst the reforms it recommended was the institution of a three-year degree course (instead of the existing two-year course), making Urdu the sole medium of instruction, and a series of regulations on the conduct of teachers and students under what was known as the University Ordinance. The power of the Vice Chancellor was increased at the expense of the university syndicate, including the power to rusticate and expel at will. The Ordinance and three-year course—which

49 Samantha Christainsen, "A Campus in Context: East Pakistan's Mass Upsurge at Local, Regional and International Scales," *South Asia Multidisciplinary Academic Journal* 22 (2019), accessed May 31, 2021, http://journals.openedition.org/samaj/6491.

were formally instituted in 1963—caused widespread outrage amongst the student community, sparking large-scale agitation in defiance of martial law regulations.

After their expulsion from Karachi in 1961,[50] a dozen of the most prominent NSF leaders had found themselves scattered across the country, where they forged new student community links and established NSF chapters in Hyderabad, Sakkar, Quetta, and beyond.[51] The movement against the University Ordinance was thus able to be coordinated on an unprecedented scale; with strikes organized from Bahawalpur to Peshawar, Lahore to Hyderabad, and with the support of parallel student bodies in East Pakistan.[52] At the first grand convention of Ayub Khan's newly reconstituted Muslim League party—held at Polo Ground, Karachi, in 1963—hundreds of NSF boys stormed the stage and presented their resolutions. "Flowerpots were thrown on the ministers," wrote Faisal Sayani in a memoir essay. "Chairs went flying off in the air."[53] When the NSF leaders involved were subsequently externed, the students doubled down in protest. The female students' organization, which often worked with NSF ("they didn't go to prison, but they took care of all the organizational issues"[54]), went on a hunger strike. After several days, when the girls had become ill and weak, they were taken around the whole city on a Victoria carriage in a rally. "The entire area went on strike in support of them," remembered Khan. "The KESC workers announced their support. The port workers supported us. They breathed new life into the movement." The governor was sent to negotiate with the students and, in a rare act of capitulation, the three-year degree course was revoked.

The example of the anti-Sharif Commission protests illustrates the way in which encounters with authority deeply shaped the activism of students. Clashes both physical (with police during protests) and intellectual or moral (with figures of authority and institutions—i.e., the figure of the Vice Chancellor) lay at the heart of most interviewees' narratives of resistance. The rhetoric of international socialism—and calls for a radical transformation of society overall—thus appears more as a vehicle for expressing immediate

50 For the Lumumba and Jabalpur demonstrations, mentioned above.

51 Naqi, interview; Qadri, interview.

52 Tahir, *Political Dynamics*, 493.

53 Faisal Sayani, "A Song of Batons and Jails," *The Friday Times*, September 30, 2016, accessed May 31, 2021, https://www.thefridaytimes.com/a-song-of-batons-and-jails/.

54 Khan, interview.

anti-regime positions, in which opposition to Ayub's rule could be equated to broadly defined anti-imperialist politics. Experiences of state intervention and repression were understood as signs of the invisible hand of US imperialism, decisions dictated by the regime's dependence on American aid. In the era of decolonization, the desire for national sovereignty was the foundation on which political ambitions and aspirations ultimately rested. "The bulk of students were basically nationalists," speculated Jamil in his recollections. "The anti-imperialist jargon—it was about not being dictated to by anyone, not being dependent on anyone [...] and a deep suspicion of America."[55]

In this way, the policies of the Sharif Commission were understood as only one item on a long list of state reforms representative of Ayub Khan's broader "modernization" agenda: An American-backed project of international development to be achieved through an aggressive focus on industrial and social development. The rapid economic growth achieved through these autocratic measures consolidated wealth in the hands of a small minority—with over two thirds of industrial capital held by the infamous "22 families"—at the expense of the working class and increasingly impoverished masses.[56] In 1968, when Ayub Khan decided to celebrate "the Decade of Development", the NSF unilaterally condemned the idea and announced that it would commemorate a "Decade of Decadence" instead. They organized protests around a "week of demands", which included the restoration of parliamentary democracy on the basis of adult franchise, the revocation of One Unit, a secular foundation for the state, educational reforms, and a withdrawal from military alliances with the USA. Student mobilizations, which began in October of that year, began to grow into mass civil disobedience, particularly after police opened fire on a student rally in Rawalpindi. Three students died, triggering nationwide outrage and protests—including a rent strike, bus and railway strike, and what is known as a "wheel jam" strike in the capital of Islamabad.[57] Intellectuals, journalists, professionals, and industrial workers took to the streets in urban centers across West and

55 Jamil, interview.

56 Riaz Ahmed Shaikh, "1968—Was it Really A Year of Social Change in Pakistan?" *Sixties Radicalism and Social Movement Activism: Retreat or Resurgence?*, eds. Bryn Jones and Mike O'Donnell (London: Anthem Press, 2010), 73–88, here: 74.

57 Khan, *Pakistan's Other Story*, 143.

East Pakistan.[58] By March, Ayub Khan was forced to step down, handing over power to General Yahya Khan.

Despite their character of immediate, spontaneous, and ferocious urgency, the mass mobilizations of 1968–1969 were, at least for NSF students, the culmination of a longstanding resistance against authoritarian rule. The methods of civil disobedience—strikes, sit-ins, *gherao* (encirclement), vandalism, even violence—were familiar, employed in agitations throughout Khan's dictatorship[59] and relating, ultimately, to a longer history of contentious politics in the subcontinent (dating back to the anti-colonial movement and beyond).[60] Certain strategies of student indiscipline, however, also point to the ways this language of protest reflected an overarching form of "resistance" that was historically specific and anti-authoritarian in nature. To remain with the examples related above: NSF students targeted the convention launching Ayub Khan's sham political party, storming the stage and wreaking havoc at what was meant to be a decorous state affair. In response to Ayub's "Decade of Development", they organized protests around the theme of "Decade of Decadence" instead. The visceral, unruly displays at protests and rallies often involved the purposeful performance of civil disobedience, clashes with police, and arrests; as well as including a rich repertoire of sloganeering ("*Ayub Khan Murdabad!*") and popular poetry that often operated in the registers of irony, irreverence, and scorn. Take Jalib's popular poem, "*Musheer*" (Advisor), written in the voice of Ayub Khan's advisor:

> "I said to him, I said to him/You are the light of God/You are intellect, you are reason/the nation is with you […] Those few that speak out/Are all mischief-makers/Rip out their tongues/Throttle their throats/I said to him."[61]

Protest scripts like these, through the use of humiliation and even mockery, conveyed not only opposition to the regime (and its particular policies or actions), but an understanding of the fundamental illegitimacy of its vision of politics and citizenship. Through the forms and tactics of their resistance, students made physical and visible an understanding of the inherently anti-

58 Shaikh, "1968," 84.

59 Other examples include the movement against One Unit, protests after the 1965 war debacle, and after the election results of 1964.

60 For an introduction to the question of how the political methods of anticolonial agitation translated to postcolonial contexts, see: Dipesh Chakrabarty, "In the Name of Politics: Democracy and the Power of the Multitude in India," *Public Culture* 19, no. 1 (2007): 35–58.

61 Habib Jalib, *Jalib-Naama* (Lahore: Jang Publications, 1991), 90.

democratic nature of the state—drawing implicit connections between, for example, police suppression of student rallies and the suppression of civil liberties ("*Musheer*"), the government's "modernization" agenda and its pro-imperialist intent (the "Decade of Decadence"), the pretense of electoral politics and the real erosion of democratic rights (storming the Muslim League Convention). The "resistance" performed by students, in other words, was both universalizable *and* specific; an effort to redefine the very terms and possibilities of politics against the particular contexts and limitations of Khan's regime. Against the suppressive and depoliticizing vision of citizenship (i.e., limited adult franchise, diminished provincial autonomy, and repressed civil liberties), students intervened and, arguably, enacted their own ideal of democratic politics through collective protest. In their condemnations of the state—whether rhetorical/ideological or physical/performative—they contended not only for an overthrow of the regime, but a fundamental reformulation of the horizons and possibilities of the political.

Conclusion: The Question of Legacies

Upon taking power, Yahya Khan immediately announced general elections on the basis of adult franchise—to be held in August 1970—as well as the dissolution of the One Unit policy. These are what might be taken as the concrete "successes" of the anti-Ayub movement: The ousting of an authoritarian regime, the restoration of democracy, and a gesture towards regional autonomy. Yet it quickly became clear that the dynamics of power in Pakistan—between the establishment, the state, and the military in particular—remained fundamentally unchanged. Many have put the blame for this on Zulfikar Ali Bhutto, whose newly founded Pakistan's People's Party (PPP) rode the wave of social agitation to a sweeping electoral victory in 1970, before reverting to an authoritarian mode of governance.[62] As early as 1972, Bhutto began purging his party of its left-wing elements, who were critical of his failure to implement the socialist reforms he had promised. Meraj Muhammad Khan, who was a founding member of the PPP and served as the first Minister of Labor in Bhutto's cabinet, was among those who found themselves behind bars as a political prisoner of the administration he had

62 Toor has termed his rule a form of "authoritarian populism"; see Toor, *State of Islam*, 117.

helped bring to power. But is it enough to say that the PPP—with its pseudo-socialist rhetoric, forged largely from the fires stoked by the student movement—simply co-opted, and ultimately betrayed, the "real" progressivism of 1968, which might otherwise have offered an opportunity for transformative social change? These are the kinds of questions that continue to preoccupy many ex-student leaders and activists over half a century later. Many relayed their own theories regarding the failure of the left—some pointed to organizational deficiency, others to the lack of "grassroots" working-class links, still others to the disorder brought by the Sino-Soviet split and the breakdown of internationalist solidarities. "This was a false dawn,"[63] lamented Aijaz Qureshi, one interviewee. "As young people, we thought NSF would bring revolution," recalled Qadri. "We talked about it romantically but, looking back, it was not [revolutionary] and therefore it failed. When history is being written—NSF failed."[64]

Despite the blows dealt by its fraught association with the PPP and increased factionalization, the NSF continued to be a prominent force in student politics throughout the 1970s. This decade also saw the meteoric rise of the *Islami Jamiat-e Taleba*, which became the primary rival to shifting progressive alliances and played an instrumental role in challenging (and ultimately, undoing) Bhutto's government. The tumultuous dynamism of campus politics in this era—sometimes referred to as the "golden age" of student politics in Pakistan[65]—suggests another reading of the anti-Ayub movement; as the inauguration, rather than the apogee, of a distinctive style of democratic student political action. Not long after, however, under the retrogressive military dictatorship of General Zia-ul-Haq (1977–1988), student unions were banned in the country (and remain so to this day), and student activism was increasingly taken over by political and religious parties. Zia's regime also intensified the suppression and systematic dismantling of progressive politics, witnessing the escalation of sectarian and religion-based violence, as well as the decline of the political left on a global scale. The question of legacies then, is always an ambiguous one at best—as different temporal and spatial framings reveal alternative and overlapping inheritances, not only in the registers of success and failure, but also of novelty, resurgence, and transformation.

63 Aijaz Qureshi, interview, Karachi, Pakistan, June 23, 2012.

64 Qadri, interview.

65 Paracha, "Student Politics".

In revisiting the history of the National Students Federation, I have tried to decouple progressive student activism from the successes of the Pakistani "left" at large—in order to replace a familiar narrative of failure by one of burgeoning new forms of activism, indicative of an expanding and rapidly transforming political sphere. The NSF—from its antecedents in the DSF to its role in the mass uprisings against Ayub Khan—represents one view of the broader shift in political and social relations that took place in Pakistan in this era, a shift which brought new political actors, ideas, and expectations into the realm of the popular and the public. Amongst the many factors that shaped their politics, I have tried to highlight just a few here—including *muhajir* identity, urban growth, left-wing cultural politics, and the experience of authoritarianism, as well as how these were inflected by the expectations of decolonization and the rhetoric of global anti-imperialism.

The challenge to the state that was constituted by this multivalent activism cannot be reduced to a generalizable binary of oppression against resistance but was, in fact, laden with multiple layers of meaning ranging from the local to the global. In projecting and enacting these overlapping meanings, students did not just aim to topple a dictatorship (an action which, in hindsight, had little "revolutionary" effect), they intervened against the suppressive and depoliticizing conception of citizenship proffered by state authoritarianism. The situation of "crisis" they helped bring about was thus an expression of not only grievance and frustration, but of a more complex opposition—shaped by student identity and their ideals of political action. Tracing the NSF's politics this way—with attention to its organic construction through student life, identity, and experiences—we might arrive at an activism that was neither "successful" nor "unsuccessful", but rather the product of, and perhaps only possible within, its own historical moment.

Exhaustion as Rebellion: The Identity Crisis of Salaried Women in South Korea and Kim Sŭng-ok's Novella, "A Night Walk" (1969)

Chan Yong BU

Introduction[1]

In a collection of essays translated as *The Salaried Masses* in English, German philosopher Siegfried Kracauer sought to theorize the psychology of salaried employees, whose numbers skyrocketed in 1920s Germany thanks to the development of modern large-scale enterprises. Focusing on this icon of modernization and urbanization, Kracauer contests the potential of decoding white-collar workers whose lives were "more unknown than that of the primitive tribes."[2] Against the simplified description of office workers as completely powerless servants to the capitalist system, Kracauer analyzes the explosive potential of their unnoticed desires. This theorization of salaried employees' dual identities as guardians of economic progress and mysterious entities resonates with Korean writer Kim Sŭng-ok's 1969 novella, "A Night Walk", which depicts the ostensibly sudden "depravity" of a bank clerk as a figure craving wanton sex to nullify her social status.[3]

This chapter analyzes the identity crisis of salaried employees in the novella as the epitome of the self-contradictions intrinsic to Park Chung-hee's authoritarian regime (1961–1979) in the Republic of Korea (hereafter South Korea). Historically, Park seized power in a military coup in 1961 against the Second Republic of Korea, which was established following the revolution

1 I want to thank Meher Ali, who provided insightful comments and suggestions. I am also grateful for Sin Hyŏng-gi's illuminating feedback in the early stages of the article's development. Regarding the names of Korean figures, both the body of this chapter and the citations follow Korean naming conventions, which list the family name first and given name second.

2 Siegfried Kracauer, *The Salaried Masses: Duty and Distraction in Weimar Germany*, trans. Quintin Hoare (London: Verso, 1998), 28–32.

3 Kim Sŭng-ok, "Yahaeng," in *Saengmyŏng yŏnsŭp*: *Kim Sŭng-ok taep'yo chungdanp'yŏnsŏn* (P'aju: Munhak Tongne, 2014), 441–465.

of April 19, 1960. The "April 19 Revolution" marks a watershed in South Korea's history for dethroning the authoritarian regime of Rhee Syngman, the first President of South Korea, which prohibited any kind of political activity in the name of national security, grossly violated the freedom of the press, and even rigged the vice-presidential election. Although the Second Republic, a parliamentary government under President Yun Bo-seon and Prime Minister Chang Myon, was established after the fall of Rhee's regime, Park justified his coup by claiming the Second Republic had failed to respond to the nationwide mandate for reform. As literary scholar Sin Hyŏng-gi points out, the Park regime foregrounded its slogan of "making a clear sweep of past depravity as the rightful successor to April 19", which claimed that the revolution was not complete until an administratively stable and morally upright regime was established.[4] In other words, the Park regime was established on the discourse of a yet to be resolved national crisis by claiming itself to be the savior of the people.

Against the people's expectations, it soon turned out that Park's proclamation of succeeding the April 19 revolutionaries was but a political means to wield irrefutable power behind the moral slogan of "cleansing" the administrative and spiritual remnants of corrupt past regimes. According to political scientist Yi Yŏng-ch'ŏl, the military regime of Park Chung-hee was a "developmental authoritarian state", which found the rationale for the regime's legitimacy less from its representativeness than from successful economic development. The government led the market, keeping a strong grip on the financial sphere while retaining its superiority over enterprises in the name of collaboration. These developmentalist traits are combined with more general features of authoritarianism, such as a political system that favors the current power group and the enforcement of obedience to a central authority at the expense of personal freedoms. "Maintaining the appearance of democracy" was also important for Park in forging a stronger alliance with the US; he had to foreground the regime's "democratic" identity against its Cold War counterparts through supporting their allies' democratization.[5]

Kim Sŭng-ok's works are known for delicately probing into the psychological landscape of individuals in the 1960s authoritarian society that betrayed its self-identification as the successor to the April 19 Revolution. Born

4 Sin Hyŏng-gi, "Punyŏltoen man-bogaek - Kim Sŭng-ok ŭi 1960-yŏndae sosŏl ilkki," *Sanghŏ hakpo* 11 (2003): 199–225, here: 199–201.

5 Yi Yŏng-ch'ŏl, "Chaep'yŏn ŭi chŏngch'i wa nodong ŭi chaep'yŏn," *Han'guk haengjŏng hakpo* 33, no.1 (1999): 279–294, here: 284–286.

in 1941, Kim experienced the April 19 Revolution and Park's May 16 military coup while in his freshman year at Seoul National University; he started his literary career the following year. Named as one of the representative "419 generation" (419 *sedae*) authors, most of Kim's works from this period have been acclaimed by literary critics for reflecting on what it means to remember the revolution under the authoritarian Park regime. However, this does not mean that Kim's works present an explicit call for another revolution to subvert the Park regime. Rather, they speak about freedom and exploration of self through their implausibility under the Park regime, which provokes a strong sense of disorientation in the protagonists. For instance, his two magnum opuses, *Seoul: 1964, Winter* and *Record of a Journey to Mujin*, both present educated male protagonists in their 20s and early 30s, the generation and gender group once articulated as the main driving force behind the April 19 Revolution, who can neither find a clear meaning in life nor form humanitarian bonds with others, and eventually become engulfed by the blinding urban space developed by the Park regime.[6] While the frequent foregrounding of unending disorientation in his novels may even evoke charges of quietism, Sin Hyŏng-gi lucidly points out that it is the very routinization of identity crisis, or schizophrenia, in Kim's literary works that harbors the potential for resistance against the molding of well-disciplined patriotic subjects under the authoritarian regime.[7]

How does illustrating the identity crisis of salaried employees in "A Night Walk", especially that of a salaried woman, fit Kim's larger project of critically engaging with the authoritarian regime of Park Chung-hee? Park seized power in a coup and set "national modernization" as its mantra, sugarcoating its brutality in the name of restoring the country devastated by North Korea by accumulating wealth. Foregrounded in this procedure of myth molding was quantified economic growth, such as gross domestic product. The rise of large-scale enterprises and a centralized national

6 Kim Sŭng-ok, "Sŏul, 1964-yŏn kyŏul (Seoul: 1964, Winter)," in *Saengmyŏng yŏnsŭp: Kim Sŭng-ok taep'yo chungdanp'yŏnsŏn* (P'aju: Munhak Tongne, 2014), 257–286; Kim Sŭng-ok, "Mujin kihaeng (Record of a Journey to Mujin)," in *Saengmyŏng yŏnsŭp*, 220–256. "Seoul: 1964, Winter" and "Record of a Journey to Mujin" are currently the only two works by Kim that have been translated into English. For English translations cf. Kim Sŭng-ok, "Seoul: 1964, Winter," in *Land of Exile: Contemporary Korean Fiction*, eds. and trans. Marshall R. Pihl, Bruce Fulton, and Ju-Chan Fulton (Armonk: M.E. Sharpe/UNESCO Publishing, 1993), 84–101; Kim Sŭng-ok, *Record of a Journey to Mujin*, trans. Kevin O'Rourke (Seoul: Asia, 2012). "Yahaeng" (A Night Walk) has not been translated.

7 Sin, "Punyŏltoen man-bogaek," 203.

banking system affected the job market, greatly increasing demand for white-collar workers. In order to mitigate the serious gap between the rich and poor created by solely focusing on numeric economic growth, these salaried employees were narrativized as powerful candidates in becoming the middle class, and mobilized to attest to the "tangible" benefits of this growth in daily life. In reality, however, attaining middle-class status by fulfilling the material requisites, such as private home ownership, was barely plausible even for white-collar workers. In terms of gender politics, middle-class women were depicted as figures in charge of coordinating the family's material wealth and consuming goods wisely with their well-cultured taste. In this vein, salaried women were double-fettered by the Park regime's authoritarian policies. Taking this into account, unveiling the identity crisis of the supposedly central evidence of the regime's success, the salaried employees exposed the self-contradictions intrinsic to the authoritarian regime that its grandiose rhetoric could not hide.

"A Night Walk"

Kim's novella, "A Night Walk", presents a similar narrative structure to *Seoul: 1964, Winter* and *Record of a Journey to Mujin*. Here, the educated protagonist in Seoul, presumably in her late 20s, desperately attempts to overcome her identity crisis under Park's authoritarian state but never reaches a satisfactory result until the end of the novel. However, the novella presents features distinctive amongst other works by Kim that merit more in-depth scrutiny. "A Night Walk" specifically grapples with the identity crisis arising from the desire to enter the middle class in the context of Park's authoritarian state. Admittedly, the protagonists in Kim's works of the 1960s do not present their concerns over class issues outwardly, either because they are financially stable, or because they are more occupied with other issues, such as domestic violence. In contrast, the protagonist in "A Night Walk" is obsessed with attaining the fantasy of a middle-class life drawn by the government; what makes her sense of insecurity even more interesting is that she and her husband work in a bank, an iconic workplace for white-collar workers often equated with the middle class. However, she is still extremely concerned about her socio-economic status. As she starts to realize that the middle-class life is a fantasy constructed by the authoritarian regime to consolidate its control over the people, her identity crisis explodes. This leads the protagonist to deviate from middle-class norms by embarking on a nighttime promenade through the streets of Seoul, seeking sex with anonymous male counterparts.

In terms of criticizing the Park regime's molding and mobilization of desire to be middle class, the unusual medium the novella was published in deserves attention along with its themes. Much to the shock of literary critics, "A Night Walk" was published in the monthly, *Wŏlgan Chungang*, known for its vulgarity marked by superficial gossip and pornographic content, in contrast with highbrow literary magazines. A literary genius's seemingly idiosyncratic gesture of publishing a lascivious novella in a "low-register" magazine was often read as the early burnout of a young writer who already possessed tremendous literary talent in his early 20s; at the age of 24, he won the prestigious Tong-in Literary Prize. However, the growth of monthly magazines in the 1960s, fueling the dream of becoming middle class under the Park regime, overlaps with the concerns of the novella. Therefore, we need to regard "A Night Walk" as a literary experiment that sought to question the fundamental economy of the middle-class dream by grappling with both the material conditions and psychology propping it up.

After its release in 1969, "A Night Walk" remained on the bestseller list until the 1970s and is the third most frequently included piece in Kim's literary anthologies.[8] The novella's filmic adaptation was released in 1977 by prolific literary film director, Kim Soo-yong, and featured Shin Seong-il and Yoon Jeong-hee, the then most popular actor and actress respectively in South Korea, attracting one hundred and fifty thousand viewers—quite a commercial success at the time.[9] This consistent popularity cannot be fully explained by its lasciviousness and merits further scrutiny on its specific uniqueness even among Kim's works. Admittedly, there have been productive attempts to probe the potential of Kim's relatively unappreciated works since the 1990s, particularly those published in "low-culture" weeklies and

---

8 For instance, see "Kŭmju ŭi pesŭt'ŭsellŏ," *Maeil Kyŏngje*, March 19, 1974, 6. Although it is impossible to trace the class ratio of its readership, the major consumer demographic of *Wŏlgan Chungang* was said to consist of those financially stable enough to spend extra money on weekly magazines, and others who sought to enjoy such financial status at least temporarily by making it a habit to buy them. Kim Kyŏng-yŏn, "T'ongsok ŭi chŏngch'ihak: 1960-yŏndae huban Kim Sŭng-ok chuganji sosŏl chaedok," *Ŏmun nonjip* 62 (2015): 373–420.

9 Kim Kwang-hyŏp, "Oehwa ilsaek sinjŏng kŭkchang p'ŭro," *Tonga ilbo*, December 28, 1997, 5.

monthlies. Nonetheless, the literature on "A Night Walk" has remained mostly silent regarding its uniqueness, even among Kim's works, for featuring a salaried woman as its protagonist. Rather, "A Night Walk" has been mostly discussed in tandem with his other works under the themes of the Benjaminian *flâneur*, or with the grammar of gender-biased and even misogynist depictions of female figures throughout Kim's works.[10] Korean scholar Kim Mi-ran's work is unique in terms of reading middle-class issues in the novella through the lens of *flâneuse*, which is a gender twist on the male-centered aspect of *flâneur*. Building on Deborah Parsons' concept on female figures who probe the underlying logic of the urban landscape while refracting the male gaze of the street, Kim Mi-ran analyzes the entanglement of class and gender politics in the Park regime's promotion of middle-class culture in the 1960s. According to Kim Mi-ran, the blossoming of middle-class culture, marked by fewer obligations and a drastically increased number of educated women and their entry into white-collar jobs, granted women more freedom to embrace their sexual desires and such changes are reflected in "A Night Walk".[11] Overall, I agree with the argument regarding the critical potential of the protagonist's ostensibly promiscuous night promenade in terms of disrupting masculinized society under the authoritarian regime. Still, I would like to point out that the starting point of the protagonist's identity crisis should not be found in her "already being" middle class; rather it comes from her *aspiration* to be middle class which she believes she has not yet attained. Unlike Kim Mi-ran's reading that assumes the economic stability of the bank clerk, or white-collar work in general, equivalent to entering the middle class, the novella constantly emphasizes the protagonist's concerns about her financial insufficiency. To demonstrate this, I start with

---

10 For research focusing on the theme of the Benjaminian *flâneur*, Sin, "Punyŏltoen manbogaek," 199–225; Pak Chin-yŏng, "Han'guk hyŏndae sosŏl e nat'anan 'Yahaeng' mot'ip'ŭ wa pam sanch'aekcha yŏn'gu - Kim Sŭng-ok ŭi "Yahaeng," Hwang Chŏng-ŭn ŭi *Yahaeng*, P'yŏn Hye-yŏng ŭi *Yahaeng* ŭl taesang ŭro," *Journal of Korean Culture* 31 (2015): 151–174. For research engaging with the grammar of female representation, Yu Im-ha, "Tach'in ilsangsŏng kwa haebang ŭiji;" Kim, "T'ongsok ŭi chŏngch'ihak," 373–420; Kwak Sang-sun, "Kim Sŭng-ok tanp'yŏn sosŏl ŭi yŏsŏng inmul yŏn'gu – "Yahaeng" kwa "Sŏul ŭi talbit 0-chang" ŭl taesang ŭro," *Han'guk munhwaron kwa pip'yŏng* 14 (2010): 143–164; Chang Kyŏng-sil, Kim Sŭng-ok tanp'yŏn sosŏl ŭi yŏsŏng p'yosang e nat'anan ilt'al kwa chŏhang ŭi yangsang – "Saengmyŏng yŏnsŭ," "Mujin kihaeng," "Yahaeng" ŭl chungsimŭro," *Sunch'ŏnhyang inmun kwahak nonch'ong* 34 (2015): 71–95; Sŏng Chu-hyŏn, "Kim Sŭng-ok sosŏl kwa yŏsŏng hyŏmo," *Munhwa wa yunghap* 40, no. 2 (2018): 469–498.

11 Kim Mi-ran, "The Strategy of Individualization and Gender of Kim Seung-ok's Novel," PhD diss., (Yonsei University, 2005), 124–144.

historical and sociological research that suggests otherwise. Next, I argue that it is the discrepancy between the actual economic lives of white-collar workers and the myth of the middle-class future that mainly provoked the self-exhaustive structure of the protagonist's night walk as a counter reaction.

The Molding of a Middle-Class Future Under the Accumulation System

The protagonist, Hyŏn-ju, is a bank clerk pursuing "the happiness of daily life", a term that entered the discursive field of the 1960s in the context of middle-class life as advertised by the government. Although married to a co-worker, she hides their relationship so that she can continue working in the bank, overcome with apprehension at failing to attain a rosy future due to financial difficulties. Hyŏn-ju constantly dreams of the life she will enjoy once she and her husband save enough to create a happy family, which "off-sets their acting at the workplace, which has become a part of their anxious daily life."[12] On the last day of a short vacation, Hyŏn-ju is forcefully dragged to a motel and raped by a stranger, whose shabby appearance suggests a social status completely different from the world she believes she belongs in. While powerless at the hands of the rapist, Hyŏn-ju suddenly thinks of the situation as punishment for her "acting" at the workplace in pursuit of an unattainable mirage. Afterwards, Hyŏn-ju starts to promenade the night street, exposing herself to male salarymen and having random sex with whoever takes her to a motel as ruthlessly as the rapist did. However, as Hyŏn-ju makes it her rule to have sex only with those who grab her without conversation or eye contact, her behavior makes most of the salarymen approaching her step back in frustration. Hyŏn-ju reads the anxious response of "these salarymen no different from her husband", who are completely different from their proud appearance during the day, as the futility of the myth of national prosperity.[13] The more Hyŏn-ju seeks anonymous sex, the more it leads her in a different direction, ironically provoking her to look for the irreplaceable, distinctive face of the individual. These epistemological

12 Kim, "Yahaeng," 450.

13 Ibid., 460.

and ontological shifts eventually lead her to question the authoritarian regime's brutal mobilization of people as evidenced in the Vietnam War—part of the larger goal of consolidating regime power at the price of individual freedom—and she realizes the fostering of middle-class aspirants is yet another piece of this authoritarian scheme.

South Korea's dramatic rise in gross domestic product in the late 1960s as a result of its export-oriented development model is relevant to the novella's publication date of 1969 and its contemporary setting. This growth led to the rise of large-scale enterprise and a centralized national banking system that managed the country's growing capital influx, drastically increasing the number of salarymen in commerce and banking.[14] According to statistics, the number of salaried employees in office jobs surpassed 1.5 million, constituting more than 30 percent of Seoul's population.[15] However, a more concrete rationale for approaching Hyŏn-ju as a typical salaried employee suffering under Park's regime is that her dream of a rosy future centers on a specific object in the military regime's molding of the middle class—a house.

The obsessively detailed happy ending Hyŏn-ju hopes to reach is to be able to tell her husband, "Please invite your subordinates to dinner at our home today," offsetting "their acting at the workplace, which has become a part of their anxious daily life."[16] The emphasis on endurance in achieving a fruitful future, marked by exhibiting "our home" (*uri chip*) to others, overlaps with the craze for home ownership kindled by the regime, as well as with the discrepancy between the middle-class dream and the financial reality. According to Kim Chae-wŏn, while the actual discretionary income of salaried employees in Seoul was insufficient to own a home (which were already limited in number), home ownership was promoted as a social sign of middle-class status and increased the regional anxiety for "keeping up with the Kims" among salaried employees.[17] Another reason why the presence of the words "our home" in the novella should not be ignored is because it was only in 1967 that the specific term "my home" started to appear in the discursive field of South Korea. As sociologist Kim Han Sang points out, the

14 Yi Wan-bŏm, *1960-yŏndae ŭi chŏngch'i sahoe pyŏndong* (Seoul: Paeksan Sŏdang, 1999), 38.

15 Sŏul T'ŭkpyŏl Sisa P'yŏnch'an Wiwŏnhoe, *Sŏul 600-yŏnsa* (Seoul: Sŏul T'ŭkpyŏl Sisa P'yŏnch'an Wiwŏnhoe, 1996), 604.

16 Kim Sŭng-ok, "Yahaeng," 450.

17 Kim Chae-wŏn, "Housing Policy of Seoul and the Middle-Class Problem Recognition in the Late 1960s," *Han'guksa yŏn'gu* 175 (2016): 319–341.

words circulated through various media as a crucial symbol of the private freedom the middle class could enjoy. In contrast to Japan, Korea's promotion of attaining "my home" was more delusional than palpable, or more "aspirational than descriptive."[18]

The discourse of home ownership fever is not the only reason to focus on Hyŏn-ju's identity crisis as a salaried employee. The fact that Hyŏn-ju works as a bank clerk in particular, among many other white-collar jobs, is equally noteworthy in the context of enforced savings and restricted consumption, which were inseparable from molding the middle-class fantasy. Admittedly, until the early 1970s, banks were particularly notorious for ruthlessly firing female workers once they were married,[19] making Hyŏn-ju's hiding of her marital status more plausible. An equally important yet relatively undiscussed implication of Hyŏn-ju working in a bank is that it invokes the Park regime's obsession with "accumulation" of capital for its export-centered, loan-based, developmental model represented by the nationalization of banking and strictly enforced personal savings. Here, I particularly refer to the term "accumulation" (*ch'ukchŏk*), often deployed by economic historians to emphasize the Park regime's dominance over the flow of capital and total mobilization of personal savings under the name of industrialization, in order to emphasize Hyŏn-ju's distress under limited consumption. According to economic historian Sŏ Ik-chin, the accumulation system of Park's regime, also called the South Korean Development Model (*han'gukhyŏng sŏngjang model*), is best known for compressed growth propped up by an extremely high savings rate, mainly due to the enforced savings system.[20]

The connection between such a savings system, tacitly coerced by the developmental authoritarian state, and the government's manufacturing of the middle-class dream is well reflected in the following passage stating why Hyŏn-ju conceals her marriage:

18 Kim, "'My' Sweet Home," 119.

19 Shin Kyung-Ah, "A Work-Family Dilemma and the Change of its Discourse," *Han'guk yŏsŏnghak* 23, no. 2 (2007): 5–45, here: 14–15.

20 Sŏ Ik-chin, "Han'guk sanŏphwa ŭi palchŏn yangsik: ch'ukchŏk kwa chojŏl ŭi kwanchŏm esŏ," in *Kaebal tokchae wa Park Chŏng-hŭi sidae: uri sidae ŭi chŏngch'i kyŏngjejŏk kiwŏn*, ed. Yi Pyŏng-ch'ŏn (P'aju: Ch'angbi, 2003), 69–97.

"She [Hyŏn-ju] was overcome by the anxiety of failing to attain the happiness of daily life by solely relying on her husband's income. She couldn't give up her job right now because she wanted to increase their savings."[21]

Considered in tandem with Hyŏn-ju's aforementioned dream of inviting people to her home, the savings are prerequisites for attaining the "happiness of daily life" backed by their material possessions. Just as the ostensibly ordinary words "our home" were indeed historically specific to the rise of a new discourse surrounding a state-led, middle-class fantasy, the seemingly casual expression "happiness" was a buzzword given particular importance under the Park regime. In her illuminating research on the discourse of happiness under the Park regime in the 1960s, literary scholar Kim Ye-rim points out that the term was first narrated more with a spiritual focus as the fruit of diligence. Soon after, it began to be intertwined with strong material connotations through female-targeted magazines, marked by possessing middle-class essentials. The modifier "of daily life" attached to "happiness" here more strongly articulates the stabilization of living conditions into an enduring state. It is crucial that this discursive transition took place when the Park regime announced its investment in heavy industry, which required immense accumulated capital. It is in this vein that the women dreaming of being middle class were particularly "interpellated" by the state. Boosting the investment capacity of manufacturers and other large enterprises at the cost of suppressing personal consumption, this intervention against individual freedom was sugarcoated as wisdom and modesty in preparing for the middle-class life that "awaits".[22] In other words, the dual gestures of provoking a gendered desire for material culture marked by a home and home appliances and of mandating savings was iconic of the accumulation system begun in the mid-1960s. Taking into account that Hyŏn-ju is a female bank clerk, the combination of a gendered entity given the task of "wisely dreaming" of a patriarchal middle-class future, and the institutional incarnation of the accumulation system respectively, binds her twice over to the developmental authoritarian state's schema.

If the discussion of Hyŏn-ju's obsession with attaining middle-class life so far underlines the logic of accumulation at both personal and state level, the novella is also keen to capture the role of consumption within the socially

21 Kim, "Yahaeng," 450.

22 Kim Ye-rim, "The Cultural Politics of Developmental Nationalism and Middle-Class Home Fantasy in the Late of 1960s," *Hyŏndae munhak ŭi yŏn'gu* 32 (2007): 339–375, here: 353–359.

encouraged range that served the ultimate goal of propping up the state's accumulation system. Kim Ye-rim points out how the promotion of the middle-class fantasy deployed double-layered mechanisms of homogenization within the middle class by providing detailed material and spiritual requirements to realize it, and differentiation from the lower class to maximize the feeling of class privilege.[23] The novella reflects on this dual aspect of middle-class fantasy by depicting Hyŏn-ju's class self-distinction from non-middle-class citizens while being unsure herself about whether she would achieve the class goal. For instance, Hyŏn-ju is an avid consumer of fashion, indulging in the expensive taste of salaried employees to distance herself from low-class servers "whose status could easily be guessed by appearance."[24] A similar description can be found in the scene depicting Hyŏn-ju walking along the pedestrian overpass immediately before the rape. Here, we read an elaborate description of her outfit, "the leaf-patterned, pink one-piece instead of the bank uniform" followed by a view from the overpass overlooking the Shinsegae department store and Bank of Korea, the national bank. As Jean Baudrillard's well-known concept of "consuming the difference" describes how consumption is not merely about fulfilling physiological needs but affirming one's distinctiveness from others,[25] Hyŏn-ju's liberal spending to affirm her middle-class identity unwittingly works as an alibi to consolidate the accumulation system of Park's regime. The phrase "the pink one-piece *instead of* the bank uniform" is indeed imbued with irony, since the ostensibly contrasting objects rather converge under the simultaneously homogenizing and differentiating mechanism of the middle-class fantasy fostered by developmental authoritarianism.[26]

The novella's interest in the problem of consumption as collusion in propping up the authoritarian regime is expanded further with the author's choice of publication medium—the weekly. The fact that some of Kim Sŭng-ok's novels and novellas were published in weeklies, a very unusual publishing platform for respected authors, needs to be read as a creative pursuit of realism to cast light on the Park regime's mobilization of entertainment to distract the public from politics. Kim Kyŏng-yŏn argues that the flurry of weeklies in the mid- to late 1960s was linked to the increased

23 Kim, "The Cultural Politics of Developmental Nationalism," 351.

24 Kim, "Yahaeng," 458.

25 Jean Baudrillard, *La Société De Consommation: Ses Mythes, Ses Structures* (Paris: Denoël, 1970), 78–81.

26 Kim, "Yahaeng," 448. Italics mine.

"belief" in purchasing power thanks to the affluence the military regime had promised. In addition to the pornographic and other titillating features of weeklies that contributed to blinding people to politics, Kim Kyŏng-yŏn rightfully points out that the purchase of weeklies in itself was a performative activity to feel the ascent in class status.[27] Nonetheless, Kim Kyŏng-yŏn regards Hyŏn-ju as "typically middle class",[28] while remaining silent on the psychological struggles caused by yet to be achieved "middle-class fantasy requisites" that make her fundamentally doubt her social status despite her white-collar job and education level. Here, the parallel Kim Kyŏng-yŏn misses between the story of the novella and the medium it was published in is precisely the illusory aspect of middle-class fantasy retained by consumption as a class "performance", which did not necessarily match the actual social status of the consumers. Noteworthy in this vein is how Kim Sŭng-ok delicately casts light on the fundamental crack in the middle-class fantasy and twists the politics surrounding the government-condoned boom in weeklies by publishing "A Night Walk" through the very medium of government-condoned, middle-class, consumer culture.

Consumption and Self-Exhaustion as Protests Against Dissolution

Hyŏn-ju's situation is invocative of what Kracauer called the "spiritual homeless" in explaining the identity crisis of salaried employees, since the articulated financial stability and social privilege are illusory.[29] Hyŏn-ju's desperate, yet unguaranteed pursuit of the rosy future in which she proudly presents herself as a housewife with her "own home" makes her a typical victim suffering from spiritual homelessness. If this feeling of spiritual homelessness was depicted as more of a low-key anxiety at the beginning of the novella, it drastically becomes explosive enough to engulf Hyŏn-ju after the tragic rape she is the victim of. On her way back home after a short vacation, Hyŏn-ju encounters a man on the overpass whose appearance and behavior are the complete opposite of those at her workplace. The man suddenly grabs her wrist and drags her forcefully to a nearby motel in broad daylight

27 Kim, "T'ongsok ŭi chŏngch'ihak," 373–389.

28 Ibid., 403.

29 Kracauer, *The Salaried Masses*, 88–95.

and rapes her. The major difference between Hyŏn-ju and the rapist she encounters is not limited to the typical appearances of the salaried employee and the "thug" marked by their skin tones and clothing; more crucial are their contrasting attitudes towards class. It must be noted that the ruthless rapist's goal is neither to take vengeance on those of higher class nor to question the class divide. The formidable power of the mysterious rapist comes not just from his physical strength but also from his complete *blindness*, for he cares about nothing but the wrist in picking his victims. The rapist's motive is crucial in the context of Park's accumulation-oriented era, as it overlaps with how the regime ruthlessly consumed its citizens, regardless of the social status it granted them in the end. If we recall how Hyŏn-ju's clothing consumption and dream of home ownership were fettered to the myth of the middle class propping up the accumulation system in the larger context, the nature of the rape that happens immediately after Hyŏn-ju's observation of these two buildings is geared towards binding all victims under the singular code—the wrist—regardless of their class.

To clarify how the authoritarian regime consumed its citizens regardless of social status and link it to the structure of Hyŏn-ju's night walk following the rape, I refer to Sin Hyŏng-gi's expression of "dissolution" (*yonghae*). While juxtaposing the regime's military background as a symbol of strength with the "powerless" Second Republic, Park aggrandized himself as a morally irrefutable strong leader able to modernize a South Korea devastated by the Korean War and haunted by colonial trauma. Sin points out that the narratives (*iyagi*) of innovation (*swaesin*) and reform (*hyŏksin*) were strategically disseminated by the regime, rendering people into easily replaceable "parts that run the machine called innovation" when they fell behind the pursuit of the grand goal.[30] Naming this internalization of the regime's call for innovation facilitated by the circulation of narrative *dissolution,* Sin argues that it bred schizophrenia, which is the iconic condition the figures in Kim's works suffer from. However, Sin does not take this further and deploy the concept of dissolution to argue the specificity of salaried employees' identity crisis in terms of the accumulation system in his own reading of "A Night Walk".[31] Sin's concept of dissolution could indeed be expanded

30 Sin Hyŏng-gi, "Hyŏksin tamnon kwa Taejung ŭi wich'I," *Hyŏndae munhak ŭi yŏn'gu* 47 (2012): 263–295, here: 283; Sin, "Punyŏltoen man-bogaek," 201–202.

31 While Sin points out the problem of exhaustion in explaining Kim's more well-known novella *Seoul-1964-Winter* where the protagonist throws all of their money into the flames, the relationship between accumulation and consumption is never brought to the fore in

further, as the rape is described to evoke not just the illusoriness of the middle-class dream to Hyŏn-ju; it makes her situate the collapse within the context of the larger dissolution of salaried employees into uniform human capital whose supposedly given class is worthless. In other words, Hyŏn-ju witnesses the fundamental overlapping of structural and personal violence, by the authoritarian regime and the rapist respectively, that provokes her night walk.

As Hyŏn-ju painfully acknowledges the fact that salaried employees are as anonymously consumable as the working class, her inner instability drives her to take unprecedented action. Vaguely perceiving the affinity between the rapist's consumption of the female body and the social structure that drove her to "act" in the workplace, Hyŏn-ju walks into a street where she can appropriate the very violence inflicted upon her body and consume others without seeing them, thereby ignoring their individual traits. One remarkable description of Hyŏn-ju's night walk which demonstrates this reads:

> "The street at this time seemed highly peculiar to Hyŏn-ju for some reason. It was close to the bank. Therefore, she was familiar with the scenery of the street in daytime and early evening. Why then did it look so unfamiliar?"[32]

Considering how the author has previously constantly mentioned major nearby buildings to insinuate Hyŏn-ju's embeddedness in the accumulation system, the highlighting of the street's proximity to the bank here is significant. However, unlike the department store and Bank of Korea seen in daytime, an inexplicable eeriness strikes Hyŏn-ju as she looks at the supposedly familiar landscape at night, which anticipates her reaction against the accumulation system. While salaried employees, whose numbers skyrocketed in 1920s Germany, went to what Kracauer calls the "pleasure barracks" as a shelter to offset their spiritual homelessness and be temporarily emancipated from their situation,[33] Hyŏn-ju chooses the night street to seek redemption. Hyŏn-ju walks along slowly, exposing herself to the sexual gaze of salarymen, waiting for someone to approach her and consume her body as a product. Considering the above quote's mention of the street's proximity to the bank and the structure of the rape Hyŏn-ju constantly reflects upon, her

his reading of "A Night Walk". This could be attributed to Shim remaining silent on the accumulation system Hyŏn-ju represents and thereby not discussing consumption and self-exhaustion as a counteraction against it. Sin, "Punyŏltoen man-bogaek," 215.

32 Kim, "Yahaeng," 457.

33 Kracauer, *The Salaried Masses*, 91.

remark is about the dissolution of people into a mass to be consumed predominantly by the regime.

Another crucial point is that Hyŏn-ju always sets one condition for the consumption of her body—to never look at the other's face. That is, Hyŏn-ju refuses to see individual traits and strives to consume salaried employees as a mass of interchangeable beings. It is this ambivalence of positioning herself as a consumer and product that makes her night walk intriguing, as she retains her status *on the verge* of being relegated to a product rather than opting solely for one or the other. Considering the mention of the street's proximity to the bank and Hyŏn-ju's observation of interchangeable salaried employees just like the commodified bodies of the prostitutes on the street, what strikes her is her embeddedness in the regime's dissolution project on a larger scale.

Here, the collective entity is emerging from the process of dissolution, often labeled the masses (*taejung*) and people (*kunjung*) in pre-existing research.[34] The literature on "A Night Walk" has approached Hyŏn-ju's night promenade as a voluntary mingling with the masses/people who are suffering from an identity crisis as much as she is. However, relying on the rather abstract terms of the masses and people runs the risk of overlooking the delicate epistemological *stages* involved in Hyŏn-ju's perception of the masses/people walking on the night street. While it is true that she finds a striking similarity among the people on the streets regardless of their social status, the group she jumps into is not an already unified mass, but rather a jumble of people *on the verge of* losing their individual identities, and about to be dissolved into the masses easily mobilized by the regime. That is, the comingling with the masses pointed out by the pre-existing analysis occurs *in stages*—only after witnessing the interchangeability of people as a condition for the rise of the manipulatable and consumable masses by appropriating the violence of the military regime. The presumption of such

34 For instance, Kim Kyŏng-yŏn uses *taejung* which is conventionally translated as the "masses", and Sin Hyŏng-gi uses *kunjung*, which he explicitly translates as "people" in their analysis of "A Night Walk". In Kim's case, the masses are mostly emphasized as avid consumers of weeklies and monthlies. Sin Hyŏng-gi uses the "people" rather than "crowd", which is the more common translation for *kunjung*, to articulate the regime's interpellation for dissolution imposed upon *kunjung*. Although there exists a difference in nuance between the two terms, I pair them for my inquiry as they are both articulated as a group entity divested of individual traits and demoted to human capital to be controlled and consumed by the regime. Kim, "T'ongsok ŭi chŏngch'ihak," 373–420; Sin, "Punyŏltoen man-bogaek," 199–225.

epistemological *stages* in witnessing the accumulation system becomes clear in the quote below:

"The woman [Hyŏn-ju] realized what she had been waiting for; they were horror and chaos. Yet, above all, *the forceful hand-pulling of the rapist had to come first.* It came as no surprise that the boiling swamp of horror and chaos inside her did not seethe. The fear and chaos could engulf her *only after her wrist had been roughly pulled by the man.*"[35]

As the emphasized quotes show, Hyŏn-ju's self-disorientation requires certain steps—starting with reconfirming her own replaceability evoked by the rape. Here, the necessity of reflecting on the structure of the rape I argued above becomes more evident. While conventional analyses have focused solely on the fear and chaos she jumps into, they ignore the overlapping of violence within the accumulation system and overlook Hyŏn-ju's appropriation of such violence to discover the dissolution omnipresent in Korea.

The next stage after witnessing the system's effacement of one's identity suggested above in "the boiling swamp of horror and chaos inside her" is also crucial, for it implies how the salaried employee's self-recognition of her identity crisis has particularly explosive aspects. While the novella attributes the rapist's ruthlessness to behavior typical of a die-hard ex-convict, foregrounding the existence of the boiling swamp of horror and chaos inside Hyŏn-ju suggests her recasting of seemingly blind consumption is not accidental. This eruption of disruptive desire is akin to Kracauer's "morally pink complexion." In his essay entitled "Selection", Kracauer appropriates the expression originally used by an influential figure from a personnel department in an interview. As the interviewee underlines "pleasant appearance" as a fundamental quality of the ideal salaried employee and complements this with the expression of "a morally pink complexion," Kracauer sees through its innate violence. First, Kracauer clarifies that this expression does not merely refer to outer appearances, but also includes the combination of the total suppression of certain desires and the unity of external appearances. The pursuit of such a superficial trait is indeed beneficial in maintaining a society, as it contributes to suturing the gap between the illusory image of a rosy life and reality. Still, Kracauer goes one step further, warning that these suppressed but never extinguished desires eventually explode violently. Kracauer declares: "But beware, if morality should penetrate beneath the skin, and the pink be not quite moral enough to prevent the eruption of

35 Kim, "Yahaeng," 462. Italics mine.

desires!"[36] Kracauer's insight leads us to better grasp the rationale behind Hyŏn-ju's seemingly random switch to radical self-exhaustion on the street from someone following the government's savings policy.

Based on the discovery of the night street's landscape on her night walk, Hyŏn-ju moves on to encounter an event representing the government's ruthless consumption of the masses in the name of a larger accumulation of national power—the Vietnam War. On the news reel Hyŏn-ju sees, Korean soldiers dressed in the same uniforms and draped with flower necklaces on their return home are dissolved into the discourse of national duty and upholding world order. The memoirs of high-ranking officials in Korea's military regime demonstrate that the fundamental driving force behind this mobilization of the masses was the narrative of accumulation. For instance, then Director of the Korean Central Intelligence Agency, Kim Jong-pil, evaluates the regime's dispatch of Korean troops to the Vietnam War as "securing international trust and accumulating real combat experiences, as well as acquiring economic benefits."[37] Kim Jong-pil's justification of the troops' dispatch overlaps strikingly with his eulogy of the authoritarian regime leader Park signing the problematic contract with Japan, as Park's regime did not waste a single penny earned through the contract, tacitly situating Park as the only irrefutably moral consumer of accumulated financial and military strength.[38] As Hyŏn-ju repeats the night walk rendering herself a replaceable commodity, she conversely starts to see the irreplaceable identity of the sacrificed mass which she names "the face of our ethnicity" (*uri chongjok ŭi ŏlgul*),[39] both from the newsreels of soldiers at the dispatch ceremonies and the emasculated, intoxicated salarymen meandering the night street.

Catching Up With Madness Through Madness

Here, imitation of state violence to transcend it needs more detailed reflection regarding the meaning of anonymity. Depriving the sex partner of their personal traits and turning them into an anonymous being at night sustains

36 Kracauer, *The Salaried Masses*, 38.

37 Kim Chong-p'il, *Kim Chong-p'il chŭngŏnnok: JP ka mal hanŭn Taehan Min'guk hyŏndaesa* 1, ed. Chungang Ilbo *Kim Chong-p'il chŭngŏnnok* T'im (Seoul: Waisŭberi, 2016), 319.

38 Kim, *Kim Chong-p'il chŭngŏnnok*, 251.

39 Kim, "Yahaeng," 444.

the night walk that slowly takes the protagonist to a higher stage of enlightenment, marked by Hyŏn-ju's envisioning of the face. As Jacques Lacan pointed out, the subject's fate is determined under an eternally dialectical process,[40] so Hyŏn-ju needs to mimic the desire of the regime and the anonymity sustains her night walk as part of the dialectic process. While conventional critics undervalue the violence of the novella as mere mimicry of the dictatorial regime, this seemingly blind process carries much more potential.

Furthermore, anonymity as a rudimentary condition for Hyŏn-ju's night walk needs to be highlighted in terms of gaining sufficient *momentum* to catch up with the speed of "compressed growth",[41] a glorified modifier for the nation's numerical growth at the price of dissolving individuals into the masses and consuming them brutally as living capital. To quote Zygmunt Bauman's *Liquid Modernity*, it is impossible to discover one's own individual identity in static terms in this extremely fluid modern society.[42] As mentioned above, the protagonist's night walk is possible under the condition that she never sees the approaching salaried employee's face. This type of interaction allows her to encounter as many men as possible while rejecting those who would not "forcefully drag her wrist" to a motel "without hesitation."[43] The *efficiency*, in particular, is underlined as a major benefit of ignoring people's individual traits in the phrase: "It was a great relief for Hyŏn-ju that she could save her energy by staying silent and not looking at their faces to distinguish which one was the one she was looking for."[44]

If the night walk can be read as an extreme reaction of consumption against the authoritarian state's promotion of accumulation, this anonymous consumption of each other's bodies is essential in guaranteeing the continuity of the night walk. In this context, unlike the literature on this novella deploying Walter Benjamin's *flaneur*, which penetratingly observes the street at a relaxed pace, I would like to clarify that Hyŏn-ju's careful observation of the masses through simultaneous comingling and distancing is not incompatible with blindness and speed.

If we compare Cormac McCarthy's *No Country for Old Men* with "A Night Walk", based on their shared interest in the psychological

40 Jacques Lacan, *Le Séminaire* 3, ed. Jacques-Alain Miller (Paris: Seuil, 1991), 140.

41 Sŏ, "Han'guk sanŏphwa ŭi palchŏn yangsik," 69–97.

42 Zygmunt Bauman, *Liquid Modernity* (Cambridge: Polity Press, 2015), 48.

43 Kim, "Yahaeng," 462.

44 Ibid., 446.

insecurity provoked by the Vietnam War, the significance of speed becomes clear. In *No Country for Old Men*, Sheriff Tom Bell is overwhelmed by Anton Chigurh's inhumane violence towards his victims for financial gain. Although one is tempted to label Chigurh as an antagonist towards Bell, Bell was never a match for Chigurh from the beginning. Therefore, the seemingly typical relationship between the criminal and the sheriff is a metaphor for the post-Vietnam War situation that leaves behind anyone that cannot deal with its rapidity. Bell, an icon of the old era, never succeeds in decoding Chigurh's identity as he lacks the bare minimum speed to put him in his sights.[45] Unlike Bell's complete failure to grasp even a brief impression of his era, Hyŏn-ju's violent consumption of men on the street allows her to see beyond her daily life. As Hyŏn-ju observes the street at night, the first impression that strikes her is that of "cars speeding in a frenzy and passersby walking fast as if they were in an extreme hurry",[46] implying an overarching obsession with speed in the 1960s. Considering this necessity for speed, the anonymous consumption of bodies on the street cannot be merely regarded as feckless wandering. The pink complexion mentioned by Kracauer, and the eruption of desire into violence in the era of articulated affluence cited by Baudrillard, again explain where Hyŏn-ju acquires the explosive energy to retain her blindingly fast "speed".

Hyŏn-ju moves on to draw some meaning from her night walk in relation to the haunting images of the Vietnam War dispatch. I would like to point out that Hyŏn-ju's night walk is linked to religious words, such as "to pray" (*kido*), "believer" (*Sin-ja*), "ceremony" (*ŭisik*) and "redemption" (*kuwŏn*), particularly when describing her desperate attempt to see "the face of our ethnicity",[47] which even the regime's violence cannot annihilate. Hyŏn-ju's night walk is highly reminiscent of the rhetoric of the *yurodivy*—often translated as "holy fool"—which has its cultural roots in the Russian Orthodox Church. Unlike typical saints, the *yurodivy* not only immerse themselves in chaotic places but behave in a lowbrow manner, attaining truth in the process.[48] The aforementioned meaning of Hyŏn-ju's mimicry of the pervasive violence of anonymity shares the *yurodivy*'s pursuit of the truth. Her mimicry also features a "call from above", much like that of the *yurodivy*. During her

45 Cormac McCarthy, *No Country for Old Men* (New York: Alfred A. Knopf, 2005).

46 Kim, "Yahaeng," 459.

47 Ibid., 464.

48 Effie Poulakou-Rebelakou, "Holy Fools: A Religious Phenomenon of Extreme Behaviour," *Journal of Religion and Health* 53 (2014): 95–104.

first night walk, while still having doubts about it, she suddenly hears a voice calling her: "Where is the panting sound hitting my ears coming from? Who is calling me? Why do I now hear the sound of the wind blended with terror and confusion on this street?"[49]

This calling, which occurs in the middle of the night street where salaried employees walk quickly and cars speed by furiously, is what triggers Hyŏn-ju to indulge herself in the landscape. Her noticeable progress seems to imply that she will eventually transcend the violence and pressure inflicted on her and the entire nation.

However, the difference between the *yurodivy* and Hyŏn-ju is the latter's failure to dismantle the overarching logic of society. Despite the progress she makes in reading the military parade and linking it with the life of salaried employees, she descends into an almost complete psychological breakdown following the unbearable mental fatigue. For instance, she ends up calling her husband "honey" in the workplace in an attempt to maintain her husband as an irreplaceable being instead of as part of the anonymous masses she consumes on the night street.[50] In other words, Hyŏn-ju cannot remain fully confident in her rebellious performance nor stay completely silent on what she witnesses during her night promenade. As the ending shows, Hyŏn-ju's night walk will continue but the possibility of her overcoming the oscillation between the pursuit of irreplaceability and anonymity remains undiscussed. Why does Hyŏn-ju's night walk become mired in never-ending chaos? Also, could the ending's allusion to the permanence of salaried employees' disorientation be equated to the novella's failure to provide a concrete reflection on the military regime?

I seek to answer these two questions together by reading her failure as an allegory of Park's authoritarian regime. Whereas Hyŏn-ju's ostensible failure to discover "the face" that survives amidst the regime's ruthless dissolution has been explained through the seemingly irrefutable incompatibility between anonymity and irreplaceability,[51] I would like to argue otherwise by referring to the quote below:

49 Kim, "Yahaeng," 458.

50 Ibid., 463.

51 For instance, while Sin Hyŏng-gi rightly points out that Hyŏn-ju's schizophrenic struggle during her night walk is due to her oscillating between retaining the complete alterity of others and finding their surviving individual traits, Sin leans towards presuming the traits of people are indissoluble and attributes Hyŏn-ju's failure to go in the opposite direction, anonymizing the people on the street. Sin, "Punyŏltoen Man-bogaek," 217–218.

"Occasionally the woman [Hyŏn-ju] wondered if she could be dragged by a random man without horror and internal chaos. Just like the prostitutes, no, just like the believers attending mass without even having much to desperately pray for.

But what she was most afraid of was ending up covering her desires with such a ceremony. Although only in a vague sense, she knew she would face a complete downfall if she allowed herself to be dragged by a random man without horror and chaos, since without horror and chaos, she would only be left with ceremony. What she was craving was, yes that is right, not the doom but the redemption."[52]

Here, the reason why Hyŏn-ju is tied up in the never-ending cycle of the night walk is clarified by herself: Hyŏn-ju explicitly acknowledges that she could have attained her "redemption" had she adhered to following her "desires" (*yongmang*), but instead ended up falling into the "ceremony" (*ŭisik*), a term with strong religious connotations. Counterintuitively, Hyŏn-ju connects ceremony to empty prayers in the preceding passage and thereby makes her pursuit of "the face" not only meaningless but deceitful. This contradicts the conventional reading of Hyŏn-ju's night walk as a predestined failure in trying to reconcile anonymity and replaceability with unchanging truth. Although Hyŏn-ju at first perceives "the face" as an ineffaceable identity even within the regime's compressed growth and accumulation system, the cited paragraphs suggest what matters in the end is not whether she finds an irreplaceable value to compensate for her struggle at night; rather, the phrase renders the existence of solid truth marked by "the face" delusory. In other words, Hyŏn-ju's inner struggle is aggravated as she continues the night walk, less so because she did not choose the appropriate means, but more because it is a pilgrimage for apocryphal gnosis from the beginning.[53]

While the novel does not clarify whether Hyŏn-ju finally reaches such self-acknowledgement, passages in the preceding paragraphs in fact imply that "the face" is rendered consumable, just like the masses on the street. Where Hyŏn-ju is struck by the faces of the deployed Korean soldiers on the newsreel, she finds their faces "do not go well with the uniforms" and

52 Kim, "Yahaeng," 464.

53 Yu Im-ha already used the term "pilgrimage" (*sullye*) in describing Hyŏn-ju's night walk. However, the rationale behind Yu Im-ha's usage of the term primarily comes from the novella's explicit statement that Hyŏn-ju is seeking "redemption" and does not discuss the form of religious narrative underlying the novella. As a result, Yu's article does not fully meet the potential of theorizing pilgrimage in the novella, as it does not grapple with the problem of absolute truth the novella questions through the religious allegory. Yu, "Tach'in ilsangsŏng kwa haebang ŭiji," 275.

wonders "if this has to do with them wearing the foreign military uniform of the US."[54] On the surface, this is a typical lament of the colonized that leads us to envision the ongoing colonization of South Korea. However, what merits equal attention in Hyŏn-ju's observation is that she uses the term "our ethnicity" (*uri chongjok*) in describing the physiognomy of Korean soldiers, a more comprehensive term than "nation" (*minjok*), that is less frequently paired with the modifier "Korean".[55] How should we approach the usage of this far less common word pairing? I argue that it forebodes the seemingly radical shift of Hyŏn-ju's attitude towards "the face", foregrounding how ostensibly an essential identity is prone to consumption like a banknote, as attested by the Vietnam War. As many scholars have lucidly pointed out, Korea's dispatch of troops to the Vietnam War benefited the US in mitigating hatred towards white invaders.[56] Here, the face of Korean soldiers is purchased as the face of Asia for the price of US financial and diplomatic support and, therein, the presumed authenticity of Koreans is questioned in the rubric of the US's mobilization of an Asian ethnicity. The consumption of ethnicity represented in the case of the Vietnam War then frustrates Hyŏn-ju's painful yet supposedly rebellious night pilgrimage, not because it reminds her of a certain identity currently being oppressed and waiting to be freed, but even the face she believes to be immiscible with the accumulation system is indeed a mere product, interchangeable with the faces of other Asians and thereby only existing as an "ethnicity."

It is in this context that the concept of allegory becomes useful in arguing that Hyŏn-ju's failure to escape the system cannot be taken completely at face value. Admittedly, the term allegory has already been deployed in the reading of "A Night Walk" by Kim Kyŏng-yŏn and in the reading of Kim's *Seoul-1964-Winter* by Sin Hyŏng-gi. Kim Kyŏng-yŏn uses the concept rather generally as an equivalent of metaphor or epitome of social phenomena and Sin focuses on the fragmented relationship between individuals and society.[57] Instead, I start from the allegory's premise that the penetrating logic

---

54 Kim, "Yahaeng," 444.

55 Ibid.

56 Admittedly, historians point out that it was Park's regime that volunteered to dispatch troops to Vietnam to secure political and economic support from the US. Still, the mass dispatch of Korean troops was appealing for the US as well, and one primary reason was the "Asian face" of the Korean troops as Yun Ch'ung-no indicates. cf. Han Hong-gu, "P'et'ŭnam p'abyŏng kwa pyŏngyŏng kukka ŭi kil," in *Kaebal tokchae wa Park Chŏng-hŭi sidae*, 289–291; Yun Ch'ung-no, *Pet'ŭnam chŏnjaeng ŭi Han'guk sahoesa*, 160.

57 Kim, "T'ongsok ŭi chŏngch'ihak," 405–409.

of society cannot be directly written in the content but only be evoked through the form of the narrative in order to better describe the potential of religious allegory the novella deploys. Situating "the face" where the essence of humanity should be, the novella makes Hyŏn-ju's supposedly promising pilgrimage completely apocryphal. Her search for "the face" fundamentally overlaps with the regime's pursuit of untainted Korean spirituality, bolstered by the slogan of purifying the old evils of the nation. Building on Craig Owens's definition of allegory as a rhetorical tool that places emphasis on the similarities narrative bears to the contradictions underlying society,[58] the twist in the *yurodivy* narrative—where Hyŏn-ju is trapped in eternal chaos—cannot be regarded as irresponsible capitulation to the regime. What is important is not whether Hyŏn-ju reaches a concrete reflection on the regime; instead, the focus should be on how her constant self-destruction strikes the reader through the form of the *yurodivy* narrative to evoke the regime's truth-molding system. In addition, as we refer to the allegory as a rhetorical tool to convey messages through its "form",[59] the phrases cited above reaffirm the importance of utilizing anonymity, which I argued earlier, as the crucial momentum to catching up with the rapid modernity marked by dissolution and the accumulation system. Considered in tandem with the notion of allegory, ignoring others' faces, summarized as the term "desire" (*yongmang*), also grants the power to sustain the "form" of allegory. Hyŏn-ju continues her pilgrimage for "the redemptive truth" which she fails to find yet constantly imagined as a counterpart to her consumption of anonymous others.[60]

That is, the novelty in the allegory of the *yurodivy* in the novella does not only come from presenting how the regime's tenets of morality and innovation had destroyed individuals. Instead of naively imagining the presence of the absolute truth that is yet to be discovered as a counterpart to the regime's immorality, "A Night Walk" sheds light on the comprehensiveness of the functioning logic of the accumulation that mobilizes the very belief in authentic, untainted truth, and consumes it to consolidate the regime. Finally, "A Night Walk" suggests the possibility of expanding the original concept by questioning what sustains the form of the allegory. Hyŏn-ju's consumption of anonymous others is not only crucial in catching up with the speed

58 Craig Owens, "The Allegorical Impulse: Toward a Theory of Postmodernism," October 12 (1980): 67–86.

59 Bainard Cowan, "Walter Benjamin's Theory of Allegory," *New German Critique* 22 (1981): 109–122.

60 Kim, "Yahaeng," 464.

of the accumulation system but also works as a rudimentary condition for structuring the allegory of the *yurodivy* in the context of the military regime. Through this, the novella reveals the emptiness of the Park regime's grand promise to inherit the spirit of the April 19 Revolution and fully restore national spirit, severely damaged by colonization and the Korean War, after accumulating enough power. Therefore, against the criticism that Hyŏn-ju's ignoring of individual faces was predestined to fail in capturing the indestructible value of humanity, I argue otherwise: The novella questions if "the face" of the individual can be situated as a counterpart to faceless others from the beginning in the authoritarian regime's accumulation system boosted by mass dissolution. Taking this into account, rendering others faceless needs to be approached as a procedure for detaching oneself from pursuing the absolute truth, as it runs the risk of merely repeating, not appropriating, the state violence inflicted upon the masses.

Concluding Remarks

In his monumental *Totalitarian and Authoritarian Regimes*, Juan Linz points out that authoritarianism expresses itself not only at an institutional level but also in everyday life, therefore "penetrat[ing]" society. The ubiquitous nature of this control does not merely stem from explicit promotion of state ideology, but often a blurred political orientation to cover its severe democratic deficit and minimize the risk of facing mass backlash. It is within this frame that Linz expands the concept of limited pluralism, the most iconic, pseudo-democratic character of authoritarianism, beyond the political party system to quotidianization of control under the mask of promoting freedom.[61] This applies well to the multi-layered strategies taken by the Park Chung-hee regime in South Korea, particularly concerning its mobilization of white-collar workers. Although the authoritarianism of the Park regime in South Korea is more often associated with the term anti-communism because of its police surveillance and oppression of political freedom, the history of engineering the middle-class fantasy suggests that promoting the freedom of developing one's taste in material culture and of designing one's future was also a key piece of the puzzle in retaining the authoritarian system. The

61 Juan J. Linz, *Totalitarian and Authoritarian Regimes* (London: Lynne Rienner Publishers, 2000), 160–161.

critical importance of "A Night Walk" then lies in casting light on this diversionary aspect of middle-class fantasy that propped up authoritarianism. Although the novella frequently refers to the "fence" (*ult'ari*) imprisoning the protagonist,[62] what is at stake here is not how heavily guarded it is but how it was inconceivable until she realized its presence.

If identity crisis can be defined as a fundamental frustration of one's imagined place in society, the novella deploys the identity crisis narrative to cast light on multiple material and psychological aspects that once propped up the very self-identification of salaried employees. By doing so, it reveals how the ostensibly innocent and liberal pursuit of one's own "happiness" had blinded the people to the multi-layered mobilization strategies of the authoritarian Park regime and their embeddedness in them. As we focus on the particular narrative of saving for the future disseminated by the Park regime, the rationale behind the novella's link between the salaried employee's indeed limited liberal consumption and the Park regime's dominance in consuming human resources marked by the Vietnam War becomes evident. In this vein, probing the influence of the state model accumulation system was crucial in connecting the three major events (the rape, the night walk and the Vietnam War dispatch ceremony) within the rubric of authoritarianism in Korea. The three events, woven together from the protagonist's viewpoint, converged into unveiling the rampant violence of the Park regime where individuals are divested of the dignity and freedom for self-exploration, and demoted to anonymous, consumable objects. Therefore, my reading sought to shed light on the novelty of "A Night Walk" in delving into what Kracauer would have called "the unknown territory"[63] of salaried employees, marked by their identity crisis, as a gateway to envisioning the logic of authoritarian mass mobilization. Through this, the novella moves on to suggest blind consumption and self-exhaustion as possible modalities of resistance, particularly against the pseudo-freedom of the authoritarian regime.

---

62 For instance, Kim, "Yahaeng," 459.

63 Kracauer, *The Salaried Masses*, 28–32.

IV. Violent Crises, Crises of Violence

Necessity, Preliminarity and Moderation: The IACHR Mission in 1979 and the Argentine Junta's Response

Janis Nalbadidacis

Introduction

On August 10, 1978, US ambassador Raúl Castro met with representatives of the Argentine junta at Newbery Airport in Buenos Aires. In a letter to the State Department, he would later describe it as walking into "a lion's den".[1] Only one day before, the Assistant Secretary of State for Human Rights and Humanitarian Affairs of the United States, Patricia Derian, had made a provocative statement before the Subcommittee on Inter-American Affairs of the Committee on International Relations aimed at the Argentine junta.[2] In her statement, Derian not only pointed out ongoing violations of human rights in Argentina; she explicitly insisted on an opportunity for an on-site observation by the Inter-American Commission on Human Rights (IACHR), so that a delegation could investigate the numerous accusations and form an independent picture of events in Argentina. Namely, she mentioned the Argentine junta's reluctance to permit such a mission as one of the most important reasons for her recommendation to the Export-Import Bank of the United States to hold back a prospective loan to the military regime. In light of this news, Castro described the expression on the Argentine Foreign Minister's face throughout their meeting "as if he had just attended a funeral."[3] Obviously, the Argentine regime had strong reservations about an IACHR mission.

Scholarship unanimously agrees on the authoritarian character of the Argentine regime. The coup by the Argentine military did not come as a

1 Letter from Raúl Castro to the US State Department, August 8, 1978, 1, in: National Security Archives, Argentina Declassification Project.

2 United States of America, *Arms Trade in the Western Hemisphere: Hearings Before the Subcommittee on Inter-American Affairs of the Committee on International Relations, House of Representatives, 95th Congress, Second Session* (Washington, 1978), 175.

3 Letter from Raúl Castro to the US State Department, August 4, 1978, 1, in: National Security Archives, Argentina Declassification Project.

surprise. In late December 1975—due to the increasing violence and disastrous economic situation—the Commander-in-Chief of the Army, Lieutenant General Jorge Videla, gave the Head of Government, Isabel Perón, a 90-day ultimatum to get the situation under control.[4] From the army's point of view, that did not happen. On March 24, 1976, the military forces seized power, dissolved congress and installed a junta under the command of the three different branches of the military, represented by Jorge Videla (army), Eduardo Massera (navy), and Orlando Agosti (air force).[5] The suspension of political participation and constitutional democracy was accompanied by drastic and brutal measures against opponents. In order to avoid news of these repressive measures spreading, in March 1976 the junta instituted a very restrictive policy regarding external delegations and the investigation of human rights violations. If delegations were allowed to come to Argentina at all, they were only given very limited space to maneuver. "Every single interview we did, every place we went, was staked out," as Patricia Feeney, a member of the Amnesty International delegation, describes her experiences.[6]

The situation would be different and more difficult with an IACHR delegation, since the IACHR was an organ of the Organization of American States.[7] Hence, a delegation represented the member states, and was not just

4 Alexander Hasgall, *Regime der Anerkennung. Kämpfe um Wahrheit und Recht in der Aufarbeitung der argentinischen Militärdiktatur* (Bielefeld: Transcript, 2016), 105–106; Marcos Novaro and Vicente Palermo, *La dictadura militar, (1976–1983): Del golpe de Estado a la restauración democrática* (Buenos Aires: Ediciones Paidós, 2003), 18–19.

5 On the explicit measures the junta announced, see Junta Militar, "Acta fijando el Propósito y los Objetivos básicos Para el Procéso de Reorganización Nacionál, 24.3.1976," in *Documentos básicos y bases políticas de las Fuerzas Armadas para el Proceso de Reorganización Nacional*, ed. Junta Militar (Buenos Aires, 1980), 9–10. For further information about the complicated relations between the different branches, see the works of Canelo: Paula Canelo, *El Proceso en su laberinto: La interna militar de Videla a Bignone* (Buenos Aires: Prometeo Libros, 2008); Paula Canelo, "Las 'dos almas' del Proceso: Nacionalistas y liberales durante la última dictadura militar argentina (1976–1981)," *Páginas. Revista Digital de la Escuela de Historia* 1, no. 1 (December 2008): 70–85; Paula Canelo, *La política secreta de la última dictadura argentina (1976–1983): A 40 años del golpe de Estado* (Buenos Aires: Edhasa, 2016).

6 Patricia Feeney quoted in Ann Marie Clark, *Diplomacy of Conscience: Amnesty International and Changing Human Rights Norms* (Princeton: Princeton University Press, 2001), 76. See the report on this mission: Amnesty International, *Report of an Amnesty International Mission to Argentina, 6–15 November 1976* (London, 1977).

7 For the character and the history of the IACHR, see Robert K. Goldman, "History and Action: The Inter-American Human Rights System and the Role of the Inter-American Commission on Human Rights," *Human Rights Quarterly* 31, no. 4 (November 2009):

part of a non-profit organization which could be dealt with more restrictively and possibly be more easily compromised by false allegations. Aware of this fact, the Argentine regime did its best to ignore the IACHR's request for an on-site observation and made only empty promises.[8] In August 1978, this strategy to avoid the IACHR came to an end. By suspending the Export-Import Bank's credit, the junta found itself in quite an uncomfortable position and some of its members may have foreseen that the IACHR's mission would mean nothing good for the junta.

For a long time, the junta denied that any kind of state violence was taking place. Rather, it emphasized that its actions were guided by "Christian and Western values". As blurry and vague as these reference points were, they certainly did not include gross, systematic violations of human rights. Allegations of human rights violations had been brought up before, for example, by Amnesty International in 1976.[9] However, the IACHR had the power to bring those allegations to a new level since it was not just a non-governmental organization. Rather, it was a legally acknowledged permanent body which served to monitor the human rights situation in its member states. The IACHR mission was capable of doing severe damage to the Argentine junta's image on an international scale.[10] It could potentially even affect the domestic standing of the junta. Subsequently, the publication of the IACHR findings were perceived by the junta as a serious threat to its own legitimacy. This can be gleaned from the fact that even before the report by the IACHR was published in April 1980, the junta began distributing its own report on the IACHR mission in Argentina.[11]

For the junta, nothing less than its credibility and its founding myth of being a necessary and nation-saving intervening force in times of crisis were at stake. This interplay between the perceived legitimization crisis in 1979

856–887, here: 861–862; Diana Contreras-Garduño, "The Inter-American System of Human Rights," in *The Sage Handbook of Human Rights*, eds. Anja Mihr and Mark Gibney (London: SAGE Publications, 2014), 596–614, here: 598–602.

8 A first request by the IACHR was rejected by the Argentine junta in February 1978, Iain Guest, *Behind the Disappearances: Argentina's Dirty War Against Human Rights and the United Nations* (Philadelphia: University of Pennsylvania Press, 1990), 173.

9 Amnesty International, *Report Argentina, 6–15 November 1976.*

10 Crucial in this regard is the profound and detailed article by Novaro and Avenburg. Marcos Novaro and Alejandro Avenburg, "La CIDH en Argentina: Entre la democratización y los derechos humanos," *Desarrollo Económico* 49, no. 193 (April 2009): 61–90.

11 Junta Militar, *Observaciones y comentarios criticos del gobierno argentino al informe de la CIDH sobre la situación de los derechos humanos en Argentina* (Buenos Aires, 1980).

and the Argentine state crisis in 1976 marks the focus of this chapter. How did the Argentine junta try to present and frame past actions to the national public in order to legitimize them, as well as its claim to power? So far, scholarship in Argentina has made enormous efforts to prove the brutality of the regime by pointing out the numerous cases of torture and murder by agents of the state.[12] This was accompanied by research on the various ways the Argentine junta collaborated with other dictatorships or the CIA in the context of the Cold War.[13] The inner discrepancies in the junta as well as transformations in legitimization narratives are only rarely addressed.[14] This chapter will contribute to this strand of research by presenting a more nuanced picture of legitimization discourses in transition, focusing on the way the junta presented itself and tried to frame the findings of the IACHR commission.

Winning and Losing Credit

Money matters. As in many cases, this was definitely true for the IACHR's on-site observation in Argentina. When the junta seized power, the Argentine economy was in dire straits. Novaro and Palermo estimate that prices rose by more than 500 percent in 1976 alone.[15] While the unemployment rate fell in the following years, the inflation rate was a constant challenge as it remained above 150 percent.[16] Just how reliant the junta was on financial

---

12 Daniel Feierstein, *Genocide as Social Practice: Reorganizing Society under the Nazis and Argentina's Military Juntas* (New Brunswick: Rutgers University Press, 2014); Pilar Calveiro, *Poder y desaparición: Los campos de concentración en Argentina*, 3rd ed. (Buenos Aires: Colihue, 2006); Eduardo Luis Duhalde, *El Estado terrorista argentino: Quince años después: Una mirada crítica* (Buenos Aires: Eudeba Editorial, 1999); Marguerite Feitlowitz, *A Lexicon of Terror* (Oxford, New York: Oxford University Press, 2011).

13 William M. Schmidli, "Tracking the Cold War in Latin America," *Reviews in American History* 40, no. 2 (June 2012): 332–338; J. Patrice McSherry, *Predatory States: Operation Condor and Covert War in Latin America* (Lanham: Rowman & Littlefield Publishers, 2005); Hal Brands, *Latin America's Cold War* (Cambridge, Massachusetts: Harvard University Press, 2010); Federico Finchelstein, *The Ideological Origins of the Dirty War: Fascism, Populism, and Dictatorship in Twentieth Century Argentina* (Oxford: Oxford University Press, 2014).

14 For excellent exceptions, see the works of Canelo: Canelo, *El Proceso en su laberinto*; Canelo, "Las 'dos almas'"; Canelo, *La política secreta de la última dictadura argentina (1976–1983)*.

15 Novaro and Palermo, *La dictadura militar*, 17.

16 Ibid., 275.

support from third parties becomes obvious when one sees how quickly it made concessions to the IACHR once its credit was frozen. Just one month after a US Export-Import bank loan of 550 million dollars destined to finance the building of the Yacyretá dam was halted, the junta took significant steps towards agreeing to an on-site IACHR observation.[17] A few weeks later the suspension was lifted and, in return, on October 16, 1978, the Argentine junta declared it would allow an on-site observation by the IACHR.[18] As a former member of the IACHR delegation stresses, the on-site observation contained in its "set of rules for on-site inquiries, rules which gave us *carte blanche* to investigate, by whatever means we deemed necessary, every aspect of the human rights situation."[19] Except for institutions which were considered crucial to national security, the delegation was authorized to access any space in order to collect information about the human rights situation in Argentina, such as police departments. In addition, the delegation was authorized to collect personal complaints, to speak to representatives of different branches, including the military, religious communities, and political parties, to try to trace back specific cases of disappearances which had been brought to their attention in advance.[20] However, it would take almost another year until the IACHR arrived in Argentina in spring 1979.[21]

Retrospectively, we know that the initial years of the junta were by far the cruelest and most murderous. Even if exact numbers are difficult to validate, general estimates assume that about 80 percent of forced disappearances took place between 1976 and 1978.[22] Scholarship has identified two

17 Letter from the US embassy in Buenos Aires to the US State Department about a meeting between US Ambassador Raúl Castro and General Viola, August 9, 1978, 1–2, in: National Security Archives, Argentina Declassification Project. Tom Farer, "I Cried for You, Argentina," *Human Rights Quarterly* 38, no. 4 (November 2016): 851–927, here: 857; Novaro and Palermo, *La dictadura militar*, 290.

18 Crédito del Eximbank a Argentina por 270 millones de dólares, in: *El País*, September 29, 1978; Letter from the US embassy in Buenos Aires to the US State Department, October 18, 1978, p. 2, in: National Security Archives, Argentina Declassification Project.

19 Farer, "I Cried for You, Argentina," 856–857.

20 Comisión Interamericana de Derechos Humanos, *Informe sobre la situación de los derechos humanos en Argentina* (Washington, 1980), 6–7.

21 The junta blocked the IACHR mission several times. In the end, the mission should have taken place in May 1979. Because some of the delegation's members had other obligations, the mission had to be postponed again, from May 28, 1979, to September 1979. Novaro and Avenburg, "La CIDH en Argentina," 73–75.

22 Secretaría de Derechos Humanos y Pluralismo Cultural de la Nación (SDHN), ed., *Informe de investigación sobre víctimas de desaparición forzada y asesinato, por el accionar represivo del Estado y*

main explanations for the decline in numbers after 1978. One strand emphasizes that armed guerrilla groups, for example, the Montoneros, were largely eliminated.[23] The danger of armed resistance was vanquished, the limits of the claimed preliminarity were reached and, as such, the justification for ruling with an "iron fist" vanished. A second strand highlights the increasing international pressure and public attention on the violent state repressions in Argentina, due to spectacular cases involving foreign citizens, the FIFA World Cup which took place in Argentina in 1978, and the growing influence of the human rights movement.[24]

After a long prelude characterized by refusals, excuses, and adjustments, the IACHR delegation finally arrived in Buenos Aires on September 6, 1979. In total, the delegation consisted of eleven people—six appointed delegates and five additional support staff. The head of the delegation was the widely known and respected former Venezuelan Minister of Justice and lawyer, Andrés Aguilar.[25] More than 1,200 complaints by Argentines had already reached the offices of the IACHR in Washington D.C. by this stage.[26]

---

centros clandestinos de detención y otros lugares de reclusión clandestina (2016), accessed July 6, 2018, https://www.argentina.gob.ar/sitiosdememoria/ruvte/informe, 1566; *Nie wieder – Ein Bericht über Entführung, Folter und Mord durch die Militärdiktatur in Argentinien*, ed. Hamburger Institut für Sozialforschung (Weinheim/Basel: Beltz, 1987), 61–74; 155; Daniel Feierstein, "Los números del genocido argentino," accessed July 6, 2018, http://www.resumenlatinoamericano.org/2016/11/08/argentina-opinion-los-numeros-del-genocidio-argentino/.

23 Paul H. Lewis, *Guerrillas and Generals: The "Dirty War" in Argentina* (Westport, London: Praeger, 2002), 159–161.

24 For the events around the FIFA World Cup, see Daniel Gutman, *Somos derechos y humanos: La batalla de la dictadura y los medios contra el mundo y la reacción internacional frente a los desaparecidos* (Buenos Aires: Sudamericana, 2015), 140; Estela Schindel, *La desaparición a diario: Sociedad, prensa y dictadura (1975–1978)* (Córdoba: Eduvim, 2012), 283–298. On the growing influence of the human rights movement, see Lynsay Skiba, "Besuch bei der Junta. Der Wandel des argentinischen Menschenrechtsaktivismus und die Debatten der 1970er Jahre," in *Moral für die Welt? Menschenrechtspolitik in den 1970er Jahren*, eds. Jan Eckel and Samuel Moyn (Göttingen: Vandenhoeck & Ruprecht, 2012), 230–258; Samuel Moyn, "Die Rückkehr des verlorenen Sohnes. Einleitung: Die 1970er Jahre als Umbruchphase in der Menschenrechtsgeschichte," in *Moral für die Welt? Menschenrechtspolitik in den 1970er Jahren*, eds. Jan Eckel and Samuel Moyn (Göttingen: Vandenhoeck & Ruprecht, 2012), 7–21.

25 The other five members were Luis Demetrio Tinoco Castro, Gerardo Monroy Cabra, Carlos A. Dunshee de Abranches, Tom J. Farer, and Francisco Bertrand Galindo. Comisión Interamericana de Derechos Humanos, *Informe sobre la situación de los derechos humanos en Argentina* (Washington, 1980), 1.

26 Comisión Interamericana de Derechos Humanos, *Informe*, 7.

Nevertheless, until then, the Argentine junta succeeded in avoiding characteristic imagery which could easily have turned into paradigmatic and iconic representations of repression and, hence, raised public and international attention, as was the case with Chile some years before. There, at the beginning of Pinochet's dictatorship, thousands of people were detained in stadiums, such as the Estadio Nacional de Chile.[27] Soon, photographs of these atrocities found their way into the international media and harmed Chile's reputation. The Argentine junta had learned its lessons from the Chilean example.[28] Instead of mass arrests, the junta created a whole system of so-called *Centros Clandestinos de Detencion* (CCD) where people were held and tortured without anyone knowing where they were, including the detainees themselves.

The junta established the disappearance of people as a strategy in an unprecedented way. By denying any knowledge of the whereabouts of the respective missing persons, it not only denied any access to them but also turned the victims into abstract figures, impossible to deal with by means of the existing law—the disappeared.[29] However, even though the precise practices and strategies of repression might not have been that obvious, due to time and the extent of the brutal actions by state agents, a certain kind of repression soon became an open secret. In that way, the Argentine regime

27 Some of them even got murdered there. Hasgall, *Regime der Anerkennung*, 109; Pascale Bonnefoy Miralles, *Terrorismo de estadio: Prisioneros de guerra en un campo de deportes* (Santiago de Chile: Editorial CESOC, 2005).

28 Mara Loveman, "High-Risk Collective Action: Defending Human Rights in Chile, Uruguay, and Argentina," *American Journal of Sociology* 104, no. 2 (September 1998): 477–525, here: 496.

29 Gretchen Helmke, *Courts under Constraints: Judges, Generals, and Presidents in Argentina* (Cambridge: Cambridge University Press, 2005), 61–74. The term "*desaparecidos*" and its English counterpart "disappeared" may have been used by the junta as a euphemism. However, nowadays, it is inseparably associated with this specific historical context; the repression practices of the junta and the in-between juridical status. The appropriation of this term is well reflected by the people who "reappeared" and describe themselves as "*desaparecido*" in their accounts of this time. As such, it will be used throughout this chapter to capture this specific notion of uncertainty, oppressive vagueness and in-between juridical status. Cf. Emilio Crenzel, "The Memories of the Disappeared in Argentina," in *Desaparición. Argentina's Human Rights Trials*, ed. Gabriele Andreozzi (Oxford et al.: Lang, 2014), 275–299; Gabriel Gatti, *Surviving Forced Disappearance in Argentina and Uruguay. Identity and Meaning* (New York: Palgrave Macmillan, 2014); Mario Villani, *Desaparecido: Memorias de un cautiverio: Club Atlético, el Banco, el Olimpo, Pozo de Quilmes y ESMA* (Buenos Aires: Biblos, 2011).

clearly acted along Reemtsma's theorem which stresses that "the terror must not become so invisible that nobody notices it."[30]

In total, the commission stayed in Argentina for 17 days and opened temporary offices in various cities where people could file complaints. Whatever Tom Farer, a member of the delegation, may have expected, the actual response surprised him. This becomes clear in his description of his first day in Buenos Aires, when he returned to the temporary office following a meeting and saw the line of people: "When we arrive, late in the morning, following our meetings with the Foreign Minister and President Videla, I can't see its end. Are there a thousand people, several thousand? I am not sure."[31]

Apart from filing personal complaints, the members of the delegation arranged various meetings with representatives of different sectors and organizations in Argentine society. The meeting with some of the *Madres de Plaza de Mayo*, in particular, stuck in Farer's memory, so moving were the statements by the mothers who were desperately searching for their children: "Tears began to fall out of my eyes."[32] Still, such statements were, in the end, at most hearsay and did not serve as first-hand evidence of the actions of the Argentine junta or its representatives.

The Argentine junta had tried its best to clear up and destroy any kind of evidence before the delegation came to Argentina. Some detainees were released under the condition not to say anything, others were blackmailed or killed. For example, one of the most notorious places for holding people captive and torturing them, the Escuela de Mecánica de la Armada (ESMA), was cleared and underwent substantial renovations so that testimonies relating to these space contained discrepancies.[33] In the case of the ESMA, the junta obviously succeeded in hiding the traces of the cruel events that had taken place there since the delegation did not notice any indications of the pain people had suffered. "All we saw on our tour of the facility was innocuous, the conventional spaces of a military educational center with no sign of the blood which must have spattered walls and no echo of the screams of its doomed inhabitants."[34] Creative approaches were needed, such as

30 Jan P. Reemtsma, "'Wir sind alles für dich!' an Stelle einer Einleitung: Skizze eines Forschungsprogramms," in *Folter. Zur Analyse eines Herrschaftsmittels*, ed. Jan P. Reemtsma (Hamburg: Junius, 1991), 7–23, here: 14.

31 Farer, "I Cried for You, Argentina," 859.

32 Ibid., 868.

33 Cf. Horacio Verbitsky, *El silencio de Paulo VI a Bergoglio: Las relaciones secretas de la Iglesia con la ESMA* (Buenos Aires: Sudamericana, 2005).

34 Farer, "I Cried for You, Argentina," 870.

Farer's idea to investigate the tombstones in a cemetery where he found out that the army was digging numerous graves where they buried the unnamed.[35] As a result, the delegation collected thousands of missing persons' names—a fact that seemed to corroborate the allegations against the junta.[36] Additionally, the commission had managed to collect first-hand evidence of human rights violations by the military. Hence, the chances of a report showing the Argentine junta in a favorable light were bleak.

After the complicated prelude and the on-site observation itself, the discussions on the findings of the IACHR commission can be seen as a third stage of escalation. Once the Argentine junta realized how hopeless it was to expect a positive report, it changed its strategy. Since the IACHR's report needed time to be compiled and published, the junta tried to preempt it by publishing its own report on the IACHR mission.[37] Clearly, the junta hoped to influence the narrative by getting in first. As difficult as it may be to measure the impact of this strategy, when viewed in combination with the prohibition of the publication of the IACHR's report in Argentina, an effect on domestic politics seems likely. The international public on the other hand, largely ignored the Argentine counter-report and clearly favored the report by the IACHR delegation.[38]

It gave substantial insights into the scale of state repression in Argentina and took a clear position. Not only did the commission express its concerns about the thousands of disappeared, it clearly accused the Argentine junta of violating "the right to life, by virtue of the fact that persons belonging to or connected with government security agencies have killed numerous men and women subsequent to their being placed in detention" and "the right to personal integrity and security, by means of the systematic use of torture and other cruel, inhumane and degrading treatment."[39] As such, the IACHR report damaged the image of the junta, which stuck to its long-term narrative of a few combatants in a "dirty war" and many people of unknown destiny.[40]

---

35 Ibid., 880.

36 Helmke speaks of 5,487 *Habeas Corpus* applications in total. Helmke, *Courts under Constraints*, 127.

37 Junta Militar, *Observaciones y comentarios criticos.*

38 Comisión Interamericana de Derechos Humanos, *Informe.*

39 Ibid., 291.

40 For the "dirty war" narrative, see Hasgall, *Regime der Anerkennung*, 235–236; Robben, Antonius C. G. M., "Vom Schmutzigen Krieg zum Völkermord. Argentiniens wechselvolle Erinnerung an eine gewalttätige Vergangenheit," in *Die Erinnerte Gewalt.*

Such a narrative had already been challenged before by many individual statements. In addition, the IACHR mission gave such accusations the institutional weight of a neutral and in-depth investigation. Hence, it challenged the junta's narrative significantly, forcing it to acknowledge that crimes had been committed—at least to a certain extent—and engulfed it in a serious legitimization crisis.

In this context, the "official naming and shaming" at the Assembly of the Organization of American States on November 19, 1980, in Washington can be seen as the fourth step in dismantling the narrative of the Argentine junta.[41] While on an international level the Argentine junta and its postulated views may have been mostly disqualified, the junta went on trying to prevent as much damage as it could to its inner legitimization basis. The lines of argumentation the junta considered as valid in legitimating the past violence, and the way it tried to distance itself from its cruel past, will be discussed in the next section.

Denying, Distancing and Legitimizing

"You start from the assumption that there was torture, I start from the assumption that there was no torture."[42] Twelve years had passed since the fall of the Argentine junta when one of its leading figures, Emilio Massera, appeared in a television interview to respond to questions about the disappeared and the systematic torture under his rule. "Regarding the *transferred*, I reject that [they existed]."[43] His strategies were denial, ignoring and spreading doubt. According to Massera, questions about murder and torture were nothing more than questions of belief. In 1995, despite numerous testimonies and various forms of proof, denying and ignoring the systematic murder

Postkonfliktdynamiken in Lateinamerika, eds. Ernst Halbmayer and Sylvia Karl (Bielefeld: Transcript, 2012), 31–56.

41 Farer, "I Cried for You, Argentina," 897.

42 Transcript of an interview with Emilio Massera, July 8, 1995, n.p., in: Centro de Estudios Legales y Sociales, Serie Responsables, Sub-Serie Carpetas por Nombre, Letra H-M, Box 6.

43 Ibid. Originally, Massera uses the word *trasladar*, the meaning of which changed during the dictatorship due to its cynical use for prisoners who were taken away to be killed. Feitlowitz speaks in this context of a deformation of some words. For further discussion, see Feitlowitz, *Lexicon of Terror*, 58–59.

and torture of thousands of people by representatives of the Argentine state was still a powerful narrative.[44]

Certainly, this was true at the beginning of 1980 when the junta published its report on the IACHR mission. It denied the brutal acts by the junta, claimed different numbers of victims and questioned the methodology of the IACHR. According to the Argentine report, the IACHR report "consisted of selecting a certain number of allegations, reproducing them *in extenso*, taking them for granted without any corroboration."[45] This strategy of deny, ignore and silence is most obvious in the way the report presents the issue of the many disappeared in Argentina. First, it claims the IACHR relies on completely wrong numbers. Instead of the postulated 5,818 disappeared, the junta's report states the "Ministry of the Interior has only received reports of 3,447", hence suggesting one third of the cases the IACHR mentions are based on mere hearsay.[46] Subsequently, the report starts criticizing the implicit attribution of *forced* disappearances by emphasizing a variety of possible reasons, not least the possibility of "construed 'cases', which serve to hold the government directly responsible for the disappearances."[47] The junta considers itself as "not insensitive to this problem."[48] However, it rejects any specificity of the Argentine case in this context. This would mean creating an "absurd theoretical model."[49] The report by the junta states that, "[t]here has been no widespread violation of human rights in the Argentine Republic and the Argentine Government categorically rejects any accusation to that effect."[50] Instead, the report points at France and claims it had an even higher rate of missing persons.[51] This strategy of blurring and forcing

44 Elizabeth Jelin, "Militantes y combatientes en la historia de las memorias: Silencios, denuncias y reivindicaciones," in *Topografías conflictivas: Memorias, espacios y ciudades en disputa*, eds. Anne Huffschmid and Valeria Durán (Buenos Aires: Nueva Trilce, 2012), 43–59, here: 44–46.

45 Junta Militar, *Observaciones y comentarios criticos*, 5.

46 Ibid., 74. Exact numbers of the disappeared are still being discussed. However, it is clear that during the first two years of the military dictatorship the number of disappeared was by far higher than stated by the junta. The quite conservative estimate of the *Secretaría de Derechos Humanos y Pluralismo Cultural de la Nación* states that there were more than 6,000 forced disappearances between the years 1976–1978. SDHN, *Informe de investigación sobre víctimas de desaparición forzada y asesinato*, 1566. For ongoing debates about the exact numbers of forced disappearances, see Feierstein, "Los números".

47 Junta Militar, *Observaciones y comentarios criticos*, 64.

48 Ibid., 72.

49 Ibid., 64.

50 Ibid., 22.

51 Ibid., 72.

silence about the violence can be considered a continuous line of argumentation throughout the whole dictatorship.

However, in the report, a second line of argumentation appears most prominent. Once, Massera explained in the same interview some years after the fall of the military dictatorship, the Chilean dictator, Augusto Pinochet, gave advice to the three leading figures of the first junta—to remain in power personally. But "we wanted to have a junta with leaders who would succeed each other in power, and not establish a permanent junta so that people would believe that we wanted to stay in power, so we rotated. I think that was a mistake, not because the successors were better or worse, but because the successors were different."[52] This quotation raises an interesting point as it highlights additional room to maneuver for the second junta. It was the change at the top of the junta which allowed the second junta to frame the violence as acts of the past.

"The dark hours of terror and violence are behind us [...]."[53] Implicitly, such an expression implies acknowledgement that there had been acts of violence. This, for example, becomes clear when the report explicitly admits that "at certain moments, the guarantees of such rights [human rights] had to be restricted."[54] However, the report draws a clear line between the cruel past and a peaceful present. This becomes most obvious and concrete in the figures the report cites. It presents a strong decline in arrests, as well as victims of so-called terrorism. From an alleged 646 killings in 1976, the number supposedly fell to 181 killings. And the decline continued once more.[55] For 1978, the report states that there were only 100 killings. These numbers are accompanied by a detailed list in the annex of the report where the victims are listed by name, obviously serving to corroborate the given data.[56] Of course, these numbers are questionable and highly problematic. This becomes clear when one compares the numbers in the graph with the number of people listed in the annex. They do not match and reveal a discrepancy of up to 300 people per year. Besides such internal contradictions, the problematic nature of these claims has been made clear in further investigations by various organizations and institutions during and after the military dictatorship, such as the National Commission on the Disappearance of Persons

52 Transcript of an interview with Emilio Massera, July 8, 1995, n.p.

53 Junta Militar, *Observaciones y comentarios críticos*, 112.

54 Ibid., 59.

55 Cf. ibid., 23.

56 Cf. ibid., 151–172.

(CONADEP).[57] However, the way the numbers were presented allows us to gain interesting insights into the narrative the junta tried to build and establish.

Clearly, the question of potential victims and violent acts caused by state agents was not at the center of these statistics. In contrast, the way the report presented the killings shifted the general focus onto the situation in Argentina. Mainly, state representatives and members of the military are listed as victims.[58] The message was clear: The Argentine state was under attack. Hence, the actions carried out by the Argentine state were promoted as "self-defense".[59]

This raises the question as to who was actually considered the attacking side. By blurring words, and in line with former statements by the junta, the report frequently speaks of "terrorists" and "subversives" who threatened the country.[60] As has been pointed out in various studies, these categories were constructions of the regime —they were deliberately vague so that anyone who was not favored by the regime could fit and, hence, be declared an "enemy" or "terrorist".[61] In the statistics on victims, the losses of this construed group seem to be largely ignored.[62] Instead, they come prominently into view by looking at the second figure in the report, the arrests.[63] Such role allocation speaks for itself. While on the one hand, the Argentine state and its representatives were presented as calm guardians, the so-called "terrorists" were pictured as aggressive and destructive. In this alleged confrontation between the two parties, the so-called "civilian martyrs" are scarcely paid any attention.[64] If they are referred to at all, they remain the abstract and vague third party which suffers under the catastrophic situation

57 Hamburger Institut für Sozialforschung (HIS), *Nie wieder*, 155.

58 Cf. Junta Militar, *Observaciones y comentarios criticos*, 151–172.

59 Ibid., 110.

60 Cf. for example ibid., 10.

61 See Janis Nalbadidacis, "Laboratories of the Conditio Humana: The Role of Communism in Greek and Argentine Torture Centers During Their Last Military Dictatorships," in *The Palgrave Handbook of Anti-Communist Persecutions*, eds. Christian Gerlach and Clemens Six (Cham: Palgrave Macmillan, 2020), 97–116, here: 101; Feierstein, *Genocide as Social Practice*, 35–36.

62 Cf. Junta Militar, *Observaciones y comentarios criticos*, 151–172.

63 Cf. ibid., 76.

64 Ibid., 6.

caused by the so-called "terrorists".[65] In general, they are depicted as backing the junta's ambitions. All these aspects serve to support the image of the junta as the defender of national sovereignty.

Interestingly, the statistics all start in 1969, thus covering some years in advance of the junta's dictatorship. Both the peak in violence as well as the peak in arrests occur in 1976, according to the report. The implicit suggestion in the statistics is to look at the larger picture and to take note of the strong incline in violence until the intervention of the junta. This suggestion fits perfectly with the postulated image of the junta as the savior of the Argentine nation.

Such a narrative serves as a third line of argumentation which mainly aims at legitimizing past violence. "[T]here was a quasi-war provoked by terrorist organizations," states the junta report for the initial period of the dictatorship.[66] *In extenso*, the report describes how problems and inner conflicts in Argentina had grown since the 1970s.[67] In terms of violence, the cause of the chaotic circumstances is seen in the activities of three paramilitary organizations—the Montoneros, the Fuerzas Armadas Revolucionarias (FAR), and the Ejército Revolucionario del Pueblo (ERP).[68] The report states that the escalation in violence was caused by these organizations. In particular, the federal election in 1973 and the resulting amnesties are presented as having refueled the spiral of violence.[69] "Every day, attacks and other criminal acts occurred."[70] According to the report Argentina was ruled by a "climate of terror".[71]

At various times, the report refers to a "tremendous crisis" and describes it as the driving force for its intervention.[72] "When economic collapse, political crisis and escalating terrorism forced the Argentine armed forces to take power on March 24, 1976, the situation was critical."[73] The *coup d'état* by the military is presented as a duty in overcoming crisis and restoring

65 Cf. Feierstein, who elaborates on that category and uses it as a basis to argue that a genocide had taken place against the so-called "subversive". Feierstein, *Genocide as Social Practice*, 29.

66 Junta Militar, *Observaciones y comentarios criticos*, 61.

67 Cf. ibid., 16–22.

68 Ibid., 16.

69 Ibid., 17. For the context and the conflicts back then, see María J. Moyano, *Argentina's Lost Patrol: Armed Struggle 1969–1979* (New Haven, London: Yale University Press, 1995).

70 Junta Militar, *Observaciones y comentarios criticos*, 18.

71 Ibid., 18.

72 Ibid., 26.

73 Ibid., 19.

order. "Not to do so was to condemn it [the Argentine state] to impotence or, in more vivid words, to a form of suicide."[74] Situating the junta in a larger context by including the pre-dictatorship years and presenting the military's intervention as a turning point is a recurring *topos* throughout the entire junta report. Obviously, the report uses drastic words to conjure up a potential collapse of the Argentine state before the military intervened. It corroborates this argument by widening the temporal scope to present a certain order of violence, concluding that the terror and violence have passed and that "the aggression against its [Argentina's] way of life and the oppression of its traditions of freedom have received the virile response of a people that does not permit any form of totalitarianism."[75] Thus, the junta claimed to have overcome crisis and re-established stability.

In addition, the junta wants to widen the spatial dimension by presenting the case of Argentina as part of a worldwide conflict and as a "dramatic problem, which has arisen in different parts of the world."[76] In accordance with former discussions in Argentina, the report pictures "the terrorists" as a homogenous group with a specific political agenda and sees it as rooted in a "global strategy in the service of international imperialism."[77] Hence, it was not just the fate of the Argentine people that was at stake. Rather, the incidents in Argentina were described as exemplary for various fights aiming at "annihilating the values of Western civilization in order to establish a totalitarian and slave-owning society."[78] The junta's repeated references to democracy and human rights precisely corroborate the junta's aim of promoting a dichotomous worldview. The pattern becomes clear: Uniting and forcing silence about one's own acts and violations by polarizing and linking the situation to an overarching dichotomist Cold War narrative of good and evil, thus, hoping to serve as a kind of projection screen for other states and to gain their approval.[79]

In their own way, both attempts to contextualize the situation in Argentina served the purpose of discrediting the IACHR's report. The temporal argument emphasizes national peculiarities suggesting the IACHR did not

74 Ibid., 110.

75 Ibid., 112.

76 Ibid., 110.

77 Ibid., 16. For the preceding use of the term "Soviet imperialism" in Argentine history, see Mirko Petersen, *Geopolitische Imaginarien: Diskursive Konstruktionen der Sowjetunion im peronistischen Argentinien (1943–1955)* (Bielefeld: Transcript, 2018), 221–270.

78 Junta Militar, *Observaciones y comentarios criticos*, 110.

79 This argument is further developed in Nalbadidacis, "Laboratories," 100–105.

sufficiently take them into account. The spatial argument links the Argentine context to perceived realities in other western countries. Doing so is rooted in the idea of being an object of projection, gaining understanding of their own actions in the broader public, and avoiding being pushed aside on the international stage.

Paving the Way for "True Democracy"

"Argentine society today enjoys genuine peace and effective security within the framework of an independent justice system, with full respect for public liberties."[80] Retrospectively, such a statement reads as cynical, knowing that the regime that wrote it was responsible for numerous deaths and inflicting horrible injustice upon thousands at the time it was written. The junta was drawing a stark contrast between its initial period in 1976 and the situation in 1979. The present situation is depicted as almost ideal and idyllic in order to highlight the differences and the progress. However, distancing from the past, as well as attempts to legitimize past events, raises a different issue. According to the logic presented by the junta, the question is: How did the report justify the junta's claim to power when the fundamental crisis had been overcome?

It is striking that the report does not address this question extensively. One might be right in seeing this as a strategy to avoid opening up further discussions on the junta's legitimacy to stay in power. Instead, the report hints prominently at another document which was officially published by the Argentine junta not long before: The *Act Establishing the Political Bases of the Armed Forces for the National Reorganization Process*, published in December 1979.[81] This act was presented as a logical follow-up to the first *Act Establishing the Purpose and Basic Objectives for the National Reorganization Process*, which can be considered the key document of the Argentine junta and which was published by the junta in the early stages of the military dictatorship in March

80 *Observaciones y comentarios criticos*, ed. Junta Militar, 111 (quote), 10, 21–22.

81 The original name was *Acta fijando las bases políticas de las Fuerzas Armadas para el Proceso de Reorganización Nacional.* See Junta Militar, "Acta fijando las bases politicas de las Fuerzas Armadas para el Proceso de Reorganizacion Nacional, 19.12.1979," in Junta Militar, *Documentos básicos y bases políticas de las Fuerzas Armadas para el Proceso de Reorganización Nacional*, 53–81. The reference to this document can be found in *Observaciones y comentarios criticos*, Junta Militar, 111.

1976.[82] The suggestion of continuity becomes clear from the very beginning by referring to the former act in a quote on the first page. That quote serves to lay bare the lasting motives and aims:

"Restoring the essential values that serve as the basis for the integral management of the state, emphasizing the sense of morality, suitability and efficiency, essential to reconstituting the content of the Nation's image, eradicating subversion and promoting the economic development of national life based on balance and the responsible participation of different sectors in order to ensure the establishment of a republican, representative and federal democracy, appropriate to the reality and demands of evolution and the progress of the Argentine people."[83]

The nation, the alleged challenge to it by so-called "subversion", and democracy as the ultimate promise—this passage neatly summarizes the junta's three terminological key references. Once again, the junta relied on the nebulous ideas of "subversion"/"terrorism", with "nation" and "democracy" applied as additional reference points. According to the junta, the fate of the Argentine nation counted the most. The act even goes so far as to claim that "Argentine society has the responsibility to ensure the historical continuity of the Nation."[84] This not only reveals a somewhat ambivalent connection between nation and society imagined as two distinct spheres without overlap, it also allows the junta to picture itself as the savior of the nation and the guardian of Argentine society.[85] In a quite vague manner, the nation was described as being characterized by a specific mentality, consisting of Christian and Western values.[86] Especially with regard to so-called Western values, democracy was considered an indisputable and central component of the Argentine political landscape. Hence, the act indulges in descriptions of an ideal society, featuring the family as the "basic core of the social structure",[87] and draws the picture of a society "characterized by its pluralism, where each sector assumes its participation with responsibility for the

82 Junta Militar, "Objetivos básicos, 24.3.1976," 7–29.

83 The quotation can be found in Junta Militar, "Objetivos básicos, 24.3.1976," 15; Junta Militar, "Objetivos básicos, 19.12.1979," 55.

84 Junta Militar, *Observaciones y comentarios criticos*, 60.

85 Cf. for a discussion on this vague and controversial concept of *ser nacional* Hasgall, *Regime der Anerkennung*, 108–109; Feitlowitz, *Lexicon of Terror*, 23–24.

86 Cf. Junta Militar, "Objetivos básicos, 24.3.1976," 8; Junta Militar, "Objetivos básicos, 19.12.1979," 58.

87 Junta Militar, "Objetivos básicos, 19.12.1979," 73.

achievement of a modern state, with a high sense of morality, efficiency and greatness."[88]

Even though, the junta's discursive use of "democracy" can be seen as an empty phrase, the reference itself was important. The declared aim in all this was to achieve a "real and effective democracy"[89] or what the junta called a "true democracy".[90] According to the junta, progress had been made but there was still a long way to go. Thus, it insisted on avoiding any "haste that could impede success in achieving the final objective."[91] Defeating the alleged danger of "subversion" was considered only an initial step. Subsequently, the act draws attention to future steps which should pave the way for democracy and increasing political participation.

> "[Democratization] will continue with the analysis of legislation by the political party regime and its normalization. It begins to take shape with the publication of this document and will be followed by the enactment of the relevant laws from the second half of 1980."[92]

In framing events this way, the junta manages to present itself as a moderating force for the process of change in Argentine society between the first stage, often described as "war", and the next steps to a future democracy.

The above quotation also points out a second aspect. According to the junta, this process of taking political steps towards democracy was reflected in the publication of the act itself. It appeared just a few months before the junta's report on the IACHR mission was published and it served the purpose of giving the junta's statements about its future plans more credibility.

Conclusion

The reference to a state of exception due to a long-lasting political crisis can be considered the founding myth of the Argentine junta. The escalation in violence in pre-junta years, the economic challenges, the increasing inflation rate and, above all, the death of Juan Perón and the unstable political situation under Isabella Perón were all reasons for the military to intervene.

88 Ibid., 62.

89 Junta Militar, *Observaciones y comentarios críticos*, 93.

90 Ibid., 110.

91 Junta Militar, "Objetivos básicos, 19.12.1979," 80.

92 Ibid., 80.

Interventions by the military in unstable political situations had precedence in Argentine history. As such, the "gentlemen's coup" was not necessarily perceived as a threat; indeed, the promise to lead the country out of crisis and to get back to a stable situation was welcomed by some parts of the Argentine population. The image of the military as an authority which was able to bring order to a crisis-shaken Argentine society was crucial during the initial years and it is well reflected in the junta's various statements. At the same time, the junta presented the measures it took as guided by humanitarian and democratic ideals. This becomes especially clear in the many references to the blurry concepts of "Western and Christian values", which can be interpreted as a local adoption of the overarching dominant circulation of a Cold War narrative. Obviously, such claims stood in stark contrast to the allegations of systematic human rights violations.

In that context, the IACHR mission provoked a crisis for the junta. Before the mission, the junta may have expected to be able to control, to limit, and to manipulate the delegation's actions. However, throughout the mission, it became clear this was not the case and, by the end of the delegation's time in Argentina, it was more than likely that the IACHR's report would not be favorable to the junta. Instead, the many allegations of human rights violations and systematic torture were expected to be confirmed. Realizing that, the Argentine junta perceived the upcoming report as a serious threat to its claim to power. Clearly, the IACHR's findings were going to undermine the legitimacy of the junta by revealing that it was responsible for cruel and systematic repressions and, subsequently, exposing that it had lied about its own practices. The much-cited references to "Western and Christian values" would have been exposed as nothing more than cynical lies. Hence, the junta developed strategies to cast doubt on the integrity of the IACHR report and to limit its impact. Not only did it prohibit publication of the report in Argentina, the junta also went on the offensive by publishing its own view of the mission and presenting its perspective on the developments in Argentina. For the junta, it was paramount to present their actions in accordance with so-called "Western and Christian values" to avoid too much international pressure which, in turn, could easily weaken the junta's position in domestic politics.

In total, the chapter identifies four different strategies employed by the junta to deal with the various accusations in the IACHR report. Whereas the first strategy aimed directly at questioning the work of the IACHR delegation by accusing it of methodical shortcomings and questioning the delegation's impartiality, the other three narrative strategies approached the allegations in a broader sense. It may seem self-contradictory but hushing up and denying any kind of state violence can be considered as one of the main strategies in dealing with the allegations, if not the most dominant strategy. Especially during the initial years, the narrative of silencing and denying was prevalent. And that narrative was enduring, not least because ignorance and the claim that nothing happened served as the best line of defense in the various trials in the post-dictatorship era. However, a close look at the publications by the second junta at the end of 1979 and the beginning of 1980 reveals further attempts to frame the violence. Hence, in addition to denying the violence, the junta tried to legitimize it, as becomes clear in the references to the prevalent overarching Cold War narrative. From that perspective, the junta fought in Argentina on behalf of the so-called Western world and Christianity against "Soviet imperialism". At the same time, the junta also used the temporal dimension by emphasizing the national peculiarities of a so-called "dirty war", going back to 1969 to legitimize its violent practices and to explain the conflict in Argentina. The fourth strategy follows a similar vein which puts forward the argument that violence might have occurred but, in 1979, this can be considered a thing of the past. In adopting this latter strategy, the junta made efforts to present itself as a moderating force. According to the junta, Argentina in 1979 was ready to leave the fight against so-called terrorism behind and to take further steps towards "true democracy", namely the promise to reestablish a party system. Hence, in its description of itself, the junta accomplished a transformation from "savior of the nation" to "groundbreaker of democracy".

From the perspective of crisis, one can clearly state that references to a crisis as initial legitimization of power are likely to force the actors to find new ways to justify their legitimacy after a certain period of time. Otherwise, inevitably, the power holders will find themselves in the position of having to explain why they have not yet been able to solve the crisis. This becomes evident in the Argentine case. However, this pattern does not seem to be exclusive to authoritarian regimes. Comparative approaches might help in this regard to ascertain if there are means or reactions which can be specifically attributed to more authoritarian or more democratic regimes. All too easily, we might underestimate developments within dictatorships and subsequently regard them as monolithic blocs. The Argentine case shows that taking repressive measures was not sufficient for the junta to stay in power.

South Africa's "Total National Strategy"—Or How to Think About the Future of Apartheid in Times of Crisis, 1975–1984

Jakob Zollmann

Introduction – Notions of Crisis

South Africa in 1979: Was the country "waiting for the barbarians"? A sense of crisis had befallen the country's political leadership: The war in Angola and Namibia was dragging on, eating away financial resources from an ailing economy, while the military and state security establishment demanded constant increases from Prime Minister P.W. Botha. Despite massive military engagement by South Africa, Cuban troops and Soviet "military advisors" were thoroughly entrenched in Angola. At UN level, in the international press, and from Western governments—led by the US Carter administration since 1977—pressure was mounting on South Africa to abolish its race policies of "separate development" and "ethnic self-determination", commonly known as apartheid, and to retreat from Angola and allow Namibia's independence. Leading South African politicians, on the other hand, seeing communism on the rise in Southern Africa feared that, after the leftwing *coup d'état* in Lisbon in 1974, the resulting fall of the Portuguese empire in 1975, and the ongoing military debacles of white minority-ruled Rhodesia, Namibia would be "the-next-to-last domino"[1] before Soviet-sponsored military arrived at the gates of the Republic of South Africa and stepped up support for the armed wing of the African National Congress (ANC), *uMkhonto we Sizwe* (MK), "the enemy within".

It was in this context that South African literary scholar and novelist, John M. Coetzee (b. 1940), wrote his bestseller, *Waiting for the Barbarians*. The novel, its title quoting Constantine Cavafy's (1863–1933) famous poem, *Waiting for the Barbarians* (1904), was published to great acclaim in 1980. It received international reviews, and the eminent political message or warning

1 Richard Dale, "The UN and Decolonisation in Namibia," in *The United Nations in the World Political Economy: Essays in Honour of Leon Gordenker*, ed. David P. Forsythe (New York: Palgrave, 1989), 165–178, here: 174.

of this piece of fiction, and the particular historical place of the author and his work, were clearly identified. In the novel, a sympathetic, paternalistic magistrate serves "the Empire" by administering a frontier settlement, assuming himself to be a guardian of civilization. Due to rumors of an imminent attack by "the barbarians" beyond the frontiers, one Colonel Joll, an interrogation expert, arrives with his men from the Empire's center. Granted special "emergency powers", he undertakes "an expedition", and tortures and kills his prisoners until one "admits" that "barbarians" were indeed preparing for war. The Colonel then goes on the attack, leaving victims in his wake, one of them a crippled "barbarian" girl, with whom the magistrate becomes obsessed, nursing her wounds as if in an act of reparation. Acknowledging the hollowness of his self-perceived liberalism, the magistrate admits: "I was the lie that Empire tells itself when times are easy, he [Joll] is the truth the Empire tells when harsh winds blow." He returns the girl to her people beyond the frontier, is accused by the Colonel of treason and incarcerated. The magistrate's crisis of conscience in the face of his superiors' injustice and barbarism in the name of "the Empire" leads him to the insight: "Where civilization entailed the corruption of barbarian virtues and the creation of a dependent people, I was opposed to civilization".[2]

Coetzee made no specific reference to South Africa—as some critics noted with regret. They categorically declared the novel to be "a stark political fable of South Africa", "a 'universalized' version of South Africa",[3] or an "allegory about the misery in South Africa".[4] It was as if foreign observers of South Africa, be they politicians, journalists or literary critics, could perceive nothing but "crisis" and imminent "collapse", irrespective of politics, the economy or literature. Following the Soweto crisis, historian and journalist, R.W. Johnston, published his bestseller *How Long Will SA Survive?* and drew a "Russian analogy": As a "warning", he noted the "not inconsiderable political parallels between contemporary South Africa and pre-1917 Russia."[5]

2 Quoted in: Paul Rich, "Apartheid and the Decline of the Civilization Idea: An Essay on Nadine Gordimer's 'July's People' and J. M. Coetzee's 'Waiting for the Barbarians,'" in: *Research in African Literatures* 15/3 (1984), 365–393, here: 382.

3 Irving Howe, "A stark political fable of South Africa," *New York Times*, April 18, 1982, Sec. 7, 1.

4 Gerhard Kirchner, "Warten auf die Barbaren. Ein allegorischer Roman über die Misere in Südafrika," *Frankfurter Allgemeine Zeitung*, June 1, 1984, p. 26.

5 Richard William Johnson, *How Long Will South Africa Survive?* (London: Macmillan, 1977) 294; 20–22.

Certainly, given the notion of the all-encompassing political and moral crisis the apartheid order had created since its inception under the National Party (NP) in 1948—resulting in a perceived overly politicized literary scene in South Africa that left little space for individual perspective—, "Coetzee's novels are often valued to the extent that they escape the received conventions of politically committed literature."[6] The authoritarianism, as depicted by Coetzee, represented a form of rule that seemed all too familiar to those informed about South African politics and culture: The politics of an ideologically based pigmentocratic and illiberal regime that holds wide-ranging and unchecked powers and that remains willing and unchallenged in its ruthless persecution of any and all (perceived) "enemies".

At the same time, Coetzee's writing, like the works of other white South African novelists, was faced with changes in the political-cultural context that went beyond liberal opposition to apartheid. The "emergence of black consciousness movements and the upsurge in all forms of resistance from black communities after 1976 [the Soweto uprising], precipitated a terminal crisis of liberalism as both political ideology and literary aesthetic."[7] Political allegories, like the one Coetzee might have offered to his readers seemed, to critics, an inapposite contribution by art to the liberation of Southern Africa from the evils of apartheid,[8] a situation ripe for revolution.

The crisis of the apartheid order was thus perceived as a crisis of liberalism, since it seemed unable not only to formulate, but to implement democratic changes in favor of the disenfranchised majority.[9] Nevertheless, a liberal opposition in Cape Town's white-only Parliament had registered growing successes in national elections since the early 1970s. The sociology professor Frederik van Zyl Slabbert (1940–2010), as opposition leader of the Progressive Reform Party (1979–1986), worked hard to undermine the very moral and theological credibility of apartheid. An Afrikaner himself, the "golden boy" with "golden opportunities" outspokenly argued for a non-racial democracy with individual liberties, and won up to 20 percent of the

6 Clive Barnett, "Constructions of Apartheid in the International Reception of the Novels of J. M. Coetzee," *Journal of Southern African Studies* 25, 2 (1999), 287–301, here: 290.

7 Barnett, "Constructions of Apartheid," 295.

8 Robert Kusek, "Re-territorialising South Africa. Political Allegory in *The Master of Petersburg* by J.M. Coetzee," *Studia Litteraria Universitatis Iagellonicae Cracoviensis* 5 (2010), 67–82.

9 Sam C. Nolutshungu, *Changing South Africa: Political Considerations* (Manchester: MUP, 1982); see Ayesha Omar, "Sam C. Nolutshungu: Race, Reform, Resistance and the Black Consciousness Movement," *Comparative Political Theory* 1 (2021), 80–104.

votes.[10] His political success, based on a forceful personality and the tenet that reforms could overcome the apparent deadlock, indicated that the normative consensus among whites on apartheid was about to break.[11] German sociologist Heribert Adam and South African historian Hermann Giliomee, both well acquainted with Slabbert's politics of the possibility of change, thus recognized in 1979 the *Rise and Crisis of Afrikaner Power*.[12]

Indeed, among white Afrikaans- (but also English-) speakers—given the political and economic crisis with rising unemployment rates for them—social anxieties, pessimism, and ideological discontent regarding the future and direction of white South Africa were widespread. Yet, social psychologists in South Africa, undertaking research on "the authoritarian personality, show[ed] that certain South African groups are very authoritarian",[13] thus indicating that there was still a great deal of understanding among the white electorate for authoritarian responses to the crisis that had beset the apartheid order. As to the rationale of hardened politics by the NP government and its justification by its voters, South African psychologists recognized among their probands the willingness to see "authoritarianism as a response to stress": "South Africa's authoritarian institutions are more readily seen as a response by whites to the stress of being outnumbered four to one by a less developed people."[14] In response, contemporary liberal observers inside and outside the country noted with disdain an ever increasing "constitutional authoritarianism", implemented by the state administration ruled by the National Party (NP).[15] On the other hand, as one of South Africa's foremost

---

10 Hermann Giliomee, *The Last Afrikaner Leaders: A Supreme Test of Power* (Cape Town: Tafelberg, 2012), 207–244.

11 Albert Grundlingh, *Slabbert: Man on a Mission* (Johannesburg: Ball, 2021); *The Passion for Reason. Essays in Honour of Frederik Van Zyl Slabbert*, by various authors (Cape Town: Ball, 2010).

12 Heribert Adam and Hermann Giliomee, *The Rise and Crisis of Afrikaner Power* (Cape Town: David Philip, 1979).

13 Johan C. Mynhardt, *South African Supplement to Social Psychology*, 3rd ed., (Cape Town: Pearson, 2009), 53, ref. to his own studies from the 1970s (based on Adorno's studies on the "authoritarian personality") "finding his respondents, particularly the Afrikaans-speaking ones, to be highly authoritarian."; Theodor W. Adorno, Else Frenkel-Brunswik, Daniel J. Levinson, and R. Nevitt Sanford, *The Authoritarian Personality* (London: Verso, 2019 [1950]).

14 Patrick C. L. Heaven (ed.), *Authoritarianism: South African Studies* (Bloemfontein: De Villiers, 1980), 35; for previous research, see Heribert Adam, "The South African Power-Elite. A Survey of Ideological Commitment," in: *South Africa: Sociological Perspectives*, ed. Heribert Adam (London: OUP, 1971), 91.

15 Patrick C. L. Heaven (ed.), *Authoritarianism: South African Studies*, 35.

historians, Hermann Giliomee (b. 1938), put it, "[c]o-existing uneasily with the authoritarian state was a democracy for whites with civil rights and proper administrative procedure".[16]

The following chapter will analyze how the NP government tried to respond to the numerous problems the crisis posed to the South African state and society after 1975 with a view to upholding the white minority regime. Section I will set out the meaning of "apartheid" in the context of South African 20th century modernization processes, and the resulting gains for white society the government was intent on defending. Section II will analyze the regime's narrative of the "Total Onslaught" against Southern Africa orchestrated by world communism. Taking a view from within the NP government apparatus, Section III will evaluate the regime's response to the "Total Onslaught", the "Total National Strategy" and the resulting policies, meant to ensure the future of a (reformed) apartheid.

Apartheid as Survival Politics

Apartheid was thought to mean—as claimed by one of its architects, Prime Minister Hendrik Verwoerd (1901–1966)—"a policy of good neighborliness" between "races"; on other occasions, it was described as the "doctrine of separate development".[17] However, first of all, this policy of "apartness", as the segregation between "races" can be translated from Afrikaans, was the outcome of a deeply felt sense of crisis that, in view of 20th century modernity and political liberalism, had befallen Afrikaner nationalists since the 1930s. The resulting policy of racial segregation, as sociologist Edward Tiryakian pointed out in 1957, had an important religious component. The Dutch Reformed Church had given its "religious sanction" to the idea and its implementation.[18] Apartheid was meant to thwart the further degeneration of an alleged social order (the hierarchy between "races") ordained by God and to prevent chaos, thereby ensuring the security and survival of the

16 Hermann B. Giliomee, *Afrikaner. Biography of a People* (Cape Town: Tafelberg, 2003), 551.

17 Quoted in: Christoph Marx, *Trennung und Angst. Hendrik Verwoerd und die Gedankenwelt der Apartheid* (Berlin: DeGruyter, 2020), 391 FN 132; 188.

18 Edward A. Tiryakian, "Apartheid and Religion," *Theology Today* 14 (1957), 385–400, here: 385.

Afrikaner *volk*, its culture and language (Afrikanerdom).[19] Apartheid policies aimed at establishing a strong state in South Africa that, through social engineering along different color lines, had the power to completely transform society and all aspects of daily life according to the requirements of racial segregation. This included the subordination of the economy to comprehensive planning by the state apparatus. Based on concepts of positivism, rationality and development, apartheid was more than a technique of divide-and-rule, it was, as historian Christoph Marx points out—as did others before him—, a "future-oriented politics of modernization".[20]

During the 1960s and up until the early 1970s, the implementation of territorial, cultural, political, residential and industrial segregation policies ("grand apartheid") in South Africa under Verwoerd and, after his assassination, John Vorster (1966–1978), resulted in massive privilege and thus unheard-of modernization gains for the white population. For the first time in the country's history, the problem of *arme blankes* (white poverty)[21] seemed solved, resulting in increased approval ratings for the regime. Consequently, the early days of John Vorster's premiership, when economic growth "was rampant", also due to high prices for the export of South African raw materials, have been termed by historians as the "golden age for the white polity".[22]

However, recognizing or anticipating a crisis in the contemporary apartheid system remained a political, moral and educational possibility. Consciously or subconsciously, even before and during this "golden age", there still remained some skepticism about the longevity and survivability of the apartheid order based on state violence and discriminatory laws against the non-white majority—and not only among the English-speaking whites brought up in the spirit of what was called "Cape liberalism". Recalling his own school years in a wholly Afrikaner environment, Hermann Giliomee

19 Marx, *Trennung und Angst*, 246; 248 referring to Hermann Giliomee.

20 Marx, *Trennung und Angst*, 6, "zukunftsgerichtete Modernisierungspolitik"; 16 referring to Johannes J. Venter; see Paul B. Rich, *Hope and Despair. English Speaking Intellectuals and South African Politics 1896–1976* (London: Bloomsbury Academic, 1993), 14: "segregation [...] was part of a wider pattern of modernization of South African society."

21 Grace Davie, *Poverty Knowledge in South Africa. A social history of human science, 1855–2005* (New York: CUP, 2015); Albert Grundlingh: "'Are We Afrikaners Getting too Rich?' Cornucopia and Change in Afrikanerdom in the 1960s," *Journal of Historical Sociology* 21, no. 2 (2008), 143–165.

22 Jamie Miller, *An African Volk. The Apartheid Regime and Its Search for Survival* (Oxford: OUP, 2016), 2.

mentions an implicit "message" of crisis the children received "that uncontested white domination would not last forever".[23] Judge Dennis Davis (b. 1951), aware that his upbringing in a Jewish working-class environment made him an "outsider", remembers his time at Herzlia school in Cape Town:

> "In standard seven, I had a Hebrew teacher who spent the whole year teaching us *Cry the Beloved Country* [a famous anti-apartheid novel by Alan Paton, published in 1948] […] and he taught it in a very political way […] and we spent the whole year discussing that book. Which today looks like a kind of a wishy-washy liberal, now it wasn't so in 1965, not for a child of fourteen years old. And so yes, I think that background of where I came from, a school that really was trying to portray liberal values at its best […] So, my history was very much of growing up in a sense of realizing that there was something very wrong with the stratified society"

of South Africa. His school "produced all these kids like me, who in fact were on the left".[24]

Following the rise of the Afro-Marxist regimes in Angola and Mozambique in 1975, which was understood not solely by leading NP politicians as a watershed in Southern African history, the notion of crisis for the apartheid order not only ended the alleged "golden age", but this perception would last for the next twenty or so years until the demise of apartheid in 1994. This enduring crisis revealed the fragility of the political order meant to ensure the survival of the Afrikaner *volk* and exposed the precarity of the apartheid state's future. By 1979, South African (and foreign) academics and liberal politicians openly dissected their country's "crisis" and, looking to the future, its "options" for power sharing.[25] They were not alone in their stocktaking efforts. South Africa's ruling elite also began to weigh their options in the face of a crisis they perceived as a "Total Onslaught" by South Africa's enemies.

23 Hermann Giliomee, *Historian. An Autobiography* (Cape Town: Tafelberg, 2016), 21.

24 Dennis Davis, Constitutional Court Oral History Project, January 6, 2012, 2, accessed December 31, 2020, http://www.historicalpapers.wits.ac.za/inventories/inv_pdfo/AG3368/AG3368-D17-001-jpeg.pdf.

25 Adam and Giliomee, *The Rise and Crisis of Afrikaner Power*; Frederick van Zyl Slabbert and David Welsh, *South Africa's Options: Strategies for Sharing Power* (London: Rex, 1979).

Perceiving the "Total Onslaught"—Managing a Perception

Given the vastly increased material and rhetorical support the ANC, as South Africa's most prominent African nationalist force against apartheid, received from the newly installed Marxist governments in Luanda and Maputo, as well as their partners in the Soviet Union, Cuba, and (mostly) Eastern Europe, the government in Pretoria recognized the necessity to reformulate its perception of the political situation in Southern Africa and beyond. Indeed, notions of a "communist threat" were nothing new in South African official parlance. As early as 1950, South Africa's "Suppression of Communism Act" was supposed to be a response to the "communist" threat to South Africa's security posed by left-leaning African opposition groups eager to establish black majority rule. The Act provided an exceedingly broad definition of the meaning of "communism" and "communist". It was indeed "ironical" that the law gave South Africa's government "almost unlimited totalitarian authority, just as in communist states".[26]

As historian Stephen Ellis argued, "[t]hose most centrally involved in this contest [between the South African government and the ANC or other African liberation movements] did not doubt that South Africa was indeed at war between the early 1960s and the early 1990s." After all: "Umkhonto we Sizwe [MK] issued a formal declaration of war on December 16, 1961", intent on creating a "revolutionary" situation similar to Vietnam or Algeria.[27] What seemed new to South Africa's political elite since the late-1970s was the all-encompassing character that was supposedly engendering multiple threats to their political order—and thus to the survival of Afrikanerdom. In 1977, South Africa's Department of Defense published a white paper that set out the conviction of Defense Minister P.W. Botha and his generals that South Africa now faced a "Total Onslaught" that affected, or would soon

26 Roger B. Beck, *The History of South Africa* (Westport: Greenwood, 2000), 129; sadly, *The Palgrave Handbook of Anti-Communist Persecutions*, eds. Christian Gerlach and Clemens Six (Cham: Palgrave, 2020) does not contain an entry on South(ern) Africa or on the African continent.

27 Stephen Ellis, "The Historical Significance of South Africa's Third Force," *Journal of Southern African Studies* 24, no. 2 (1998), 261–299, here: 264; see Paul S. Landau: The ANC, MK and the ›Turn to Violence‹ (1960–1962), *South African Historical Journal* 64, no. 3 (2012), 538–563; Ian van der Waag and Albert Grundlingh (eds.), *In Different Times: The War for Southern Africa 1966–1989* (Stellenbosch, SUN Press, 2019).

affect, all aspects of the nation's life.[28] Considering continuing military confrontations between South African troops and the armies of the neighboring countries (starting with South Africa's ill-fated *Operation Savannah* in 1975/76 against Angola's capital Luanda) that mostly failed to give South Africa a durable strategic advantage, the "onslaught" seemed an empirical fact. Its perception in South Africa also gave substance to the "Soviet view prevailing in the seventies that trends in Africa favored the expansion of socialism at the expense of imperialism".[29]

However, this crisis included far more factors than military setbacks and an unwelcome sense of superiority among South Africa's arch enemies. Shortly after the publication of the white paper and based on analytical patterns set forth by Paul Eidelberg (b. 1928), a prominent Cold War critic of *détente* with the Soviet Union, General J.R. Dutton from South Africa's Chief of Staff, defined "Total Onslaught" as an "octangular strategy" of "protracted war of low intensity" as Mao Zedong had proposed. Accusing the Soviet Union and its allies of a "total war against the 'non-socialist' world order" in which, however, the "application of military force in a general war is not the primary operating factor", Dutton identified eight "operating factors" of this "war of low intensity": (1) "Military": insurgency and the threat of conventional war from the north, Angola and Botswana; (2) "political": the challenge of African nationalism; (3) "diplomatic": through the United Nations, Organization of African Unity; anti-South African moves; (4) "economic": the threat of UN sanctions; (5) "ideological": the Marxist class theory; (6) "psychological": the erosion of the idea of "separate development" (apartheid); (7) "cultural": sports boycotts and other forms of isolating Afrikanerdom; (8) "semantic": in the form of anti-apartheid "propaganda".[30]

Consequently, this multifaceted and "combined threat of communism and Black Nationalism" on South Africa's borders was portrayed as a threat not only to South Africa.[31] Rather, growing African and worldwide

28 Republic of South Africa, Dept. of Defence, *White Paper on Defence 1977* (Pretoria, 1977).

29 Ronald Dreyer, *Namibia and Southern Africa. Regional Dynamics of Decolonization 1945–1990* (London: Routledge, 1994), 95.

30 J.R. Dutton, "The military aspects of national security," in: Michael H.H. Louw (ed.) *National Security. A Modern Approach*, Pretoria: ISS 1978, 100–122, here: 105, referring to Paul Eidelberg, *Beyond Détente. Toward an American Foreign Policy* (La Salle: Sherwood Sugden, 1977), 11.

31 Matthew Graham, *The Crisis of South African Foreign Policy: Diplomacy, Leadership and the Role of the African National Congress* (London: Tauris, 2015), 50.

opposition towards apartheid was interpreted as an ongoing and ever-strengthening global communist onslaught aimed not only at the destruction of the South African order, but at taking over all of Southern Africa by communist dictatorships to the detriment of the Western world. Of the latter, South Africa remained—as Prime Minister John Vorster insisted during a conversation with conservative eminence William F. Buckley Jr.—always part of.[32] Given South Africa's strategic position, formidable military force, strong infrastructure, mineral wealth and modern manufacturing, the argument went that the country remained a major obstacle to the rise of communism towards "world domination"—and thus deserved support.

Yet, as the communist goal to "revolutionize" South Africa could not be achieved through military means alone—this would have been too costly, the government in Pretoria argued—other, indirect, non-military means were employed to bring about the downfall of the present order. In 1980, the Chief of the South African Defense Force (SADF), General Magnus Malan (1930–2011), summarized this perception shortly before his appointment as Defense Minister in the government of P.W. Botha:

> "The total onslaught is an ideologically motivated struggle and the aim is the implacable and unconditional imposition of the aggressor's will on the target state [i.e., South Africa]. The aim is therefore also total, not only in terms of the ideology, but also as regards the political, social, economic and technological areas."[33]

During these years, Africa, as the Carter administration was to learn, "was the heart of the Cold War. Africa was where the superpowers shadow-boxed",[34] and conservative critics in the United States underlined the threat emanating from the strategic "communist exploitation of nationalism" in the (former) colonies.[35] The Soviet Union's steadfast support, through arms deliveries, (military) personnel, or other means for Angola's MPLA was not only "unforeseen by Western Sovietologists", it was "unprecedented" in so

32 See the interview with Vorster: Firing Line with William F. Buckley Jr.: The Question of South Africa, March 13, 1974, accessed December 31, 2020, https://www.youtube.com/watch?v=VVWh01yCoIQ [4:58/58:17 min.].

33 Toespraak deur Generaal Magnus Malan voor die Instituut vir Strategiese Studies, Pretoria, 9.3.1980, transl. in: Deon Geldenhuys, Some Foreign Policy Implications of South Africa's Total National Strategy with Particular Reference to the "12-Point Plan," Braamfontein: South African Institute of International Affairs 1981, 3.

34 Nancy Mitchell, *Jimmy Carter in Africa: Race and the Cold War* (Stanford: Stanford University Press, 2016), 6.

35 Eidelberg, *Beyond Détente*, 169.

far as the USSR "demonstrated its ability to project power decisively thousands of miles from the Soviet mainland". Subsequently, it supported the inner-party purges, resulting in thousands of deaths following an alleged coup in 1977, and the MPLA's rebranding as a Marxist-Leninist vanguard party, the MPLA-PT (*Partido Trabalhista*). Angola and Mozambique were regarded by Moscow "as nations where 'scientific socialism' is the official ideology".[36]

This Soviet success and, most of all, the USSR's invasion of Afghanistan in December 1979, reinforced the impression of the rise of communism in the so-called "third world". South African ANC supporters inside and outside the country, such as the academic Sam Nolutshungu (1945–1997) in 1982, also pointed out with satisfaction that "whatever military difficulties South Africa might face in the future [domestically or on foreign soil] [...] the possibility that the Soviet Union might get involved on a larger scale could not be discounted."[37] In such an eventuality, the support from NATO powers would have been decisive but, given western opposition to apartheid, it seemed—also to the NP government—questionable; even though it was clear that the Reagan administration had a keen interest in keeping the Cape-route out of Soviet reach[38] and to prevent the Soviet block from further "fomenting terrorism" in Southern Africa.[39] In late 1983, the Soviet Union, seeing its ally in Angola under renewed attack from Pretoria (operation *Askari*), "officially warned South Africa that it would not tolerate the fall of the MPLA government".[40]

Though the threat of a communist-inspired coup from outside South Africa ranked highest in the perception of Pretoria's policy makers, the threat perceived as the "Total Onslaught" on the Republic was, however,

36 Kurt M. Campbell, *Soviet Policy Towards South Africa* (Basingstoke: Macmillan, 1986), 141; see Lara Pawson, *In the Name of the People: Angola's Forgotten Massacre* (London: Tauris, 2014).

37 Nolutshungu, *Changing South Africa*, 77.

38 James M. Roherty, *The International Thrust of South Africa's "Total National Strategy"* (Center for Naval Warfare Studies, Naval War College, Newport, RI, February 1984).

39 *The Role of the Soviet Union, Cuba, and East Germany in Fomenting Terrorism in Southern Africa*, Hearings before the Sub-Committee on Security and Terrorism, Committee on the Judiciary, United States Senate, (Washington: Government Printing Office, 1982).

40 Robert Davies and Dan O'Meara, "Total Strategy in Southern Africa. An Analysis of South African Regional Policy since 1978," *Journal of Southern African Studies* 11 (1985), 183–211, here: 206; see W. Scott Thompson and Brett Silvers, "South Africa in Soviet Strategy," in, *South Africa into the 1980s*, eds. Richard E. Bissel and Chester A Crocker (Boulder: Westview, 1979), 133–158.

not limited to foreign forces. Malan and P.W. Botha warned repeatedly that "communist propaganda" ("racial incitement") targeting South Africa's black population (and others) continued to foment domestic unrest against white rule. The 1976 Soweto uprising in the black "township" of Johannesburg once more made South Africa's general public aware of the possibility of unrest, even rebellion—and a global public, which through reports and, most of all, iconic photographs learnt of the brutalities of the apartheid regime.[41] Danger also seemed to loom from a different source. Considering the growing opposition to white-minority rule inside and outside the country, in 1979, the new Prime Minister Botha warned his National Party friends: "You must not proceed from the standpoint that revolution cannot come in South Africa". He added that revolution might indeed break out if his government implemented the policies demanded by South Africa's white, right-wing extremists without any consideration for the interests of the non-white population.[42] As political scientist Deon Geldenhuys argued then, this statement about an "internal threat" emanating from a white minority, was "indeed a new theme" in the political communication of the NP government.[43]

Historian Jamie Miller underlines that South Africa's government "conflated" all sorts of unrest and statements opposing its policies as "communist inspired". But this conflation and the "self-serving nature" of such epithets should not, Miller argues, "obscure the important role played by communist ideas and parties in the anti-apartheid struggle" and especially within the ANC. Prominent members of the ANC were also aligned with members of the South African Communist Party (founded in 1921/53) that, in turn, reported to the CPSU in Moscow, from where MK's weapons arsenal originated. Violent measures by the CPSU or the "sister parties", for example in Eastern Europe (Hungary 1956, Czechoslovakia 1968, Poland 1982) were vindicated by South African communists.[44]

---

41 Mitchell, *Jimmy Carter in Africa*, 75.

42 Toespraak deur Sy Edele P.W. Botha tydens "n Nasionale Party vergadering, August 27, 1979, transl. in: Geldenhuys, Some Foreign Policy Implications," 4.

43 Geldenhuys, Some Foreign Policy Implications, 4.

44 Jamie Miller, *An African Volk: The Apartheid Regime and Its Search for Survival* (Oxford: OUP, 2016) 351, FN 23, referring to Irina Filatova and Apollon Davidson, *The Hidden Threat: Russia and South Africa in the Soviet Era*, (Johannesburg: Ball, 2013); Hanno Plass, "Von Südafrika über Europa hinaus? Die South African Communist Party während der Apartheid, 1948–1990," *Jahrbuch für Historische Kommunismusforschung*

Yet, recent research has underscored—for the ANC and other liberation movements on the continent—the manifold "transnational" connections that played a role not only in the support networks between different African movements, but also in their dealings with third parties in "the West" and "the East". In the global context of the Cold War, ideological and material support against apartheid could be mustered by different actors in different geopolitical and local settings and was never static. During the 1970s and afterwards, when more and more South African critics of apartheid went into exile (or were forced to do so), "Black internationalism" played a decisive role, but was never ideologically unified, as the example of "Black anti-Communism" shows.[45] Therefore, as has been rightly emphasized, it is "much too simple to think of the 'West' as supporting the apartheid regime [...], and the 'East' as sole supporters of the Southern African liberation movements."[46]

These complexities were willfully "obscured" in the bi-polar statements by the National Party elite. Through its anti-Soviet campaigns against Angola and Mozambique, Pretoria had hoped to internationalize its internal problems of maintaining apartheid rule against the majority. The fight against "communist" guerillas or regimes, it was expected, would improve the deteriorating relations with Western governments.[47] With the inception of the Carter-administration in 1977 and growing civil society awareness all over Europe (Anti-Apartheid Movement), Western pressure to abandon apartheid and allow for a majority vote increased, whereas NP politicians accused "the West" of being blind to the gravity of the onslaught in Southern Africa and the possibility of a communist takeover. This would result in future chaos and violence in a hitherto prosperous and strategically important nation. The stalemate over Namibia, which was still occupied by South Africa despite UN resolutions demanding withdrawal, and the election

(2019), 125–138, here: 135, 137; Stephen Ellis, *External Mission: The ANC in Exile, 1960–1990* (London: Hurst, 2012).

45 "AHR Conversation Black Internationalism," *American Historical Review* 125, no. 5 (2020), 1699–1739, here:1734 [Benjamin Talton].

46 Chris Saunders, Helder Adegar Fonseca and Lena Dallywater, "Southern African Liberation Movements and the Global Cold War 'East': Transnational Activism 1960–1990," introduction in *Southern African Liberation Movements and the Global Cold War "East"*, eds. id. (Berlin: DeGruyter, 2019), 7; see also J. Alexander, J.-A. McGregor and B.-M. Tendi, "The Transnational Histories of Southern African Liberation Movements: An Introduction," *Journal of Southern African Studies* 43, no. 1 (2017), 1–12.

47 Davies and O'Meara, "Total Strategy in Southern Africa," 199.

victory of left-leaning Robert Mugabe in Zimbabwe in 1980 "completed the psychosis of onslaught in the mind of Pretoria."[48]

From the late 1970s on, South Africa's security establishment would continuously use every communication channel available to highlight the threats posed to the country (and the "Free World" in general) by the eight "operating factors" used in the "Total Onslaught". For the policy makers, it was clear that the perception of the crisis they had given the name "Total Onslaught" had to be administered or managed. General P.J. Coetzee of the SADF repeated in 1982 that the battle against the "Total Onslaught" would not be fought with guns alone: "Perhaps even more important is the battlefield of enemy propaganda and terrorist mythology" that tried to denigrate any reforms and "revolutionize" the population.[49] Recognizing the centrality of the media in the political process, whether in the domestic or international arena, political communication by the National Party government about the "Total Onslaught" was meant to develop into a sophisticated tool of defense for South African interests.

Domestically, through wide circulation of the term "Total Onslaught" in parliamentary speeches, the press, and even in academic circles, the strengthening of an (Afrikaner) defense ethic and siege culture, or circle-the-wagons mentality, was encouraged by the National Party government. This intersected with the crisis rhetoric of conservative civil society groups, who saw Afrikanerdom threatened by a "moral onslaught", some even panicking about "satanism" and the coming of "the anti-Christ". They condemned foreign "modern" influences like "'revolutionary and soul destroying' pop music as part of the Marxist ploy to use literature, music and drugs to sexually stimulate [homosexuality] and corrupt the youth of South Africa".[50] In South African English, the Afrikaans term *laager* (circle of wagons) had taken root, thus *laager* mentality or *Wagenburg-Mentalität* was an apposite term. Concerned about an increasing polarization of South Africa's white polity and the fragmentation of the ideological tenets of Afrikaner nationalism, speaking about a "Total Onslaught", orchestrated by a superpower, the USSR, was hoped to translate domestically into a closing of the ranks through the

48 M. Evans, "Neo-Apartheid, 'Total Onslaught' and 'Total Strategy'. South Africa's National Defence Policy and the Security of Afrikanerdom in the 1980s," *Historical Association of Zimbabwe. Occasional Paper* 10 (1981), 5.

49 Quoted in: Ellis, "The Historical Significance of South Africa's Third Force," 265.

50 Danielle Dunbar and Sandra Swart, "The Devil Rejoiced: Volk, Devils and Moral Panic in White South Africa, 1978–1982," *Journal of Historical Sociology* 28, no. 2 (2015), 235–263, here: 249.

creation of insiders and outsiders/dissidents. In this "Total Onslaught propaganda in defense of domestic oppression" and reform, as South African contemporaries were already describing it, the National Party was remarkably successful.[51] Eric Louw stresses that during "the 1980s white South Africans almost universally believed the 'total onslaught' idea."[52] On the other hand, attempts by the NP government to improve its standing with the foreign press and its reporting about apartheid and South Africa in general were less successful. They ended in an embarrassing corruption scandal that contributed to the fall of Prime Minister John Vorster in 1978. In the following decade, barely any of the major western media outlets would defend the idea and politics of apartheid.[53]

The three elements commonly cited to form the process of political communication, namely citizens, media, and political organizations/governments,[54] reacted differently in an authoritarian regime like South Africa than in the western democracies South African politicians claimed to be part of. The relationship between the media and politics was, of course, not shaped by principles of freedom of information and open debate. Though newspapers in South Africa could heavily criticize the government, and scholars like Deon Geldenhuys were able to publish critical analyses of the perception of "Total Onslaught" and the government's reactions to it, disciplining through intimidation (resulting in self-censorship) and legal means remained unmistakable markers of the government's authoritarian attempts to administer public perceptions of the crisis and its management by the state. Consequently, "[w]here the state sought to hide what it did, it compelled those who were able to see what was happening [mostly journalists] not to admit the testimony of their own eyes."[55]

To this end, press legislation and a "censorship bureaucracy" were always on hand for the government to repress publications "on moral and security

51 Hermann Giliomee and Lawrence Schlemmer (eds.), *Negotiating South Africa's Future* (Basingstoke: Macmillan, 1989), 23.

52 P. Eric Louw, *The Rise, Fall, and Legacy of Apartheid* (Westport: Praeger, 2004), 91; similarly, Christo B. Botha, "South Africa's total strategy in the era of Cold War, liberation struggles and the uneven transition to democracy. Review article," *Journal of Namibian Studies* 4 (2008), 75–111, here: 81.

53 Christoph Marx, "'Muldergate': Außenpolitische Propaganda und interne Machtkämpfe in Südafrika Ende der 1970er Jahre," *Geschichte in Wissenschaft und Unterricht* 69, no. 1 (2018), 51–66.

54 Brian McNair, *An Introduction to Political Communication* (New York: Routledge, 2017), 5.

55 Sarah Nuttall and Carli Coetzee (eds.), *Negotiating the Past: The Making of Memory in Modern South Africa* (Cape Town: OUP, 1998), 20.

grounds". This would have made it difficult to debate, for example, the concept of "Total Onslaught" and declare it a misperception of Soviet strategies or as using mere bogeys such as "black peril" (*swart gevaar*) and "red menace" to instill paranoia.[56] Such critical assessments by South Africans of "the supposed 'Soviet threat' in the sub-continent" were mostly published outside the country.[57] South Africa's black newspapers were "singled out for particularly harsh treatment." Contemporary critics went so far as to speak of a "'Total Onslaught' against the Press": "For, as the South African government comes under increasing pressures from opponents of apartheid at home and abroad, so too does freedom of expression within South Africa diminish".[58]

Establishing the "Total National Strategy"—Managing a Crisis

The increasingly harsher treatment of the media was merely one aspect of the NP government's reaction to the crisis it named "Total Onslaught". South Africa was, so the government argued, obliged to develop a "Total National Strategy" to withstand the revolutionary forces of the "Total Onslaught" with all of South Africa's national resources. With such a "Total National Strategy", the NP government devised the idea that through the coordination of military, political and developmental policies, the future of South Africa as a state based on (a reformed) apartheid could be salvaged—this was presented as the "only effective counterstrategy".[59] In the exceedingly broad definition of the above-mentioned 1977 white paper the "Total National Strategy" was:

"[T]he comprehensive plan to utilize all the means available to a state according to an integrated pattern in order to achieve the national aims [as set forth in the preamble of the constitution] within the framework of the specific policies. A total

56 Philip Frankel, *Pretoria's praetorians: Civil-military relations in South Africa* (Cambridge: CUP, 1984).

57 Sam C. Nolutshungu, "Strategy and Power: South Africa and Its Neighbours," in *South Africa: No Turning Back*, ed. Shaun Johnson (London: Palgrave, 1988), 335–352, here: 336.

58 William A. Hachten and C. Anthony Giffard, *The Press and Apartheid: Repression and Propaganda in South Africa* (Madison: UWP, 1984), 146; 165; xiii; 3.

59 Dutton, "The military aspects of national security," 106.

national strategy is, therefore, not confined to a particular sphere, but is applicable at all levels and to all functions of the state structure."[60]

One of the intellectual fathers of this "comprehensive plan" was purportedly the French general, André Beaufre (1902–1975). A soldier who had seen most of the French theaters of wars of decolonization, Beaufre emphasized the (military) necessity to give due consideration to the non-military aspects of warfare, including a battle for the "hearts and minds" of the population. A "total strategy" was therefore ignoring boundaries between the military and civil society. Beaufre's analysis of *La guerre révolutionnaire* (1972) "became influential in Cold War US military circles and was taught at Fort Leavenworth Defense College", where Magnus Malan also graduated. Defense Minister Botha was acquainted with Beaufre's ideas and, during the 1970s and 1980s, they were widely taught in South African military colleges.[61]

Problematizing the effects of a blurring between the military and civil realms, General Dutton considered that the "function" of the "total strategy [...] would then be to allocate relative values and priorities to [the eight aforementioned "factors in total war"] and to reconcile the conflicting requirements", not only between the different branches of government, but also the private sector. He admitted that:

"[t]wo of the most thorny problems to be resolved [in the political process] would arise from: (a) Total strategy without violation of essential democratic principles [presumably where they existed for the white polity]; (b) Balance in the allocation of national resources to the various spheres of activity. This would include the determination of priorities."[62]

Since South Africa's incursion into Angola in 1975, this "allocation" prioritized to an unprecedented degree all security related branches of the government: Armed forces, police, secret service(s). Through "emergency laws", they all increasingly violated "essential democratic principles" even for the white population. On the most basic level, purportedly to "safeguard the integrity" of the country and to "secure the maintenance of law and order" for the survival of the state, the "Total National Strategy" resulted in a massive investment in the state's "defense" capacities and a militarization of South African society. Faced with a UN arms embargo, during his tenure as

60 Republic of South Africa, Dept. of Defence, *White Paper on Defence 1977*, Pretoria, 1977, 5.

61 Louw, *The Rise, Fall, and Legacy of Apartheid*, 91; see Giliomee, *The Afrikaners*, 588; Frankel, *Pretoria's praetorians*.

62 Dutton, "The military aspects of national security," 119.

SADF Chief (1976–1980), General Malan was, along with his Defense Minister and future Prime Minister P.W. Botha, instrumental in reorganizing and increasing the SADF into a force capable of preventing external interference with the domestic South African order.

The unsuccessful *Operation Savannah* in Angola, against MPLA and Cuban forces, had indicated weaknesses in the conventional warfare capacity of the SADF, especially inadequacies in infantry and artillery.[63] Seeing the Soviet arms build-up and convinced that "the enemy" in its "Total Onslaught" would use all means available, from coercive to persuasive, it seemed paramount to Botha and Malan that South Africa possessed, in the present and future, Southern Africa's most formidable armed forces, trained in both counterinsurgency warfare and conventional mechanized operations. Being prepared to be employed inside and outside the state territory, the SADF was meant to give South Africa a strategic position that would be too costly to challenge and thereby take away any military options imagined by the regime's adversaries. The defense budget doubled from 700 million rand in 1974/5 to 1,400 million in 1977/78 and rose to 1,800 million rand in 1980; allowing for a total mobilization force of up to 404,500 men, consisting of a small permanent force of around 12,000 white conscripts (for whom national service was extended to two years in 1977), citizen force reserve, and non-white volunteers (up to 40 percent of the SADF) equipped with modern, foreign and domestic-built weaponry.[64]

This unprecedented massive reallocation of financial and personal resources (including setting up secret funds) to the military (SADF), South African Police (SAP), the Department of Defense (DOD), the intelligence services (NIS), the State Security Council (SSC), and the speedy development of a domestic arms industry (ARMSCOR) was not only proof of the "forceful personality" of Defense Minister P.W. Botha, who managed to sideline the "doves" in the administration.[65] This predatory budget allocation administered by a few "strong men" also attests to the authoritarian character of South Africa's system of government since it could do so

63 Rodney Warwick, "Operation Savannah: A Measure of SADF Decline, Resourcefulness and Modernisation," *Scientia Militaria* 40, 3 (2012), 354–397.

64 Chester A. Crocker, "Current and projected military balances in Southern Africa," in *South Africa into the 1980s*, eds. Richard E. Bissel and Chester A Crocker, (Boulder: Westview, 1979), 71–107.

65 Kenneth W. Grundy, "The Angolan Puzzle: Varied Actors and Complex Issues," *Issue. A Journal of Opinion* 15 (1987), 35–41, here: 37.

without much consideration for parliament or other elements of the democratic process.

Since the late 1970s, the number of South African casualties in the Angolan theater of war against Angolan and Cuban troops rose to over 100 annually. In addition, the number of border "incidents" and mine explosions increased due to incursions of SWAPO combatants, eager to fight for Namibia's independence.[66] The crisis obliged the state, so the NP government argued, to apply its "total national strength" not only to react to, but to eliminate the causes of this crisis—domestic and foreign. To this end, the government, according to Malan, aimed at "the management of South Africa's four power bases" that were under attack (namely political/diplomatic; economic; social/psychological; security) "as an integrated whole". Consequently, a "National Security Management System" was put in place as the institutionalization of the Total National Strategy. It consisted of the following components:

"1) the State Security Council—a cabinet committee [already established in 1972] headed by the Prime Minister; 2) the working committee of the State Security Council; 3) the security planning branch of the Prime Minister's Office; 4) a number of interdepartmental committees; 5) a number of joint management centers and the Department of National Intelligence 'to provide the essential strategic background'."[67]

This all-encompassing state security architecture, centralized around P.W. Botha's Prime Minister's office and aimed at the coordination of all government institutions, attests to a thoroughly authoritarian strategy. It was based on the belief in the manageability of external threats and internal civil unrest through ever tightening security measures. It also, as Adam and Giliomee underlined in 1979, attested to a "new role of the state", a new form of "crisis management"[68] that spoke to Botha's confidence in the "overpowering strength of the state."[69] Sidelining the police forces favored by his predecessor Vorster, Botha ensured that within the South African government,

66 Lauren Dobell, *Swapo's Struggle for Namibia, 1960–1991: War by Other Means*, (Basel: Schlettwein, 1998); Gary Baines and Peter Vale (eds.), *Beyond the Border War. New Perspectives on Southern Africa's Late Cold War Conflicts* (Pretoria: Unisa Press, 2008); Leopold Scholtz, *The SADF in the Border War: 1966–1989* (Cape Town: Tafelberg, 2013).

67 All quotations from Gen. Malan transl. in: Geldenhuys, Some Foreign Policy Implications, 9–10.

68 Adam and Giliomee, *The Rise and Crisis of Afrikaner Power*, 12.

69 Giliomee, *The Afrikaners*, 586.

his followers, the so-called "securocrats", originating mostly from the Department of Defense, were well placed to exercise control over the political decision-making process and implementation at all levels of government. Following this "silent *coup d'état*" within the National Party,[70] these men based their understanding of the implementation of the "Total National Strategy" on the conviction "that security structures could be used as institutions for managing political change" necessary to withstand the "Total Onslaught".[71] In the critical analysis by political scientist Philip Frankel the "Total National Strategy" was:

"a counter-revolutionary programme devised by a particular group of power holders as a self-protective device through the distilled combination of their own historical and cultural background [the Afrikaner *kommando* tradition of the South African war (1899–1902)] with the practical experience of others [like Beaufre] in the art of containing revolution."[72]

In "times of national crisis when the security or even the continued existence of the State and its people is at stake," as General Dutton stated before the press,[73] implementing an armed suppression approach seemed appropriate to the policy makers. Encouraged through means provided by the "Total National Strategy", South Africa's domestic secret services developed into, as critics argued, a "myriad [of] government 'dirty tricks' departments".[74] They "came to constitute entities effectively outside the scope and control of civilian agencies" and parliamentary control,[75] resulting in the massive extension of surveillance and intra-service rivalries. They were responsible for covert operations, including extra-judicial killings; detainment without trial was as ubiquitous as torture in South Africa's prisons. Or, as J.M. Coetzee had put it in his *Waiting for the Barbarians*, ruthless means were "the truth the Empire tells when harsh winds blow."

70 M. Evans, "Neo-Apartheid, 'Total Onslaught' and 'Total Strategy,'" 12.

71 Ellis, "The Historical Significance of South Africa's Third Force," 266.

72 Philip Frankel, *Pretoria's praetorians: Civil-military relations in South Africa* (Cambridge: CUP, 1984), 68–69.

73 General J.R. Dutton quoted in *The Star* (Johannesburg), October 3, 1977, 7.

74 Jan-Bart Gewald, "Who Killed Clemens Kapuuo?" *Journal of Southern African Studies* 30 (2004), 559–576, here: 560; see Chris Alden, *Apartheid's Last Stand: The Rise and Fall of the South African Security State* (London: Macmillan, 1996); A. de Villiers Minnaar, I. Liebenberg and C. Schutte (eds.), *The Hidden Hand: Covert Operations in South Africa* (Pretoria, Human Sciences Research Council, 1994).

75 Botha, "South Africa's total strategy," 75.

South African techniques of rule over "revolutionized" Africans and the counterinsurgency means necessary to do so were learnt in the context of the decolonization wars. Already under Vorster, South African policemen fought against SWAPO incursions, first from Zambia and, since 1975, also from Angola. More importantly, up to 2,000 South African security officials were heavily involved in fighting African "rebels" from ZIPRA, ZANUPF and other groups in Rhodesia, who were intent on defeating the white-minority regime. The Rhodesian forces, in turn, were commanded by battle-hardened British officers who had experienced the decolonization wars in Kenya and British Malaya. Furthermore, South Africa had sent "a dozen policemen" to train "on detachment in Algeria in the last days of French rule", some of whom were instrumental in setting up clandestine hit-and-run squads in the 1980s. The "key lesson learned by South African policemen on detachment in Rhodesia was the value of intelligence in irregular warfare".[76] A fact that meant capturing and torturing guerillas to provide intelligence and, ideally, turning them against their own men by incorporating them as irregular (colonial) troops (*askari*) to hunt down their own former "comrades".[77]

However, despite the almost desperate attempts to learn from the crises of previous colonial regimes and their (failed) attempts to (re-)gain the monopoly of violence through counterinsurgency, and to end the crisis that decolonization was for the colonial administrations, soon Botha, Malan and other policy makers recognized that there would be no military solution to the "Total Onslaught" against South Africa. Despite an undeniable fanaticism among lower and middle charges in South Africa's security apparatus, it became clear that—no matter how well founded and equipped—military and police could win time but not the war. Despite continuous "raids" within South Africa and the neighboring states supporting the ANC's struggle (the destabilization measures of 1982/83 aiming to compel the "frontline states" into "non-aggression pacts")[78], SADF and the police failed to "defeat" the enemy. They could not even prevent the ANC and its armed wing, MK, from continuing to shock the country through counterraids,

76 Ellis, "The Historical Significance of South Africa's Third Force," 269; 267; see Seegers, *The Military in the Making of Modern South Africa*, (London: Tauris, 1996); Johnson, *How long*, 13.

77 Jacob Dlamini, *Askari: A Story of Collaboration and Betrayal in the Anti-apartheid Struggle* (Johannesburg: Jacana, 2014).

78 Davies and O'Meara, "Total Strategy in Southern Africa," 198–205.

embarrassing the securocrats and their many forces. For example, in December 1982, after South African agents had just assassinated anti-apartheid activist Ruth First, MK sabotaged South Africa's only nuclear power plant, Koeberg near Cape Town, "causing millions of rands in damage."[79] As historian Jacob Dlimani shows in his analysis of South African security police work, the state apparatus never had the efficiency and oversight it claimed it had.[80]

At the new height of Soviet-US animosity in the early 1980s, when Ronald Reagan and Yuri Andropov exchanged hostile rhetoric,[81] the South African regime could sense some respite in its foreign affairs. And yet, even the most hawkish of the "securocrats" and Botha himself accepted that communism's alleged "Total Onslaught" was also to be countered by non-military means. Botha, who saw himself as a pragmatic reformer and modernizer of apartheid, was convinced that the survival of the state depended on accommodating some of the grievances of the disenfranchised population, including the black majority that lived in abject poverty compared to the white population. Within the ranks of the National Party, this insight made him a *verligte* (enlightened) politician, who argued hard with the *verkramptes* (conservatives), who feared that the threats of materialism, modernity, equality, individualism, capitalism and communism would bring social decadence and moral corruption to Afrikanerdom. In contrast, Botha and his followers saw the improvement of the constitutional position of the "non-white" population, the socio-economic conditions in rural areas, and in the black townships where, with increasing regularity, "insurrections" threatened apartheid's "law and order" as essential in proving wrong those commentators who claimed that "the revolution was around the corner".[82] The disenfranchised majority was to be convinced that it had more to gain from a reform of the present apartheid order than from a future communist

79 "Chronology," *Historical Dictionary of South Africa*, eds. Christopher Saunders and Peter Limb (Lanham: Rowman, 2021), xxxix.

80 Jacob Dlamini, *The Terrorist Album: Apartheid's Insurgents, Collaborators, and the Security Police* (Cambridge, Mass.: Harvard UP, 2020).

81 Simon Miles, *Engaging the Evil Empire. Washington, Moscow, and the Beginning of the End of the Cold War* (Ithaca: Cornell UP, 2020), 84.

82 As summarized by Shula Marks and Stanley Trapido, "South Africa since 1976: An Historical Perspective," in *South Africa: No Turning Back*, ed. Shaun Johnson (London: Palgrave, 1988), 1–51, here: 1, calling such characterization as insufficient in describing "the complexities of the current situation."

"black dictatorship", as government officials called the regimes in Mozambique and Angola.

This was, on the one hand, a question of communication (or propaganda) that needed to be appropriate in conveying the message that the National Party government would be honest in its reform policies to adapt or abrogate (some) old Verwoerdian apartheid regulations and, perhaps, would allow for the development of a "non-white" urban middle class. Such "propaganda" was, in the terminology of general André Beaufre and his "Cold War counterrevolutionary warfare model", part of the "indirect strategy" (the "political struggle") that involved "both sides in a complex mix of 'winning hearts and minds' and instilling fear—that is, struggling for the love and respect of citizens". As Eric Louw emphasizes, this argumentation was a "major input into Botha's world view."[83]

Botha's (constitutional) reforms of 1983 not only made him South Africa's first executive state president from 1984 to 1989. He also introduced the tricameral parliament with representation divided according to skin color/"ethnicity": House of Assembly (representation of "Whites"), House of Representatives (representation of "Coloreds"), House of Delegates (representation of "Indians"), but still excluding the black majority ("Bantu", who were, so the cynical argument of the NP went, represented in the parliament of "their homelands", the "independent" "Bantustans"). Such "reforms" were soon denounced as "neo-apartheid" and rejected internationally at UN level. On other occasions too, the government's authoritarian actions were accompanied by measures of (limited) political reform that dismantled some apartheid structures. This included the (indirect) permission of all kinds of engagements between the exiled ANC and groups inside South Africa, and also, since 1986, with representatives of the government.[84] As anti-apartheid activist Kumi Naidoo (b. 1965) proudly explained, it was clear that these measures and "reforms" (he put the word in scare quotes) had "been primarily provoked by resistance activity" inside and outside the country.[85] Historians agree that "this [African] resistance engendered significant shifts in government policies". The NP government was

83 Louw, *The Rise, Fall, and Legacy of Apartheid*, 91; see 73–74.

84 Ulrich van der Heyden, *Der Dakar-Prozess. Der Anfang vom Ende der Apartheid in Südafrika* (Kiel: Solivagus, 2018).

85 Kumi Naidoo, "Internal Resistance in South Africa: The Political Movements," in *South Africa: No Turning Back*, ed. Shaun Johnson (London: Palgrave, 1988), 172–205, here: 172.

actively forced to react and did so both by liberalizing some apartheid rules and militarizing society and foreign policy. Even though this widened the gulf between the *verligtes* and *verkramptes*, through reform and repression, the government "succeeded in containing or at least defining limits to popular insurgency".[86]

On the other hand, next to the propaganda of liberalization of apartheid, livelihoods had to be practically improved. Aware of the crisis that had befallen millions of Africans in their "independent" "homelands" due to failed economic policies, falling gold prices, and an enduring drought from 1982 to 1984, politicians and generals alike publicly explained that South Africa's struggle against ANC and SACP revolutionaries was 20 percent military and 80 percent socioeconomic. Or, as one general phrased it: "If South Africa lost the socio-economic struggle, we need not bother to fight the military one."[87] And it was also here, in the context of economic and social policies, that the South African state with its massively overstretched and exceedingly unaffordable military apparatus failed utterly—just as it failed to avert, through reforms and other measures of the TNS, the crisis that apartheid had been for millions since 1948. By the mid-1980s, it became increasingly clear that all political, constitutional and military measures and reforms implemented by the NP under this strategy would not suffice to salvage the apartheid system but, as Dan O'Meara put it, within the ruling circles "nothing else was on offer, no long term vision of how to proceed" in a possible future outside the bounds of the politics of "race"/"ethnicity".[88]

Indeed, since the 1960s, academics, politicians and journalists had discussed a plethora of alternatives to apartheid and "plan[s] for the future" of South Africa, from confederation to partition—but these plans had little impact on NP government policies. Rightly, a scholar characterized South Africa as a "real graveyard of social science prophecies".[89] Given this

86 Tom Lodge, "Resistance and Reform 1974–1994," in *Cambridge History of South Africa. Vol 2: 1885–1994*, eds. Robert Ross, Anne Kelk Mager, and Bill Nasson (Cambridge: CUP, 2011), 409–491, here: 409.

87 Quoted in Hermann Giliomee and Bernard Mbenga, New History of South Africa (Cape Town: Tafelberg, 2007), 367.

88 Dan O'Meara, *Forty Lost Years: The Apartheid State and the Politics of the National Party 1948–1994* (Athens: Ohio University Press, 1996), 326.

89 Quoted in: Erich Leistner, "Auf dem Weg zu einer neuen Ordnung in Südafrika," *Hamburger Jahrbuch für Wirtschafts- und Gesellschaftspolitik* 22 (1977), 191–203, here: 191; see Welsh and van Zyl Slabbert, *South Africa's Options*; Jakob Zollmann, "Negotiated Partition of South Africa—An Idea and its History (1920s–1980s)," *South African Historical Journal* 73 (2021), 406–434.

stalemate, in 1989, an embittered P.W. Botha was forced to resign due to a power struggle within the NP. The collapse of world communism and the end of the Cold War conflict would then play an important argumentative role in the political combats fought to abolish apartheid between 1990 and 1994.

Conclusion

The National Party government's Total National Strategy is a prime example of the ambivalence of the term "crisis". "Crisis" is not merely an objective diagnosis or description of the notion of, for example, an unfavorable political, economic, or military situation. The socially constructed character of a "crisis" and its perception and interpretation as permitting or calling for measures beyond the hitherto political routines gives the term suggestive power that, in turn, invites for its political instrumentalization. This ambivalence is also the reason why the TNS holds a distinctive position within the historiography of the demise of apartheid. While some contemporary researchers, who saw South Africa as an important part of the Western defense against Soviet imperialism, lauded the TNS as the "most explicit plan of action for the implementation of policy to be found anywhere in the world today [1984]",[90] others proved far more skeptical, calling it a "counter-revolutionary program" and "a self-protective device" of a ruthless power elite that stubbornly refused to understand that its time is up.[91]

In retrospect, the policies stemming from the Total National Strategy are judged by historians in unmistakably negative terms. Prime Minister Botha is said to have taken "the country to the brink of disaster while clinging to delusions of grandeur and infallibility" with the TNS's "reform element […] carried out half-heartedly, lacking conviction".[92] The attempt to establish and invest political capital in the "homelands" for Africans held "a fatal attraction that blinded [the NP government] to the need for imaginative responses" to the crisis.[93] All these policies were informed by a political tenet evolving in the period under review here that has since been described as

90 Roherty, *The International Thrust of South Africa's "Total National Strategy,"* 3.

91 Frankel, *Pretoria's praetorians*, 68–69.

92 Botha, "South Africa's total strategy in the era of Cold War," 80, 84.

93 Giliomee and Mbenga, *New History of South Africa*, 372.

"power sharing without losing control".[94] As contradictory as this tenet may appear, in the authoritarian context of the apartheid regime—that ordered secret death squads to hunt down "enemies of the state" while publicly announcing reforms and liberalization—the dominating will to continue controlling the South African state and its resources still allowed for a degree of flexibility. In an adverse domestic and international environment, Prime Minister P.W. Botha saw himself, as mentioned previously, first and foremost as a reformer; in this light, the National Party announcement in 1979 must be understood: "Apartheid is dead".[95] Botha thought of himself as a leader who had learnt from the crisis following 1975 that the policy of separate development of "races" must be changed, must be "modernized" in order to survive the 20th century—the future was imagined as holding this possibility.

Considering the objectives of South Africa's adversaries to abolish apartheid and introduce the one-man-one-vote principle, the TNS was thus, on the one hand, an (at least indirect) acknowledgment by South Africa's political elite that apartheid had in fact caused a "crisis"—and it was termed as such. It was undeniable and the National Party did not deny (any longer) that the country's long-cherished stability was an illusion. On the other hand, South Africa's government, eager to avoid a crisis of legitimacy among its white voter base, was intent on underlining the "manageability" of the crisis. The TNS was declared to be the sole and indispensable strategy to manage this crisis. Furthermore, through its propaganda about the "Total Onslaught", the NP government aimed at managing how society, all "races", interpreted and reacted to the crisis and its purported causes. "Crisis" descriptions such as the "Total Onslaught" against South Africa by a multitude of adversaries with a multitude of "tools" were also a rhetorical strategy to motivate and to vindicate demands for change and "reforms", be it the massive increase of all sorts of military and security budgets, or the abrogation of some apartheid legislation. All reformist initiatives had to be declared as being compatible with the TNS. Through the juxtaposition of "Total Onslaught" and "Total National Strategy", an "either–or situation" was argumentatively created that was a call for action: Either South Africa acts in defense of its (reforming apartheid) order, or communism will take over.

At its inception, TNS was thought to be a strategy well planned and funded enough to not only cope with South Africa's current crisis brought

94 Giliomee, *The Last Afrikaner Leaders*, 139.

95 Quoted in: Giliomee and Mbenga, *New History of South Africa*, 368.

about by the independence of Angola, Mozambique (and later Zimbabwe) and the international sanctions, but also to prevent future crises like a growing involvement of the USSR in Southern African affairs or increased domestic turmoil and black defiance against apartheid rule. In contemporary South African novels, the "specter of regional revolution, of African nationalism quite literally flooding South Africa" haunted the imagination of readers (and voters).[96] However, in the end, the changes implemented under the TNS merely managed to win time for the besieged National Party government.[97]

96 James Graham, *Land and Nationalism in Fictions from Southern Africa* (New York: Routledge, 2009), 56.

97 Following the death of P.W. Botha in 2006, even his erstwhile adversaries pointed out the relevance of the "reforms" he implemented in the apartheid system. Helen Suzman was quoted by the BBC as declaring: "There were of course a number of important changes introduced during his regime. These were important steps forward." And President Nelson Mandela "remembere[d] him for the steps he took in paving the way towards the eventual peacefully negotiated settlement," PW Botha: Reaction in quotes (November 1, 2006), accessed December 31, 2020, http://news.bbc.co.uk/2/hi/africa/6105178.stm.

Emergency as Normalcy: An Afterword

Armin Nassehi

Some date the beginning of modernity to All Saints' Day in 1755, when a tsunami triggered by an earthquake 200 kilometers off the coast of Portugal destroyed Lisbon.[1] It was a senseless event that could not be subordinated to a world plan or even God's will, if only because Alfama, the city's red-light district, was largely spared the destruction. There have always been catastrophes, so why should this one be considered the starting point of modernity? At a minimum, the experience of this senseless event with all its evil effects revived the age-old question of how God, given his omnipotence and kindness, could allow such calamity. This so-called *theodicy question*, of course, was now no longer solved primarily in religious terms, but ultimately by separating nature from culture, necessity from freedom, and coincidence from sense.

Modernity, therefore, begins with separating different areas of life and logics of argumentation from each other. Immanuel Kant, for example, wrote a scientific theory of earthquakes and tsunamis in the wake of Lisbon. Although it turned out to be wrong in the end, it served to perceive the events as mere effects of natural forces that ultimately had nothing to do with the question of a decent and good life.

The lesson drawn from Lisbon was twofold. On the one hand, it was learned that it was not the tsunami itself, nor the many deaths and the destruction that constituted a crisis, but the fact that it was not possible to adequately interpret what was happening. On the other hand, it became increasingly clear that the new age had to take its fate into its own hands, that it no longer wanted to believe in the omnipotence of God but in its own creative power. As is widely acknowledged, this was to develop into a

1 This essay is a revised and condensed translation of Armin Nassehi's, "Der Ausnahmezustand als Normalfall: Modernität als Krise," *Kursbuch* 48, no. 170 (2012): 34–49. We are very grateful to Murmann Verlag for allowing a revised translation to be included in this volume. This essay has been translated by Linda O'Grady and Martin Wagner.

"wiser" age, if not a triumphant one, which, just as the theories of progress in the vein of, for example, Auguste Comte suggest, attempted to replace old theological and metaphysical patterns with rational and scientific ones. Ultimately, however, this merely shifted the question of theodicy, because its solution could now no longer be attributed to God's omnipotence, but to the course of history.

We sometimes imagine the Enlightenment as all too triumphant and self-confident. However, it was much more characterized by the sense of uncertainty that narratives of crisis management now had to be derived out of themselves, because no other criteria were available anymore. But in order to endure the inadequacy of the current times, a presence was needed that could not be too apparent in order to actually make such an attribution. If, up to then, it was still God as presence and absence at the same time, modernity invented itself by being able to assess the future as the absent presence which postpones into the future what at present was not yet solvable. This transition was fluid, emancipating itself slowly and rather cautiously from the recourse to the religious, as one can learn from Hans Joas' study on *Die Sakralität der Person* ("The Sacrality of the Person").[2] Just as the imperfect world of sin could previously be seen as a test of God and thus as an opportunity for the effort to overcome sin, it now became possible to portray the present in all its unreasonableness as reasonable. Even the contingencies of nature were then no longer evil, but merely of an uncertain nature, and irrational people and conditions became transitory stages in the fundamental solvability of the problem.

Ultimately, modernity was a child of the experience of crisis—how the different experiences and logics of life could be combined: For example, the realms of necessity and freedom in the face of a tsunami like the one in 1755, or the regulative idea of rationality and good reasons in the face of the unreasonableness of empirical people. With the prospect of reconciliation in the future, even the unreasonable present can then be experienced rationally—the culmination is probably Hegel's assertion of the reasonableness of all that is real in the preface to his *Philosophy of Right* of 1821.[3] Here, crisis experience is obscured by the fact that it can be interpreted as a necessary

---

2 Hans Joas, *Die Sakralität der Person: Eine neue Genealogie der Menschenrechte*, 3rd ed. (Berlin: Suhrkamp, 2012).

3 Georg Wilhelm Friedrich Hegel, *Grundlinien der Philosophie des Rechts oder Naturrecht und Staatswissenschaft im Grundrisse: Mit Hegels eigenhändigen Notizen und den mündlichen Zusätzen*, 16th ed. (Frankfurt am Main: Suhrkamp, 2020).

step on the way to historical salvation. Interpretations from the *Philosophy of Right* that the worst state is still better than no state, because the reality of the moral idea and thus the reasonableness of what is precisely real is represented in it, are obvious attempts to "sublate" (*aufheben*) the crisis experience of the world. An earthquake on All Saints' Day, even in one of the most Catholic countries in the world, can no longer have an effect on this sublation. Then, one can have both: The experience of suffering and the unreasonable, as well as the expectation of salvation and the reasonable.

Susan Neiman has published a study on evil and is surprised this connection succeeded. It would have been sufficient to simply separate nature and culture, reason and unreason. Neiman says that "nothing is easier than stating the problem of evil in nontheist terms. One can state it, for example, as an argument with Hegel: not only is the real not identical with the rational; they aren't even related. To make this observation, you need no theory. Any observation of the world that continues for more than a couple of minutes should do."[4]

That it does not need a *grand theory*, sounds as if the grand theory has not gained this insight. But I think one has to reverse the relationship: *One needs grand theory to cover the independence of the real from the reasonable!* In other words: Modernity gave itself grand narratives in order to cope with its own experiences of the disparate, of crisis, and of the sense of uncertainty. The grand narratives of modernity have always been narratives of crisis management. The narrative of reason was supposed to defeat the unreasonableness that was always found in empirical people. The narrative of the nation appeared where society had to reconcile order and progress after the great revolution but experienced that it was already enough to give a name to communities that were becoming more complex and ungovernable, so that one could address commands and promises. The narrative of freedom is the most difficult one: It performs a *theodicy of free will* by postulating free choices on the one hand, but only enabling them by limiting them to the *right* choices. Freedom has been bought with submission—submission to the necessity of the reasonable, to the better argument and its good reasons, or at least to the dictates of professional producers of good reason.

Modernity brings two things into the world: The claim of the individual motive for action and the problem of constraining motives. Modernity experienced itself as crisis because people were now supposed to do what they

4 Susan Neiman, *Evil in Modern Thought: An Alternative History of Philosophy* (Princeton: Princeton University Press, 2002), 5.

wanted to do, but possibly did not want to do what they were supposed to do. Order thus became more and more contingent because the old relationships of domination became fragile. The old order could not get into crisis because it was not sane. Whether divine or vassal rule, whether obedience or tradition—everything conformed to an order that one only had to recognize. The old rule could govern with an iron fist, that is, it could still force society and its actors to do what had to be done. Now, however, a detour had to be taken via motive and good reasons. This makes decisions uncertain, makes the world ambiguous, and increases the cost of rule and control.

Modernity experiences itself as crisis because it no longer has any grip on society, because it remains inaccessible, precisely because there is no overall rationality with which to govern society and oneself. It is true that the central narratives of modernity were above all *politicized* narratives, i.e., narratives that programmatically and futilely made the claim to control society as a whole—but this is only an indication that keeping a grip on society is difficult.

Theories of modernity have always struggled to integrate the biggest crises of this age into the narratives of the promises of modernity. I am referring to the political dictatorships of the twentieth century, the differences within which I am not neglecting here. They temporarily succeeded in integrating society, in reconciling the conflicting moments of modernity, in abolishing the fundamental ungovernability of the world. We know the cost of this. Such overall integration of society can obviously only be achieved at the price of violence. And perhaps this is the dark side of modernity: That totalitarian rule and war are ultimately also attempts to deal with the fundamental crisis of modernity. Possibly, the functional purpose of the war between the European states after the Peace of Westphalia of 1648, but even more so in the nineteenth and early twentieth centuries, is to mobilize societies, that is, to *sublate* their differentiation in the literal Hegelian sense.

War was ultimately the great generator of order in a world in which, unlike the old world, the forces of society diverged. If one wants to formulate modernity: The central pillars of society, such as economy and politics, science and religion, and art and education, develop completely different internal logics, conditions for success, theories of reflection, manners of expectation and functions and, on the one hand, become more independent of each other; on the other hand, they always remain crisis-ridden because they do not really relate to each other. The sociological term for this is *functional differentiation*—and this is not a program or even a political idea or a solution concept, but simply the basic experience of modernity—that things present themselves differently from different perspectives. Categorically, two things followed from this—paradoxically, *on the one hand*, the loss of a central social perspective and, *on the other hand*, the need for such a perspective.

Modernity therefore experiences itself as crisis because it experiences the resistance of society to intervening approaches. The economy reacts economically to political conditions and often counteracts the political intention. The education system is not able to solve problems as quickly as is demanded by the political public or enterprises. Science generates contradictory analyses because it primarily solves scientific problems. Economic, political, and legal forms elude ethical justification algorithms. Economic prosperity and its parameters nevertheless generate economic hardship and injustice.

The potency of modernity lies precisely in the fact that the different logics regard their societal importance as importance logical to themselves. Thus, the enormous potency of the market and the capitalist economy is indeed an ingenious problem solver—but only from an economic point of view. Thus, economic success can be accompanied by consequences that are not very socially acceptable. And political success is measured by success within the political process, but not by whether identified problems have been solved. Wittgenstein's famous aphorism that the solution of all scientific problems may not yet have solved any problem in life must also be seen in this context.[5] In this respect, it is precisely the most powerful theories of reflection that generate the most naive concepts of society. The neoliberal paradigm of solving all problems through the economical use of resources and corresponding incentive structures is just as ridiculous as the belief in the fundamental solvability of all problems by participation or the complete ethicization of decision algorithms. And if I call them ridiculous here, this in no way means that these programs are not effective or significant—on the contrary, some of them are the best and most successful of their kind.

The crisis of modernity is based on the experience that the concepts we possess are obviously not sufficient—we experience something as crisis-ridden when it eludes our grasp in the sense of an objective force that "deprives a subject of a piece of sovereignty to which it is normally entitled," as Jürgen Habermas once put it in *Legitimationsprobleme im Spätkapitalismus* of

5 Ludwig Wittgenstein, *Tractatus Logico-Philosophicus: Logisch-philosophische Abhandlung* (London: Kegan Paul, 1922), §6.52.

1973.[6] That is pretty accurate—and yet this formulation is still impregnated with the idea that crisis can, in principle, be overcome by sovereignty. But probably the basic structure of modernity is characterized by the fact that exactly this sovereignty has long since ceased to belong to the subject—at least not in the sense that things adhere to what the actor might have wanted. The crisis of modernity is therefore not an objective crisis, but one that arises from the fact that this society never stands still and reacts with a logic of its own that eludes any sovereign. Modernity is ultimately ungovernable—and this applies as much to the experience of complex social spheres as it does to individual lifestyles.

You can lament this—but you can also consider the alternative. There may be much to learn from the current Chinese path to a modern industrial society. The success of this path may lie in the fact that it is even easier to govern the country with an iron fist—the peculiar combination of turbo-capitalism and the sulfurous smell of a communist regime creates a narrative that can function as long as there are stable growth rates and as long as this growth can be generated by successively including ever more groups of the population into this dynamic. The semantics of economic growth parameters, underpinned by a new cultural self-confidence, will possibly suffice for this narrative for some time to come. Here, in fact, everything still looks as if everyone is pulling in the same direction. It is possible to pretend that an *overall societal* perspective can be narrated, because the conflicting parts can still be accordingly bundled. The renunciation of the complexity's imposition of a democratic political system does the rest. But a new narrative of coming to terms with crisis will have to be created, at the latest, when the narrative of growth and a hardening currency no longer suffice. Europe knows a thing or two about this at the moment.

But back to the problem of stimulating integral societal perspectives: In European history, such perspectives have always been the desire of intellectual self-descriptions and modern theories of reflection, whether formulated in more socialist or more conservative terms. The dark side of European history, of course, is that it was precisely the dark side of Europe that offered an integral societal perspective not as a program, not as a normative idea, not as a promise, but as an empirical experience. This was the role played by the classic European war of nations. Max Horkheimer's famous aphorism that whoever wants to speak about capitalism must not be silent about

6 Jürgen Habermas, *Legitimationsprobleme im Spätkapitalismus* (Frankfurt am Main: Suhrkamp, 1973), 10.

fascism is correct in principle—only it is a considerable understatement and truncation.[7] Capitalism here stands for the basic experience of a differentiated modern society—and fascism is only the extreme name for, to put it mildly, the internal and external defensiveness of the Western nations.

For a long time, the (nations-)war was ultimately the only phenomenon able to generate an *overall societal* perspective. War has always been able to bundle the differentiated logics of functional systems—and, thus, all the individual factors that are cited as conditions of modern state war turn into a strange description of the simultaneous strategic use and suspension of functional differentiation: War as an *economic* bundling program for the production of war material, war as a *scientific* program for the perfection of technology, war as a *pedagogical* program for training in a cognitive and physical regard, war as an *artistic* program for the aestheticization of "Storms of Steel", war as a *mass media* program for the implementation of simple lines of conflict and the production of a common space of meaning, war as a *legal* program for the suspension of freedom of movement, and, of course, war as a *political* program for the production of that collectivity which can be expected to make binding decisions.

Not to be misunderstood: No dark history of modernity is told here, no negative dialectic, no history of decay. What can be read from the dark sides of modernity, however, is its basic structure; a structure that these dark sides of modernity are precisely trying to deny and overcome. In this respect, war was indeed the force that united the diverging factors of society. Sovereign, Carl Schmitt said, is he who can decide on the state of exception.[8] It is no wonder that this generation was fascinated by war, by the belligerent deed, by decisionism, because it could be modern and anti-modern at the same time. It is *modern* to want to unite the divergent factors, and it is *anti-modern* to do so. What was not possible is to endure the state of exception, but to want to govern it, to decide on it, where decisions are virtually counteracted by the complexity of society.

To put it in a formula: Whoever wants to overcome the fundamental crisis of modernity, which excludes the classic idea of sovereignty, plunges society into crisis all the more. This is what has connected the dictatorships of the twentieth century, the belligerent tradition of classical-modern

7 Max Horkheimer, "Die Juden und Europa," *Zeitschrift für Sozialforschung/Studies in Philosophy and Social Science* 8 (1939), 115–137, here: 115.

8 Carl Schmitt, *Politische Theologie: Vier Kapitel zur Lehre von der Souveränität*, 11th ed. (Berlin: Duncker & Humblot, 2021), 13.

statehood since the Westphalian model of the seventeenth century, also the colonialism of the nineteenth and twentieth centuries and possibly the fascination with the "Iron-fist rule" China of the twenty-first century. Everywhere, it is the attempt to overcome the digital crisis with analog solutions.

Authors

Meher Ali is a doctoral student in the Department of History at Princeton University. She studies modern South Asia, focusing on questions of mass politics, social movements, and urban political culture in Pakistan. She received her M.A. from the University of Chicago and has previously been awarded Fulbright and AIIS Fellowships.

Jörg Baberowski is Professor of East European History at Humboldt-Universität zu Berlin and speaker of the Research Network, "*Landschaften der Verfolgung*" (Landscapes of Persecution). He has been widely published on the history of violence, Stalinism, and the Russian Revolution, including *Scorched Earth: Stalin's Reign of Terror* (Yale University Press, 2016); *Räume der Gewalt* (S. Fischer, 4th ed., 2018); *Der sterbliche Gott: Revolution und Diktatur in Russland* (C.H. Beck, 2022).

Chan Yong Bu is a Ph.D. candidate in East Asian Studies at Princeton University. Chan Yong received his B.A. in Korean Language and Literature from Yonsei University and is currently writing his dissertation on audiovisual media and literature featuring heavy industry in East Asia.

Amerigo Caruso is an Assistant Professor of Modern and Contemporary History at the University of Bonn. His current research project investigates the practice and theory of emergency powers in nineteenth- and twentieth-century Europe. He is the author of *"Blut und Eisen auch im Innern": Soziale Konflikte, Massenpolitik und Gewalt in Deutschland vor 1914* (Campus, 2021), an exploration of social conflicts and political violence in late Imperial Germany.

Duygu Coşkuntuna is a Ph.D. candidate at Princeton University, Department of Near Eastern Studies. Her book on the late Ottoman mentalities, *Minds of Passage: An Interpretation of the Memoirs of Young Turks (1908–1923)*, was published by Libra Kitap in 2014. Her current research focuses on the German-Ottoman war experience at the Ottoman fronts during World War I.

Stephen G. F. Hall is a Lecturer at the University of Bath. He completed his Ph.D. in 2020 at the School of Slavonic and East European Studies, University College London. His research investigates authoritarian learning in the post-Soviet space and has appeared in *East European Politics*, the *Journal of Eurasian Studies* and *Russian Politics*. His monograph *The Authoritarian International: Tracing How Authoritarian Regimes Learn in the Post-Soviet Space* is forthcoming with Cambridge University Press.

Carolin Kautz is a research fellow and Ph.D. candidate at Georg-August University Göttingen. She studied Modern Chinese Studies and Political Science in Göttingen and Beijing and is currently working on the Chinese Communist Party, more specifically on ideology, Party discipline, and corruption. Her work has been published in the *Journal of Chinese Political Sciences*, *ASIEN – The German Journal on Contemporary Asia* and the *British Journal of Chinese Studies*.

Rob Konkel is a Ph.D. candidate in History at Princeton University. He is a global historian specializing in political economy, geopolitics, and development. Currently, he is writing a global history of the interwar period through the lens of strategic metallic minerals. His work has appeared in the *Journal of Global History*.

Grzegorz Krzywiec is an Associate Professor at the Institute of History of the Polish Academy of Sciences. He has mainly published on Polish anti-Semitism, Polish-Jewish relations, and right-wing politics in Eastern Europe. His publications include *Polska bez Żydów. Studia dziejów idei, wyobraźni i praktyk antysemickich na ziemiach polskich przed Wielką Wojną, 1905–1914* (Instytut Historii PAN, 2017) and *Chauvinism, Polish Style: The Case of Roman Dmowski. Beginnings: 1886–1905* (Peter Lang, 2016). He is currently investigating the history of Polish fascism from a Central and Eastern European perspective.

Bertram Lang is a research fellow and Ph.D. candidate at Goethe University Frankfurt. His academic areas of interest include China's non-profit sector,

Sino-European relations, and the politics of corruption. Bertram studied Political Science and Chinese Studies in Freiburg, Aix-en-Provence, Nanjing, and Bruges and previously worked as an analyst at the Mercator Institute for China Studies. His research has appeared in the *Journal of Contemporary Asia*, in *Crime, Law and Social Change*, the *Journal of Current Chinese Affairs* and the *Journal of Civil Society*.

Alexander Libman is Professor of Russian and East European Politics at Freie Universität Berlin. His research focuses on comparative authoritarianism studies. His main publications include *Historical Legacies of Communism* (Cambridge University Press, 2021, with Anastassia Obydenkova) and *Authoritarian Regionalism in the World of International Organizations* (Oxford University Press, 2019, with Anastassia Obydenkova), as well as articles in *American Political Science Review, World Politics, Comparative Political Studies* and *Comparative Politics*.

Janis Nalbadidacis is a research fellow at Humboldt-Universität zu Berlin. He is a historian of Southeastern Europe and Latin America and specializes in the history of torture. His book, *In den Verliesen der Diktatur: Folterzentren während der Militärdiktaturen in Griechenland (1967–1974) und Argentinien (1976–1983)*, has recently appeared with Campus.

Armin Nassehi is Professor of General Sociology and Theory of Society at Ludwig-Maximilians-Universität München and a member of "Corona" expert councils of the federal governments of North Rhine-Westphalia and Bavaria. He has been widely published on political and cultural sociology, notably on contemporary challenges to society, including *Unbehagen: Theorie der überforderten Gesellschaft* (C.H. Beck, 2021); *Muster: Theorie der digitalen Gesellschaft* (C.H. Beck, 3rd ed., 2019); *Gesellschaft der Gegenwarten: Studien zur Theorie der modernen Gesellschaft II* (Suhrkamp-Verlag, 2011).

Stefan Schubert completed his Ph.D. in Modern History at the Albert-Ludwigs-Universität Freiburg. As a member of the Collaborative Research Center 948 "Heroes – Heroizations – Heroisms", he worked on the correlations between the status of a war hero and political leadership in the first half of the 20th century in France and Germany. He has written several articles for the online encyclopedia, *Compendium heroicum*.

Martin Wagner is a research fellow and Ph.D. candidate at Humboldt-Universität zu Berlin. Having studied History and Chinese Studies in Berlin, Beijing, and Moscow, he is currently working on a comparative history of post-Stalinist and post-Maoist transformations. His research has appeared in *Historische Zeitschrift*, *Geschichte und Gesellschaft*, *Comparativ* and *Jahrbücher für Geschichte Osteuropas.*

Jakob Zollmann is a research fellow at the Center for Global Constitutionalism, WZB Berlin Social Science Center. He has mainly published on the history of colonialism in Africa and legal history, including *Koloniale Herrschaft und ihre Grenzen: Die Kolonialpolizei in Deutsch-Südwestafrika* (Vandenhoeck & Ruprecht, 2010) and *Naulila 1914: World War I in Angola and International Law* (Nomos, 2016).